# Free Will

Jonathan Edwards' Psychological, Ethical, and Theological
Philosophy in his *Freedom of the Will*

A careful and strict

# ENQUIRY

INTO

The *modern* prevailing Notions

OF THAT

# FREEDOM of WILL,

Which is supposed to be essential

TO

*Moral Agency, Vertue* and *Vice, Reward* and *Punishment, Praise* and *Blame.*

---

By JONATHAN EDWARDS, A.M.

Pastor of the Church in *Stockbridge.*

---

Rom. ix. 16. *It is not of him that willeth* ——

---

BOSTON, N.E.

Printed and Sold by S. KNEELAND, in Queen-street.
MDCCLIV.

# Free Will

Jonathan Edwards' Psychological, Ethical, and Theological Philosophy in his *Freedom of the Will*

EDITED BY PETER B. JUNG

RESOURCE *Publications* • Eugene, Oregon

FREE WILL

Jonathan Edwards' Psychological, Ethical, and Theological Philosophy in his *Freedom of the Will*

Copyright © 2019 Peter B. Jung. All rights reserved. Except for brief quotations in critical publications or reviews, no part of this book may be reproduced in any manner without prior written permission from the publisher. Write: Permissions, Wipf and Stock Publishers, 199 W. 8th Ave., Suite 3, Eugene, OR 97401.

Resource Publications
An Imprint of Wipf and Stock Publishers
199 W. 8th Ave., Suite 3
Eugene, OR 97401

www.wipfandstock.com

PAPERBACK ISBN: 978-1-5326-6140-2
HARDCOVER ISBN: 978-1-5326-6141-9
EBOOK ISBN: 978-1-5326-6142-6

Manufactured in the U.S.A. 03/18/19

# Contents

Editor's Introduction | 1

Author's Preface | 34

**Part I: Wherein are Explained Various Terms and Things Belonging to the Subject of the Ensuing Discourse**

SECTION 1
Concerning the Nature of the Will | 41

SECTION 2
Concerning the Determination of the Will | 45

SECTION 3
Concerning the Meaning of the Terms Necessity, Impossibility, Inability, Etc.; and of Contingence | 54

SECTION 4
Of the Distinction of Natural and Moral Necessity, and Inability | 62

SECTION 5
Concerning the Notion of Liberty, and of Moral Agency | 70

**Part II: Where It Is Considered, whether There Is, or Can Be Any Such Sort of Freedom of Will, as That wherein Arminians Place the Essence of the Liberty of All Moral Agents; and Whether Any Such Thing Ever Was, or Can Be Conceived of**

SECTION 1
Showing the Manifest Inconsistence of ohe Arminian Notion of Liberty of Will, Consisting in the Will's Self-Determining Power | 77

SECTION 2
Several Supposed Ways of Evading the Foregoing Reasoning, Considered | 82

SECTION 3
Whether Any Event Whatsoever, and Volition in Particular, can Come to Pass without a Cause of Its Existence | 89

SECTION 4
Whether Volition can Arise without A Cause, through the Activity of the Nature of the Soul | 96

SECTION 5
Showing, That if the Things Asserted in These Evasions should Be Supposed to Be True, They Are Altogether Impertinent, and Can't Help the Cause of Arminian Liberty; and How (This Being the State of the Case) Arminian Writers are Obliged to Talk Inconsistently | 100

SECTION 6
Concerning the Will's Determining in Things Which are Perfectly Indifferent, in the View of the Mind | 105

SECTION 7
Concerning the Notion of Liberty of Will Consisting in Indifference | 113

SECTION 8
Concerning the Supposed Liberty of the Will, as Opposite to All Necessity | 122

SECTION 9
Of the Connection of the Acts of the Will with the Dictates of the Understanding | 126

SECTION 10
Volition Necessarily Connected with the Influence of Motives; with Particular Observations on the Great Inconsistence of Mr. Chubb's Assertions and Reasonings, About the Freedom of the Will | 134

SECTION 11
The Evidence of God's Certain Foreknowledge of the Volitions of Moral Agents | 149

SECTION 12
God's Certain Foreknowledge of the Future Volitions of Moral Agents, Inconsistent with Such a Contingence of Those Volitions, as Is Without All Necessity | 168

SECTION 13
Whether We Suppose the Volitions of Moral Agents to be Connected with Anything Antecedent, or Not, Yet They Must be Necessary in Such a Sense as to Overthrow Arminian Liberty | 183

**Part III: Wherein Is Inquired, Whether Any Such Liberty of Will as Arminians Hold, Be Necessary to Moral Agency, Virtue and Vice, Praise, and Dispraise, Etc.**

SECTION 1
God's Moral Excellency Necessary, Yet Virtuous and Praiseworthy | 189

SECTION 2
The Acts of the Will of the Human Soul of Jesus Necessarily Holy, Yet Truly Virtuous, Praiseworthy, Rewardable, etc. | 193

SECTION 3
The Case of Such as are Given Up of God to Sin, and of Fallen Man in General, Proves Moral Necessity and Inability to be Consistent with Blameworthiness | 208

SECTION 4
Command, and Obligation to Obedience, Consistent
with Moral Inability to Obey | 216

SECTION 5
That Sincerity of Desires and Endeavors, Which is Supposed to Excuse in the
Nonperformance of Things in Themselves Good, Particularly Considered | 227

SECTION 6
Liberty of Indifference, Not Only Not Necessary to Virtue, but Utterly Inconsistent
with It; and All, Either Virtuous or Vicious Habits or Inclinations, Inconsistent
with Arminian Notions of Liberty and Moral Agency | 235

SECTION 7
Arminian Notions of Moral Agency Inconsistent with All Influence of Motive
and Inducement, in Either Virtuous or Vicious Actions | 244

## Part IV: Wherein the Chief Grounds of the Reasonings of Arminians, in Support and defense of Their Notions of Liberty, Moral Agency, etc. and against the Opposite Doctrine, Are Considered

SECTION 1
The Essence of the Virtue and Vice of Dispositions of the Heart, and Acts
of the Will, Lies Not in Their Cause, but Their Nature | 253

SECTION 2
The Falseness and Inconsistence of That Metaphysical Notion of Action, and
Agency, Which Seems to be Generally Entertained by the Defenders
of the Arminian Doctrine Concerning Liberty, Moral Agency, Etc. | 260

SECTION 3
The Reasons Why Some Think It Contrary to Common Sense, to Suppose Those
Things which Are Necessary, to be Worthy of Either Praise or Blame | 268

SECTION 4
It Is Agreeable to Common Sense, and the Natural Notions of Mankind,
to Suppose Moral Necessity to be Consistent with Praise and Blame,
Reward and Punishment | 275

SECTION 5
Concerning Those Objections, That This Scheme of Necessity Renders All Means
and Endeavors for the Avoiding of Sin, or the Obtaining Virtue and Holiness,
Vain, and to No Purpose; and That It Makes Men No More than Mere Machines
in Affairs of Morality and Religion | 284

SECTION 6
Concerning That Objection against the Doctrine which Has Been Maintained,
That It Agrees with the Stoical Doctrine of Fate, and the Opinions of Mr.
Hobbes | 292

SECTION 7
Concerning the Necessity of the Divine Will | 296

SECTION 8
Some Further Objections against the Moral Necessity of God's Volitions
Considered | 305

SECTION 9
Concerning That Objection against the Doctrine Which Has Been Maintained,
That It Makes God the Author of Sin | 320

SECTION 10
Concerning Sin's First Entrance into the World | 337

SECTION 11
Of a Supposed Inconsistence of These Principles,
with God's Moral Character | 340

SECTION 12
Of a Supposed Tendency of These Principles to Atheism and Licentiousness | 346

SECTION 13
Concerning That Objection against the Reasoning, by Which the Calvinistic Doctrine is Supported, That It is Metaphysical and Abstruse | 350

The Conclusion | 357

APPENDIX 1: (Edwards's) Remarks on the "Essays on the Principles of Morality and Natural Religion (by Henry Home, Lord Kames, 1751)," in a Letter to a Minister of the Church of Scotland | 367

APPENDIX 2: (Edwards's) Letter to John Erskine, August 3, 1757, "To Mr. Erskine" | 381

APPENDIX 3: Last Letter from John Erskine to Jonathan Edwards, January 24, 1758. | 387

APPENDIX 4: Thomas Reid's Reading Notes on Edwards's *Freedom of the Will* | 391

APPENDIX 5: Proposals for printing *Freedom of the Will* | 400

Index | 403

# Editor's Introduction

## PREFACE

This introduction aims to analyze contradictory interpretations of Edwards's *Freedom of the Will*[1] and his doctrine of will and to provide a general survey of the book, in which the editor attempts to reconcile those contradictions. Contrary to the position of many scholars, Edwards maintains that man has freedom of will, the so-called free will, and yet it does not clash with the necessity of God's determination because God does not "necessitate men to do a thing contrary to his will," and human "will is determined by the greatest motive" that man is pleased to follow.

However, that belief does not mean that Edwards asserts what his Arminian antagonists unanimously insist: that man does have self-determining power, or free will, and acts freely without any force or necessity, and that freedom of the will is necessary for man's moral acts and man can be blamed for his actions. At the end of this introduction and the main text, readers can be certain that Edwards's theory of will basically echoes St. Augustine, John Calvin, and Petrus van Mastricht for the theological application of will and John Locke for the psychological basis of will.

## 1. RESEARCH TRENDS IN *FREEDOM OF THE WILL*

### (1) James Dana, the first critic of *Freedom of the Will*

Edwards received no criticism while he was alive concerning his publication of *Freedom of the Will* (1754). However, after Edwards died, James Dana (1735–1812)[2]

---

1. Edwards' original title is normally shortened to *Freedom of the Will*. However, this edition is titled as *Free Will*, hereafter the former is abbreviated as *FOW*, which indicates the Yale edition's first volume.

2. James Dana graduated from Harvard in 1753 and was called by the Wallingford Church, but his opponents called a consociation meeting and charged him with heterodoxy. The church (1758–1789), however, enforced his ordination. His doctrinal matter became minor. Then he succeeded Chauncey Whittelsey of the New Haven Church. See William Buell Sprague, *Annals of the American Pulpit: Presbyterian* (New York: R. Carter and Brothers, 1859), 565–71; Conrad Wright, *The Beginnings of Unitarianism in America*, 74.

became the leading critic of Edwards with *An Examination of the Late Reverend President Edwards's Inquiry on Freedom of the Will* (1770) and *An Examination of the Same Continued* (1773). Somewhat later, Samuel West (1730–1807) criticized Edwards in *Essays on Liberty and Necessity* (1793).[3]

These critiques have been reviewed by Conrad Wright, who claimed in 1954 that New England was divided into Calvinists holding the doctrine of necessity, and Arminians holding the doctrine of the freedom of the will. Nevertheless, he stated, "Most New England Calvinists asserted that man is a free moral agent in about the same terms that the Arminians used," and, "Necessity was regarded as a doctrine not of the Calvinists, but of freethinkers."[4]

Dana's position was described in a letter to Andrew Eliot (1718–1778),[5] who also opposed Edwards's *FOW*. According to Wright, Dana's position was clearly neither Calvinistic nor an outspoken form of Arminianism.[6] Furthermore, Wright suggests that Dana and Eliot did not believe will to be an autonomous and self-determining faculty of the mind, and in their eyes, Edwards was identified as a freethinker. Wright's suggestion means that there were no specific differences in the understanding of the mind between Edwards and his opponents.[7] Nevertheless, Wright concluded that Dana maintained the doctrine of the freedom of the will but rejected the doctrine of necessity as determinism and fatalism. He misunderstood Edwards's system of theistic determinism and insisted that Edwards's interpretation was similar to that of ancient and modern fatalists such as "Hobbes, Spinoza, Collins, Leibnitz, the authors of Cato's letters, [and] Hume, among the Atheists and Deists."[8]

## (2) Paul Ramsey, the Editor of the Yale Edition of *FOW*

Paul Ramsey, the editor of the Yale edition of *FOW*, identifies Edwards's moral purpose in writing *Freedom of the Will*. He traces the theological and philosophical trajectories and delineates Edwards "combat[ing] [the] contingency and self-determination"[9] of Arminians and articulating the Calvinist doctrine of will. Ramsey, as an ethicist, asserts that Edwards maintained "[A] passionate conviction that the decay to be observed in religion and morals followed the decline in doctrine since the founding of New England."[10]

---

3. James Dana, *An Examination of the Late Reverend President Edwards's 'Inquiry on Freedom of the Will'* (Boston: Daniel Keeland, 1770); idem, *An Examination of the Same Continued* (New Haven: Thomas and Samuel Green, 1773); Samuel West, *Essays on Liberty and Necessity* (1793).

4. Conrad Wright, *The Beginnings of Unitarianism in America*, 92–93.

5. "James Dana to Andrew Eliot, July 9, 1773," in Andrews-Eliot Papers, *Massachusetts Historical Society*, 11.

6. Wright, 106n36.

7. Wright, 94, 107.

8. Dana, *Examination of the Late Reverend President Edwards*, 132.

9. Paul Ramsey, "Editor's Introduction," *Freedom of the Will* (hereafter *FOW*), WJE 1:2.

10. WJE 1:2.

Arminians of the seventeenth century, according to Ramsey, emphasized God's side of a divine-human relationship, but their teaching that divine grace is resistible resulted in accentuating "the ethical and the human among later Arminians," and eventually falling into Pelagianism, deism, and natural religion. Therefore, for Ramsey, Arminianism is regarded as "a loose term for all forms of the complaint of the aggrieved moral nature against the harsh tenets of Calvinism."[11]

Methodologically, Edwards's "design" of *FOW* was to expose the Arminian notions of free will, human action, and moral responsibility as erroneous.

### (3) Norman Fiering

Fiering advances two areas of Edwards's scholarship. He first asserts, like Ramsey, that Edwards's moral theology was expounded in *FOW*. Also, he realizes Edwards's engagement in *Original Sin* and *True Virtue*,[12] with eighteenth-century moralists like the Third Earl of Shaftesbury (1671–1713), Francis Hutcheson (1694–1746), and George Turnbull (1698–1748), who claimed: "religion and virtue are one and the same thing."[13] Secondly, Fiering asserts that moral theology was related to Arminianism, as Edwards accomplished his main theological task to demonstrate that

> [D]eterminism, even in the form of the Calvinist absolute decrees of God, was not inconsistent with praise and blame, and reward and punishment, or, in effect, with merit and demerit.[14]

Accordingly, the Arminians in *FOW* are identified with a single group of "all of the advocates of liberty,"[15] and as such constituted a continuation of the free will debate at Harvard, which commenced in the late seventeenth century.[16]

### (4) Allen Guelzo

Like Fiering, Guelzo asserts that the theological controversy of the will was a central issue in mid-eighteenth-century New England.[17] Guelzo traces the origin of the free will controversy to British and Continental philosophers and also discusses the Old Lights,[18] who were opposed to Edwards and eventually rejected Calvinism and favored

11. *WJE* 1:3.

12. *Two Dissertations on the End for Which God Created the World* and *The Nature of True Virtue* (written in 1755, published in 1765), *WJE* 8; *Original Sin* (completed in May 1757, published in 1758), *WJE* 3.

13. Norman Fiering, *Jonathan Edwards's Moral Thought and its British Context* (Chapel Hill: University of North Carolina Press, 1981), 8.

14. Fiering, 292.

15. *FOW*, 176, 463.

16. Fiering, 263.

17. It is not a surprise to find a "will" work of Benjamin Franklin, "A Dissertation of Liberty and Necessity," (1725), in *The Papers of Benjamin Franklin* vol. 1, ed. Leonard Labaree (Yale University Press, 1959).

18. There is no conclusive evidence to recount who first used the terms "Old Light" or "Old

Arminianism, Unitarianism, or deism.[19] The main factor that separated the Old Lights from the New Lights was in their views on intellectualism and voluntarism, according to Guelzo; the former regarded the intellect or reason as superior to the will or heart, while the latter believed the opposite. The Old Lights, representatives of the Old Calvinists, embraced the intellectualism of Scottish philosophers like Samuel Langdon (1723–1797), who believed that sin arises from the mind rather than from the heart or will.[20] According to Guelzo in agreement with Fiering, the Old Lights dismissed Edwards's understanding of the will, which implies that the will plays a role in human acts and that the will can choose what the intellect rejects.[21] However, the Arminians endorsed the primacy of the human will over the intellect, an "ethical voluntarism."[22] Guelzo contends, however, that Edwards adopted the Augustinian description of will in *FOW*, asserting, "The will is not active in causing or determining, but [is] purely the passive subject,"[23] and, "The acts of the will have some connection with the dictates or views of the understanding."[24] Edwards's position on the relation of the intellect (or understanding or mind) and the will does not show that he merely embraced Augustine's idea, but that he did so more thoroughly than Calvin's idea, which is that

> [T]he human soul consists of two faculties, understanding, and will. Let the office, moreover, of understanding be to distinguish between objects, as each seems worthy of approval or disapproval; while that of the will, to choose and follow what the understanding pronounces good, but to reject and flee what it disapproves.[25]

---

Calvinism" and "New Light" or "New Divinity." The terms were first used after the First Great Awakening. Old and New Lights took different positions on the spiritual revival and its experiences like enthusiasm. New Lights like Hopkins embraced the revivals, while Old Lights like Charles Chauncy and Ezra Stiles were suspicious of the revivals and Hopkinsianism as well. See Guelzo, *Edwards on the Will*, 88–89. "The term 'New Divinity' was first used as a pejorative in 1765 about Hopkins' argument that an unregenerate but awakened sinner who used the means of grace appeared guiltier in God's eyes than an unawakened sinner." See Joseph A. Conforti, *Samuel Hopkins and the New Divinity movement* (MI: Christian University Press, 1981), 4.

19. Allen C. Guelzo, *Edwards on the Will: A Century of American Theological Debate* (Middletown, CT: Wesleyan University Press, 1989; reprint, Eugene, OR: Wipf and Stock Publishers, 2007), 143.

20. Samuel Langdon, *Remarks on the Leading Sentiments of Dr. Hopkins's System of Doctrines* (Exeter, NH: Henry Ranlet, 1794), 24.

21. Augustine, *On the Free Choice of the Will, On Grace and Free Choice, and Other Writings*, tr. Peter King (Cambridge University Press, 2010), 3–10. Cf. Norman Fiering, *Moral Philosophy at Seventeenth-Century Harvard: A Discipline in Transition* (The University of North Carolina Press, 1981), 138–46; and Guelzo, 152, 255.

22. Bonnie Kent distinguishes between three forms of voluntarism: psychological, ethical, and theological. For her detailed discussion of voluntarism, see Bonnie Kent, *Virtues of the Will: The Transformation of Ethics in the Late Thirteenth Century* (Washington D.C.: The Catholic University of America Press, 1995), 261; and Lilli Alanen, *Descartes's Concept of Mind* (Harvard University Press, 2003), 230.

23. *FOW*, 272.

24. *FOW*, 217.

25. Calvin, *Institutes of the Christian Religion* (edited by John T. McNeill) I.xv7. 194–96. Cf.

Guelzo, moreover, traces this knowledge of the will through the writings of Turretin, Mastricht, Ames, and the Fransican Scotis tradition to Augustine.[26] Thus, according to Guelzo, James, Dana, and others dismissed Edwards's Augustinian voluntarism and concluded that Edwards departed from Old Calvinism; hence, the New Lights departed from New England orthodoxy.[27] Samuel Spring (1746–1819), who described the Old Lights as "a jumble of Arminianism and Antinomianism,"[28] was branded by Edwards's student Samuel Hopkins (1721–1803) as a "moderate Calvinist" or "moderate Arminian."[29] Furthermore, Guelzo observes the more important question, whether or not the will is free, rather than what the will and its liberty are, and how free it is, if it is free at all. Guelzo finds the three positions in the free will debate to be: (1) sometimes (soft determinism); (2) always (libertarianism); (3) never (hard determinism).[30] To understand Edwards's position on this issue, it is necessary to look back at the history of the Reformed theology of his era. The core of the theological conflict between the Reformed party and Arminians rested in their irreconcilable positions on predestination, yet its philosophical controversy centered over the problem of free will. The Reformed doctrine of the will was misunderstood as a form of Stoic fatalism and Hobbes' "doctrine of necessity"[31] that maintains the notion that man's actions are determined by the effects of antecedent causes. In contrast, just as the Reformed scholastics of the sixteenth and seventeenth centuries had asserted, Edwards held that divine grace and human liberty are compatible.[32] Thus, if Edwards were a compatibilist, it would affirm that he was neither a so-called "hard determinist" who held that free will and determinism are incompatible, nor a "libertarian," a "soft determinist" or a "reconciliationist." Guelzo depicts Edwards as the last,[33] though, stating,

---

Aristotle, *Nicomachean Ethics*, VI. 2 (LCL edition, 328 f.); Plato, *Phaedrus* 253 D (LCL Plato I. 492 f.), and Augustine, *On Rebuke and Grace* xi. 32 (MPL 44.936; tr. NPNF V. 484 f.).

26. Guelzo, 3–4.

27. Guelzo, 163–34. See also Wright, *The Beginnings of Unitarianism in America*, 107. Guelzo asserts that the criticism of Dana is ignorant and ineffectual.

28. Samuel Spring, *Moral Disquisitions and Strictures* (Newburyport, MA: John Mycall, 1854), 153.

29. Samuel Hopkins, "The Signs of Men are so under the Direction and Control of God as to Glorify Him," in *Works of Samuel Hopkins* 3:762.

30. Guelzo, 7, 255. William L. Reese offers the three possible solutions: (1) total freedom; (2) limited freedom; and (3) zero freedom. Cf. William L. Reese, *Freedom: A Study Guide with Readings* (New York: Humanity Books, 2000), 16.

31. Willem J. van Asselt, "Introduction," in *Reformed Thought on Freedom, The Concept of Free Choice in Early Modern Reformed Theology*, Willem J. van Asselt, J Martin Bac, and Roef T. de Velde (Grand Rapids, MI: Baker Academic, 2010), 15n2. Cf. *FOW*, 384

32. See Willem J. van Asselt, "Introduction," 15 n2. Its editors perceive six modern Reformed scholastics on the whole as compatibilists: Girolamo Zanchi, Franciscus Junius, Franciscus Gomarus, Gisbertus Voetius, Francesco Turrettini, and Bernardinus de Moor.

33. Guelzo, 7, 255.

Edwards, as a reconciliationist, attributed all events to God's causal efficacy, but he nonetheless extorted freedom from causality (as reconciliationsts routinely do) by hairsplitting the meaning of freedom.[34]

Nevertheless, Guelzo's view of "reconciliationism," which is identified with "soft determinism," does not entail the nature of universal compatibilism, stating that Edwards "extorted freedom from causality," and yet he later altered his view on the subject and stated, "Edwards was a *compatibilist*: liberty and necessity are compatible with each other."[35] Besides that, Edwards does not use the term "reconciliation" or attempt to reconcile freedom and necessity by sacrificing something, but rather argues that they are "consistent,"[36] or in modern terms, "compatible,"[37] by using his contemporary philosophical or metaphysical method. Edwards argues that there is no inconsistency between the doctrines of divine predestination and human liberty; that is to say, a soul chooses what God has determined "in its pleasure"[38] because they are compatible, and they do not presuppose such a liberty as that of Lord Kames Henry Home (1696–1782), with his libertarian liberty, which is contrary to and incompatible with the necessity.[39]

Robert Kane, however, assesses Edwards as "a classical compatibilist," as stated in Part II of *FOW*.[40] Stephen Wilson agrees, labeling Edwards's stance in *FOW* as "a kind of compatibilism,"[41] even though he perceives that Edwards "allowed for some dimension of human cooperation in the redemptive process."[42]

### (5) James A. Harris

His "Jonathan Edwards against Arminianism"[43] in his *Of Liberty and Necessity: The Free Will Debate in Eighteenth-Century British Philosophy* (2005) also presents the idea that free will was a central problem in eighteenth-century British intellectual circles,

---

34. Guelzo, 255.

35. Allen Guelzo, "Freedom of the Will," in *The Princeton Companion to Jonathan Edwards*, ed. Sang Hyun Lee (Princeton University Press, 2005), 126.

36. *FOW*, 231, 238, 254, 272, 299, 300, 309, 373, 405, 407, 419, 429, 448, 458.

37. The word "compatible" is a modern synonym of the old word that Jonathan Edwards (hereafter abbreviated JE except specific cases) then used. As for "reconciliationism," Bernard Berofsky clarifies it is the belief that "determinism" is true, but "incompatibilism" is false. See Bernard Berofsky (ed.), *Free Will and Determinism* (New York: Harper and Row, 1966), ix.

38. *FOW*, 370.

39. JE, "*Remark on the Essay on the Principles of Morality and Natural Religion*," Related Correspondence, in *FOW*, 453. Cf. Lord Kames Henry Home, *Essays on the Principles of Morality and Natural Religion* (Edinburgh, 1751).

40. Robert Kane, *A Contemporary Introduction to Free Will* (Oxford University Press, 2005), 148.

41. *FOW*, 405–06. Cf. Stephen Wilson, *Virtue Reformed: Rereading Jonathan Edwards* (Leiden, Boston: Brill, 2005), 193.

42. Wilson, *Virtue Reformed*, 220.

43. James A. Harris, *Of Liberty and Necessity: The Free Will Debate in Eighteenth-Century British Philosophy* (New York: Oxford University Press, 2005), 108–130.

including theology. Harris places Locke as a foundational figure in the question of human faculty and begins his discussion with Locke, as Edwards did in *FOW*. According to Harris, Locke's method and principles were useful in Edwards's arguments to combat Arminianism. Following Perry Miller, Harris notes that the passivity of perception was criticized by many in early New England, but it attracted Edwards to Locke, and the latter most influenced the former in formulating his doctrine of the will. Edwards agreed with Locke's claim that "What had been called faculties are really only different capacities or powers possessed by the agent;" that is to say, for Edwards, the will is "the unitary and functional nature of the organism."[44] In that manner, Edwards could defeat Arminianism through a widespread framework of "autonomous mental 'faculties.'"[45] Yet Harris identifies the points Edwards attacked; these are Locke's account of human liberty and his claim that "The will is determined by uneasiness rather than by perception of the greater good." Additionally, in *FOW* Edwards disagreed with and demolished Locke's "experimentalism," which argues that all knowledge is to be gained exclusively through experience, though he partially embraced Locke's "empiricism."[46] In Harris' view, Locke and Edwards have some similarities but more differences,[47] and he identifies the libertarians as Arminian and anti-Calvinist, which Edwards refutes in *FOW*. Although Edwards in part embraced British philosophies as his methods, he maintained his Calvinist argument against libertarian Arminianism.

## (6) Richard Muller and Paul Helm

One of the most recent and significant scholarly discussions concerning Edwards's doctrine of the will is the debate between Richard Muller and Paul Helm. Muller criticizes the traditional interpretation of Edwards's theological tradition on the doctrine of the will[48] and insists that Edwards's doctrine did not originate from the Reformed tradition, but from Thomas Hobbes' philosophical determinism. Muller thereby appeals to "Unitarian universalist minister" Joseph Priestley's criticism:

> The creed of the necessitarian is the very reverse of that of the Calvinist,... The doctrine of philosophical necessity is... a modern thing... Of Calvinists, I believe Mr. Jonathan Edwards to be the first. . .But the inconsistency of his scheme with what is properly called Calvinism, appeared by dropping several of the essential parts of that system.[49]

44. Harris, 109–11.
45. Harris, 109–11.
46. For further discussion, see Harris, *Of Liberty and Necessity*, 109–11, and also see 111 n14. Locke's notion that knowledge comes only from sensory experience influenced Edwards's epistemology.
47. Harris, 121–22.
48. Richard Muller, "Jonathan Edwards and the Absence of Free Choice: A Parting of Ways in the Reformed Tradition," *JESO* 1, no. 1 (2011).
49. Joseph Priestly, *The Doctrine of Philosophical Necessity* (London, 1777), 157, 160–61. Cf. Richard Muller, "Jonathan Edwards and the Absence of Free Choice: A Parting of Ways in the Reformed Tradition," *JESO* 1 (no. 1, 2011): 6. Muller points to more similar criticisms to object to Edwards's

Furthermore, Muller declares that the Reformed tradition, without exactly defining the "older Reformed tradition," "had consistently argued free choice to consist not merely in spontaneity but also in [the] freedom of contrariety and contradiction," yet Edwards held onto the "not only heterodox but heretical" determinism that was opposite to its tradition and the *Westminster Confession*.[50] Helm's response is:

> So when Muller claims that "The older language of primary and secondary causality, of formal and final causality, of necessity and contingency, and of free choices as a species of contingency had been replaced," he exaggerates. Indeed, Edwards would in principle have no objection to being tarred with a Stoical or Hobbesian brush, should the facts warrant it, any more than would the Orthodox to being tarred with an Aristotelian brush.[51]

The criticisms mentioned above of Edwards's arguments regarding the will then give rise to an array of questions such as: "Is the will free?"; "What determines the will?"; "Isn't Edwards's God the author of sin?"; "Isn't Edwards determinist or fatalist?"; and "Was Edwards Reformed?"

## 2. EDWARDS'S WRITING MOTIVATION AND PROCESS

Jonathan Edwards (1703–1758) began his ministry in October 1726 at Northampton and then was dismissed by the church on June 22 (*A Farewell Sermon*, July 1, 1750) because he had an Arminian controversy with his parishioners over qualifications for church membership, in particular. The grounds for the controversy and for the theological alteration of the work of his grandfather and predecessor, Solomon Stoddard (1643–1729), were latent from the beginning.[52] Edwards expressed his concern about Arminianism from his early ministry and kept his anti-Arminian vice in sermons and writings. Around August 1751, right after he moved out to Stockbridge, he began to write about it, he almost completed it in April 1753, and it was published in December 1754.

It was coincident with his lifelong concern that the central issue of the theology in mid-eighteenth-century New England was free will, for which the theological disagreement was clearly manifested in particular by the Calvinists' theistic determinism that God determines everything and the Arminians' libertarianism that men have the free will of self-determining. Edwards observed that the primary principle of Arminianism lies in the doctrine of free will, so he designed to write his magnum

---

Calvinist necessitarianism.

50. Muller, "Jonathan Edwards and the Absence of Free Choice," *JESO* 1 (no. 1, 2011): 10, 18.

51. Paul Helm, "Jonathan Edwards and the Parting of Ways," *JESO* 4 (no. 1, 2014): 57.

52. Solomon Stoddard also appraised "The Half-Way Covenant," and it was approved at the synod of 1662. Yet, about two decades later, Stoddard was concerned for those who had been baptized but were barred from communion just for lack of conversion experience, and he sought to evolve the Half-Way Covenant and, in the *Reforming Synod,* proposed open communion as a "converting ordinance."

opus, *Freedom of the Will*. It is a reduction of the full original title: *A Careful and Strict Enquiry into the Modern Prevailing Notions of that Freedom of Will which is supposed to be essential to Moral Agency, Virtue and Vice, Reward and Punishment, Praise and Blame*. Its theological purpose[53] was to provide anti-Arminian polemics on the will as a prologue to his "The Uncompleted Summa"[54]: "*A Rational Account of the Main Doctrines of the Christian Religion*."[55]

## 3. CONTENTS AND STRUCTURE OF THE TEXT

In "Part One," Edwards first introduces the Lockean notion of will and its determination by "motive," which is presented by John Locke in his *An Essay Concerning Human Understanding*.[56] Edwards defines the will like the "faculty or power or principle of mind by which it is capable of choosing," which he inherited from Calvin.[57] Regarding Locke's influence on Edwards, Guelzo reasonably maintains that Edwards at first accepted Locke's reasoning, but he later rejected it and was greatly influenced by the Third Earl of Shaftesbury and Francis Hutcheson. Guelzo argues that Edwards adopted the Augustinian doctrine of will in his theory of *FOW*: the will plays the primary role in human action. Additionally, Edwards disagreed on Locke's "experimentalism" in his *FOW*, but he partially embraced it.[58]

Edwards first introduces the Lockean notion of will and its determination by "motive," which is dealt with in the previous section,[59] and then he debates the problem of the necessity and liberty of the will in the introductory "Part One" of his *FOW*. In his defining sections, Edwards heavily employs the basic principles of Locke's *Human Understanding* and applies the "common" and "metaphysical or philosophical" notions of terms like necessity and freedom.[60]

In "Part Two," he proves the Arminian notion of the liberty of the will to be senseless. According to Edwards's understanding of Arminianism regarding the will, Arminians assert that the will itself has freedom/liberty; it can freely do any acts without necessity; that is to say, the will has its own power and freedom.[61] Likewise, the most central point of Arminian thought is "the notion of a self-determining power in

---

53. Guelzo, 2–4.
54. Perry Miller, *Jonathan Edwards* (New York: William Sloane Associates, 1949), 285.
55. *WJE* 6: 397. See Paul Ramsey "Introduction," *FOW*, 32.
56. John Locke, *Essay*, bk. II.ch.21, nos. 14–21; 1:319–24. JE restated Locke's concept of liberty in *FOW*, 164.
57. *FOW*, 137.
58. For further discussion, see Harris, 109–11, and also see 111 n14.
59. *FOW*, 137–148.
60. *FOW*, 151, 373.
61. *FOW*, 164–65.

the will."[62] Edwards concludes that such an idea of liberty is not only maintained by Arminians, but also by Pelagians and other anti-Calvinists for an entirely different signification, and that it is contrary even to the common notion of the will that humanity has "vulgarly" conceived.

In "Part Three," he refutes the Arminian supposition that such liberty of the will is necessary to moral agency, and that without it, there are no moral acts, virtue or vice, and reward or punishment.

In "Part Four," he defends his necessitarianism as different from Hobbes' mechanism and fatalism. Concerning this doctrine, Edwards strictly follows Calvin's idea by insisting on the compatibilist theory that the liberty of the will and God's predetermination are not contradictory but harmonious with each other. Augustine, Calvin, and Edwards agreed on the states of the will respectively as follows: "Man has *not so much freedom now* as he had before the fall, in this respect: now he has a will against a will, an inclination contrary to his reason and judgment."[63]

In his "Conclusion," Edwards recaptures the most controversial points between Calvinists and Arminians, displays that the Arminian doctrine of the self-determining freedom of the will disputes the five points of Calvinism, and reiterates them.[64]

## 4. TRAJECTORIES IN *FREEDOM OF THE WILL*

The assumption that the will has "freedom" or "liberty" and "self-determining" or "autonomous"[65] power, and so it does not require the necessity, is the central premise of the Arminians. In their view, all men are intelligent beings and moral agents, and they make moral decisions by themselves without any necessity or any divine assistance. This notion could not help but provoke their antipathy "concerning the moral perfections of God." It is plain that Edwards kept in mind Whitby's questions, which resulted in bringing men into doubt:

> Who can blame a person for doing what he could not help?"; "Why doth God command, if man hath not free will and power to obey?"; "Who will not cry out, that it is folly to command him, that hath not liberty to do what is commanded; and that it is unjust to condemn him, that has it not in his power to do what is required?[66]

---

62. *FOW*, 164, 171, 186, 189. Cf. *FOW*, 225, 453, 466.

63. "*The 'Miscellanies'*: no. 436. "Adam's Fall. Original Sin. Free Will," *WJE* 13:484. Cf. Calvin, *Institutes*, II. ii, 255–289. This is the title of II. ii, 255.

64. Interestingly, JE included the five points of Calvinism in his "Conclusion" chapter. This may indicate his intentions in writing the book. *FOW*, 430–439.

65. JE never used the term "autonomous," but Ramsey prefers to call it "self-determining." See "Editor's Introduction," 75, 83.

66. *FOW*, 299.

The Arminians proclaimed, according to Edwards, that the will itself has freedom/liberty; it can freely commit any acts without necessity, and it is free from any compulsion or coaction. That is to say that the will has its own power and freedom. The Arminian notion of the liberty of the will, according to Edwards, could be summarized by:

> (1) That it consists in a self-determining power in the will, or a certain sovereignty the will has over itself, and its own acts, whereby it determines its own volitions; so as not to be dependent in its determinations, on any cause without itself, nor determined by anything prior to its own acts.

> (2) Indifference belongs to liberty in their notion of it, or that the mind, previous to the act of volition be, *in equilibrio*. (3) Contingence is another thing that belongs and is essential to it; not in the common acceptation of the word, as that has been already explained, but as opposed to all necessity, or any fixed and certain connection with some previous ground or reason of its existence.[67]

Edwards concludes that such a notion of liberty is not only maintained by Arminians, but also by Pelagians and other anti-Calvinists for an entirely different meaning, and that it is contrary even to the common notion of humanity.

The common notion of humanity was employed in Locke's *An Essay Concerning Human Understanding*. According to Locke, liberty is that power and opportunity for one to do and conduct as he will, or according to his choice, without taking into account the meaning of the word, anything of the cause or origin of that choice, or how the person came to have such a volition.[68]

Edwards reaffirms Locke's definition of the liberty of the will, especially in defining the faculties of men such as the will, soul, and mind, and the properties of the will, such as volition or liberty. Then he differentiates between the universal concept of freedom and the Arminian one.

Edwards's definition of the will as the "faculty or power or principle of mind by which it is capable of choosing" is inherited from Calvin.[69] The latter's primary premise is that reason is gravely wounded through sin, and evil desires very much enslave the will. Then Calvin defines the will as "a faculty of the reason to distinguish between good and evil, a faculty of the will to choose one or the other" from studying Origen and other thinkers who held very similar views, such as Bernard, Anselm, Peter Lombard and the Scholastics, and Thomas Aquinas.[70] Calvin, however, was most influenced by Augustine[71] resonating with Martin Luther, who defines the

---

67. *FOW*, 164–65.
68. John Locke, *Essay*, bk. II.ch.21, nos. 14–21; 1:319–24. JE restates Locke's concept of liberty in *FOW*, 164.
69. *FOW*, 137.
70. For their detailed definitions, see Calvin, *Institutes*, II.ii.4.
71. Calvin, "Augustine's doctrine of 'free will,'" *Institutes*, I.ii.8; II.iv.13–14.

will as a choosing or preferring faculty and asserts that man has no free will,[72] an idea commonly held in the era of the Reformation.[73] This inheritance of the Reformation did not hinder Edwards from consulting with John Locke[74] and his *Essay on Human Understanding* (1690).[75]

## 5. JOHN LOCKE'S INFLUENCES ON EDWARDS[76]

Sereno Edwards Dwight (1786–1850), a maternal great-grandson of Edwards, tells us that

> "In the second year of his collegiate course, while at Wethersfield, Edwards read Locke on the Human Understanding with peculiar pleasure.... From his own account of the subject, he was inexpressibly entertained and delighted with that profound work, when he read it at the age of fourteen; enjoying a far higher pleasure in the perusal of its pages, 'than the most greedy miser finds, when gathering up handfuls of silver and gold, from some newly discovered treasure.'"[77]

It is a key to unlock what Edwards agrees and disagrees with in John Locke's (1632–1704) *Essay Concerning Human Understanding*. About the will, Edwards's main proposition is that "the will itself is not *an agent* that has a will.... He that has the liberty of doing according to his will, is the *agent* or *doer* who is possessed of the will."[78] This idea is exactly imported from Locke's *Essay*, which argues, "Liberty, which is but a power, belongs only to *agents*, and cannot be an attribute or modification of the will, which is also but a power.... Liberty ... is the power a *man* has to do or forbear doing ... The will is nothing but one power, and freedom another power or

---

72. Martin Luther, *On the bondage of the will* (*De Servo Arbitrio*), written in answer to the diatribe *of Erasmus on free-will*, tr. by Henry Cole (London: T. Bensley, 1823), 62–63. Compare with Edwards's *FOW*, 137, 164–65.

73. Heinrich Heppe, *Reformed Dogmatics*, trans. G.T. Thomson (Grand Rapids, MI: Baker, 1950), 224.

74. JE imported Locke's theories into his *Notes on the Mind*, *Original Sin*, "Miscellanies," no. 1060, and the "Interleaved Bible" (Romans 6:19), see *WJE* 26: 90; 3:78; 24:1002; 20:421. According to Thuesen, Edwards cited Locke twenty-nine times in his works, yet he cited Calvin only three times in *Religious Affections*. See also *WJE* 26: 434, 450–51.

75. According to Samuel Hopkins' 1765 biography, Edwards first read it in his second year at Yale College, but the Catalogue letter leaf supports the idea that Edwards first read it in 1724, while he was a graduate student or a tutor. Sometime later, Edwards acquired his own copy of the *Essay*, lending it to his son Timothy in 1754, as the "Account Book" reveals.

76. Paul Copan, "Jonathan Edwards's Philosophical Influences: Lockean or Malebranchean?," *Journal Evangelical Theological Society* 44, no. 1 (2001): 107–124.

77. Sereno Edwards Dwight, *The Life of President Edwards* (G. & C. & H. Carvill, 1830), 30, quoted in Ramsey, "Introduction," *FOW*, 47.

78. *FOW*, 163.

ability."[79] Edwards also rejects the tripartite view that holds that the soul is a composite of the reason, the will, and the appetites. However, he adopts Locke's bipartite view that soul is the understanding and the will. Edwards reformulates his notion of elements of soul or mind, that "man has reason and understanding, and has a faculty of will, and so is capable of volition and choice; and in that, his will is guided by the dictates or views of his understanding,"[80] by adopting Locke's idea that "the understanding and the will are two faculties of the mind."[81] They both belong to a school of modern faculty psychology that views the human mind as composed of separate departments, which are as Locke put it "powers to do one action,"[82] and as Edwards wrote, "that faculty or power or principle of . . . choosing."[83] As Ramsey observes, they have a different position on the relation between the two faculties, and Locke views that the two faculties are distinct and independent, but Edwards argues that they act like one and cannot oppose and contradict each other[84] and "the will always follows the last dictate of the understanding."[85] Edwards holds a different view than Augustine, who supposes the self-contradiction in the will.[86] However, Edwards allows that there is the conflict between man's consent and dissent, similar to Augustine's war between will and love for God and the desire for minor things, but he does not count it as a matter of the will but of the understanding or the motive, which can be solved before the will chooses. As for Augustine, it could be seen in man before grace.[87] Locke distinguishes the will from the desire or preference, but Edwards opposes that distinction "by which his opponents might drag in some notion of freedom under the guise of opposition among the affections,"[88] and as Ramsey detected, his New England Arminians adopted Locke's idea and attempted to make room mainly for the doctrine for the freedom of the will in the interstitial spaces left open by the latter's view of the will.[89]

According to Edwards, the factor of the determination of the will is the strongest motive, i.e. the greatest apparent good, that which is "pleasing to the mind," or the absence of what is "considered as evil or disagreeable."[90] However, in the first edition of *Essay*, Locke had the same view as Edwards, but later in the second edition, he

79. John Locke, *An Essay Concerning Human Understanding* (Eliz. Holt, 1700), bk. II, ch. 21, no. 14, p. 128.

80. *FOW*, 370.

81. Locke, *Essay*, bk. II, ch.21, no. 6.

82. Locke, *Essay*, bk. II, ch.21, no. 18.

83. *FOW*, 137.

84. *FOW*, 157, 205, 305; "The Mind," *WJE* 6:337, 362, 365.

85. *FOW*, 148.

86. Ramsey, 50.

87. *FOW*, 51.

88. Clarence Henry Faust, *Jonathan Edwards's View of Human Nature* (University of Chicago, 1935), xlvii, quoted in Ramsey, 52.

89. Ramsey, 52.

90. *FOW*, 143.

changed it for the greater good to present uneasiness, which, as he notes, the will avoids or removes. The loopholes left open to the freedom of the will in the second edition allowed for providing the will with greater freedom by admitting that "the mind ha[s] . . . a power to *suspend* the execution and satisfaction of any of its desires and so all one after another is at liberty to consider the objects of them examine them on all sides and weigh them with others. In this lies the liberty man has."[91]

## 6. EDWARDS'S NOTION OF THE WILL

Paraphrasing Locke's *Essay*, Edwards recreates in *FOW* his definition of the liberty of the will from a Calvinist perspective as follows: (a) Common and universal notion of liberty: Anyone has the freedom/liberty/opportunity/power "to do as he pleases." The will acts freely as men please;[92] (b) Arminian notion: The will, in indifference, sovereignly determines all of its free actions. Man or the will has the power to cause and determine "that God has given."[93] The person or soul "acting voluntarily, determines."[94]; (c) Edwards's notion: As a faculty of man, "The will [, in truth,] signifies nothing but a power or ability to prefer or choose."[95] The will does not have "such [an Arminian]" power of choosing, but it "do[es] what he pleases." The "will is always determined by the strongest motive, by that view of the mind,"[96] and "under necessity,"[97] or (not always) "guided by the dictates or views of his understanding."[98]

Edwards only sets a threefold state of the will: before the Fall, after the Fall of sinners, and after the Conversion of saints. Man's will before the Fall is righteous and imperfect and "more free." It "is enslaved" in sin and less free after the Fall, but it is again free after Conversion by Grace. Consequently, he does not only deny the Arminian notion of the freedom of the "uncaused" will and the mechanism as well, but he also argues for the Reformed doctrine of the liberty of the "caused" will.

## 7. AUGUSTINE, CALVIN, AND MASTRICHT: FREE OR NOT

Edwards applies the common notion when he reconstructs his definition of the will and its liberty and uses it to expose the contradiction in the Arminian definition of them. Nevertheless, many fail to grasp what Edwards means by these ambiguous

---

91. Locke, *Essay*, bk. II, ch. 21, no. 47.
92. *FOW*, 163.
93. *FOW*, 189.
94. *FOW*, 172.
95. JE deleted "in truth" and quoted from Locke's *Essay*, bk. II, ch.21, no. 17.
96. *FOW*, 148.
97. *FOW*, 156, 278.
98. *FOW*, 370. Cf. *FOW*, 148, "In some sense, the will always follows the last dictate of the understanding . . . It is not true, that the will always follows the last dictate of the understanding."

phrases: "man is fully and perfectly free"[99]; "men act voluntarily, and do what they please"[100]; "in them alone was the man was free"[101]; "a man...can do as he chooses"[102]; and "there is no need of any such liberty."[103] They misunderstand these assertions on his part that the absolute freedom of the will is of an Arminian character, and they overlook the fact that the foundation of Edwards's thought is laid in Calvin and Mastricht.

For example, Calvin employs Augustine's doctrine of will and clarifies its ambiguity: "Augustine also recognizes no independent activity of the human will;"[104] "Augustine does not eliminate man's will, but makes it wholly dependent upon grace."[105] Elsewhere, Calvin states that the "will is not taken away by grace, but is changed from evil into good . . . the human will does not obtain grace by freedom, but obtains freedom by grace;"[106] "[t]hus there is left to man such free will, if we please so to call it."[107] Concerning this doctrine, Edwards stringently follows Calvin's idea by insisting on the compatibilist doctrine that the liberty of the will and God's predetermination are not contradictory but harmonious with each other. Although Edwards does not refer to or quote Calvin's works, he imports some causation ideas from Calvin and Mastricht respectively, as follows:

> he causes them to be inclined where and when he will, either to bestow benefits, or to inflict punishments;[108]
>
> [t]he Reformed are of [the] opinion that all effects, whether they be contingent or necessary, happen surely and undeviatingly, provided their causes have been aroused and predetermined by the divine influx.[109]

As Mastricht notes, "The Reformed," such as Girolamo Zanchi (1516–1590) and Franciscus Gomarus (1563–1641), asserted the fourfold state of "free will [free choice] (*liberum arbitrium, αὐτεξούσιον*),"[110] the liberty before the Fall, after the Fall,

---

99. *FOW*, 164. Defined according to the common notion.
100. *FOW*, 147. The same as above.
101. *FOW*, 325. In certain circumstances.
102. *FOW*, 371.
103. *FOW*, 433. The liberty indicates "self-determining power."
104. Calvin, *Institutes*, II.iii.13.
105. Calvin, *Institutes*, II.iii.308.
106. Calvin, *Institutes*, II.iii.14.
107. Calvin, *Institutes*, II.iii.14. Cf. John Calvin, *The Bondage and Liberation of the Will: A Defence of the Orthodox Doctrine of Human Choice against Pighius*, trans. Graham I. Davies, ed. Ans Lane (Grand Rapids, MI: Baker, 1996), 69–70. In it, Calvin does "*deny that choice is free,...because [man's] will is corrupt he is held captive under the yoke of sin.*"
108. Calvin, *Institutes*, II.iii.9.
109. Petrus van Mastricht, *Theoretico Practica Theologia*, III.x.30, 17. Cf. Heppe, 266, 272; Adriaan C. Neele, *Petrus van Mastricht: Reformed Orthodoxy: Method and Piety* (Leiden: Brill, 2008).
110. The following editors prefer the term "free choice" to "free will." See Willem J. van Asselt, J

under grace, and in glory.[111] Gomarus, however, developed it more precisely than his predecessors, as the liberty before the Fall and after the Fall and before Conversion, in Conversion, and after Conversion.[112] All of them acknowledged the volition, acts, and liberty of the will within the limits that do not concede the Arminian notion of autonomous liberty.

One may notice that Augustine, Calvin, and Edwards agree on the states of the will respectively as follows: "Without the Spirit man's will is not free, since it has been laid under by shackling and conquering desires;"[113] "Man Has Now Been Deprived of Freedom of Choice and Bound Over to Miserable Servitude;"[114] "Man has *not so much freedom now* as he had before the fall, in this respect: now he has a will against a will, an inclination contrary to his reason and judgment."[115]

## 8. EDWARDS'S CHIEF ANTAGONISTS

In his *FOW*, Edwards disputes his three main antagonists: first, Thomas Chubb, an Arian deist, and his *A Collection of Tracts*; second, Daniel Whitby, an Arminian Anglican, and his "*Discourse on the Five Points*"; and third, Isaac Watts, "not properly Pelagian[s] nor Arminian[s]"[116] and yet a moderate Calvinist, and his *An Essay on Freedom of Will in God and in Creatures*. These three English divines were not all Arminian movers in eighteenth-century New England, but in Edwards's view, they were admittedly the chief English liberals. It was mainly Chubb who influenced Robert Breck to become a notorious Arminian in Edwards's locality. Edwards reaffirms that the opponents formulated the New England Arminianism of the eighteenth century.

### (1) Thomas Chubb (1679-1747)

Chubb read widely, and in 1701 he was brainwashed by the "historical preface" of William Whiston's *Primitive Christianity Revived* (1710). Chubb was dismissed on the grounds of his Arian unorthodoxy, although he was a successor of Isaac Newton at Cambridge.[117] Afterwards, he was involved in religious controversy. He was criticized

---

Martin Bac, and Roef T. de Velde, eds., *Reformed Thought on Freedom: The Concept of Free Choice in Early Modern Reformed Theology* (Texts and Studies in Reformation and Post-Reformation Thought, Grand Rapids, Baker, 2010), 5–6.

111. Willem J. van Asselt, *Reformed Thought on Freedom*, 89.

112. Willem J. van Asselt, *Reformed Thought on Freedom*, 138–143.

113. Augustine, *Letters* cxlv. 2 (MPL 33. 593; tr. NPNF VLL. 293). Cf. Calvin, *Institutes*, II.ii.8, 265.

114. This is the title of II. ii, 255. Calvin, *Institutes* II. ii, 255–289.

115. "*The 'Miscellanies'*: no. 436. Adam's Fall. Original Sin. Free Will," *WJE* 13:484.

116. "To the Reverend John Erskine, July 7, 1752." *WJE* 16:491.

117. The term "*Natural Philosophy*" is derived from Newton's *Philosophiae Naturalis Principia Mathematica* (1687) and was used much later in the title *Treatise on Natural Philosophy* (published in 1876 and reprinted in 1879) by Kelvin and Tait. Cotton Mather read the *Optics* and by 1712 had pronounced Newton "the *Perpetual Dictator* of the Learned World in the Principles of Natural

as an Arianist[118] for having written a treatise, *The Supremacy of the Father Asserted*, which Whiston helped him to correct and print in 1715.[119] Chubb's treatises were circulating among New Englanders like Edwards's,[120] and yet they were banned[121] and they could not be held by the libraries of Yale or Harvard College until Arminianism and other liberalisms became prevalent in the late eighteenth century.[122]

Therefore, Edwards also considered Chubb the first of his principal antagonists because the latter expressively "agrees, for the most part, with Arminians, in his notion of the freedom of the will," and because his "notion of the freedom of the will" had become "a leading article in the Arminian scheme."[123] Edwards and Chubb then clashed in their contradictory positions on the will; the former criticized the latter, asserting "there is none more unintelligible"[124] than Chubb's phrase concerning "the passive ground or reason of that action" that he regarded as the "motives and excitements to the action of the will" conceded "in all the writings of Duns Scotus,

---

Philosophy" in his *Thoughts for the Day of Rain in two essays* (Boston: B. Green, 1712), iii.

118. Thomas L. Bushell, *The Sage of Salisbury: Thomas Chubb 1679-1747* (New York: Philosophical Library, 1967), 143. Voltaire once praised Chubb's abilities as a thinker. It should also be noted, however, that Chubb's thoughts perplexed Voltaire. For example, Voltaire did not entirely deny the validity of the dogma of original sin, but Chubb did. See also Leslie Stephen, "Thomas Chubb," *Dictionary of National Biography*, ed. Sidney Lee, Volume 10 (New York: Macmillan, 1887), 298. Furthermore, in his *True Deism* (1749), Caleb Fleming accused Chubb of "modern deism," that is, "denying or disbelieving that God has made any express revelation of his love to the world, in the teachings of Christ and his apostles." Cf. Caleb Fleming, *True Deism, the Basis of Christianity: or, Observations on Mr. Thomas Chubb's Posthumous works* (London, 1749), vi.

119. Thomas L. Bushell, *The Sage of Salisbury: Thomas Chubb 1679-1747*, 8-9.

120. JE owned Chubb's *A Collection of Tracts of Various Subjects*, London (1 vol. of 1730, 2nd ed., 2 vols of 1754), which appears in the "Account Book." Cf. "Catalogue," *WJE* 26:324.

121. The first book banned in the New England colonies was T*he Meritorious Price of our Redemption, Justification, &c.* (printed in London, 1650), which was written by William Pynchon, founder of Springfield, Massachusetts. Charles Stearns, "Memoir of William Pynchon," *New England Historical and Genealogical Review* 13 (October 1859): 287.

122. William H. Bond and Hugh Amory, eds., "The 1723, 1773, 1790 Catalogues," PRINTED CATALOGUES OF THE HARVARD COLLEGE LIBRARY, 1723-1790 (Boston Colonial Society of Massachusetts, 1996), C162, C270-1, C317, C207, C271, C256; James E. Mooney, ed., "*The 1743, 1755, 1791 Catalogues*," Eighteenth-Century Catalogues of the Yale College Library (Yale University Beinecke Library, 2001). Chubb's books were only available from the *1790 Catalogue of Harvard College*, in which the majority are listed, including *The Supremacy of the Father Asserted*. Aside from these, Chubb wrote a multitude of treatises on various theological questions. Among over fifty popular deistic tracts are the following: *Supremacy of the Father vindicated* (1715, first work); *Discourse Concerning Reason* (1731); *An Enquiry into the Ground and Foundation of Religion, wherein it is shown that Religion is founded on Nature* (1738); *The True Gospel of Jesus Christ Vindicated* (1739), and *Discourse on Miracles* (1741).

123. *FOW*, 132. It is certain that Edwards disliked Thomas Chubb, who severely influenced Robert Breck, an Arminian candidate and then minister of Springfield, where "the late lamentable Springfield contention" arose.

124. *FOW*, 228.

or Thomas Aquinas."[125] In Edwards's view, Chubb could not be ranked merely as an Arminian because he "went far beyond the Arminians."[126]

## (2) Daniel Whitby (1638–1726)

Whitby had long been favored in the Church of England and became a prominent writer against Popery, but was also "first an evangelical Arminian, and then gradually a Unitarian."[127] In 1683, he anonymously published *The Protestant Reconciler*, a plea for a fuller communion between churchmen and dissenters. The book was condemned by the University of Oxford to be burned, and he was forced to renounce its most important principles. His most famous work is *A Paraphrase and Commentary on the New Testament*, which was held in esteem as an Arminian exposition.[128] In connection with this, he later produced *The Necessity and Usefulness of the Christian Revelation* (1705) and *Discourses on the Five Points* (1710).[129] The latter work stands out as the definitive exposition of Arminian doctrines against Calvinism, and it was abridged and often reprinted in New England as Whitby on the *Five Points*. Writing to Joseph Bellamy on January 15, 1747, Edwards informed him that he still "ha been reading Whitby, which ha engaged [him] pretty thoroughly in the study of the Arminian controversy."[130]

Whitby on the *Five Points* is a major focus in Edwards's *FOW*.[131] Whitby's books are detailed with criticisms of Calvinism, and in chapter IV of *Discourses on the Five Points*, Edwards insists that full freedom of the will exists, writing particularly about the "Liberty of the Will of Man in a state of Trial and Probation."

## (3) Isaac Watts (1674–1748)

Watts maintained Arminian doctrine: as Edwards described the former's doctrine, "moral necessity and impossibility is in effect the same thing [as] physical and natural necessity and impossibility."[132] Known as the greatest hymn writer, Watts was born in

---

125. *FOW*, 212.

126. *FOW*, 132.

127. Frank Hugh Foster, *A Genetic History of the New England Theology* (The University of Chicago Press, 1907), 274.

128. Samuel Austin Allibone, *A critical dictionary of English literature and British and American authors*, vol. 8 (Philadelphia: J. B. Lippincott company, 1871), 2681.

129. "A discourse concerning, I. The true import of the words of election and reprobation; and the things signified by them in the Holy Scripture. II. The extent of Christ's redemption. III. The grace of God; where it is enquired, whether it be vouchsafed sufficiently to those who improve it not, and irresistibly to those who do improve it; and whether men be wholly passive in the work of their regeneration? IV. The liberty of the will in a state of tryal and persecution. V. The perseverance or defectibility of the saints; with some reflections on the state of heathens, the providence and prescience of God (London, 1710; 2nd ed., corr., 1735)." Cf. *Catalogues of Books*, *WJE* 26:246, 352.

130. "To the Reverend Joseph Bellamy," *WJE* 16:217.

131. Ramsey, "Editor's Introduction," *FOW*, 81–89.

132. *FOW*, 381. Cf. Watts, *Essay*, Sec. 7, dif. 3: in *Works* 6:275.

Southampton, England, in 1674, and was brought up in a Nonconformist family. As a result, he was the only dissenter among the three most prominent antagonists.

Analyzing the main arguments in Watts's *Essay on Freedom of Will in God and in Creatures* (London, 1732), Edwards reasserts that the point is conceived as a landmark of Arminianism in the former's notion of "the soul's having power to cause and determine its own volitions, as a being to whom God has given a power of action,"[133] which is to say that the soul or will acts without any external cause. Watts, however, implies that liberty is necessary to moral agents and yet necessity is inconsistent with their moral acts and duties.[134]

Guelzo notes that "Calvinists, even great and famous ones like Isaac Watts, took appropriate note and abandoned the predestination ship."[135] Likewise, Watts declared himself as a moderate Calvinist in his works,[136] and he defended the doctrine of election, but he rejected that of reprobation.[137] Watts, according to Edwards, gradually changed his position, held to the Pelagian notion of the freedom of the will, agreed with Arminian arguments and consequently departed from Calvinism.

## 9. MAIN ARGUMENTS

### (1) Theistic Determinism versus Arminian Libertarianism

A point of controversy between Calvinists and Arminians, then, was the problem of determinism versus libertarianism. This issue escalated when *FOW* was published. In Edwards's viewpoint, "some degree of liberty" is universally supposed to be incompatible with the moral necessity of men's volitions, but it is compatible with "a sort of liberty" which he maintains. The libertarians of "a higher sort or degree of freedom" hold to the self-determination in the will and the liberty of contingency and indifference.[138]

---

133. Isaac Watts, *An Essay on Freedom of Will in God and in Creatures* (London, 1732), 68–69, sec, 6, *obj.* 2 and *ans.*; reprinted in *The Works of the Reverend and Learned Isaac Watts, D.D.*, ed. Jennings and Doddridge, 1st ed., 6 vols. (London, 1753); 6 vols, (London, 1811), 6:265. Cf. *FOW*, 187, in "Section 4. Whether volition can rise without a cause, through the activity of the nature of the soul."

134. *FOW*, 417. Cf. Guelzo, 66–69.

135. Daniel Whitby, *A Discourse Concerning: I. The true import of the words election and reprobation . . . II. The extent of Christ's redemption. III. The grace of God . . . IV. The liberty of the will . . . V. The perseverance or detectability of the saints* (London: Printed for John Wyat, 1710), 13.

136. One might not find better resources of the criticism of Watts than those referred to in Ramsey's Editor's Introduction to *Freedom of the Will*. The latter heavily relies on Roland N. Stromberg, *Religious Liberalism in Eighteenth-Century England* (Oxford: Oxford University Press, 1954), 116; Jeremy Belknap, *Memoirs of the Lives, Characters and Writings of Dr. Isaac Watts and Dr. Philip Doddridge* (Boston, 1793), 24.

137. Watts's *The Ruin and Recovery of Mankind* (1740) inspired John Wesley to import Watts's doctrine, and *Serious Considerations Concerning the Doctrines of Election and Reprobation* (1740) is composed by extracting from its chapter 13.

138. *FOW*, 455.

Nonetheless, an "Arminian, Pelagian, or Epicurean," whom Edwards pegged as libertarian, has a notion of the liberty that is "power in the mind to determine itself, but not by its choice or according to its pleasure" and that is to be exercised by "a determination arising contingently out of a state of absolute indifference."[139] Such an absurd sort of liberty would lead one to suppose the existence of the "sovereignty of the will, self-determining power, self-motion, self-direction, arbitrary decision, liberty *ad utrumvis*, power of choosing differently in given cases, etc., as long as they will."[140]

Arminian libertarianism implies that the will is always at liberty, always free, and "itself determines all free acts of the will,"[141] and also that such a notion of free will is opposite to that of necessity, i.e., casual or theistic determinism. Edwards identifies the strongest motive or God as the first cause (*causa prima*), which determines a person to choose what they please, rather than otherwise.[142] Even so, God's sovereign determination does not "necessitate men to do a thing contrary to his will" or by "force, compulsion, and coaction," but God determines them to choose and do freely as they will by the strongest motive in the mind.[143] Such freedom of the will, Edwards holds, is compatible with such a causal determinism; that is to say, he insists upon theistic compatibilism.

## (2) Doctrine of Necessity vs. Stoical Fatalism and Hobbes' Mechanism

Edwards classifies ancient Stoics as Arminians because they assert similar doctrines. These Stoics included Epicurus, who maintained contingence but excluded necessity,[144] and also some other theists like Hobbes, who followed "the Stoical doctrine of fate" and the "doctrine of necessity."[145] So Whitby supposes that Stoics maintained a doctrine similar to that of Calvinists, and yet he "alleges agreement of the Stoics with the Arminians."[146] Of course, Edwards does not reject all truth of liberty and necessity that was demonstrated by Hobbes, but he also does not admit "the universal fatality [fatalism]" that "is inconsistent with any liberty that is possible" and "with the world's being in all things subject to the disposal of an intelligent wise agent,"[147] and the universal mechanism,[148] "[m]aking men mere machines."[149]

---

139. *FOW*, 454.

140. *FOW*, 454–55.

141. *FOW*,, 171.

142. Cf. *FOW*, 141: "It is that *motive*, which, as it stands in the view of the mind, is the strongest, that determines the will."

143. *FOW*, 164, 142.

144. *FOW*, 420

145. *FOW*, 192, 193, 372. For other deistic antagonists of Edwards, see Gottfried Wilhelm Leibniz, 114–16; Samuel Clarke, 217, 224, 263; George Turnbull, 217–18; Lord Kames Henry Home, 443–45.

146. *FOW*, 372.

147. *FOW*, 374.

148. The universal mechanism is found in the opening passages of the *Leviathan* by Thomas Hobbes (1651).

149. *FOW*, 430.

As Locke could formulate his principles of human understanding and action by responding to issues raised by Newton's *Principia,* Edwards was influenced by Newton through Locke. Consequently, Edwards adapted the Newtonian determinism that antecedent causes determine the processes of actions, but he rejected Hobbes' mechanistic determinism.[150]

In fact, English Arminians first raised the issues of fatalism and mechanism to object to the Calvinist doctrine of necessity by indicating that Calvinists agreed with Hobbes about many things, but Edwards defends it by reporting on the Arminian objection, stating that

> [T]he Arminians agree with Mr. Hobbes in many more things than the Calvinists. As, in what he is said to hold concerning original sin, in denying the necessity of supernatural illumination, in denying infused grace, in denying the doctrine of justification by faith alone; and other things.[151]

Thus, Edwards disputes Arminians' misunderstanding of the theistic and causal determinism as mechanism and fatalism and formulates his necessitarianism to be compatible with the freedom of the will, which is formulated in the Calvinist tradition.[152]

## 10. EDWARDS'S CONCLUSION: "FIVE POINTS OF CALVINISM"

The "grand issue" for Edwards, relating to the doctrine of the will, is interestingly central to the "five points" concluding *FOW*. In his own *Conclusion*, "by clearing and establishing" the Calvinist doctrine of will, Edwards undermines the five chief objections of Arminians against Calvinism, that is, the five trajectories of the freewill controversy that resonate with the *Canons of Dort* (1618–19) ratified in the Synod of Dort held to solve the Remonstrant and Contra-Remonstrant controversy in 1618–19, as the following Table I shows:

---

150. Ryan D. Tweney, "Jonathan Edwards and Determinism," *Journal of the History of the Behavioral Sciences* 33(4) (Fall 1997): 366.

151. *FOW*, 374.

152. "Although Calvin does not avow compatibilism in so many words, his views on providence and predestination, as well as his doctrine of the bondage of the will to sin and the need for efficacious grace, fit snugly with compatibilism. Calvin is also a resolute opponent of 'Stoic fate,' arguing that in that scheme God himself is subject to fate." See Paul Helm, "8. Calvin the Compatibilist," in *Calvin at the Centre* (Oxford and New York: Oxford University Press, 2010), 227–272.

| T.U.L.I.P. or, The Five Points of Calvinism | Cannons of Dort[153] | Five Points of Edwards[154] |
|---|---|---|
| I. Total Depravity | 3rd + 4th Human Corruption, Conversion to God, and the Way It Occurs | Total depravity and corruption of man's nature |
| II. Unconditional Election | 1st Divine Election and Reprobation | Efficacious grace |
| III. Limited Atonement | | Absolute, eternal, personal election |
| IV. Irresistible Grace | | |
| | | Die for all, . . .yet particular |
| V. Perseverance of the Saints | 5th The Perseverance of the Saints | Perseverance of saints |

Edwards first makes a list of the five objections of Arminians against Calvinism, and then explains it concretely.

### (1) "The total depravity and corruption of man's nature"

Edwards notes, "From these things it will inevitably follow." He puts "man's nature" first, for he views it as the core part in reconstructing the Calvinist doctrine of "total corruption and depravity"[155] and the inability of men, according to the "teaching and maintaining" of "the first Reformers and others that succeeded them," and he calls it "Calvinistic."[156]

### (2) "Efficacious grace"

Arminius himself declares that "Gratia est non vis irresistibilis (Grace is not an irresistible one)."[157] But to Edwards, divine grace is conceived as "divine assistance" or "God's

---

153. The *Canons* were originally written in Latin: *Acta Synodi Nationalis* (Leiden: Elsevier, 1620), *Actes du synode national, tenu à Dordrecht l'an 1618 & 1619 ensemble des jugementtant des théologiens étrangersqueceux des Provinces-Unies des Pays-Bas. Mis en Français, par Richard Jean de Nérée* (Leiden : Isaac Elsevir) / added author(s): Richard Jean de Nerée, and its first English translation was more recently discovered: *T H E I V D G E M E N T OF THE S Y N O D E Holden at D O R T, Concerning the fiue Articles: As also their sentence touching CONRADVS VORSTIVS* (Theatrum Orbis Terrarum, 1619, 83 pages); *Canons, ratified in the National Synod of the Reformed Church, held at Dordrecht in the years 1618 & 1619* (trans. by anonymous in 1812), Thomas Scott, *The Articles of the Synod of Dort* (London in 1817, Philadelphia Presbyterian Board of Publication, 1856' reprint, Sprinkle Publications, 1993), Philip Schaff in *Creeds of Christendom*, vol. I:550–80 (translated and printed in 1877), Anthony Hoekema in 1968, and a new translation adopted by the 1986 at the Synod of the Christian Reformed Church (CRC), USA. In the study *T H E IVDGEMENT OF THE SYNODE Holden at DORT* is primarily consulted. For detailed five points, see page 3–56.

154. *FOW*, 432–436.

155. *FOW*, 373.

156. *FOW*, 437.

157. Art. Non., in *Opera*, 959; *Works* II:722. Quoted in Stanglin, *Assurance*, 81; Idem, *Arminius, Arminianism, and Europe: Jacobus Arminius*, 15.

assistance or influence," which "is always efficacious to do that which we are assisted to," which is "all that God intends it shall be efficacious [to]; that is, when God assists, he assists to all that he intends to assist to."[158] In his view, when grace is bestowed on a man, it sovereignly affects his will, which was deprived because of the Fall. However, Arminius holds that grace and man's free will cooperate to bring an individual to salvation, as he said elsewhere: "A man receives by his own free choice the grace . . . as grace saves, so the free will is saved, and the subject of grace is man's free will."[159] So for them, grace is not the primary cause of man's salvation, but just a concomitant one. Such doctrine of grace and will challenge Edwards, so he oppositely identifies grace with "divine influence" and proves it to be "efficacious, yea, and irresistible too."[160] "Irresistible" means that it is ever impossible for the moral necessity of grace to "be violated by any resistance." It is God's "determining efficacy and power" that works out the good as God's virtue in the heart of man, and God "does decisively, in his providence, order all the volitions of moral agents, either by positive influence or permission."[161]

In summary, Edwards establishes the doctrine of "irresistible grace," i.e., "determining efficacious grace," which frees man's enslaved will to will "the good" or "to resist his own will."[162] When "the effect of grace is the will," it is not "possible for a man to will a thing and not will it at the same time."[163]

## (3) "Absolute, eternal, personal election"

Arminians hold "election of nations and societies, and general election of the Christian church, and *conditional election* of particular persons," (italics mine) which signify that "God could not decree before the foundation of the world, to save all that should believe in and obey Christ, unless he had absolutely decreed that salvation should be provided, and effectually wrought out by Christ."[164]

The main objection of Arminians against the doctrine of "God's absolute, eternal, personal election in particular" is, however, that if God foreknows and predestines "the volitions of moral agents" and "the future moral state and acts of men," then the warnings, expostulations, rewards, and punishments must not have to be established. This would make God the author of sin.

---

158. "No. 5. Irresistible Grace," *The Miscellanies*, WJE 13:207.

159. "Examination of Perkins's Pamphlet," *The Works of Arminius* III:470.

160. JE prefers "efficacious" to "irresistible," because the latter term "is relative . . . and is insufficient to withstand the power, or hinder the effect." *FOW*, 149. "JE disliked the Calvinist use of the word 'irresistible' for grace since that gives the impression that human beings are like dumb blocks of wood that do not participate in their own decisions. JE stressed that "we are free in our willing: we choose what we want. In Grace God moves our will, but it is our will," McClymond and McDermott, 363.

161. *FOW*, 433.

162. "No.5. Irresistible Grace," *The Miscellanies*, WJE 13:170–71.

163. *WJE* 13:170–71.

164. *FOW*, 286. Note that, owing to this sentence, many scholars misinterpret Edwards as an infralapsarian.

Edwards refutes these Arminian objections on the ground of "God's certain foreknowledge" in *FOW*.[165] He shows that "God has an absolute and certain foreknowledge of the *free* actions of moral agents" (italics added by the author). That is, "If God doesn't foreknow, he can't foretell such events."[166] The volitions of men are foreseen, so they are foreknown and then foretold by God. The following shows his conception of unconditional election by God:

> If God did not foreknow the fall of man, nor the redemption by Jesus Christ, nor the volitions of man since the fall; then he did not foreknow the saints in any sense; neither as particular persons, nor as societies or nations; either by election, or mere foresight of their virtue or good works; or any foresight of anything about them relating to their salvation; or any benefit they have by Christ, or any manner of concern of theirs with a Redeemer.[167]

Therefore, at this point, Edwards reveals his supralapsarianism again,[168] saying the elect are elected "by his eternal design or decree,"[169] and "from eternity,"[170] that is, before the foundation of the world.

### (4) "Particular...redemption"

This doctrine is what, in his youth, Edwards disagreed with: the doctrine of "God's sovereignty, in choosing whom he would to eternal life, and rejecting whom he please," namely 'double predestination'—condemning it as "horrible doctrine." By experiencing his "first conviction," he came to admire it as "sweet doctrine."[171]

However, Arminius insisted on 'unlimited atonement,' i.e., 'universal redemption,' which means Jesus died for all humanity, i.e., 'unlimited atonement,' to which Edwards seems to agree in saying that "Christ in some sense may be said to *die for all*, and to redeem all visible Christians, yea, the whole world by his death; yet there must be something *particular* in the design of his death."[172] He elsewhere explains in detail:

> Now Arminians, when [they] say that Christ died for all, cannot mean, with any sense, that he died for all any otherwise than to give all an opportunity to be saved; and that, Calvinists themselves never denied. He did die for all in this sense; it is past all contradiction.[173]

---

165. *FOW*, "Part II, SECTION 11. THE EVIDENCE OF GOD'S CERTAIN FOREKNOWLEDGE OF THE VOLITIONS OF MORAL AGENTS," 239–256.

166. *FOW*, 239.

167. *FOW*,, 252–53.

168. JE, "SUPRALAPSARIANS," MSC no.292, *WJE* 13:383–84.

169. *FOW*, 435.

170. *FOW*, 434.

171. "Personal Narrative," *WJE* 16:792.

172. *FOW*, 435.

173. *The "Miscellanies": (Entry Nos. a-z, aa-zz, 1–500)*, *WJE* 13:174.

Edwards states that 'limited atonement' implies that "there must be something *particular* in the design of his death . . . God has the actual salvation or redemption of a certain number . . . only . . . of the salvation of the elect in giving Christ to die."[174]

### (5) "Perseverance of Saints"

As described by Edwards, this doctrine is of "the infallible and necessary perseverance of saints," and it is defined as "the continuance of professors in the practice of their duty, and being steadfast in a holy walk, through the various *trials* that they meet with," in his *Religious Affections*,[175] and as "a note of sincerity" in sermons,[176] and as "steadfastness" and "certainty of events" in a letter related to *FOW*.[177] This doctrine was condemned by Arminians as "repugnant to the freedom of the will; that it must be owing to man's own self-determining power,"[178] and became one of the most controversial issues since the contention between Augustine and Pelagius.

Arminians, according to Edwards, chronically oppose the belief that perseverance is "infallible and necessary," because, firstly, they suppose it to be "repugnant to the freedom of the will" that depends on "man's own self-determining power." Secondly, they assume that if man has no such freedom, his obedience and efforts would not be his praiseworthy virtue, nor would they be a matter of commands and promises, and he would not be warned against his apostasy. Edwards removes the inconstancies of their objections by representing "steadfastness and perseverance" as "the virtue of the saints" and the subject of God's commands or warnings.

In conclusion, according to Edwards, the principal issue of the Arminian teachings in New England was centralized in the understanding of the doctrine of the freedom of the will. He was historically informed of and returned to the tenets of the *Canons of Dort*, including the doctrines of election, predestination, grace and perseverance of the saints.

## 11. PUBLISHING HISTORY AND MODERNIZATION AND ANNOTATIONS OF THE TEXT

### (1) Brief Publishing History of Edwards's Works and *Freedom of the Will*

For most readers, it is necessary to overview a brief publishing history of Edwards's collected works and in particular *Freedom of the Will*, in order to observe the reception and influence of the latter.

---

174. *FOW*, 435.
175. *Religious Affections, WJE* 2:389.
176. "Signs of Godliness," *WJE* 21:480; "Matt. 7:21," *WJE Online* 45.
177. *FOW*, 436.
178. *FOW*, 435–36.

First, diverse editions of the collected works of Edwards were printed and reprinted even during the first half of the 19th Century, and *Freedom of the Will* was appraised as an important piece and included in all these collected editions:[179]

1) *Works of President Edwards*, ed. E. Williams and E. Parsons. 8 vols. (Vol. I containing *Memoirs of Mr. Edwards* by Samuel Hopkins)[180], Leeds, 1806–1811; reprinted in a new edition, London, 1817;

2) *Works of President Edwards*, ed. Samuel Austin. 8 vols. (Vol. I containing *Memoirs of the Late Reverend Jonathan Edwards* by Samuel Hopkins), Worcester, 1808–9; reprinted with additions, including the supplementary volumes edited by Ogle and an index, New York, 1847, and various titles since;

3) *Works of President Edwards*, ed. by Sereno E. Dwight. 10 vols. (Vol. I containing a *Memoir of his Life* by Dwight), New York, 1829, 1830;

4) *Works of Jonathan Edwards*, ed. by Edward Hickman. 2 vols., London, 1834; with an essay on the Genius and Writings of Edwards by Henry Rogers and the *Memoir* by Dwight that was revised and corrected by E. Hickman, London, 1834; reprinted in one volume, London, 1835; 10 vols., Edinburgh, 1847, reissued by The Banner of Truth Trust in 2 vols., Edinburgh in 1974, reprinted in 1976, 1979, 1984, 1987, 1990, 1992;

5) *Works of President Edwards*, in 4 vols., a reprint of the Worcester edition, with additions and a copious general index. (Vol. I containing *Memoirs of President Edwards* by Samuel Hopkins), New York, 1843; Boston, 1843; Philadelphia, 1843.

6) *Works of President Edwards*, in 6 vols., a supplementary to the New York's four volume edition, 1843), Edinburgh, Glasgow, London, New York, 1847.

7) *Works of Jonathan Edwards*, ed. by Edward Hickman. 2 vols., London, 1834; with an essay on the Genius and Writings of Edwards by Henry Rogers and the *Memoir* by Dwight, that was revised and corrected by E. Hickman, London, 1834; reprinted in one volume, London, 1835; 10 vols., Edinburgh, 1847, reissued by The Banner of Truth Trust in 2 vols., Edinburgh in 1974, reprinted in 1976, 1979, 1984, 1987, 1990, 1992.

179. I made a list of these works on the basis of Ola Winslow's *Jonathan Edwards* of 1939; Thomas H. Johnson, *The Printed Writings of Jonathan Edwards 1703–1758* (Princeton University Press, 1940), 112–127; M. X. Lesser, "An Honor Too Great: Jonathan Edwards in Print Abroad," in *Jonathan Edwards at Home and Abroad: Historical Memories, Cultural Movements, Global Horizons*, ed. David William Kling and Douglas A. Sweeney (University of South Carolina Press, 2003), 304–313.

180. Samuel Hopkins's *Memoirs* was reprinted from Samuel Hopkins, *The Life and Character of the Late Reverend Mr. Jonathan Edwards, President of the College of New Jersey: Together with a Number of his Sermons on Various Important Subjects* (Boston: S. Kneeland, 1765).

8) *Works of President Edwards*, in 4 vols., a reprint of the Worcester edition, with additions and a copious general index. (Vol. I containing *Memoirs of President Edwards* by Samuel Hopkins), New York, 1843; Boston, 1843; Philadelphia, 1843. *Works of President Edwards*, in 6 vols., a supplementary to the New York's four volume edition, 1843), Edinburgh, Glasgow, London, New York, 1847.

Second, the first English edition of *Freedom of the Will* was published as a monography in Boston, 1754. The second edition was printed in Boston in 1762 and reprinted in London in 1762. The third edition added "Remarks on Lord Kames' *Essays*" as an appendix and was printed in London in 1768, Glasgow in 1790, and Albany in 1804. The fourth edition was printed in London in 1775 and Wilmington in 1790. The fifth edition was printed as follows: London,1790; London, 1816; Edinburgh: Oliver and Boyd, 1818; Edinburgh: Thomas Turnbull, 1818; London, 1818; with "An Introductory Essay" by Isaac Taylor,[181] the author of *Natural History of Enthusiasm*, Liverpool, 1827; New York, 1828; Edinburgh, 1830; new edition with "An Introductory Essay" by Isaac Taylor, London, 1831; with an Index, Andover and New York, 1840; London and Edinburgh, 1845; New York, 1851; Liverpool, 1855.

In addition to English versions, there is a Dutch translation, Utrecht, 1774, and a Welsh translation, Bangor, 1865.

## (2) Modernization of the Text

The primary aim of this edition is to provide 21st century readers with the original style and vivid voice of Edwards's eighteenth-century writing. Many editing peculiarities in the 1754's original edition were removed by Paul Ramsey, the editor of the Yale edition, in 1957 in order to modernize it. In his edition, all capitalization is removed and lower case is used. But in this edition, some of capitalizations and italicization that are considered by this editor to vivify the author's unique tone have been restored.

In this edition's text are [square brackets] used to mark off the original author's emphasis or explanations, and (parentheses) used to do so for paginations and Bible references, excepting the footnotes.

This editor indented passages that are not direct quotations with the intention of helping readers grasp the point of a passage or to explain the author's argumentation in a paragraph. Edwards's discussions are very logical and lengthy, and so hundreds of signposts, summaries, and Q&As in italics were needed in this edition.

All old spellings such as "it Self (=> itself)," "chuse (=> choose)," "spake (=> spoke)," "shew (=> show)" and even "shewn (=> shown)"[182] are modernized, as are contractions such as "don't (=> doesn't)," and "ben't (=> isn't or aren't)," according to

---

181. In 1859 Taylor expanded *Essay* and published it as "Logic in Theology" in his book *Logic in Theology, and other Essays*. Also note that in the 1877 reprinted edition by Edward Hopewell, its subjects were classified by "Free Will and Determinism."

182. Ramsey did retain it, but in this edition it is modernized, as well as some contractions like "ben't," a negative contraction that meant "isn't" or "aren't" in written English in the 1600s.

their person and tense. In this edition, some exceptions are made to capitalization or spelling when it might preserve Edwards's authentic accentuation. Edwards used italics for actual and indirect quotations, but this edition omits italics, and quotations are indented.

The original sources of footnotes are always identified by referring to the author's name, such as "Edwards" or "Ramsey," but the name of this editor is deliberately omitted.

### (3) Annotations of the Text

Annotations are given in this edition with great hesitation, because they could undermine the original intention of the author and interfere with the creative understanding and interpretation of an educated reader. Nevertheless, as is already acknowledged by most experts and many readers who have been uncomfortable because of the difficulty of the text, full annotations are highly demanded. This is the first attempt to give full annotations since 1754. They serve to help readers read quickly to gain a sense of what each paragraph is about and what arguments the author conducts in it.

Edwards's important ideas are hidden in the text, so they are highlighted by headlines, summaries, and questions that are inserted between paragraphs. The annotations show Edwards's philosophical and theological points. Their meanings are explained, and any confusing words or phrases are defined in the footnotes.

## 12. RECEPTION AND INFLUENCE OF *FREEDOM OF THE WILL*

Perry Miller stated that Edwards's magnum opus, *Freedom of the Will*, "has been most widely spread abroad of all his works"[183] and selected it to be Volume No. 1 of the Yale edition of Edwards's works. Its first edition was published in Boston in 1754; the second and third in London in 1762[184] and 1768. The fourth English edition appeared in London in 1775, followed by two more British editions in 1790. According to Ramsey's tally, during the first half of the nineteenth century, of the ten separate editions—collected works excepted—six were brought out in England and four in New England.[185] Moreover, the first non-English version was a Dutch translation[186] in 1774; then it was translated into the Welsh language in 1865. Its readership, especially in English-speaking Great Britain, was so wide that Edwards's work attracted some notable proponents for, and opponents of, the doctrine of the will. Among the proponents were Andrew Fuller, William Godwin, John Collett, John Ryland, Jr., and Ed-

---

183. Perry Miller, "General Editor's Note," *FOW*, vii.

184. Anonymous, "Review of Freedom of the Will," *Monthly Review of Literary Journal* 27 (1762 December): 434–38.

185. Paul Ramsey, "Editor's Introduction," *FOW*, 118–19.

186. Een bepaald en nauwkeurig onderzoek van de thans heerschende denkbeelden over de vrijheid van den wil, (. . .) lof en schande te behoren (Utrecht, 1774)

ward Williams. Opponents included Lord Kames, George Hill, John Newton, David Hume, Joseph Priestley, William Hamilton, Dugald Stewart, Samuel Taylor Coleridge, James Dana, Stephen West, Samuel West, and Henry Philip Tappan.

This phenomenon continued in the late 18th century and afterwards became very complicated: Princeton Presbyterians Archibald Alexander and John Witherspoon embraced Thomas Reid's Scottish Common Sense Realism, which argued that all human beings are endowed with common sense and their feelings and actions are governed by its basic principles. The faculty of common sense brings out *intuitive knowledge* in man—that is, innate and immediate knowledge—but *certain knowledge* is to be acquired through empirical observation of the external world.[187] Although Reid read and summarized Edwards's *Freedom of the Will*[188] and, as James Harris permits,[189] embraced his key principles, he disputed Edwards's Calvinistic Necessarianism. Nevertheless, Samuel Baird, James Henry Thornwell, and Henry Boynton Smith later advocated for Edwards, as did Scottish Presbyterians Thomas Chalmers, John McLeod Campbell and James Orr.[190] The fact that Edwards's philosophical thesis on the will was apparently employed by Lord Kames and Reid in Scotland as well as by many intellectuals in New England demonstrates this new viewpoint: that Edwards, rather than merely being influenced by European theologians and philosophers, in fact influenced them, not only theologically but also philosophically. Nevertheless, further research is needed to find out which other European philosophers, like Kames and Reid, reacted to this work.

## 13. EDWARDS'S FUNDAMENTAL QUESTIONS OF THE WILL:

(1)   What is the will? Pt. I. St. 1.

(2)   What is the volition? Pt. I. St. 2.

(3)   What determines the will? Pt. I. St. 2.

(4)   What influences, directs, or determines the mind or will to come to such a conclusion or choice as it does? What is the cause, ground or reason? Why it concludes thus, and not otherwise? Pt. I. St. 2.

(5)   What is the cause and reason of the soul's exerting such an act? Pt. II. St. 2.

---

187. Among Reid's major works were *Inquiry into the Human Mind on the Principles of Common Sense* (1764), *Essays on the Intellectual Powers of Man* (1785), and *Active Powers of the Human Mind* (1788).

188. Harris, 191. I am grateful to James Harris for drawing my attention to Reid's summary note and thought.

189. Harris, 217.

190. Mark Noll, "Jonathan Edwards, Edwardsean Theologies, and Presbyterians," in *After Jonathan Edwards: The Courses of the New England Theology*, ed. Oliver D. Crisp and Douglas A. Sweeney (Oxford University Press on Demand, 2012), 178–196.

(6) How a spirit endowed with activity comes to act, as why it exerts such an act, and not another; or why it acts with such a particular determination? Pt. II. St. 7.

(7) Wherein consists the mind's liberty in any particular act of volition? Pt. II. St. 2.

(8) How can the mind first act? What motives shall be the ground and reason of its volition and choice? Pt. III. St. 1.

(9) Is there, or can be any such thing, as a volition which is contingent in such a sense, as not only to come to pass without any necessity of constraint or coaction, but also without a *necessity of consequence*, or an infallible connection with anything foregoing. Whether, if it were so, this would at all help the cause of liberty. Whether volition is a thing that ever does, or can come to pass, in this manner, contingently? Pt. II. St. 8.

(10) Do we act freely? Pt. I. St. 5.

(11) How is the will related to the intellect, or how the act of willing is knowledge or knowing? Pt. II. St. 9.

(12) Whether intellect or will ought to have first place? Pt. II. St. 9.

(13) How does the understanding move the will? Pt. II. St. 9.

(14) Is free will compatible with necessary determinism? Pt. I. St. 3.

(15) What conditions must obtain for an action to be worthy of praise or blame? Pt. I. St. 5; Pt. IV. St. 3.

(16) Are we responsible for our actions? Pt. III. St. 3.

(17) What kind of freedom is necessary to be morally accountable beings? Pt. II. St. 8.

(18) Why should we thank God for His goodness, any more than if He were forced to be good, or any more than we should thank one of our fellow creatures who did us good, not freely, and of good will, or from any kindness of heart, but from mere compulsion, or extrinsical necessity? Pt. III. St. 1.

(19) Why does God command, if man has not free will and power to obey? Pt. III. St. 4.

(20) What need of Christ's dying, to satisfy for the imperfections of our obedience? Pt. III. St. 4.

(21) Will it be as the libertarian claim—that we could have acted otherwise? Pt. III. St. 5.

(22) Or will it be along the lines of a compatibilist—we are free as long as we can do as we please? Pt. I. St. 2; Pt. I. St. 3; Pt. II. St. 5.

(23) Why do they choose sin? Pt. IV. St. 9, 10.

(24) Why might not God as well have first made them with a fixed prevailing principle of sin in their heart? Pt. IV. St. 10.

(25) How does Adam's sin create a certainty of everyone else's depraved behavior? Pt. IV. St. 10.

(26) How is it possible that a morally unfallen individual like Adam could commit a sin? Pt. IV. St. 10.

(27) How sin come into the world? Pt. IV. St. 10.

(28) Was the Fall part of the divine decree? Pt. IV. St. 9.

(29) Was reprobation considered as an act of God's sovereignty? Pt. IV. St. 7.

(30) To what degree his writings express the potential of human power (liberty)? Pt. II. St. 1.

(83)[191] What is the true idea of God's decrees? Pt. II. St. 12.

(84) Are God's acts or volitions successive? Or do they successively take place in the divine mind? Pt. IV. St. 8.

(85) Did God decree the existence of sin? Pt. IV. St. 9.

(86) For what end did God decree the existence of sin? Pt. IV. St. 9.

(87) In what sense is sin agreeable to the will of God? Pt. IV. St. 9.

(88) Is the present system of the universe the best possible? Pt. IV. St. 8.

(89) What is the difference between the secret and revealed will of God? Pt. IV. St. 9.

(90) In what sense and in what manner did God introduce sin into the world? Pt. IV. St. 9.

(91) How do you answer the objection that this makes God the author of sin? Pt. IV. St. 9.

(92) If the influence of God destroys the creature's free agency, can that influence produce sin in the creature? Pt. IV. St. 9.

(93) If the divine influence does not destroy the creature's free agency, in what sense, liable to objection, is God the author of sin? Pt. IV. St. 9.

(94) What is necessary to constitute a moral agent? Pt. I. St. 5.

(95) What is that liberty, which is necessary to moral agency? Pt. I. St. 5.

(96) Do we always act from motive? Or what do you mean by motive? Pt. I. St. 2 and 4.

---

191. The questions no. 83–111 are taken out from "The Theological Questions," which was made by Jonathan Edwards, Jr., for they are related to the topic of this book. For that the numbers are not changed. No. 83–111, "The Theological Questions of President Edwards, Senior, and Dr. Edwards, his son," *WJE Online* 39.

## Free Will

(97) Is a capacity to know our duty, necessary to moral agency? Pt. I. St. 5.

(98) Is self-determination necessary to moral agency? Pt. I. St. 5.

(99) Are we conscious that our volitions are not effected by any cause without ourselves? Pt. I. St. 4.

(100) Must our volitions be self-determinate in order that they may be our own? Pt. I. St. 4.

(101) Are men moral agents? Pt. I. St. 5.

(102) What is the difference between natural and moral necessity and ability? Pt. III. St. 3; Pt. IV. St. 7; Pt. III. St. 4.

(103) How can absolute moral necessity and inability be consistent with free agency? Pt. IV. St. 12; Pt. III. St. 3.

(104) How can the doctrine of universal absolute decrees be consistent with free agency in man? Pt. II. St. 12.

(105) Is it consistent with human liberty that God should efficiently produce volition in the human heart? Pt. II. St. 12.

(106) Is it equally consistent with human liberty, that God should efficiently produce in the human heart an evil volition as a good one? Pt. IV. St. 10.

(107) If God were to produce an evil volition in the human heart, would it prove that God were a sinner, or that he loves sin? Pt. IV. St. 9.

(108) If moral necessity be inconsistent with liberty, can God be the author of sin? Pt. IV. St. 9.

(109) How do you make it appear that men may be accountable, though they be not the efficient causes of their own volitions? Pt. II. St. 11.

(110) If all the volitions of men be decreed, how are they in a state of probation? Pt. II. St. 11.

(111) How do you prove a particular, special providence in every event? Pt. IV. St. 9.

# Author's Preface

*Arminians hate to be called "Arminian."*

Many find much fault with the calling professing Christians[1] that differ one from another in some matters of opinion by distinct names, especially calling them by the names of particular men who have distinguished themselves as maintainers and promoters of those opinions; as the calling some professing Christians "Arminians," from Arminius; others "Arians," from Arius; others "Socinians," from Socinus, and the like. They think it unjust in itself, as it seems to suppose and suggest that the persons marked out by these names received those doctrines which they entertain out of regard to, and reliance on, those men after whom they are named, as though they made them their rule; in the same manner, as the followers of Christ are called "Christians" after his name, whom they regard and depend upon as their great Head and Rule. Whereas, this is an unjust and groundless imputation on those that go under the aforementioned denominations. Thus [say they] there is not the least ground to suppose that the chief divines, who embrace the scheme of doctrine which is by many called Arminianism,[2] believe it the more because Arminius believed it, and that there is no reason to think any other than that they sincerely and impartially study the Holy Scriptures and inquire after the mind of Christ, with as much judgment and sincerity as any of those that call them by these names; that they seek after truth and are not careful whether they think exactly as Arminius did; yea, that in some things they actually differ from him.

---

1. [The word "professing" means to affirm openly. So a "professing Christian" is one who affirms their faith openly. Edwards saw many who outwardly declared their belief but did not actually prove in their moral actions to be real believers. Hereafter Paul Ramsey's footnotes in Yale edition are marked as "[Ramsey, . . .]"; Edwards's original footnotes in the first edition of 1754 remain unchanged. Otherwise footnotes are made by the editor of this edition, if they are not marked specifically.]

2. [Arminianism is known as the theological system of the Dutch theologian, Jacobus Arminius (1560–1609). He rejected the doctrine of predestination of the first Reformers, which claimed that prior to the Fall God preordained the salvation of some souls. Until Jonathan Edwards (1703–1758) and other Calvinists posed a problem of it, there was no serious awareness of it in New England during the early eighteenth century.]

***Edwards (hereafter JE) claims Arminians differ from Jacobus Arminius.***

This practice is also esteemed actually injurious on this account, that it is supposed naturally to lead the multitude to imagine the difference between persons thus named and others to be greater than it is; yea, as though it were so great that they must be as it were another species of beings. And they object against it as arising from an uncharitable, narrow, contracted spirit, which they say commonly inclines persons to confine all that is good to themselves and their own party, make a wide distinction between themselves and others, and stigmatize those that differ from them with odious names.

They say, moreover, that the keeping up such a distinction of names has a direct tendency to uphold distance and disaffection and keep alive mutual hatred among Christians, who ought all to be united in friendship and charity; however, they can't in all things think alike.

***Arminians (hereafter Ar) show the negative consequences of calling Christians by their theologian's name.***

***Edwards responds that that is true and yet is due to their foul intention. Additionally, he argues why a distinctive is necessary to demonstrate their differences and to argue easily.***

I confess, these things are very plausible. And I will not deny, that there are some unhappy consequences of this distinction of names, and that men's infirmities and evil dispositions often make an ill improvement of it. But yet I humbly conceive, these objections are carried far beyond reason. The generality of mankind are disposed enough, and a great deal too much, to uncharitableness, and to be censorious and bitter towards those that differ from them in religious opinions: which evil temper of mind will take occasion to exert itself, from many things in themselves innocent, useful and necessary. But yet there is no necessity to suppose, that the thus distinguishing persons of different opinions by different names, arises mainly from an uncharitable spirit. It may arise from the disposition there is in mankind (whom God has distinguished with an ability and inclination for speech) to improve the benefit of language, in the proper use and design of names, given to things which they have often occasion to speak of, or signify their minds about; which is to enable them to express their ideas with ease and expedition, without being encumbered with an obscure and difficult circumlocution. And the thus distinguishing persons of different opinions in religious matters, may not imply, nor infer any more than that there is a difference, and that the difference is such as we find we have often occasion to take notice of, and make mention of. That which we have frequent occasion to speak of (whatever it be, that gives the occasion) this wants a name: and it is always a defect in language, in such cases, to be obliged to make use of a description, instead of a name. Thus we have often occasion to speak of those who are the descendants of the ancient inhabitants of France, who were subjects or heads of the government of that land, and spoke the language peculiar to it; in distinction from the descendants of the inhabitants of Spain, who belonged to that community, and spoke the language of that country. And therefore we find the great need of distinct names to signify these different sorts of people, and the great convenience of those distinguishing words, "French," and "Spaniards"; by which the signification of our minds is quick and easy, and our speech is delivered from the burden of a continual reiteration of diffuse descriptions, with which it must otherwise be embarrassed.

**JE posits that a distinction by using names is a consequence.**

That the difference of the opinions of those, who in their general scheme of divinity agree with these two noted men, Calvin, and Arminius, is a thing there is often occasion to speak of, is what the practice of the latter, itself confesses; who are often, in their discourses and writings, taking notice of the supposed absurd and pernicious opinions of the former sort. And therefore the making use of different names in this case can't reasonably be objected against, or condemned, as a thing which must come from so bad a cause as they assign. It is easy to be accounted for, without supposing it to arise from any other source than the exigence and natural tendency of the state of things; considering the faculty and disposition God has given mankind, to express things which they have frequent occasion to mention, by certain distinguishing names. It is an effect that is similar to what we see arise, in innumerable cases which are parallel, where the cause is not at all blameworthy.

**JE clarifies that he does not object to being labeled a Calvinist but does not fully adhere to Calvin's teachings.**

Nevertheless, at first I had thoughts of carefully avoiding the use of the appellation "Arminian" in this treatise. But I soon found I should be put to great difficulty by it; and that my discourse would be so encumbered with an often-repeated circumlocution, instead of a name, which would express the thing intended, as well and better, that I altered my purpose. And therefore I must ask the excuse of such as are apt to be offended with things of this nature, that I have so freely used the term "Arminian" in the following discourse. I profess it to be without any design, to stigmatize persons of any sort with a name of reproach, or at all to make them appear more odious. If when I had occasion to speak of those divines who are commonly called by this name, I had, instead of styling them Arminians, called them "these men," as Dr. Whitby does Calvinistic divines; it probably would not have been taken any better, or thought to show a better temper, or more good manners. I have done as I would be done by, in this matter. However, the term "Calvinist" is in these days, among most, a term of greater reproach than the term "Arminian"; yet I should not take it at all amiss, to be called a Calvinist, for distinction's sake: though I utterly disclaim a dependence on

Calvin, or believing the doctrines which I hold, because he believed and taught them; and cannot justly be charged with believing in everything just as he taught.

### *JE states that most Arminians hold free will; some are extreme, but not all of them hold corrupt doctrine.*

But lest I should really be an occasion of injury to some persons, I would here give notice, that though I generally speak of that doctrine, concerning free will and moral agency, which I oppose, as an Arminian doctrine; yet I would not be understood, that every divine or author whom I have occasion to mention as maintaining that doctrine, was properly an Arminian, or one of that sort which is commonly called by that name. Some of them went far beyond the Arminians: and I would by no means charge Arminians in general with all the corrupt doctrine, which these maintained.

Thus for instance, it would be very injurious, if I should rank Arminian divines in general, with such authors as Mr. Chubb. I doubt not, many of them have some of his doctrines in abhorrence; though he agrees, for the most part, with Arminians, in his notion of the freedom of the will. And on the other hand, though I suppose this notion to be a leading article in the Arminian scheme, that which, if pursued in its consequences, will truly infer, or naturally lead to all the rest; yet I don't charge all that have held this doctrine, with being Arminians. For whatever may be the consequences of the doctrine really, yet some that hold this doctrine, may not own nor see these consequences; and it would be unjust, in many instances, to charge every author with believing and maintaining all the real consequences of his avowed doctrines.

And I desire it may be particularly noted, that though I have occasion in the following discourse, often to mention the author of the book entitled, *An Essay on the Freedom of the Will, in God and the Creature*,[3] as holding that notion of freedom of will, which I oppose; yet I don't mean to call him an Arminian: however, in that doctrine he agrees with Arminians, and departs from the current and general opinion of Calvinists. If the author of that essay be the same as it is commonly ascribed to, he doubtless was not one that ought to bear that name. But however good a divine he was in many respects, yet that particular Arminian doctrine which he maintained, is never the better for being held by such an one: nor is there less need of opposing it on that account; but rather is there the more need of it; as it will be likely to have the more pernicious influence, for being taught by a divine of his name and character; supposing the doctrine to be wrong, and in itself to be of an ill tendency.

I have nothing further to say by way of preface; but only to bespeak the reader's candor, and calm attention to what I have written.

---

3. [Isaac Watts authored in 1732.]

***JE insists that the knowledge of God and of ourselves is most important. The latter is about our understanding and will, in which all virtue and religion reside and of which science is the most important.***

The subject is of such importance, as to *demand* attention, and the most thorough consideration. Of all kinds of knowledge that we can ever obtain, the knowledge of God, and the knowledge of ourselves, are the most important. As religion is the great business, for which we are created, and on which our happiness depends; and as religion consists in an intercourse between ourselves and our Maker; and so has its foundation in God's nature and ours, and in the relation that God and we stand in to each other; therefore, a true knowledge of both must be needful in order to true religion. But the knowledge of ourselves consists chiefly in right apprehensions concerning those two chief faculties of our nature, the *understanding* and *will*.[4] Both are very important: yet the science of the latter must be confessed to be of greatest moment; inasmuch as all virtue and religion have their seat more immediately in the will, consisting more especially in right acts and habits of this faculty. And the grand question about the freedom of the will, is the main point that belongs to the science of the will.

Therefore, I say, the importance of this subject greatly *demands* the attention of Christians, and especially of divines. But as to my manner of handling the subject, I will be far from presuming to say, that it is such as *demands* the attention of the reader to what I have written. I am ready to own, that in this matter I depend on the reader's *courtesy*. But only thus far I may have some color for putting in a *claim*; that if the reader be disposed to pass his censure on what I have written, I may be fully and patiently heard, and well attended to, before I am condemned. However, this is what I would humbly *ask* of my readers; together with the prayers of all sincere lovers of truth, that I may have much of that Spirit which Christ promised his disciples, which guides into all truth; and that the blessed and powerful influences of this Spirit would make truth victorious in the world.

---

4. [Locke's definitions are crucial for reading Edwards's *FOW*: "The power of thinking is called the understanding, and the power of volition is called the will." John Locke, *An Essay Concerning Human Understanding* (the 7th edition: London, 1716), bk. II, ch. 6, no. 2.]

# PART I

Wherein are Explained Various Terms and Things Belonging to the Subject of the Ensuing Discourse

# Section 1

## Concerning the Nature of the Will

It may possibly be thought, that there is no great need of going about to define or describe the "will"; this word being generally as well understood as any other words we can use to explain it: and so perhaps it would be, had not philosophers, metaphysicians and polemic divines brought the matter into obscurity by the things they have said of it. But since it is so, I think it may be of some use, and will tend to the greater clearness in the following discourse, to say a few things concerning it.

*JE defines the will as "that by which the mind chooses anything."*

And therefore I observe, that the will (without any metaphysical refining) is plainly, that by which the mind chooses anything. The faculty of the will[1] is that faculty or power or principle of mind by which it is capable of choosing: an act of the will is the same as an act of choosing or choice.

*JE defines the will as "that by which the soul chooses."*

If any think it is a more perfect definition of the will, to say, that it is that by which the soul either chooses or refuses; I am content with it: though I think that it is enough to say, it's that by which the soul chooses: for in every act of will whatsoever, the mind chooses one thing rather than another; it chooses something rather than the contrary, or rather than the want or nonexistence of that thing. So in every act of refusal, the mind chooses the absence of the thing refused; the positive and the negative are set before the mind for its choice, and it chooses the negative;[2] and the mind's making its choice in that case is properly the act of the will: the will's determining between the

---

1. [JE holds two faculties in the soul: the understanding and the will or inclination or the mind or heart; in the latter there are some properties like affections, by which men "either as liking or disliking, pleased or displeased, approving or rejecting." See Jonathan Edwards, *Religious Affections*, WJE 2:96.]

2. [JE refers to the negative things, like refusing, disapproving, disliking, rejecting, forbidding, etc.]

two is a voluntary determining; but that is the same thing as making a choice. So that whatever names we call the act of the will by—choosing, refusing, approving, disapproving, liking, disliking, embracing, rejecting, determining, directing, commanding, forbidding, inclining or being averse, a being pleased or displeased with—all may be reduced to this of choosing. For the soul to act voluntarily, is evermore to act electively.

### Locke defines the will as "a power or ability to prefer or choose."

Mr. Locke[3] says, "The will signifies nothing but a power or ability to prefer or choose." And in the foregoing page says, "The word 'preferring' seems best to express the act of volition"; but adds, that "it does it not precisely; for" (says he) "though a man would prefer flying to walking, yet who can say he ever wills it?"[4]

### JE argues that Locke's definition of the will is erroneous and points that ongoing preferring brings out successive acts of the will.

But the instance he mentions doesn't prove that there is anything else in "willing" but merely "preferring": for it should be considered what is the next and immediate object of the will, with respect to a man's walking, or any other external action; which is not his being removed from one place to another; on the earth, or through the air; these are remoter objects of preference; but such or such an immediate exertion of himself. The thing nextly chosen or preferred when a man wills to walk, is not his being removed to such a place where he would be, but such an exertion and motion of his legs and feet, etc., in order to it. And his willing such an alteration in his body in the present moment, is nothing else but his choosing or preferring such an alteration in his body at such a moment, or his liking it better than the forbearance of it.

### JE continues that, in the will, there should be such alterations of preferring or choosing or desiring or pleasing or liking, through successive moments.

And God has so made and established the human nature, the soul being united to a body in proper state, that the soul preferring or choosing such an immediate exertion or alteration of the body, such an alteration instantaneously follows. There is nothing else in the actings of my mind, that I am conscious of while I walk, but only my preferring or choosing, through successive moments, that there should be such alterations of my external sensations and motions; together with a concurring habitual expectation that it will be so; having ever found by experience, that on such an immediate preference, such sensations and motions do actually instantaneously, and constantly arise. But it is not so in the case of flying: though a man may be said remotely to choose or prefer flying; yet he doesn't choose or prefer, incline to or desire, under circumstances in view, any immediate exertion of the members of his body in order to do it; because he has no expectation that he should obtain the desired end by any such exertion; and

3. [JE cites John Locke, bk. II, ch. 21, no. 17.]
4. [John Locke, bk. II, ch. 21, no. 15.]

he doesn't prefer or incline to any bodily exertion or effort under this apprehended circumstance, of its being wholly in vain.

So that if we carefully distinguish the proper objects of the several acts of the will, it will not appear by this, and suchlike instances, that there is any difference between "volition" and "preference"; or that a man's choosing, liking best, or being best pleased with a thing, are not the same with his willing that thing; as they seem to be according to those general and more natural notions of men, according to which language is formed. Thus an act of the will is commonly expressed by its pleasing a man to do thus or thus; and a man's doing as he wills, and doing as he pleases, are the same thing in common speech.

**JL observes that the will and desire conflict with each other: e.g., a man under coercion to persuade another.**

Mr. Locke says, "The will is perfectly distinguished from desire; which in the very same action may have a quite contrary tendency from that which our wills set us upon. A man" (says he) "whom I cannot deny, may oblige me to use persuasions to another, which, at the same time I am speaking, I may wish may not prevail on him. In this case it is plain the will and desire run counter."

**JE insists that a man never, at any instance, wills anything contrary to his desires, or desires anything contrary to his will.**

I don't suppose, that "will" and "desire" are words of precisely the same signification: "will" seems to be a word of a more general signification, extending to things present and absent. "Desire" respects something absent. I may prefer my present situation and posture, suppose sitting still, or having my eyes open, and so may will it. But yet I can't think they are so entirely distinct, that they can ever be properly said to run counter. A man never, in any instance, wills anything contrary to his desires, or desires anything contrary to his will.

The aforementioned instance, which Mr. Locke produces, doesn't prove that he ever does. He may, on some consideration or other, will to utter speeches which have a tendency to persuade another, and still may desire that they may not persuade him: but yet his will and desire don't run counter at all: the thing which he wills, the very same he desires; and he doesn't will a thing, and desire the contrary in any particular. In this instance, it is not carefully observed, what is the thing willed, and what is the thing desired: if it were, it would be found that will and desire don't clash in the least. The thing willed on some consideration, is to utter such words; and certainly, the same consideration so influences him, that he doesn't desire the contrary; all things considered, he chooses to utter such words, and doesn't desire not to utter them. And so as to the thing which Mr. Locke speaks of as desired, viz. that the words, though they tend to persuade, should not be effectual to that end, his will is not contrary to this; he doesn't will that they should be effectual, but rather wills that they should not, as he desires.

### *JE defines the will and desire as being the same in their nature.*

In order to prove that the will and desire may run counter, it should be shown that they may be contrary one to the other in the same thing, or with respect to the very same object of will or desire: but here the objects are two; and in each, taken by themselves, the will and desire agree. And it is no wonder that they should not agree in different things, however little distinguished they are in their nature. The will may not agree with the will, nor desire agree with desire, in different things. As in this very instance which Mr. Locke mentions, a person may, on some consideration, desire to use persuasions, and at the same time may desire they may not prevail; but yet nobody will say, that desire runs counter to desire; or that this proves that desire is perfectly a distinct thing from desire. The like might be observed of the other instance Mr. Locke produces, of a man's desiring to be eased of pain, etc.

### *JE observes that in the soul is there an inclination to prefer one thing to another.*

But not to dwell any longer on this, whether desire and will, and whether preference and volition be precisely the same things or no; yet, I trust it will be allowed by all, that in every act of will there is an act of choice; that in every volition there is a preference, or a prevailing inclination of the soul, whereby the soul, at that instant, is out of a state of perfect indifference,[5] with respect to the direct object of the volition. So that in every act, or going forth of the will, there is some preponderance of the mind or inclination, one way rather than another; and the soul had rather have or do one thing than another, or than not to have or do that thing; and that there, where there is absolutely no preferring or choosing, but a perfect continuing equilibrium,[6] there is no volition.

---

5. ["Indifference" means here not apathy demonstrated by an absence of emotional reactions, the trait of lacking enthusiasm for or interest in things generally, but state unbiased impartial unconcern.]

6. [Equilibrium theory is contrary to determinism that many Scholastics maintained, that when two motives are in equilibrium, the will is not restricted by any external causes and chooses any motive freely. But JE holds that such equilibrium does exist in man; yet his will is determined by the strongest motive.]

# Section 2

## Concerning the Determination of the Will

***Edwards defines "determining the will" as causing the will to make a choice.***

By "determining the will," if the phrase be used with any meaning, must be intended, causing that the act of the will or choice should be thus, and not otherwise: and the will is said to be determined, when, in consequence of some action, or influence, its choice is directed to, and fixed upon a particular object. As when we speak of the determination of motion, we mean causing the motion of the body to be such a way, or in such a direction, rather than another.

***Ar claims that the will determines itself.***

To talk of the determination of the will, supposes an effect, which must have a cause. If the will be determined, there is a determiner. This must be supposed to be intended even by them that say, the will determines itself. If it be so, the will is both determiner and determined; it is a cause that acts and produces effects upon itself, and is the object of its own influence and action.

***What determines the will?***

With respect to that grand inquiry, what determines the will, it would be very tedious and unnecessary at present to enumerate and examine all the various opinions, which have been advanced concerning this matter; nor is it needful that I should enter into a particular disquisition of all points debated in disputes on that question, whether the will always follows the last dictate of the understanding. It is sufficient to my present purpose to say, it is that motive, which, as it stands in the view of the mind, is the strongest, that determines the will.—But it may be necessary that I should a little explain my meaning in this.

***Edwards outlines the determination procedure as motive→ to mind→ to volition.***

45

By "motive," I mean the whole of that which moves, excites or invites the mind to volition, whether that be one thing singly, or many things conjunctly. Many particular things may concur and unite their strength to induce the mind; and when it is so, all together are as it were one complex motive. And when I speak of the "strongest motive," I have respect to the strength of the whole that operates to induce to a particular act of volition, whether that be the strength of one thing alone, or of many together.

Whatever is a motive, in this sense, must be something that is extant in the view or apprehension of the understanding, or perceiving faculty. Nothing can induce or invite the mind to will or act anything, any further than it is perceived, or is some way or other in the mind's view; for what is wholly unperceived, and perfectly out of the mind's view; can't affect the mind at all. It is most evident, that nothing is in the mind, or reaches it, or takes any hold of it, any otherwise than as it is perceived or thought of.

### Edwards defines motive as a previous tendency in the mind that perceives objects and considers them good. The will is always determined by the strongest motive.

And I think it must also be allowed by all, that everything that is properly called a motive, excitement or inducement to a perceiving willing agent, has some sort and degree of tendency, or advantage to move or excite the will, previous to the effect, or to the act of the will excited. This previous tendency of the motive is what I call the "strength" of the motive. That motive which has a less degree of previous advantage or tendency to move the will, or that appears less inviting, as it stands in the view of the mind, is what I call a "weaker motive." On the contrary, that which appears most inviting, and has, by what appears concerning it to the understanding or apprehension, the greatest degree of previous tendency to excite and induce the choice, is what I call the "strongest motive." And in this sense, I suppose the will is always determined by the strongest motive.

### JE elaborates that things in the mind have their strength to move the will.

Things that exist in the view of the mind, have their strength, tendency or advantage to move or excite its will, from many things appertaining to the nature and circumstances of the thing viewed, the nature and circumstances of the mind that views, and the degree and manner of its view; which it would perhaps be hard to make a perfect enumeration of.

But so much I think may be determined in general, without room for controversy, that whatever is perceived or apprehended by an intelligent and voluntary agent, which has the nature and influence of a motive to volition or choice, is considered or viewed *as good*; nor has it any tendency to invite or engage the election of the soul in any further degree than it appears such. For to say otherwise, would be to say, that things that appear have a tendency by the appearance they make, to engage the mind to elect them, some other way than by their appearing eligible to it; which is absurd.

And therefore it must be true, in some sense, that the will always is as the greatest apparent good is. But only, for the right understanding of this, two things must be well and distinctly observed.

1. It must be observed in what sense I use the term "good"; namely, as of the same import with "agreeable." To appear good to the mind, as I use the phrase, is the same as to appear agreeable, or seem pleasing to the mind. Certainly, nothing appears inviting and eligible to the mind, or tending to engage its inclination and choice, considered as evil or disagreeable; nor indeed, as indifferent, and neither agreeable nor disagreeable. But if it tends to draw the inclination, and move the will, it must be under the notion of that which *suits* the mind. And therefore that must have the greatest tendency to attract and engage it, which, as it stands in the mind's view, suits it best, and pleases it most; and in that sense, is the greatest apparent good: to say otherwise, is little, if anything, short of a direct and plain contradiction.

***John Locke supposes "determining the will" means to avoid uneasiness, which is the same as to choose easiness or agreeableness.***

The word "good," in this sense, includes in its signification, the removal or avoiding of evil, or of that which is disagreeable and uneasy. It is agreeable and pleasing, to avoid what is disagreeable and displeasing, and to have uneasiness removed. So that here is included what Mr. Locke supposes determines the will. For when he speaks of uneasiness as determining the will, he must be understood as supposing that the end or aim which governs in the volition or act of preference, is the avoiding or removal of that uneasiness; and that is the same thing as choosing and seeking what is more easy and agreeable.

***JE supposes that volition always chooses objects which appear most agreeable.***

2. When I say, the will is as the greatest apparent good is,[1] or (as I have explained it) that volition has always for its object the thing which appears most agreeable; it must be carefully observed, to avoid confusion and needless objection, that I speak of the direct and immediate object of the act of volition; and not some object that the act of will has not an immediate, but only an indirect and remote respect to. Many acts of volition have some remote relation to an object, that is different from the thing most immediately willed and chosen.

---

1. [During Edwards's lifetime, with regard to *Freedom of the Will* (1754), no immediate and notable critic appeared in New England. After his death, however, James Dana (1695–1760) became the spearhead among critics against Edwards, with his *An Examination of the Late Reverend President Edwards's 'Inquiry on Freedom of the Will'* (1770) and *An Examination of the Same Continued* (1773), along with Samuel West (1730–1807) and his *Essays on Liberty and Necessity* (1793).]

### JE demonstrates volition's immediate objects: e.g., whether to drink it or not.

Thus, when a drunkard has his liquor before him, and he has to choose whether to drink it, or no; the proper and immediate objects, about which his present volition is conversant, and between which his choice now decides, are his own acts, in drinking the liquor, or letting it alone; and this will certainly be done according to what, in the present view of his mind, taken in the whole of it, is most agreeable to him. If he chooses or wills to drink it, and not to let it alone; then this action, as it stands in the view of his mind, with all that belongs to its appearance there, is more agreeable and pleasing than letting it alone.

### The present pleasure which man expects by drinking and the future misery which he concerns are his volition's indirect objects.

But the objects to which this act of volition may relate more remotely, and between which his choice may determine more indirectly, are the present pleasure the man expects by drinking, and the future misery which he judges will be the consequence of it: he may judge that this future misery, when it comes, will be more disagreeable and unpleasant, than refraining from drinking now would be. But these two things are not the proper objects that the act of volition spoken of is nextly conversant about. For the act of will spoken of is concerning present drinking or forbearing to drink. If he wills to drink, then drinking is the proper object of the act of his will; and drinking, on some account or other, now appears most agreeable to him, and suits him best. If he chooses to refrain, then refraining is the immediate object of his will, and is most pleasing to him. If in the choice he makes in the case, he prefers a present pleasure to a future advantage, which he judges will be greater when it comes; then a lesser present pleasure appears more agreeable to him than a greater advantage at a distance. If on the contrary a future advantage is preferred, then that appears most agreeable, and suits him best. And so still the present volition is as the greatest apparent good at present is.

### JE notes that where there is the greatest apparent good, or what appears most agreeable, there is always the will.

I have rather chosen to express myself thus, that the will always *is* as the greatest apparent good, or as what appears most agreeable, is, than to say that the will is *determined* by the greatest apparent good, or by what seems most agreeable; because an appearing most agreeable or pleasing to the mind, and the mind's preferring and choosing, seem hardly to be properly and perfectly distinct. If strict propriety of speech be insisted on, it may more properly be said, that the voluntary action which is the immediate consequence and fruit of the mind's volition or choice, is determined by that which appears most agreeable, than the preference or choice itself; but that the act of volition itself is always determined by that in or about the mind's view of the object, which causes it to appear most agreeable.

### Section 2—Concerning the Determination of the Will

*JE asks what makes an object in view agreeable? He answers that it is the object itself and mindset and circumstances.*

I say, in or about the mind's view of the object, because what has influence to render an object in view agreeable, is not only what appears in the object viewed, but also the manner of the view, and the state and circumstances of the mind that views.—Particularly to enumerate all things pertaining to the mind's view of the objects of volition, which have influence in their appearing agreeable to the mind, would be a matter of no small difficulty, and might require a treatise by itself, and is not necessary to my present purpose.

I shall therefore only mention some things in general.

*The volition chooses an object appearing agreeable. What makes it so?*

I. *The object itself does so.*
 1. *It chooses what appears beautiful.*
 2. *It chooses according to its circumstances.*
 3. *It chooses temporally nearer pleasure.*

I. One thing that makes an object proposed to choice agreeable, is the apparent nature and circumstances of the object. And there are various things of this sort, that have a hand in rendering the object more or less agreeable; as,

1. That which appears in the object, which renders it beautiful and pleasant, or deformed and irksome to the mind; viewing it as it is in itself.

2. The apparent degree of pleasure or trouble attending the object, or the consequence of it. Such concomitants and consequents being viewed as circumstances of the object, are to be considered as belonging to it, and as it were parts of it; as it stands in the mind's view, as a proposed object of choice.

3. The apparent state of the pleasure or trouble that appears, with respect to distance of time; being either nearer or farther off. It is a thing in itself agreeable to the mind, to have pleasure speedily; and disagreeable, to have it delayed: so that if there be two equal degrees of pleasure set in the mind's view, and all other things are equal, but only one is beheld as near, and the other far off; the nearer will appear most agreeable, and so will be chosen. Because, though the agreeableness of the objects be exactly equal, as viewed in themselves, yet not as viewed in their circumstances; one of them having the additional agreeableness of the circumstance of nearness.

II. *According to the manner of mind's view of an object,*
 1. *The volition chooses the more certain pleasure;*
 2. *It chooses an object in more apparent understanding.*

II. Another thing that contributes to the agreeableness of an object of choice, as it stands in the mind's view, is the manner of the view. If the object be something which appears connected with future pleasure, not only will the degree of apparent pleasure have influence, but also the manner of the view, especially in two respects.

1. With respect to the degree of judgment, or firmness of assent, with which the mind judges the pleasure to be future. Because it is more agreeable to have a certain happiness, than an uncertain one; and a pleasure viewed as more probable, all other things being equal, is more agreeable to the mind, than that which is viewed as less probable.

2. With respect to the degree of the idea of the future pleasure. With regard to things which are the subject of our thoughts, either past, present or future, we have much more of an idea or apprehension of some things than others; that is, our idea is much more clear, lively, and strong.

### JE observes that a certain knowledge is gained by immediate sensation and contemplation.

Thus, the ideas we have of sensible things by immediate sensation, are usually much more lively than those we have by mere imagination, or by contemplation of them when absent. My idea of the sun, when I look upon it, is more vivid, than when I only think of it. Our idea of the sweet relish of a delicious fruit is usually stronger when we taste it, than when we only imagine it. And sometimes, the ideas we have of things by contemplation, are much stronger and clearer, than at other times. Thus, a man at one time has a much stronger idea of the pleasure which is to be enjoyed in eating some sort of food that he loves, than at another.

### JE notes that the idea influences the mind to excite choice or volition.

Now the degree, or strength of the idea or sense that men have of future good or evil, is one thing that has great influence on their minds to excite choice or volition. When of two kinds of future pleasure, which the mind considers of, and are presented for choice, both are supposed exactly equal by the judgment, and both equally certain, and all other things are equal, but only one of them is what the mind has a far more lively sense of, than of the other; this has the greatest advantage by far to affect and attract the mind, and move the will.

### JE notes that men choose pleasures, of which their mind has a livelier sense.

It is now more agreeable to the mind, to take the pleasure it has a strong and lively sense of, than that which it has only a faint idea of. The view of the former is attended with the strongest appetite, and the greatest uneasiness attends the want of it; and it is agreeable to the mind, to have uneasiness removed, and its appetite gratified.

### JE lists the three compounded factors of choosing an object as the greater, livelier, and probable pleasure.

And if several future enjoyments are presented together, as competitors for the choice of the mind, some of them judged to be greater, and others less; the mind also having a greater sense and more lively idea of the good of some of them, and of others a less; and some are viewed as of greater certainty or probability than others; and those enjoyments that appear most agreeable in one of these respects, appear least so in others: in this case, all other things being equal, the agreeableness of a proposed object of choice will be in a degree some way compounded of the degree of good supposed by the judgment, the degree of apparent probability or certainty of that good, and the degree of the view or sense, or liveliness of the idea the mind has, of that good; because all together concur to constitute the degree in which the object appears at present agreeable; and accordingly volition will be determined.

### *Another factor that contributes to the agreeableness or disagreeableness of an object of choice is the temper and state of the mind.*

I might further observe, the state of the mind that views a proposed object of choice, is another thing that contributes to the agreeableness or disagreeableness of that object; the particular temper which the mind has by nature, or that has been introduced and established by education, example, custom, or some other means; or the frame or state that the mind is in on a particular occasion. That object which appears agreeable to one, does not so to another. And the same object doesn't always appear alike agreeable to the same person, at different times. It is most agreeable to some men, to follow their reason; and to others, to follow their appetites: to some men, it is more agreeable to deny a vicious inclination, than to gratify it; others it suits best to gratify the vilest appetites. It is more disagreeable to some men than others, to counteract a former resolution. In these respects, and many others which might be mentioned, different things will be most agreeable to different persons; and not only so, but to the same persons at different times.

### *A Distinct Ground of the Agreeableness of Objects: the frame and the state of the mind.*

But possibly it is needless and improper, to mention the frame and state of the mind, as a distinct ground of the agreeableness of objects from the other two mentioned before; viz. the apparent nature and circumstances of the objects viewed, and the manner of the view: perhaps if we strictly consider the matter, the different temper and state of the mind makes no alteration as to the agreeableness of objects, any other way, than as it makes the objects themselves appear differently beautiful or deformed, having apparent pleasure or pain attending them: and as it occasions the manner of the view to be different, causes the idea of beauty or deformity, pleasure or uneasiness to be more or less lively.

### *Volition chooses objects and actions which appear most agreeable and pleasing.*

However, I think so much is certain, that volition, in no one instance that can be mentioned, is otherwise than the greatest apparent good is, in the manner which has been explained. The choice of the mind never departs from that which, at that time, and with respect to the direct and immediate objects of that decision of the mind, appears most agreeable and pleasing, all things considered. If the immediate objects of the will are a man's own actions, then those actions which appear most agreeable to him he wills.

### *Men choose to do what is most agreeable to them rather than what they please.*

If it be now most agreeable to him, all things considered, to walk, then he now wills to walk. If it be now, upon the whole of what at present appears to him, most agreeable to speak, then he chooses to speak: if it suits him best to keep silence, then he chooses to keep silence. There is scarcely a plainer and more universal dictate of the sense and experience of mankind, than that, when men act voluntarily, and do what they please, then they do what suits them best, or what is most agreeable to them. To say, that they do what they please, or what pleases them, but yet don't do what is agreeable to them, is the same thing as to say, they do what they please, but don't act their pleasure; and that is to say, that they do what they please, and yet don't do what they please.

### *The will always follows the last dictate of the understanding* or *reason.*

It appears from these things, that in some sense, the will always follows the last dictate of the understanding. But then the understanding must be taken in a large sense, as including the whole faculty of perception or apprehension, and not merely what is called reason or judgment.

If by the dictate of the understanding is meant what reason declares to be best or most for the person's happiness, taking in the whole of his duration, it is not true, that the will always follows the last dictate of the understanding. Such a dictate of reason is quite a different matter from things appearing now most agreeable; all things being put together which pertain to the mind's present perceptions, apprehensions or ideas, in any respect.

### *The will is normally determined by the dictate of reason or sometimes by other factors. ILL: The scales lean towards the side with greater weight.*

Although that dictate of reason, when it takes place, is one thing that is put into the scales, and is to be considered as a thing that has concern in the compound influence which moves and induces the will; and is one thing that is to be considered in estimating the degree of that appearance of good which the will always follows; either as having its influence added to other things, or subducted from them. When it concurs with other things, then its weight is added to them, as put into the same scale; but when it is against them, it is as a weight in the opposite scale, where it resists the influence of other things: yet its resistance is often overcome by their greater weight, and so the act of the will is determined in opposition to it.

***JE's final position is that the view of the mind of the previous tendency to excite volition results in the strongest motive, which in turn leads the will to be determined.***

The things which I have said may, I hope, serve, in some measure, to illustrate and confirm the position I laid down in the beginning of this section, viz. that the will is always determined by the strongest motive, or by that view of the mind which has the greatest degree of previous tendency to excite volition. But whether I have been so happy as rightly to explain the thing wherein consists the strength of motives, or not, yet my failing in this will not overthrow the position itself; which carries much of its own evidence with it, and is the thing of chief importance to the purpose of the ensuing discourse: and the truth of it, I hope, will appear with greater clearness, before I have finished what I have to say on the subject of human liberty.[2]

---

2. [JE's doctrine of human liberty of will can be applied in salvation, as follows: "Certainly, anyone who wants to come to Christ may come to him. That is why Jonathan Edwards insisted that *the will is not bound*. However, this *liberty is what makes our refusal to seek* God so unreasonable and increases our guilt Who is it who wills to come? . . . No one, except those in whom the Holy Spirit has already performed the entirely irresistible work of the new birth. . ." See James Montgomery Boice, and Philip Graham Ryken, *The Doctrines of Grace: Rediscovering the Evangelical Gospel* (Crossway, 2002), 85.]

# Section 3

## Concerning the Meaning of the Terms Necessity, Impossibility, Inability, Etc.; and of Contingence

The words "necessary," "impossible," etc., are abundantly used in controversies about free will and moral agency; and therefore the sense in which they are used, should be clearly understood.

***The word "must" means "there being a necessity."***

Here I might say, that a thing is then said to be necessary, when it must be, and cannot be otherwise. But this would not properly be a definition of necessity, or an explanation of the word, any more than if I explained the word "must," by there being a necessity. The words "must," "can," and "cannot" need explication as much as the words "necessary" and "impossible"; excepting that the former are words that children commonly use, and know something of the meaning of earlier than the latter.

***The word "necessary" means that a thing must be without any impossibility and resistibility.***

The word "necessary," as used in common speech, is a relative term; and relates to some supposed opposition made to the existence of the thing spoken of, which is overcome, or proves in vain to hinder or alter it. That is necessary, in the original and proper sense of the word, which is, or will be, notwithstanding all supposable opposition. To say, that a thing is necessary, is the same thing as to say, that it is impossible it should not be: but the word "impossible" is manifestly a relative term, and has reference to supposed power exerted to bring a thing to pass, which is insufficient for the effect; as the word "unable" is relative, and has relation to ability or endeavor which is insufficient; and as the word "irresistible" is relative, and has always reference to resistance which is made, or may be made to some force or power tending to an effect, and is insufficient to withstand the power, or hinder the effect. The common notion of necessity and impossibility implies something that frustrates endeavor or desire.

Here several things are to be noted.

1. Things are said to be necessary *in general*,

***Things are "necessary" even though men oppose anyhow.***

which are or will be notwithstanding any supposable opposition from us or others, or from whatever quarter. But things are said to be necessary *to us,*

***Things are "necessary" even though men oppose entirely.***

which are or will be notwithstanding all opposition supposable in the case *from us*. The same may be observed of the word "impossible" and other suchlike terms.

***"Necessary," "impossible," and "irresistible" mean that we cannot help opposing a thing and endeavoring otherwise.***

2. These terms "necessary," "impossible," "irresistible," etc., do especially belong to the controversy about liberty and moral agency, as used in the latter of the two senses now mentioned, viz. as necessary or impossible *to us*, and with relation to any supposable opposition or endeavor *of ours*.

***A misconception of "necessity" is as some supposable opposition of our wills or some voluntary exertion or effort to the contrary.***

3. As the word "necessity," in its vulgar and common use, is relative, and has always reference to some supposable insufficient opposition; so when we speak of anything as necessary *to us*, it is with relation to some supposable opposition of our wills, or some voluntary exertion or effort of ours to the contrary. For we don't properly make opposition to an event, any otherwise than as we voluntarily oppose it. Things are said to be what must be, or necessarily are, *as to us*, when they are, or will be, though we desire or endeavor the contrary, or try to prevent or remove their existence: but such opposition of ours always either consists in, or implies opposition of our wills.

***"Necessary" means that we can't do otherwise, and so it is "impossible," "irresistible," and "unable."***

It is manifest that all suchlike words and phrases, as vulgarly used, are used and accepted in this manner. A thing is said to be necessary, when we can't help it, let us do what we will.[1] So anything is said to be impossible to us, when we would do it, or

---

1. [Allen Guelzo's early view of JE's position of relationship between liberty and necessity was "reconciliationism," which is identified with "soft determinism." Yet he later altered his view and stated, "Edwards was a *compatibilist*: liberty and necessity are compatible with each other." Edwards argues that there is no inconsistency between the doctrines of divine predestination and human liberty; because they are compatible. Stephen Wilson and Robert Kane, however, assess Edwards as a compatibilist. as the latter stated in Part II of *FOW*. See *FOW*, 405–06; Allen Guelzo, "Freedom of the Will," in *The Princeton Companion to Jonathan Edwards*, ed. Sang Hyun Lee (Princeton University Press, 2005), 126; Robert Kane, *A contemporary introduction to free will* (Oxford University Press,

would have it brought to pass, and endeavor it; or at least may be supposed to desire and seek it; but all our desires and endeavors are, or would be vain. And that is said to be irresistible, which overcomes all our opposition, resistance, and endeavor to the contrary. And we are to be said unable to do a thing, when our supposable desires and endeavors to do it are insufficient.

**JE supports the common sense of the words but precautions the vulgar and scientific senses of them.**

We are accustomed, in the common use of language, to apply and understand these phrases in this sense: we grow up with such a habit; which by the daily use of these terms, in such a sense, from our childhood, becomes fixed and settled; so that the idea of a relation to a supposed will, desire and endeavor of ours, is strongly connected with these terms, and naturally excited in our minds, whenever we hear the words used. Such ideas, and these words, are so united and associated, that they unavoidably go together; one suggests the other, and carries the other with it, and never can be separated as long as we live. And if we use the words, as terms of art, in another sense, yet, unless we are exceeding circumspect and wary, we shall insensibly slide into the vulgar use of them, and so apply the words in a very inconsistent manner: this habitual connection of ideas will deceive and confound us in our reasonings and discourses, wherein we pretend to use these terms in that manner, as terms of art.

**JE: The proper opposition or insufficient will or endeavor is not allowed, and so it is supposable and smothered up. Such terms are not proper to describe a supposable opposition, will or endeavor.**

4. It follows from what has been observed, that when these terms "necessary," "impossible," "irresistible," "unable," etc., are used in cases wherein no opposition, or insufficient will or endeavor, is supposed, or can be supposed, but the very nature of the supposed case itself excludes and denies any such opposition, will or endeavor; these terms are then not used in their proper signification, but quite beside their use in common speech. The reason is manifest; namely, that in such cases, we can't use the words with reference to a supposable opposition, will or endeavor. And therefore, if any man uses these terms in such cases, he either uses them nonsensically, or in some new sense, diverse from their original and proper meaning.

As for instance; if a man should affirm after this manner, that it is necessary for a man, and what must be, that a man should choose virtue rather than vice, during the time that he prefers virtue to vice; and that it is a thing impossible and irresistible, that it should be otherwise than that he should have this choice, so long as this choice continues; such a man would use these terms "must," "irresistible," etc., with perfect insignificance and nonsense, or in some new sense, diverse from their common use;

---

2005), 148; Stephen Wilson, *Virtue Reformed: Rereading Jonathan Edwards* (Brill, 2005), 193, 220.]

which is with reference, as has been observed, to supposable opposition, unwillingness and resistance; whereas, here, the very supposition excludes and denies any such thing: for the case supposed is that of being willing, and choosing.

***Misuses of these terms by metaphysicians consist in describing 1) unthinkable cases, 2) God's existence, and 3) the inclinations and actions of God, angels, and men.***

5. It appears from what has been said, that these terms "necessary," "impossible," etc., are often used by philosophers and metaphysicians in a sense quite diverse from their common use and original signification: for they apply them to many cases in which no opposition is supposed or supposable. Thus, they use them with respect to God's existence before the creation of the world, when there was no other being but he: so with regard to many of the dispositions and acts of the Divine Being, such as his loving himself, his loving righteousness, hating sin, etc. So they apply these terms to many cases of the inclinations and actions of created intelligent beings, angels and men; wherein all opposition of the will is shut out and denied, in the very supposition of the case.

***Philosophical necessity is the certainty of things.***

Metaphysical or philosophical necessity is nothing different from their[2] certainty. I speak not now of the certainty of knowledge, but the certainty that is in things themselves, which is the foundation of the certainty of the knowledge of them; or that wherein lies the ground of the infallibility of the proposition which affirms them.

What is sometimes given as the definition of philosophical necessity, namely, *that by which a thing cannot but be, or whereby it cannot be otherwise,* fails of being a proper explanation of it, on two accounts:

> first, the words "can" or "cannot" need explanation as much as the word "necessity"; and the former may as well be explained by the latter, as the latter by the former. Thus, if anyone asked us what we mean, when we say, a thing cannot but be, we might explain ourselves by saying, we mean, it must necessarily be so; as well as explain necessity, by saying, it is that by which a thing cannot but be. And secondly, this definition is liable to the aforementioned great inconvenience: the words "cannot" or "unable" are properly relative, and have relation to power exerted, or that may be exerted, in order to the thing spoken of; to which, as I have now observed, the word "necessity," as used by philosophers,[3] has no reference.

2. [JE, Jr., changed the wording, but this edition recovered the original "their."]

3. [Joseph Priestley (1734–1804) was named "Unitarian universalist minister," but he held an extreme position opposing freewill, saying, "All things past, present, and to come, are precisely what the Author of Nature intended them to be and has made provision for them." See Joseph Priestley, *The Doctrine of Philosophical Necessity Illustrated* (London, 1777), 7,8. "The creed of the necessitarian is the very reverse of that of the Calvinist, . . ." Nevertheless, he criticizes JE for "The doctrine of philosophical necessity is. . .a modern thing. . . Of Calvinists, I believe Mr. Jonathan Edwards to be

***Philosophical necessity is the connection and existence of things, which is affirmed in the proposition despite a supposable opposition.***

Philosophical necessity is really nothing else than the full and fixed connection between the things signified by the subject and predicate of a proposition, which affirms something to be true. When there is such a connection, then the thing affirmed in the proposition is necessary, in a philosophical sense; whether any opposition, or contrary effort be supposed, or supposable in the case, or no. When the subject and predicate of the proposition, which affirms the existence of anything, either substance, quality, act or circumstance, have a full and certain connection, then the existence or being of that thing is said to be necessary in a metaphysical sense. And in this sense, I use the word "necessity," in the following discourse, when I endeavor to prove that necessity is not inconsistent with liberty.

The subject and predicate of a proposition, which affirms existence of something, may have a full, fixed, and certain connection several ways.

***JE notes three ways of connection between subject and predicate of a proposition. First, things have a connection in their own nature.***

(1) They may have a full and perfect connection *in and of themselves*; because it may imply a contradiction, or gross absurdity, to suppose them not connected. Thus many things are necessary in their own nature. So the eternal existence of being generally considered, is necessary in itself: because it would be in itself the greatest absurdity, to deny the existence of being in general,[4] or to say there was absolute and universal nothing; and is as it were the sum of all contradictions; as might be shown, if this were a proper place for it. So God's infinity, and other attributes are necessary. So it is necessary in its own nature, that two and two should be four; and it is necessary, that all right lines drawn from the center of a circle to the circumference should be equal. It is necessary, fit and suitable, that men should do to others, as they would that they should do to them. So innumerable metaphysical and mathematical truths are necessary in themselves; the subject and predicate of the proposition which affirms them, are perfectly connected of themselves.

***Second, in the past, they were connected and in the present they are fixed and certain.***

(2) The connection of the subject and predicate of a proposition, which affirms the

---

the first...But the inconsistency of his scheme with what is properly called Calvinism, appeared by dropping several of the essential parts of that system." Idem, pp.157, 160–61.]

4. [Being as being (ens inquantum ens) or being in general or common being (ens commune) is the subject matter of metaphysics. For Edwards, God is the only real cause or substance underlying physical and mental phenomena. As God in the Bible is stated as the highest Being, in *FOW* JE describes Him as "being in general," the "sum of all being." In conceiving such God, JE employed the notion from Nicolas Malebranche (1638–1715): "Being without any limitation, Being infinite, and in general." *Recherche de la Verité*, bk. III, Pt. 2, ch. 8. Quoted from ed. Wallace E. Anderson's Introduction, *WJE* 6:72.]

existence of something, may be fixed and made certain, because the existence of that thing is already come to pass; and either now is, or has been; and so has as it were made sure of existence. And therefore, the proposition which affirms present and past existence of it, may by this means be made certain, and necessarily and unalterably true; the past event has fixed and decided the matter, as to its existence; and has made it impossible but that existence should be truly predicated of it. Thus the existence of whatever is already come to pass, is now become necessary; it is become impossible it should be otherwise than true, that such a thing has been.

### *Third, as necessary things are connected with one another, and consequentially there is a certain connection between the subject and predicate of a proposition.*

(3) The subject and predicate of a proposition which affirms something to be, may have a real and certain connection *consequentially*; and so the existence of the thing may be consequentially necessary; as it may be surely and firmly connected with something else, that is necessary in one of the former respects. As it is either fully and thoroughly connected with that which is absolutely necessary in its own nature, or with something which has already received and made sure of existence. This necessity lies in, or may be explained by the connection of two or more propositions one with another. Things which are perfectly connected with other things that are necessary, are necessary themselves, by a necessity of consequence.

And here it may be observed, that all things which are future, or which will hereafter begin to be, which can be said to be necessary, are necessary only in this last way. Their existence is not necessary in itself; for if so, they always would have existed. Nor is their existence become necessary by being made sure, by being already come to pass. Therefore, the only way that anything that is to come to pass hereafter, is or can be necessary, is by a connection with something that is necessary in its own nature, or something that already is, or has been; so that the one being supposed, the other certainly follows.

And this also is the only way that all things past, excepting those which were from eternity, could be necessary before they came to pass, or could come to pass necessarily; and therefore the only way in which any effect or event, or anything whatsoever that ever has had, or will have a beginning, has come into being necessarily, or will hereafter necessarily exist. And therefore, this is the necessity which especially belongs to controversies about the acts of the will.

### *Metaphysical necessity is that things are necessary, either with a general or particular necessity.*

It may be of some use in these controversies, further to observe concerning metaphysical necessity, that (agreeable to the distinction before observed of necessity, as vulgarly understood) things that exist may be said to be necessary, either with a *general* or *particular* necessity.

### General necessity is the necessary existence of general things.

The existence of a thing may be said to be necessary with a general necessity, when all things whatsoever being considered, there is a foundation for certainty of their existence;[5] or when in the most general and universal view of things, the subject and predicate of the proposition, which affirms its existence, would appear with an infallible connection.

### Particular necessity is the necessary existence of a particular event, thing, person, or time.

An event, or the existence of a thing, may be said to be necessary with a particular necessity, or with regard to a particular person, thing or time, when nothing that can be taken into consideration, in or about that person, thing or time, alters the case at all, as to the certainty of that event, or the existence of that thing; or can be of any account at all, in determining the infallibility of the connection of the subject and predicate in the proposition which affirms the existence of the thing; so that it is all one, as to that person, or thing, at least, at that time, as if the existence were necessary with a necessity that is most universal and absolute. Thus there are many things that happen to particular persons, which they have no hand in, and in the existence of which no will of theirs has any concern, at least, at that time; which, whether they are necessary or not, with regard to things in general, yet are necessary to them, and with regard to any volition of theirs at that time; as they prevent all acts of the will about the affair. I shall have occasion to apply this observation to particular instances in the following discourse. Whether the same things that are necessary with a particular necessity, be not also necessary with a general necessity, may be a matter of future consideration.

Let that be as it will, it alters not the case, as to the use of this distinction of the kinds of necessity.

### JE notes that metaphysicians added the meaning of the terms.

These things may be sufficient for the explaining of the terms "necessary" and "necessity," as terms of art, and as often used by metaphysicians, and controversial writers in divinity, in a sense diverse from, and more extensive than their original meaning, in common language, which was before explained.

### JE defines "necessary" and "necessity" as contrary to "impossible" and "impossibility." Therefore, impossibility is the same as a negative necessity or a necessity that a thing should not be.

5. [JE Jr., changed the wording here to "their Existence" in his personal copy, and Ramsey changed it to "its Existence," but JE's original phrase was right contextually and is restored in this edition.]

## Section 3—Concerning the Meaning of the Terms Necessity, Impossibility, Inability, Etc.

What has been said to show the meaning of the terms "necessary" and "necessity," may be sufficient for the explaining of the opposite terms, "impossible" and "impossibility." For there is no difference, but only the latter are negative, and the former positive. Impossibility is the same as negative necessity, or a necessity that a thing should not be. And it is used as a term of art in a like diversity from the original and vulgar meaning, with necessity.

The same may be observed concerning the words "unable" and "inability." It has been observed, that these terms, in their original and common use, have relation to will and endeavor, as supposable in the case, and as insufficient for the bringing to pass the thing willed and endeavored. But as these terms are often used by philosophers and divines, especially writers on controversies about free will, they are used in a quite different, and far more extensive sense; and are applied to many cases wherein no will or endeavor for the bringing of the thing to pass, is or can be supposed, but is actually denied and excluded in the nature of the case.

**"Contingent" means that it happens by chance or accident without connection with its causes or antecedents and no means of foresight.**

As the words "necessary," "impossible," "unable," etc., are used by polemic writers, in a sense diverse from their common signification, the like has happened to the term "contingent." Anything is said to be contingent, or to come to pass by chance or accident, in the original meaning of such words, when its connection with its causes or antecedents, according to the established course of things, is not discerned; and so is what we have no means of the foresight of. And especially is anything said to be contingent or accidental with regard to us, when anything comes to pass that we are concerned in, as occasions or subjects, without our foreknowledge, and beside our design and scope.

**"Contingent" is used for something which has absolutely no previous ground or reason.**

But the word "contingent" is abundantly used in a very different sense; not for that whose connection with the series of things we can't discern, so as to foresee the event; but for something which has absolutely no previous ground or reason, with which its existence has any fixed and certain connection.

# Section 4

## Of the Distinction of Natural and Moral Necessity, and Inability

That necessity which has been explained, consisting in an infallible connection of the things signified by the subject and predicate of a proposition, as intelligent beings are the subjects of it, is distinguished into moral and natural necessity. I shall not now stand to inquire whether this distinction be a proper and perfect distinction; but shall only explain how these two sorts of necessity are understood, as the terms are sometimes used, and as they are used in the following discourse.

*JE: "moral necessity" is the necessity of obligation, being under bonds of duty and conscience and the connection of things.*

The phrase "moral necessity" is used variously: sometimes it is used for a necessity of obligation. So we say, a man is under necessity, when he is under bonds of duty and conscience, which he can't be discharged from. So the word "necessity" is often used for great obligation[1] in point of interest. Sometimes by "moral necessity" is meant that apparent connection[2] of things, which is the ground of moral evidence[3]; and so is distinguished from absolute necessity, or that sure connection of things, that is a foundation for infallible certainty.

---

1. [JE never read Immanuel Kant (1724–1804), who synthesized early modern rationalism and empiricism and necessity and will. According to the latter, to make moral *obligation* possible is *autonomy*, the *moral law* of one's own reason. "Necessitation by the moral law, to act with accordance with it, obligation." (V 27:481), quoted in Lara Denis, and Oliver Sensen, *Kant's Lectures on Ethics* (Cambridge University Press, 2015), 145; Natalia Marandiuc, "Human Will, Divine Grace, and Virtue: Jonathan Edwards Tangos with Immanuel Kant" in *Jonathan Edwards and Scotland*, ed., Kenneth P. Minkema, Adriaan C. Neele, and Kelly Van Andel (Edinburgh: Dunedin, 2011), 129–46.]

2. [Ramsey defines "connection" as "cause." *FOW*, 118.]

3. [Moral evidence refers to that evidence obtained by those convictions of the mind, the use of the senses, the testimony of men, and analogy or induction. *A Law Dictionary Adapted to the Constitution and Laws of the United States of America* (1855), 188.]

### Section 4—Of the Distinction of Natural and Moral Necessity, and Inability

*JE defines "moral necessity" as high degree of probability in conduct and behavior.*

In this sense, "moral necessity" signifies much the same as that high degree of probability, which is ordinarily sufficient to satisfy, and be relied upon by mankind, in their conduct and behavior in the world, as they would consult their own safety and interest, and treat others properly as members of society.

*JE defines "moral necessity" as necessity of connection and consequence, to arise from moral causes (strength and connection) and certain volitions and actions.*

And sometimes by "moral necessity" is meant that necessity of connection and consequence, which arises from such moral causes, as the strength of inclination, or motives, and the connection which there is in many cases between these, and such certain volitions and actions. And it is in this sense, that I use the phrase "moral necessity" in the following discourse.

*JE defines "natural necessity" as instances in which men are under the force of natural causes.*

By "natural necessity," as applied to men, I mean such necessity as men are under through the force of natural causes; as distinguished from what are called moral causes, such as habits and dispositions of the heart, and moral motives and inducements.

*Instances of "Natural Necessity"*

Thus men placed in certain circumstances, are the subjects of particular sensations by necessity: they feel pain when their bodies are wounded; they see the objects presented before them in a clear light, when their eyes are opened: so they assent to the truth of certain propositions, as soon as the terms are understood; as that two and two make four, that black is not white, that two parallel lines can never cross one another: so by a natural necessity men's bodies move downwards, when there is nothing to support them.

But here several things may be noted concerning these two kinds of necessity.

*Moral necessity or natural necessity can equal absolute necessity; the will is determined by the strongest motive, yet the former cannot resist the latter which is stronger.*

1. Moral necessity may be as absolute, as natural necessity.[4] That is, the effect may be as perfectly connected with its moral cause, as a naturally necessary effect is with its natural cause. Whether the will in every case is necessarily determined by the strongest motive, or whether the will ever makes any resistance to such a motive, or can ever

---

4. [JE's moral absolutism: JE maintains there are absolute standards in judging actions to be right or wrong, regardless of the context of the act, in Part III and IV, *FOW*. Cf. Norman Fiering, *Jonathan Edwards's Moral Thought and its British Context* (Chapel Hill: University of North Carolina Press, 1981), 107, 144; R.G. Frey, *Absolutism and its consequentialist critics* (Rowman & Littlefield, 1994), 110.]

oppose the strongest present inclination, or not; if that matter should be controverted, yet I suppose none will deny, but that, in some cases, a previous bias and inclination, or the motive presented, may be so powerful, that the act of the will may be certainly and indissolubly connected therewith.

**When the will resists motives or previous bias, the will faces some difficulty, and the will overcomes or submits to them, according to its power. A connection is the moral necessity between moral causes and moral effects.**

When motives or previous bias are very strong, all will allow that there is some difficulty in going against them. And if they were yet stronger, the difficulty would be still greater. And therefore, if more were still added to their strength, to a certain degree, it would make the difficulty so great, that it would be wholly impossible to surmount it; for this plain reason, because whatever power men may be supposed to have to surmount difficulties, yet that power is not infinite; and so goes not beyond certain limits. If a man can surmount ten degrees of difficulty of this kind, with twenty degrees of strength, because the degrees of strength are beyond the degrees of difficulty; yet if the difficulty be increased to thirty, or a hundred, or a thousand degrees, and his strength not also increased, his strength will be wholly insufficient to surmount the difficulty. As therefore it must be allowed, that there may be such a thing as a sure and perfect connection between moral causes and effects; so this only is what I call by the name of "moral necessity."

**Moral necessity and natural necessity are different. A moral habit or motive or cause is dominant in the act or the will.**

2. When I use this distinction of moral and natural necessity, I would not be understood to suppose, that if anything comes to pass by the former kind of necessity, the nature of things is not concerned in it, as well as in the latter. I don't mean to determine, that when a moral habit or motive is so strong, that the act or the will infallibly follows; this is not owing to the nature of things. But these are the names that these two kinds of necessity have usually been called by; and they must be distinguished by some names or other; for there is a distinction or difference between them, that is very important in its consequences. Which[5] difference does not lie so much in the nature of the connection, as in the two terms connected. The cause with which the effect is connected, is of a particular kind; viz. that which is of a moral nature; either some previous habitual disposition, or some motive exhibited to the understanding. And the effect is also of a particular kind; being likewise of a moral nature; consisting in some inclination or volition of the soul, or voluntary action.

---

5. [Paul Ramsey, editor of Yale edition of *FOW*, changed the original sentence, in p. 22 of the first edition of 1754, ". Which..." To ": which...," but this edition restores it into the original. Cf. *FOW*, 158. Hereafter abbreviated "Corrected" when corrected from the first edition by using the "Supplemental Errata" list combined of Errata slip and JE Jr.'s handwritten changes. See this edition's appendix.]

## Section 4—Of the Distinction of Natural and Moral Necessity, and Inability

***"Mere nature" is without anything of choice. "Nature" and "choice" are completely and universally distinct. Men cannot make choices by breaking laws of nature in the material world.***

I suppose, that necessity which is called natural, in distinction from moral necessity, is so called. The word "nature" is often used in opposition to "choice"; not because nature has indeed never any hand in our choice; but this probably comes to pass by means that we first get our notion of nature from that discernible and obvious course of events, which we observe in many things that our choice has no concern in; and especially in the material world; which, in very many parts of it, we easily perceive to be in a settled course; the stated order and manner of succession being very apparent. But where we don't readily discern the rule and connection [though there be a connection, according to an established law, truly taking place], we signify the manner of event by some other name. Even in many things which are seen in the material and inanimate world, which don't discernibly and obviously come to pass according to any settled course, men don't call the manner of the event by the name of nature, but by such names as "accident," "chance," "contingence," etc. So men make a distinction between "nature" and "choice"; as though they were completely and universally distinct.

***Rather, men make choices under the influence of nature.***

Whereas, I suppose none will deny but that choice, in many cases, arises from nature, as truly as other events. But the dependence and connection between acts of volition or choice, and their causes, according to established laws, is not so sensible and obvious. And we observe that choice is as it were a new principle[6] of motion and action, different from that established law and order of things which is most obvious, that is seen especially in corporeal and sensible things;

***Misunderstanding of the relation between nature and human choice: They are distinctive and separate.***

and also that choice often interposes, interrupts and alters the chain of events in these external objects, and causes them to proceed otherwise than they would do, if let alone, and left to go on according to the laws of motion among themselves. Hence it is spoken of, as if it were a principle of motion entirely distinct from nature, and

---

6. [JE used the word "principle" in the sense of the Latin *principium* or the Greek *arché*. The word "principle" means a source or beginning or spring of disposition and action. But it also means the direction, shape, or contours of human hearts and lives, as in the root of our word "archetype" or the *arché* or formative power of Plato's ideas, such as justice or beauty, or triangularity. So when the first verse of St. John's Gospel reads, "In the beginning was the Word," that in Greek is *en arché* and in Latin *inprincipio*. The verse not only points to the source and beginning of all things, without whom "was not anything made that was made." These verses also tell us something about the channel in which the whole creation runs, its shape, meaning, and direction." Quoted from Editor's Introduction, Ethical Writings, ed. Paul Ramsey (*WJE* Online 8:16)]

properly set in opposition to it. Names[7] being commonly given to things, according to what is most obvious, and is suggested by what appears to the senses without reflection and research.

### *Men's will cannot resist the moral necessity.*

3. It must be observed, that in what has been explained, as signified by the name of "moral necessity," the word "necessity" is not used according to the original design and meaning of the word: for, as was observed before, such terms "necessary," "impossible," "irresistible," etc., in common speech, and their most proper sense, are always relative; having reference to some supposable voluntary opposition or endeavor, that is insufficient. But no such opposition, or contrary will and endeavor, is supposable in the case of moral necessity; which is a certainty of the inclination and will itself; which does not admit of the supposition of a will to oppose and resist it. For it is absurd, to suppose the same individual will to oppose itself, in its present act; or the present choice to be opposite to, and resisting present choice: as absurd as it is to talk of two contrary motions, in the same moving body, at the same time. And therefore the very case supposed never admits of any trial, whether an opposing or resisting will can overcome this necessity.

### *Moral inability is from the opposition or want of inclination.*

What has been said of natural and moral necessity, may serve to explain what is intended by natural and moral *inability*.[8] We are said to be *naturally* unable to do a thing, when we can't do it if we will, because what is most commonly called nature doesn't allow of it, or because of some impeding defect or obstacle that is extrinsic to the will; either in the faculty of understanding, constitution of body, or external objects. *Moral* inability consists not in any of these things; but either in the want of inclination; or the strength of a contrary inclination; or the want of sufficient motives in view, to induce and excite the act of the will, or the strength of apparent motives to the contrary. Or both of these may be resolved into one; and it may be said in one word, that moral inability consists in the opposition or want of inclination. For when a person is unable to will or choose such a thing, through a defect of motives, or prevalence of contrary motives, it is the same thing as his being unable through the want of

---

7. [Restored, from "to it—names being. . . ." "Names" refer to "contingence," "fate," "accident," "chance," etc.]

8. [Sam Storm: "If I fail to save a drowning child because I cannot swim (a natural inability), I am subject to a natural necessity and thus blameless. If I refuse to save a drowning child because I don't care (a moral inability), I am subject to a moral necessity and deserving of condemnation. When Martin Luther stood before the Diet of Worms in 1521 and declared, "Here I stand. I can do no other," it wasn't because his legs were incapable of carrying him out of the presence of his accusers. His "inability" to do anything other was the "necessary" product of a will that "freely" defied the Roman Catholic Church." See Sam Storm, "The Will: Fettered Yet Free (Freedom of the Will)" in *A God Entranced Vision of all Things: the Legacy of Jonathan Edwards*, ed. John Piper and Justin Taylor (Wheaton, IL: Crossway Books, 2004), 209.]

an inclination, or the prevalence of a contrary inclination, in such circumstances, and under the influence of such views.

### Instances of Moral Inability

To give some instances of this moral inability: A woman of great honor and chastity may have a moral inability to prostitute herself to her slave. A child of great love and duty to his parents, may be unable to be willing to kill his father. A very lascivious man, in case of certain opportunities and temptations, and in the absence of such and such restraints, may be unable to forbear gratifying his lust. A drunkard, under such and such circumstances, may be unable to forbear taking of strong drink. A very malicious man may be unable to exert benevolent acts to an enemy, or to desire his prosperity: yea, some may be so under the power of a vile disposition, that they may be unable to love those who are most worthy of their esteem and affection.

### Moral inability may be overcome by a strong habit.

A strong habit of virtue and great degree of holiness may cause a moral inability to love wickedness in general, may render a man unable to take complacence in wicked persons or things; or to choose a wicked life, and prefer it to a virtuous life. And on the other hand, a great degree of habitual wickedness may lay a man under an inability to love and choose holiness; and render him utterly unable to love an infinitely holy Being, or to choose and cleave to him as his chief good.

Here it may be of use to observe this distinction of moral inability, viz. of that which is general and habitual, and that which is particular and occasional.

### General and habitual moral inability is the inability to exert such acts of benevolence.

By a *general and habitual* moral inability, I mean an inability in the heart to all exercises or acts of will of that nature or kind, through a fixed and habitual inclination, or an habitual and stated defect, or want of a certain kind of inclination. Thus a very ill-natured man may be unable to exert such acts of benevolence, as another, who is full of good nature, commonly exerts; and a man, whose heart is habitually void of gratitude, may be unable to exert such and such grateful acts, through that stated defect of a grateful inclination.

### Particular and occasional moral inability is the inability of the will or heart to perform a particular act.

By *particular and occasional* moral inability, I mean an inability of the will or heart to a particular act, through the strength or defect of present motives, or of inducements presented to the view of the understanding, on this occasion. If it be so, that the will is always determined by the strongest motive, then it must always have an inability, in this latter sense, to act otherwise than it does; it not being possible, in any case, that the will should, at present, go against the motive which has now, all things considered, the greatest strength and advantage to excite and induce it.

### General and chronic moral inability denotes that men's strong habit can sink their desires and efforts; it can resist their will.

The former of these kinds of moral inability, consisting in that which is stated, habitual and general, is most commonly called by the name of "inability"; because the word "inability," in its most proper and original signification, has respect to some stated defect. And this especially obtains the name of "inability" also upon another account: I before observed, that the word "inability" in its original and most common use, is a relative term[9]; and has respect to will and endeavor, as supposable in the case, and as insufficient to bring to pass the thing desired and endeavored. Now there may be more of an appearance and shadow of this, with respect to the acts which arise from a fixed and strong habit, than others that arise only from transient occasions and causes.

### Acts of the will, present and future, can conflict one another, but present ones cannot conflict one another.

Indeed, will and endeavor against, or diverse from present acts of the will, are in no case supposable, whether those acts be occasional or habitual; for that would be to suppose the will, at present, to be otherwise than, at present, it is. But yet there may be will and endeavor against future acts of the will, or volitions that are likely to take place, as viewed at a distance. It is no contradiction, to suppose that the acts of the will at one time, may be against the acts of the will at another time; and there may be desires and endeavors to prevent or excite future acts of the will; but such desires and endeavors are, in many cases, rendered insufficient and vain, through fixedness of habit: when the occasion returns, the strength of habit overcomes, and baffles all such opposition.

### Future acts of the will can be transiently changed. The will and reason cannot resist a strong habit, that is, the moral inability.

In this respect, a man may be in miserable slavery and bondage to a strong habit. But it may be comparatively easy to make an alteration with respect to such future acts, as are only occasional and transient; because the occasion or transient cause, if foreseen, may often easily be prevented or avoided. On this account, the moral inability that attends fixed habits, especially obtains the name of "inability." And then, as the will may remotely and indirectly resist itself, and do it in vain, in the case of strong habits; so reason may resist present acts of the will, and its resistance be insufficient; and this is more commonly the case also, when the acts arise from strong habit.

---

9. [A relative term is a logical term that is not self-sufficient or absolute and so it requires reference to any number of other objects in order to denote a definite object or relationship.]

### Section 4—Of the Distinction of Natural and Moral Necessity, and Inability

*Moral inability signifies natural inability due to a lack of the will and disposition.*

But it must be observed concerning[10] moral inability, in each kind of it, that the word "inability" is used in a sense very diverse from its original import. The word signifies only a natural inability, in the proper use of it; and is applied to such cases only wherein a present will or inclination to the thing, with respect to which a person is said to be unable, is supposable.

*Some instances of general and habitual moral inability:*

It can't be truly said, according to the ordinary use of language, that a malicious man, let him be never so malicious, can't hold his hand from striking, or that he is not able to show his neighbor kindness; or that a drunkard, let his appetite be never so strong, can't keep the cup from his mouth.

*It is true that man can do it if he wills, and false that he can't if he wills.*

In the strictest propriety of speech, a man has a thing in his power, if he has it in his choice, or at his election: and a man can't be truly said to be unable to do a thing, when he can do it if he will. It is improperly said, that a person can't perform those external actions, which are dependent on the act of the will, and which would be easily performed, if the act of the will were present. And if it be improperly said, that he cannot perform those external voluntary actions, which depend on the will, it is in some respect more improperly said, that he is unable to exert the acts of the will themselves; because it is more evidently false, with respect to these, that he can't if he will: for to say so, is a downright contradiction: it is to say, he *can't* will, if he *does* will. And in this case, not only is it true, that it is easy for a man to do the thing if he will, but the very willing is the doing; when once he has willed, the thing is performed; and nothing else remains to be done. Therefore, in these things to ascribe a nonperformance to the want of power or ability, is not just; because the thing wanting is not a being *able*, but a being *willing*. There are faculties of mind, and capacity of nature, and everything else, sufficient, but a disposition: nothing is wanting but a will.

---

10. [Corrected from "concerned" to "concerning."]

# Section 5

## Concerning the Notion of Liberty, and of Moral Agency

***"Liberty" is power, opportunity, or advantage, that anyone has, to do as he pleases.***

The plain and obvious meaning of the words "freedom" and "liberty," in common speech, is power, opportunity, or advantage, that anyone has, to do as he pleases. Or in other words, his being free from hindrance or impediment in the way of doing, or conducting in any respect, as he wills.[1] And the contrary to liberty, whatever name we call that by, is a person's being hindered or unable to conduct as he will, or being necessitated to do otherwise.

***Liberty and its contrary have such a faculty, power, or property, as is called "will."***

If this which I have mentioned be the meaning of the word "liberty," in the ordinary use of language; as I trust that none that has ever learned to talk, and is unprejudiced, will deny; then it will follow, that in propriety of speech, neither liberty, nor its contrary, can properly be ascribed to any being or thing, but that which has such a faculty, power or property, as is called "will." For that which is possessed of no such thing as will, can't have any power or opportunity of doing according to its will, nor be necessitated to act contrary to its will, nor be restrained from acting agreeably to it.

***Neither liberty nor its contrary belongs to the will itself. The will is a faculty, power, or property, but not an agent who has a power to make choices.***

And therefore to talk of liberty, or the contrary, as belonging to the very will itself, is not to speak good sense; if we judge of sense, and nonsense, by the original and proper signification of words. For the will itself is not an agent that has a will: the power of

---

1. [JE, I say not only "doing," but "conducting" because a voluntary forbearing to do, sitting still, keeping silence, etc., are instances of persons' conduct, about which liberty is exercised, though they are not properly called "doing."]

choosing, itself, has not a power of choosing. That which has the power of volition or choice is the man or the soul, and not the power of volition itself. And he that has the liberty of doing according to his will, is the agent or doer who is possessed of the will; and not the will which he is possessed of.

### Man or soul has the freedom of doing according to his will, but the will itself does not.

### ILL: *a bird let loose has power and liberty to fly.*

We say with propriety, that a bird let loose has power and liberty to fly; but not that the bird's power of flying has a power and liberty of flying. To be free is the property of an agent, who is possessed of powers and faculties, as much as to be cunning, valiant, bountiful, or zealous. But these qualities are the properties of men or persons; and not the properties of properties.

### There are two kinds of anti-freedom: constraint (compulsion, coaction) and restraint (hindrance, inability).

There are two things that are contrary to this which is called liberty in common speech. One is *constraint*; the same is otherwise called force, compulsion, and coaction; which is a person's being necessitated to do a thing *contrary* to his will. The other is *restraint*; which is his being hindered, and not having power to do *according* to his will. But that which has no will, can't be the subject of these things. I need say the less on this head, Mr. Locke having set the same thing forth, with so great clearness, in his *Essay on the Human Understanding*.[2]

### A common notion of liberty is the power and opportunity for one to do and conduct his will, or according to his choice.

But one thing more I would observe concerning what is vulgarly called liberty; namely, that power and opportunity for one to do and conduct as he will, or according to his choice, is all that is meant by it; without taking into the meaning of the word, anything of the cause or original of that choice; or at all considering how the person came to have such a volition; whether it was caused by some external motive, or internal habitual bias; whether it was determined by some internal antecedent volition, or whether it happened without a cause; whether it was necessarily connected with something foregoing, or not connected. Let the person come by his volition or choice how he will, yet, if he is able, and there is nothing in the way to hinder his pursuing and executing his will, the man is fully and perfectly free, according to the primary and common notion of freedom.

### Arminians and Pelagians use the freedom in an entirely different sense.

---

2. Locke, *Essay*, bk. II, ch. 21, nos. 14–21; 1:319–24. "Liberty belongs not to the will." Locke, *Essay*, bk. II, ch. 21, nos. 14.

What has been said may be sufficient to show what is meant by liberty, according to the common notions of mankind, and in the usual and primary acceptation of the word: but the word, as used by Arminians, Pelagians[3] and others, who oppose the Calvinists, has an entirely different signification. These several things belong to their notion of liberty:

*Ar—1. The freedom consists of a self-determining power in the will, or a certain sovereignty in it.*

1. That it consists in a self-determining power in the will, or a certain sovereignty the will has over itself, and its own acts, whereby it determines its own volitions; so as not to be dependent in its determinations, on any cause without itself, nor determined by anything prior to its own acts.

*Ar—2. The freedom comes from indifference and even state between soberness and its reverse.*

2. Indifference belongs to liberty in their notion of it, or that the mind, previous to the act of volition be, *in equilibrio*.

*Ar—3. The freedom comes not from necessity but from contingence.*

3. Contingence is another thing that belongs and is essential to it; not in the common acceptation of the word, as that has been already explained, but as opposed to all necessity, or any fixed and certain connection with some previous ground or reason of its existence.[4]

*Moral actions do not come out of the will's freedom but the man himself who does them freely.*

They suppose te essence of liberty so much to consist in these things, that unless the will of man be free in this sense, he has no real freedom, how much so ever he may be at liberty to act according to his will.

*A moral agent is a moral actor to be denominated for he has moral faculty or sense and capacity.*

A moral agent is a being that is capable of those actions that have a moral quality, and which can properly be denominated good or evil in a moral sense, virtuous or vicious, commendable or faulty. To moral agency belongs a moral faculty, or sense of moral

---

3. [Pelagius (ca. AD 354—ca. AD 420/440), a British-born or Irish monk, was condemned as a heretic by the Synod of Carthage in about 418, for he denied the doctrines of original sin and total depravity and predestination of St. Augustine, defending innate human goodness and free will.]

4. [JE holds almost the same opinion on contingence as Spinoza, as Richard Mason states "*Contingency* is related to a 'deficiency in our knowledge.'" In reality, 'nothing in nature is contingent.'" Richard Mason, *The God of Spinoza: A Philosophical Study* (Cambridge University Press, 1997), 62.]

good and evil, or of such a thing as desert[5] or worthiness of praise or blame, reward or punishment; and a capacity which an agent has of being influenced in his actions by moral inducements or motives, exhibited to the view of understanding and reason, to engage to a conduct agreeable to the moral faculty.

**Where there is no moral faculty or sense, there are no moral actions and judgment: e.g., sun, fire, animals.**

The sun is very excellent and beneficial in its action and influence on the earth, in warming it, and causing it to bring forth its fruits; but it is not a moral agent: its action, though good, is not virtuous or meritorious. Fire that breaks out in a city, and consumes great part of it, is very mischievous in its operation; but is not a moral agent: what it does is not faulty or sinful, or deserving of any punishment. The brute creatures are not moral agents: the actions of some of them are very profitable and pleasant; others are very hurtful: yet, seeing they have no moral faculty, or sense of desert, and don't act from choice guided by understanding, or with a capacity of reasoning and reflecting, but only from instinct, and are not capable of being influenced by moral inducements, their actions are not properly sinful or virtuous; nor are they properly the subjects of any such moral treatment for what they do, as moral agents are for their faults or good deeds.

**There is a circumstantial difference between the moral agency of a ruler and a subject, in moral inducements, capacity, and knowledge of moral good and evil.**

Here it may be noted, that there is a circumstantial difference between the moral agency of a ruler and a subject. I call it circumstantial, because it lies only in the difference of moral inducements they are capable of being influenced by, arising from the difference of circumstances. A ruler acting in that capacity only, is not capable of being influenced by a moral law, and its sanctions of threatenings and promises, rewards and punishments, as the subject is; though both may be influenced by a knowledge of moral good and evil. And therefore the moral agency of the Supreme Being, who acts only in the capacity of a ruler towards his creatures, and never as a subject, differs in that respect from the moral agency of created intelligent beings.

God's actions, and particularly those which he exerts as a moral governor, have moral qualifications, are morally good in the highest degree. They are most perfectly holy and righteous; and we must conceive of him as influenced in the highest degree, by that which, above all others, is properly a moral inducement; viz. the moral good which he sees in such and such things: and therefore he is, in the most proper sense, a moral agent, the source of all moral ability and agency, the fountain and rule of all virtue and moral good; though by reason of his being supreme over all, it is not

---

5. [Desert (desertus) in philosophy is the condition of being deserving of the rewards of meritocracy.]

possible he should be under the influence of law or command, promises or threatenings, rewards or punishments, counsels or warnings.

***Man as a moral agent was created in the natural spiritual and moral image of God, and was endowed with essential qualities; the understanding and the capacity of discerning, and so he is deserved of praise or blame.***

The essential qualities of a moral agent are in God, in the greatest possible perfection; such as understanding, to perceive the difference between moral good and evil; a capacity of discerning that moral worthiness and demerit, by which some things are praiseworthy, others deserving of blame and punishment; and also a capacity of choice, and choice guided by understanding, and a power of acting according to his choice or pleasure, and being capable of doing those things which are in the highest sense praiseworthy. And herein does very much consist that image of God wherein he made man (which we read of, Genesis 1:26, 27 and ch. 9:6), by which God distinguished man from the beasts,[6] viz. in those faculties and principles of nature, whereby he is capable of moral agency. Herein very much consists the *natural* image of God; as his *spiritual* and *moral* image, wherein man was made at first, consisted in that moral excellency, that he was endowed with.[7]

---

6. [For the main difference between men and beasts, see "The Mind," *WJE* 6:374]

7. [JE holds there are attributes and principles and twofold images of God in man, such as the natural and the spiritual or moral ones, which are not to be identified but distinguished. In his view, the former is imperfectly intact for man such as inferior strength and natural ability, understanding/knowledge/reason/conscience/affections/will, greatness of God, dominion over creatures, and the latter is totally lost superior image, such as holiness and moral excellency. The "natural ability" even after the Fall is not eradicated by the original sin. And the "natural difficulty" remains in men, and yet the Holy Spirit assists men's natural abilities. *FOW*, 351; *Religious Affections*, *WJE* 2:207, 256; *Original Sin*, *WJE* 3:381; idem, *True Virtue*, *WJE* 8:590.]

# PART II

Where It Is Considered, whether There Is, or Can Be Any Such Sort of Freedom of Will, as That wherein Arminians Place the Essence of the Liberty of All Moral Agents; and Whether Any Such Thing Ever Was, or Can Be Conceived of

# Section 1

## Showing the Manifest Inconsistence of the Arminian Notion of Liberty of Will, Consisting in the Will's Self-Determining Power

*JE questions whether, as Arminians insist, the freedom of the will is necessary for moral agency.*

Having taken notice of those things which may be necessary to be observed, concerning the meaning of the principal terms and phrases made use of in controversies concerning human liberty, and particularly observed what liberty is, according to the common language, and general apprehension of mankind, and what it is as understood and maintained by Arminians; I proceed to consider the Arminian notion of the freedom of the will, and the supposed necessity of it in order to moral agency, or in order to anyone's being capable of virtue or vice, and properly the subject of command or counsel, praise or blame, promises or threatenings, rewards or punishments; or whether that which has been described, as the thing meant by liberty in common speech, be not sufficient, and the only liberty, which makes, or can make anyone a moral agent, and so properly the subject of these things.

*JE questions whether, as Arminians insist, the will itself has the self-determining power to determine all of its free acts.*

In this part, I shall consider whether any such thing be possible or conceivable, as that freedom of will which Arminians insist on; and shall inquire whether any such sort of liberty be necessary to moral agency, etc. in the next part.[1]

1. [The will is free? Arminians insist "the freedom of will" or "perfectly free will" or "free will," but JE argues that there is no freedom in the will itself but in man. That is, man is free whether to obey or disobey the morals or necessity, and God is so only in doing good. Nevertheless, many fail to grasp what Edwards means by these ambiguous phrases: "man is fully and perfectly free"; "men act voluntarily, and do what they please"; "in them alone was the man was free"; "a man. . .can do as he

And first of all, I shall consider the notion of a self-determining power in the will: wherein, according to the Arminians, does most essentially consist the will's freedom; and shall particularly inquire, whether it be not plainly absurd, and a manifest inconsistence, to suppose that the will itself determines all the free acts of the will.

***Arminians posit that the will itself determines all the free acts of the will.***

***JE counters that human actions are to be ascribed to an agent and not to the will or power of the agent itself.***

Here I shall not insist on the great impropriety of such phrases, and ways of speaking, as "the will's determining itself"; because actions are to be ascribed to agents, and not properly to the powers of agents; which improper way of speaking leads to many mistakes, and much confusion, as Mr. Locke observes.[2] But I shall suppose that the Arminians, when they speak of the will's determining itself, do by the will mean "the soul willing."[3]

***Ar: The will is the determiner. That is, the soul has power of willing or acting voluntarily.***

I shall take it for granted, that when they speak of the will, as the determiner, they mean the soul in the exercise of a power of willing, or acting voluntarily. I shall suppose this to be their meaning, because nothing else can be meant, without the grossest and plainest absurdity. In all cases, when we speak of the powers or principles of acting, as doing such things, we mean that the agents which have these powers of acting, do them, in the exercise of those powers.

So when we say, valor fights courageously, we mean, the man who is under the influence of valor fights courageously. When we say, love seeks the object loved, we mean, the person loving seeks that object. When we say, the understanding discerns, we mean the soul in the exercise of that faculty. So when it is said, the will decides or determines, the meaning must be, that the person in the exercise of a power of willing and choosing, or the soul acting voluntarily, determines.

---

chooses"; or "there is no need of any such liberty." *FOW*, 164, 147, 325, 371, 433.]

2. [Edwards's relationship to John Locke: Tappan provides some clue to how much he adopts Locke by saying, "Locke fully adopts the Necessitarian view of liberty," that is held by Edwards. Both agree liberty is a power of the soul, and deny Arminian notion of the will of the self-determining power. And they agree the soul or mind is composed of two faculties of the understanding and the will, but JE disagree with JL's possibility of conflict between them. See Henry Philip Tappan, *A treatise on the will: containing A review of [J.] Edwards's Inquiry into the freedom of the will [&c.]* (Glasgow: Lang Adamson & Co., 1857), 592; Paul Ramsey, Editor's Introduction, *WJE* 1:47–65; Paul Helm, "John Locke and Jonathan Edwards: A Reconsideration," Journal *of the History of Philosophy* 7 (1969): 51–61.]

3. [William of Occam (1287–1349) states the most characteristic *activity* of God is *willing*, and likewise in his view: "The intellect is the soul thinking; the will is the soul willing." David W. Clark, "Ockham on Human and Divine Freedom," *Franciscan Studies* 38 (1978): 132–33. JE might have not read Occam but the former regards it to be Arminian notion of the will as "the soul willing" as the same definition of Occam.]

# Section 1—Showing the Manifest Inconsistence of the Arminian Notion of Liberty of Will

*Ar: The will determines all its own free acts; the will determines the will.*

Therefore, if the will determines all its own free acts, the soul determines all the free acts of the will in the exercise of a power of willing and choosing; or, which is the same thing, it determines them of choice; it determines its own acts by choosing its own acts.

If the will determines the will, then choice orders and determines the choice: and acts of choice are subject to the decision, and follow the conduct of other acts of choice. And therefore if the will determines all its own free acts, then every free act of choice is determined by a preceding act of choice, choosing that act. And if that preceding act of the will or choice be also a free act, then by these principles, in this act too, the will is self-determined; that is, this, in like manner, is an act that the soul voluntarily chooses; or which is the same thing, it is an act determined still by a preceding act of the will, choosing that.

**Arminian Contradiction: Insisting the will itself determines all its acts, they do not say that the person or soul determines them.**

And the like may again be observed of the last mentioned act. Which brings us directly to a contradiction: for it supposes, an act of the will preceding the first act in the whole train, directing and determining the rest; or a free act of the will, before the first free act of the will. Or else we must come at last to an act of the will, determining the consequent acts, wherein the will is not self-determined, and so is not a free act, in this notion of freedom: but if the first act in the train, determining and fixing the rest, be not free, none of them all can be free; as is manifest at first view, but shall be demonstrated presently.

**In the Arminian view, the will determines itself and its acts. According to JE, the will's act is determined by an act of volition preceding them.**

If the will, which we find governs the members of the body, and determines and commands their motions and actions, does also govern itself, and determine its own motions and acts, it doubtless determines them the same way, even by antecedent volitions. The will determines which way the hands and feet shall move, by an act of volition or choice: and there is no other way of the will's determining, directing or commanding anything at all. Whatsoever the will commands, it commands by an act of the will. And if it has itself under its command, and determines itself in its own actions, it doubtless does it the same way that it determines other things which are under its command.

*Ar: The will's free self-determination equals that it determines its actions by following its command, and its volitions by itself.*

*JE: Every volition arises from antecedent volition.*

So that if the freedom of the will consists in this, that it has itself and its own actions under its command and direction, and its own volitions are determined by itself, it will follow, that every free volition arises from another antecedent volition, directing and commanding that: and if that *directing* volition be also free, in that also the will is self-determined; that is to say, that directing volition is determined by another going before that; and so on, till we come to the first volition in the whole series: and if that first volition be free, and the will self-determined in it, then that is determined by another volition preceding that.

Which is a contradiction; because by the supposition, it can have none before it, to direct or determine it, being the first in the train. But if that first volition is not determined by any preceding act of the will, then that act is not determined by the will, and so is not free, in the Arminian notion of freedom, which consists in the will's self-determination. And if that first act of the will, which determines and fixes the subsequent acts, be not free, none of the following acts, which are determined by it, can be free.

### JE: Man is free, but his will is not free because it is determined by its preceding act.

If we suppose there are five acts in the train, the fifth and last determined by the fourth, and the fourth by the third, the third by the second, and the second by the first; if the first is not determined by the will, and so not free, then none of them are truly determined by the will: that is, that each of them are as they are, and not otherwise, is not first owing to the will, but to the determination of the first in the series, which is not dependent on the will, and is that which the will has no hand in the determination of. And this being that which decides what the rest shall be, and determines their existence; therefore the first determination of their existence is not from the will. The case is just the same, if instead of a chain of five acts of the will, we should suppose a succession of ten, or a hundred, or ten thousand. If the first act be not free, being determined by something out of the will, and this determines the next to be agreeable to itself, and that the next, and so on; they are none of them free, but all originally depend on, and are determined by some cause[4] out of the will: and so all freedom in the case is excluded, and no act of the will can be free, according to this notion of freedom.

### ILL: A long chain of ten thousand links: If the first link moves, it will cause the rest of the links to consecutively move; the first link is moved by something else. Likewise, man's motion and direction are determined by something other than his will.

If we should suppose a long chain, of ten thousand links, so connected, that if the first link moves, it will move the next, and that the next; and so the whole chain must be determined to motion, and in the direction of its motion, by the motion of the first link; and that is moved by something else: in this case, though all the links, but one,

---

4. [JE explains by using metaphors like a train and chain of cause, motive, will, volition, and effect (act), in which the first cause is God, and he is called a causationist.]

are moved by other parts of the same chain; yet it appears that the motion of no one, nor the direction of its motion, is from any self-moving or self-determining power in the chain, any more than if every link were immediately moved by something that did not belong to the chain.

***JE: The will does not cause man's acts, nor is it free to determine them at all.***

If the will be not free in the first act, which causes the next, then neither is it free in the next, which is caused by that first act: for though indeed the will caused it, yet it did not cause it freely; because the preceding act, by which it was caused, was not free. And again, if the will is not free in the second act, so neither can it be in the third, which is caused by that; because, in like manner, that third was determined by an act of the will that was not free. And so we may go on to the next act, and from that to the next; and how long so ever the succession of acts is, it is all one; if the first on which the whole chain depends, and which determines all the rest, isn't a free act, the will is not free in causing or determining any one of those acts; because the act by which it determines them all, is not a free act; and therefore the will is no more free in determining them, than if it did not cause them at all. Thus, this Arminian notion of liberty of the will, consisting in the will's self-determination, is repugnant to itself, and shuts itself wholly out of the world.[5]

---

5. [Concerning the question whether or not the will is free, JE answers elsewhere that man "had more freedom of will" before the Fall. See JE, "FALL AND FREE WILL," MSC No.291, *WJE* 13:383.]

# Section 2

## Several Supposed Ways of Evading the Foregoing Reasoning, Considered

*Ar: The will itself determines its volition and act.*

*JE: The prior act determines the will's act.*

If to evade the force of what has been observed, it should be said, that when the Arminians speak of the will's determining its own acts, they don't mean that the will determines its acts by any preceding act, or that one act of the will determines another; but only that the faculty or power of will, or the soul in the use of that power, determines its own volitions; and that it does it without any act going before the act determined; such an evasion would be full of the most gross absurdity. I confess, it is an evasion of my own inventing; and I don't know but I should wrong the Arminians, in supposing that any of them would make use of it. But it being as good a one as I can invent, I would observe upon it a few things.

*Arminian Arguments and Contradictions:*

*The 1st Arminian argument: The will or soul's power can determine its act and volition without the preceding act.*

*JE's counterargument: The volition cannot be determined without the preceding act of the will.*

First, if the faculty or power of the will determines an act of volition, or the soul in the use or exercise of that power, determines it, that is the same thing as for the soul to determine volition by an *act* of will. For an exercise of the power of will, and an act of that power, are the same thing. Therefore to say, that the power of will, or the soul in the use or exercise of that power, determines volition, without an act of will preceding the volition[1] determined, is a contradiction.

1. [Volition [F., fr. L. volo I will, velle to will, be willing] One can find JE imported his definition

*The 2nd Arminian argument: The will's willing and choosing power chooses an act of volition and then determines its act.*

*JE: If so, why doesn't it choose the other acts? It is because the will is caused by the preceding act.*

Secondly, if a power of will determines the act of the will, then a power of choosing determines it. For, as was before observed, in every act of will, there is choice, and a power of willing is a power of choosing. But if a power of choosing determines the act of volition, it determines it by choosing it. For it is most absurd to say, that a power of choosing determines one thing rather than another, without choosing anything. But if a power of choosing determines volition by choosing it, then here is the act of volition determined by an antecedent choice, choosing that volition.

*The 3rd Arminian argument: The will determines its volition without a prior act.*

*JE: Such determining is its act and also a cause.*

Thirdly, to say, the faculty, or the soul, determines its own volition, but not by any act, is a contradiction. Because for the soul to direct, decide, or determine anything, is to act; and this is supposed; for the soul is here spoken of as being a cause in this affair, bringing something to pass, or doing something; or, which is the same thing, exerting itself in order to an effect, which effect is the determination of volition, or the particular kind and manner of an act of will.

But certainly, this exertion or action is not the same with the effect, in order to the production of which it is exerted; but must be something prior to it.

*The 4th Arminian argument: There is sovereignty in the will and power to determine its volitions.*

*JE: The determination of volition is an act of the will, which is an exercise of that supposed power and sovereignty.*

Again, the advocates for this notion of the freedom of the will, speak of a certain sovereignty in the will, whereby it has power to determine its own volitions. And therefore the determination of volition must itself be an act of the will; for otherwise it can be no exercise of that supposed power and sovereignty.

*The 5th Arminian Dilemma:*
  *A. The will determines its act by its freedom.*
  *B. The will is active and exercises its own act.*

---

from Locke: 1. The act of willing or choosing; the act of forming a purpose; the exercise of the will. Volition is the actual exercise of the power the mind has to order the consideration of any idea, or the forbearing to consider it. 2. Volition is an act of the mind, knowingly exerting that dominion it takes itself to have over any part of the man, by employing it in, or withholding it from, any particular action. bk. II, Ch. 28.]

### JE: C. The will's determination is also its act, which is followed by the prior act, and so it has no freedom in self-determining power.

Again, if the will determines itself, then either the will is active in determining its volitions, or it is not. If it be active in it, then the determination is an *act* of the will; and so there is one act of the will determining another. But if the will is not active in the determination, then how does it exercise any liberty in it? These gentlemen suppose that the thing wherein the will exercises liberty, is in its determining its own acts. But how can this be, if it is not active in determining? Certainly the will, or the soul, can't exercise any liberty in that wherein it doesn't act, or wherein it doesn't exercise itself. So that if either part of this dilemma[2] be taken, this scheme of liberty, consisting in self-determining power, is overthrown.

### JE's objection against the freedom consisting in self-determining power

If there be an act of the will in determining all its own free acts, then one free act of the will is determined by another; and so we have the absurdity of every free act, even the very first, determined by a foregoing free act. But if there be no act or exercise of the will in determining its own acts, then no liberty is exercised in determining them. From whence it follows, that no liberty consists in the will's power to determine its own acts: or, which is the same thing, that there is no such thing as liberty consisting in a self-determining power of the will.

### Arminian Appeal: "Please don't suppose hastily 'this act to be prior to the volition determined.'"

If it should be said, that although it be true, if the soul determines its own volitions, it must be active in so doing, and the determination itself must be an act; yet there is no need of supposing this act to be prior to the volition determined; but the will or soul determines the act of the will *in willing*; it determines its own volition, *in* the very act of volition; it directs and limits the act of the will, causing it to be so and not otherwise, *in* exerting the act, without any preceding act to excite[3] that.

If any should say after this manner, they must mean one of these three things: either

(1) that the determining act, though it be before the act determined in the order of nature, yet is not before it in the order of time. Or (2) that the determining act is not before the act determined, either in the order of time or nature, nor is truly distinct

---

2. [Dilemma (Greek: δίλημμα "double proposition") is a form of argument involving a choice between equally unfavorable alternatives, or can be said as a problem offering two possibilities, neither of which is practically acceptable. The dilemma is sometimes used as a rhetorical device, in the form "you must accept either A, or B"; here A and B would be propositions each leading to some further conclusion. As "If A, then c; if B, then C. Either A or B. Therefore, C."]

3. [Corrected from "exert" to "excite."]

from it; but that the soul's determining the act of volition is the same thing with its exerting the act of volition: the mind's exerting such a particular act, is its causing and determining the act. Or (3) that volition has no cause, and is no effect; but comes into existence, with such a particular determination, without any ground or reason of its existence and determination.

### JE: *The determining act, the cause, exists temporally prior to the act determined, the effect.*

I shall consider these distinctly.

(1) If all that is meant, be, that "the determining act is not before the act determined in order of time," it will not help the case at all, though it should be allowed. If it be before the determined act in the order of nature, being the cause or ground of its existence, this as much proves it to be distinct from it, and independent on it, as if it were before in the order of time.

### ILL: *Distinctive cause and effect of motion of a natural body, a builder and his house, a father and his begotten son, a chain of many links.*

As the cause of the particular motion of a natural body in a certain direction, may have no distance as to time, yet can't be the same with the motion effected by it, but must be as distinct from it, as any other cause, that is before its effect in the order of time: as the architect is distinct from the house which he builds, or the father distinct from the son which he begets.

### JE: *The first act of the will is the act determining without the act of the will, and doing so, all the rest are not free acts determined.*

And if the act of the will determining be distinct from the act determined, and before it in the order of nature, then we can go back from one to another, till we come to the first in the series, which has no act of the will before it in the order of nature, determining it; and consequently is an act not determined by the will, and so not a free act, in this notion of freedom. And this being the act which determines all the rest, none of them are free acts.

As when there is a chain of many links, the first of which only is taken hold of and drawn by hand; all the rest may follow and be moved at the same instant, without any distance of time; but yet the motion of one link is before that of another in the order of nature; the last is moved by the next, and that by the next, and so till we come to the first; which not being moved by any other, but by something distinct from the whole chain, this as much proves that no part is moved by any self-moving power in the chain, as if the motion of one link followed that of another in the order of time.

### Ar: *The determining act is not temporally before the determined act nor is distinct from it.*

**JE: Both are linked as cause and effect and are not free from each other.**

(2) If any should say, that the determining act is not before the determined act, either in the order of time, or of nature, nor is distinct from it; but that the *exertion* of the act is the *determination* of the act; that for the soul to exert a particular volition, is for it to cause and determine that act of volition: I would on this observe, that the thing in question seems to be forgotten, or kept out of sight, in a darkness and unintelligibleness of speech; unless such an objector would mean to contradict himself.

**What is volition?**

The very act of volition itself is doubtless a determination of mind; i.e. it is the mind's drawing up a conclusion, or coming to a choice between two things, or more, proposed to it. But determining among external *objects* of choice, is not the same with determining the *act* of choice itself, among various possible acts of choice.

**What influences or determines the will to make a choice?**

The question is, what influences, directs, or determines the mind or will to come to such a conclusion or choice as it does? Or what is the cause, ground or reason, why it concludes thus, and not otherwise? Now it must be answered, according to the Arminian notion of freedom, that the will influences, orders and determines itself thus to act. And if it does, I say, it must be by some antecedent act. To say, it is caused, influenced and determined by something, and yet not determined by anything antecedent, either in order of time or nature, is a contradiction. For that is what is meant by a thing's being prior in the order of nature, that it is some way the cause or reason of the thing, with respect to which it is said to be prior.

**Ar: The will influences or determines itself.**

**JE: It has some cause, is it distinct from and is before its effect.**

If the particular act or exertion of will, which comes into existence, be anything properly determined at all, then it has some cause of its existing, and of its existing in such a particular determinate manner, and not another; some cause, whose influence decides the matter: which cause is distinct from the effect, and prior to it. But to say, that the will or mind orders, influences and determines itself to exert such an act as it does, by the very exertion itself, is to make the exertion both cause and effect; or the exerting such an act, to be a cause of the exertion of such an act. For the question is, What is the cause and reason of the soul's exerting such an act? To which the answer is, the soul exerts such an act, and that is the cause of it. And so, by this, the exertion must be prior in the order of nature to itself, and distinct from itself.

**Ar: The soul itself exerts an act of the will without any cause; the latter has the liberty consisting in self-determining power.**

## Section 2—Several Supposed Ways of Evading the Foregoing Reasoning, Considered

***JE: Their contention raises confusion by their senseless words.***

(3) If the meaning be, that "the soul's exertion of such a particular act of will, is a thing that comes to pass *of itself*, without any cause"; and that "there is absolutely no ground or reason of the soul's being determined to exert such a volition, and make such a choice, rather than another";

I say, if this be the meaning of Arminians, when they contend so earnestly for the will's determining its own acts, and for liberty of will consisting in self-determining power; they do nothing but confound themselves and others with words without a meaning.

***To the question of what determines the will,***

***Ar. response is,—"The will itself."***

***JE's response is,—"Something."***

In the question, What determines the will? and in their answer, that the will determines itself, and in all the dispute about it, it seems to be taken for granted, that something determines the will; and the controversy on this head is not, whether anything at all determines it, or whether its determination has any cause or foundation at all: but where the foundation of it is, whether in the will itself, or somewhere else. But if the thing intended be what is above-mentioned, then all comes to this, that nothing at all determines the will; volition having absolutely no cause or foundation of its existence, either within, or without. There is a great noise made about self-determining power, as the source of all free acts of the will: but when the matter comes to be explained, the meaning is, that no power at all is the source of these acts, neither self-determining power, nor any other, but they arise from nothing; no cause, no power, no influence, being at all concerned in the matter.

### *Arminian Notion of Liberty of Will*

However, this very thing, even that the free acts of the will are events which come to pass without a cause, is certainly implied in the Arminian notion of liberty of will; though it be very inconsistent with many other things in their scheme, and repugnant to some things implied in their notion of liberty. Their opinion implies, that the particular determination of volition is without any cause; because they hold the free acts of the will to be *contingent* events; and contingence is essential to freedom in their notion of it. But certainly, those things which have a prior ground and reason of their particular existence, a cause which antecedently determines them to be, and determines them to be just as they are, don't happen contingently. If something foregoing, by a causal influence and connection, determines and fixes precisely their coming to pass, and the manner of it, then it doesn't remain a contingent thing whether they shall come to pass or no.

## Part II—Where It Is Considered, whether There Is, or Can Be Any Such Sort of Freedom of Will

And because it is a question, in many respects, very important in this controversy about the freedom of will, whether the free acts of the will are events which come to pass without a cause? I shall be particular in examining this point in the two following sections.

# Section 3

## Whether Any Event Whatsoever, and Volition in Particular, can Come to Pass without a Cause of Its Existence

*What is cause? "Positive efficiency or influence to produce a thing, or bring it to pass."*

Before I enter on any argument on this subject, I would explain how I would be understood, when I use the word "cause" in this discourse: since, for want of a better word, I shall have occasion to use it in a sense which is more extensive, than that in which it is sometimes used. The word is often used in so restrained a sense as to signify only that which has a positive efficiency or influence to produce a thing, or bring it to pass. But there are many things which have no such positive productive influence; which yet are causes in that respect, that they have truly the nature of a ground or reason why some things are, rather than others; or why they are as they are, rather than otherwise.

*JE: Motions and causes of all things are different, yet they are connected to and dependent on one another; e.g., sunbeam, sun, spring, winter.*

Thus the absence of the sun in the night, is not the cause of the falling of the dew at that time, in the same manner as its beams are the cause of the ascending of the vapors in the daytime; and its withdrawment in the winter, is not in the same manner the cause of the freezing of the waters, as its approach in the spring is the cause of their thawing. But yet the withdrawment or absence of the sun is an antecedent[1], with which these effects in the night and winter are connected, and on which they depend; and is one thing that belongs to the ground and reason why they come to pass at that

---

1. [As an antonym of consequent, antecedent is the first half of a hypothetical proposition, like If P, then Q. Not P. Therefore, not Q. JE gave the example, If the daytime is short in winter, then it is cold. The day is not short. Therefore, it is not cold.]

time, rather than at other times; though the absence of the sun is nothing positive, nor has any positive influence.

### *Two causes: natural and moral causes; the latter alone is the true cause.*

It may be further observed, that when I speak of connection of causes and effects, I have respect to moral causes, as well as those that are called natural in distinction from them. Moral causes may be causes in as proper a sense, as any causes whatsoever; may have as real an influence, and may as truly be the ground and reason of an event's coming to pass.

Therefore, I sometimes use the word "cause," in this inquiry, to signify any antecedent, either natural or moral, positive or negative, on which an event, either a thing, or the manner and circumstance of a thing, so depends, that it is the ground and reason, either in whole, or in part, why it is, rather than not; or why it is as it is, rather than otherwise;

### *Any antecedent leads to a consequent event.*

or, in other words, any antecedent with which a consequent event is so connected, that it truly belongs to the reason why the proposition which affirms that event, is true; whether it has any positive influence, or not. And in an agreeableness to this, I sometimes use the word "effect" for the consequence of another thing, which is perhaps rather an occasion than a cause, most properly speaking.

### *All events create the cause of another event.*

I am the more careful thus to explain my meaning, that I may cut off occasion, from any that might seek occasion to cavil and object against some things which I may say concerning the dependence of all things which come to pass, on some cause, and their connection with their cause.[2]

### *Nothing can begin to exist without a cause.*

Having thus explained what I mean by cause, I assert, that nothing ever comes to pass without a cause. What is self-existent must be from eternity, and must be unchangeable: but as to all things that *begin to be*, they are not self-existent, and therefore must have some foundation of their existence without themselves.

### *Why do all things begin to exist? What is the cause?*

---

2. [Edwards's occasionalism is originated from his belief of God's absolute sovereignty: God is the only real cause and the only true substance. The created substances cannot be efficient causes of events, but God is the first cause of all events. This theory is articulated, yet not as a "modified" but "consistent" occasionalism, by Oliver Crisp, "How Occasional was Edwards's Occasionalism?" in *Jonathan Edwards: Philosophical Theologian*, ed., Paul Helm and Oliver Crisp (Aldershot: Ashgate, 2003), 69–77.]

## Section 3—Whether Any Event Whatsoever, and Volition in Particular, can Come to Pass

That whatsoever begins to be, which before was not, must have a cause why it then begins to exist, seems to be the first dictate of the common and natural sense which God hath implanted in the minds of all mankind, and the main foundation of all our reasonings about the existence of things, past, present, or to come. And this dictate of common sense[3] equally respects substances and modes, or things and the manner and circumstances of things.

***ILL: A body at rest begins to move, and a moving body changes its direction, . . . for it has a cause or reason.***

Thus, if we see a body which has hitherto been at rest, start out of a state of rest, and begin to move, we do as naturally and necessarily suppose there is some cause or reason of this new mode of existence, as of the existence of a body itself which had hitherto not existed. And so if a body, which had hitherto moved in a certain direction, should suddenly change the direction of its motion; or if it should put off its old figure, and take a new one; or change its color: the beginning of these new modes is a new event, and the mind of mankind necessarily supposes that there is some cause or reason of them.

If this grand principle of common sense[4] be taken away, all arguing from effects to causes ceases, and so all knowledge of any existence, besides what we have by the most direct and immediate intuition.

Particularly all our proof of the being of God ceases: we argue his being from our own being, and the being of other things, which we are sensible once were not, but have begun to be; and from the being of the world, with all its constituent parts, and the manner of their existence; all which we see plainly are not necessary in their own nature, and so not self-existent, and therefore must have a cause. But if things, not in themselves necessary, may begin to be without a cause, all this arguing is vain.

***Ways to Prove God's Existence: Ar: Naturally, there is no foundation for the knowledge of the existence of God, nor the existence of a being eternal, absolute, and***

---

3. [JE delineates "common sense" to be equal to the knowledge and experience which most people already have, or which the person using the term believes that they do or should have. However, this is not a plain definition in common dictionaries.]

4. [Common sense (Latin *sensus communis*, Greek κοινός αἴσθησῃ) is originally the power of uniting mentally the impressions conveyed by the five physical senses, thus "ordinary understanding, without which one is foolish or insane," meaning "good sense" is from 1726. However, JE uses it in terms of Calvinistic "common grace" or "common revelation" but does not vulgarize the special grace or revelation. After JE's death in 1758, Thomas Reid (1710–1796) summarized JE's *FOW* in four pages and developed his common sense philosophy as a disciple of George Turnbull, whom JE disputes in this book of him. Objecting to the idealism of George Berkeley, empiricism of John Locke, and skepticism of David Hume, Reid discovered the common sense in language, phenomenon, perception, judgment, mathematic, logic, causation, etc., and set these principles of all science, and held a realistic idea. And he influenced to schools of Scottish Common Sense Realism. See Gordon Graham, *Scottish Philosophy in the Nineteenth and Twentieth Centuries* (Oxford University Press, 2015), 73.]

*universal. However, we have sufficient strength of mind to have a clear idea and therefore we can intuitively see it.*

**JE: *The intuitive evidence is not enough to prove God's existence, but we do so: 1) a posteriori, or from what is after, i.e., from effects; 2) by argumentation, not intuition; 3) a priori, or "from what is before," i.e., from the proved necessity of his existence.***

Indeed, I will not affirm, that there is in the nature of things no foundation for the knowledge of the being of God without any evidence of it from his works. I do suppose there is a great absurdity, in the nature of things simply considered, in supposing that there should be no God, or in denying being in general, and supposing an eternal, absolute, universal nothing: and therefore that here would be foundation of intuitive evidence that it cannot be, and that eternal, infinite, most perfect Being must be; if we had strength and comprehension of mind sufficient, to have a clear idea of general and universal being, or, which is the same thing, of the infinite, eternal, most perfect divine Nature and Essence. But then we should not properly come to the knowledge of the being of God by arguing; but our evidence would be intuitive: we should see it, as we see other things that are necessary in themselves, the contraries of which are in their own nature absurd and contradictory; as we see that twice two is four; and as we see that a circle has no angles. If we had as clear an idea of universal infinite entity, as we have of these other things, I suppose we should most intuitively see the absurdity of supposing such being not to be; should immediately see there is no room for the question, whether it is possible that being, in the most general abstracted notion of it, should not be. But we have not that strength and extent of mind, to know this certainly in this intuitive independent manner: but the way that mankind come to the knowledge of the being of God, is that which the Apostle speaks of,

Rom. 1:20, "The invisible things of Him, from the creation of the world, are clearly seen; being understood by the things that are made; even his eternal power and Godhead."

We first ascend, and prove *a posteriori*, or from effects, that there must be an eternal cause; and then secondly, prove by argumentation, not intuition, that this being must be necessarily existent; and then thirdly, from the proved necessity of his existence, we may descend, and prove many of his perfections a priori.

**Edwards's Principle of Cause and Effect: *Nothing can come to pass without a cause.***

But if once this grand principle of common sense be given up, that what is not necessary in itself, must have a cause; and we begin to maintain, that things may come into existence, and begin to be, which heretofore have not been, of themselves, without any cause;

all our means of ascending in our arguing from the creature to the Creator, and all our evidence of the being of God, is cut off at one blow. In this case, we can't prove that there is a God, either from the being of the world, and the creatures in it, or from the manner of their being, their order, beauty and use. For if things may come into existence without any cause at all, then they doubtless may without any cause answerable to the effect. Our minds do alike naturally suppose and determine both these things; namely, that what begins to be has a cause, and also that it has a cause proportionable and agreeable to the effect. The same principle which leads us to determine, that there cannot be anything coming to pass without a cause, leads us to determine that there cannot be more in the effect than in the cause.

**Arminian Hypothesis:** *As things may come to pass without a cause, acts of the will come to pass without a cause.*

Yea, if once it should be allowed, that things may come to pass without a cause, we should not only have no proof of the being of God, but we should be without evidence of the existence of anything whatsoever, but our own immediately present ideas and consciousness. For we have no way to prove anything else, but by arguing from effects to causes: from the ideas now immediately in view, we argue other things not immediately in view: from sensations now excited in us, we infer the existence of things without us, as the causes of these sensations: and from the existence of these things, we argue other things, which they depend on, as effects on causes. We infer the past existence of ourselves, or anything else, by memory; only as we argue, that the ideas, which are now in our minds, are the consequences of past ideas and sensations. We immediately perceive nothing else but the ideas which are this moment extant in our minds. We perceive or know other things only by means of these, as necessarily connected with others, and dependent on them. But if things may be without causes, all this necessary connection and dependence is dissolved, and so all means of our knowledge is gone. If there be no absurdity or difficulty in supposing one thing to start out of nonexistence, into being, of itself without a cause; then there is no absurdity or difficulty in supposing the same of millions of millions. For nothing, or no difficulty multiplied, still is nothing, or no difficulty: nothing multiplied by nothing doesn't increase the sum.

And indeed, according to the hypothesis I am opposing, of the acts of the will coming to pass without a cause, it is the case in fact, that millions of millions of events are continually coming into existence contingently, without any cause or reason why they do so, all over the world, every day and hour, through all ages.

So it is in a constant succession, in every moral agent. This contingency, this efficient Nothing, this effectual No-Cause, is always ready at hand, to produce this sort of effect, as long as the agent exists, and as often as he has occasion.

**JE:** *There is some cause in an event.*

If it were so, that things only of one kind, viz. acts of the will, seemed to come to pass of themselves; but those of this sort in general came into being thus; and it were an event that was continual, and that happened in a course, wherever were capable subjects of such events; this very thing would demonstrate that there was some cause of them, which made such a difference between this event and others, and that they did not really happen contingently. For contingence is blind, and does not pick and choose for a particular sort of events. Nothing has no choice. This No-Cause, which causes no existence, can't cause the existence which comes to pass, to be of one particular sort only, distinguished from all others. Thus, that only one sort of matter drops out of the heavens, even water, and that this comes so often, so constantly and plentifully, all over the world, in all ages, shows that there is some cause or reason of the falling of water out of the heavens; and that something besides mere contingence has a hand in the matter.

***Arminian Supposition: Things come into existence, without any cause or antecedent.***

***JE's Objection: Under the supposition, they could not be particular for all ages, and could come into their existence only where there is room for them, or a subject capable of them, and whenever there is an occasion for them.***

If we should suppose Nonentity to be about to bring forth; and things were coming into existence, without any cause or antecedent, on which the existence, or kind or manner of existence depends; or which could at all determine whether the things should be; stones, or stars, or beasts, or angels, or human bodies, or souls, or only some new motion or figure in natural bodies, or some new sensations in animals, or new ideas in the human understanding, or new volitions in the will; or anything else of all the infinite number of possibles;

then certainly it would not be expected, although many millions of millions of things are coming into existence in this manner, all over the face of the earth, that they should all be only of one particular kind, and that it should be thus in all ages, and that this sort of existences should never fail to come to pass where there is room for them, or a subject capable of them, and that constantly, whenever there is occasion for them.

***Arminian Objection: It is possible for things to come into existence without a cause, so free acts of the will are different existences of a particular nature from others that come into pass without a cause.***

If any should imagine, there is something in the sort of event that renders it possible for it to come into existence without a cause; and should say, that the free acts of the will are existences of an exceeding different nature from other things; by reason of which they may come into existence without any previous ground or reason of it, though other things cannot; if they make this objection in good earnest, it would be an evidence of their strangely forgetting themselves: for they would be giving an account of some ground of the existence of a thing, when at the same time they would maintain there is no ground of its existence.

Therefore, I would observe, that the particular nature of existence, be it never so diverse from others, can lay no foundation for that thing's coming into existence without a cause; because to suppose this, would be to suppose the particular nature of existence to be a thing prior to the existence; and so a thing which makes way for existence, with such a circumstance, namely without a cause or reason of existence.

But that which in any respect makes way for a thing's coming into being, or for any manner or circumstance of its first existence, must be prior to the existence. The distinguished nature of the effect, which is something belonging to the effect, can't have influence backward, to act before it is.

### JE: Volition cannot arise without a cause, nor can do anything, and has no influence.

The peculiar nature of that thing called volition, can do nothing, can have no influence, while it is not. And afterwards it is too late for its influence: for then the thing has made sure of existence already, without its help. So that it is indeed as repugnant to reason, to suppose that an act of the will should come into existence without a cause, as to suppose the human soul, or an angel, or the globe of the earth, or the whole universe, should come into existence without a cause. And if once we allow, that such a sort of effect as a volition may come to pass without a cause, how do we know but that many other sorts of effects may do so too? It is not the particular kind of effect that makes the absurdity of supposing it has being without a cause, but something which is common to all things that ever begin to be, viz. that they are not self-existent, or necessary in the nature of things.

# Section 4

## Whether Volition can Arise without A Cause, through the Activity of the Nature of the Soul

*Isaac Watts supposes that corporeal beings are passive and cannot come to pass without a sufficient reason, but spirits are active and they do so without it.*

*JE argues that all things cannot do so without a cause or reason.*

The author of the *Essay on the Freedom of the Will in God and the Creatures*, in answer to that objection against his doctrine of a self-determining power in the will (pp. 68, 69),[1] "that nothing is, or comes to pass, without a sufficient reason why it is, and why it is in this manner rather than another," allows that it is thus in corporeal things, "which are properly and philosophically speaking passive beings"; but denies that it is thus in "spirits, which are beings of an active nature, who have the spring of action within themselves, and can determine themselves." By which it is plainly supposed, that such an event as an act of the will, may come to pass in a spirit, without a sufficient reason why it comes to pass, or why it is after this manner, rather than another; by reason of the activity of the nature of a spirit. But certainly this author, in this matter, must be very unwary and inadvertent. For,

*IW: Spirits are active, and their own determination is a cause.*

1. The objection or difficulty proposed by this author, seems to be forgotten in his answer or solution. The very difficulty, as he himself proposes it, is this: how an event can "come to pass without a sufficient reason why it is, or why it is in this manner rather than another"? Instead of solving this difficulty, or answering this question with regard to volition, as he proposes, he forgets himself, and answers another question quite diverse, and wholly inconsistent with this, viz. what is a sufficient reason why it

---

1. [Isaac Watts, *An Essay on Freedom of Will in God and in Creatures* (London, 1732), 68–69, sec. 6, obj. 2.]

is, and why it is in this manner rather than another? And he assigns the active being's own determination as the cause, and a cause sufficient for the effect; and leaves all the difficulty unresolved, and the question unanswered, which yet returns, even, how the soul's own determination, which he speaks of, came to exist, and to be what it was without a cause?

The activity of the soul may enable it to be the cause of effects; but it doesn't at all enable or help it to be the subject of effects which have no cause; which is the thing this author supposes concerning acts of the will. Activity of nature will no more enable a being to produce effects, and determine the manner of their existence, *within* itself, without a cause, than *out of* itself, in some other being. But if an active being should, through its activity, produce and determine an effect in some external object, how absurd would it be to say, that the effect was produced without a cause!

*IW: The dynamic nature of a soul causes it to do a particular act.*

*JE: The active nature of a soul can cause common acts, but it cannot be its own cause for why it does a particular act because it requires a particular tendency to action.*

2. The question is not so much, how a spirit endowed with activity comes to act, as why it exerts such an act, and not another; or why it acts with such a particular determination? If activity of nature be the cause why a spirit (the soul of man for instance) acts, and doesn't lie still; yet that alone is not the cause why its action is thus and thus limited, directed and determined. Active nature is a *general* thing; it is an ability or tendency of nature to action, generally taken; which may be a cause why the soul acts as occasion or reason is given; but this alone can't be a sufficient cause why the soul exerts such a *particular* act, at such a time, rather than others. In order to do this, there must be something besides a *general* tendency to action; there must also be a *particular* tendency to that individual action. If it should be asked, why the soul of man uses its activity in such a manner as it does; and it should be answered, that the soul uses its activity thus, rather than otherwise, because it has activity; would such an answer satisfy a rational man? Would it not rather be looked upon as a very impertinent one?

*IW: As a being like an object can act and produce its effect in himself, so the first exercise of his activity is the cause of it.*

*JE: Nonsense! His activity itself cannot be a cause of it. The determination of the first action, or exercise of the activity itself, can be a cause.*

3. An active being can bring no effects to pass by his activity, but what are consequent upon his acting: he produces nothing by his activity, any other way than by the exercise of his activity, and so nothing but the fruits of its exercise: he brings nothing to pass by a dormant activity. But the exercise of his activity is action; and so his action, or exercise of his activity, must be prior to the effects of his activity. If an active being produces an effect in another being, about which his activity is conversant, the effect

being the fruit of his activity, his activity must be first exercised or exerted, and the effect of it must follow. So it must be, with equal reason, if the active being is his own object, and his activity is conversant about himself, to produce and determine some effect in himself; still the exercise of his activity must go before the effect, which he brings to pass and determines by it. And therefore his activity can't be the cause of the determination of the first action, or exercise of activity itself, whence the effects of activity arise; for that would imply a contradiction; it would be to say, the first exercise of activity is before the first exercise of activity, and is the cause of it.

***IW: An active substance in the soul is a cause to determine act. Its first act produces different effects.***

***JE: In the same nature are no diverse causes or influences, neither such an effect.***

4. That the soul, though an active substance, can't *diversify* its own acts, but by first acting; or be a determining cause of *different* acts, or any different effects, sometimes of one kind, and sometimes of another, any other way than in consequence of its own diverse acts, is manifest by this; that if so, then the *same* cause, the same causal power, force or influence, *without variation in any respect*, would produce *different* effects at different times. For the same substance of the soul before it acts, and the same active nature of the soul before it is exerted (i.e. before in the order of nature) would be the cause of different effects, viz. different volitions at different times. But the substance of the soul before it acts, and its active nature before it is exerted, are the same without variation. For it is some act that makes the first variation in the cause, as to any causal exertion, force or influence.

But if it be so, that the soul has no different causality, or diverse causal force or influence, in producing these diverse effects; then it is evident, that the soul has no influence, no hand in the diversity of the effect; and that the difference of the effect can't be owing to anything in the soul; or which is the same thing, the soul doesn't determine the diversity of the effect; which is contrary to the supposition. It is true, the substance of the soul before it acts, and before there is any difference in that respect, may be in a different state and circumstances: but those whom I oppose, will not allow the different circumstances of the soul to be the determining causes of the acts of the will; as being contrary to their notion of self-determination and self-motion.

***IW: As an active voluntary elective free being, the soul makes its choice and produces effects actively, voluntarily, and selectively.***

***JE: The soul does not, by its activity, produce all acts of will or choices itself.***

5. Let us suppose, as these divines do, that there are no acts of the soul, strictly speaking, but free volitions; then it will follow, that the soul is an active being in nothing further than it is a voluntary or elective being; and whenever it produces effects actively, it produces effects voluntarily and electively. But to produce effects thus, is the same

thing as to produce effects in consequence of, and according to its own choice. And if so, then surely the soul doesn't by its activity produce all its own acts of will or choice themselves: for this, by the supposition, is to produce all its free acts of choice voluntarily and electively, or in consequence of its own free acts of choice, which brings the matter directly to the aforementioned contradiction, of a free act of choice before the first free act of choice.

According to these gentlemen's own notion of action, if there arises in the mind a volition without a free act of the will or choice to determine and produce it, the mind is not the active voluntary cause of that volition; because it doesn't arise from, nor is regulated by choice or design. And therefore it can't be, that the mind should be the active, voluntary, determining cause of the first and leading volition that relates to the affair. The mind's being a designing cause, only enables it to produce effects in consequence of its design; it will not enable it to be the designing cause of all its own designs. The mind's being an elective cause, will only enable it to produce effects in consequence of its elections, and according to them; but can't enable it to be the elective cause of all its own elections; because that supposes an election before the first election. So the mind's being an active cause enables it to produce effects in consequence of its own acts, but can't enable it to be the determining cause of all its own acts; for that is still in the same manner a contradiction; as it supposes a determining act conversant about the first act, and prior to it, having a causal influence on its existence, and manner of existence.

*IW: The soul has the power to cause and determine its volitions.*

*JE: That means the soul has God-given power to always excite its volitions at its pleasure.*

I can conceive of nothing else that can be meant by the soul's having power to cause and determine its own volitions, as a being to whom God has given a power of action, but this; that God has given power to the soul, sometimes at least, to excite volitions at its pleasure, or according as it chooses. And this certainly supposes, in all such cases, a choice preceding all volitions which are thus caused, even the very first of them. Which runs into the aforementioned great absurdity.

Therefore, the activity of the nature of the soul affords no relief from the difficulties which the notion of a self-determining power in the will is attended with, nor will it help, in the least, its absurdities and inconsistencies.

# Section 5

Showing, That if the Things Asserted in These Evasions should Be Supposed to Be True, They Are Altogether Impertinent, and Can't Help the Cause of Arminian Liberty; and How (This Being the State of the Case) Arminian Writers are Obliged to Talk Inconsistently

*JE: Every free act of the will is to be determined by some act of the will that precedes it.*

What was last observed in the preceding section may show, not only that the active nature of the soul can't be a reason why any act of the will is, or why it is in this manner, rather than another; but also that if it could be so, and it could be proved that volitions are contingent events, in that sense, that their being and manner of being is not fixed or determined by any cause, or anything antecedent; it would not at all serve the purpose of Arminians, to establish the freedom of the will, according to their notion of its freedom, as consisting in the will's determination of itself; which supposes every free act of the will to be determined by some act of the will going before to determine it; inasmuch as for the will to determine a thing, is the same as for the soul to determine a thing by *willing*; and there is no way that the will can determine an act of the will, than by willing that act of the will, or, which is the same thing, choosing it.

*Arminian notions of the freedom of the will:*

*The will determines something which the soul does not determine willingly.*

*Something is to be done by the will when the soul doesn't do with its will.*

*The will can determine an act of the will.*

## Section 5—Showing, That if the Things Asserted in These Evasions should Be Supposed to Be True

***JE: The will to determine a thing is the same as for the soul to determine a thing by willing, and there is no way that the will determines an act of the will.***

So that here must be two acts of the will in the case, one going before another, one conversant about the other, and the latter the object of the former, and chosen by the former. If the will doesn't cause and determine the act by choice, it doesn't cause or determine it at all; for that which is not determined by choice, is not determined voluntarily or willingly: and to say, that the will determines something which the soul doesn't determine willingly, is as much as to say, that something is done by the will, which the soul doesn't do with its will.

So that if Arminian liberty of will, consisting in the will's determining its own acts, be maintained, the old absurdity and contradiction must be maintained, that every free act of will is caused and determined by a foregoing free act of will.

Which doesn't consist with the free act's arising without any cause, and being so contingent, as not be fixed by anything foregoing. So that this evasion must be given up, as not at all relieving, and as that which, instead of supporting this sort of liberty, directly destroys it.

And if it should be supposed, that the soul determines its own acts of will some other way, than by a foregoing act of will; still it will not help the cause of their liberty of will. If it determines them by an act of the understanding, or some other power, then *the will* doesn't determine *itself*; and so the self-determining power of the will is given up. And what liberty is there exercised, according to their own opinion of liberty, by the soul's being determined by something besides its own choice? The acts of the will, it is true, may be directed, and effectually determined and fixed; but it is not done by the soul's own will and pleasure: there is no exercise at all of choice or will in producing the effect: and if will and choice are not exercised in it, how is the liberty of the will exercised in it?

***Ar: Every free act of will is to be determined by the soul's free choice or preceding free act of will.***

***JE: Even if they insist the first free act is to be determined by another preceding free act, that contradicts their notion of liberty, and a gross contradiction arises in it.***

So that let Arminians turn which way they please with their notion of liberty, consisting in the will's determining its own acts, their notion destroys itself. If they hold every free act of will to be determined by the soul's own free choice, or foregoing free act of will; foregoing, either in the order of time, or nature; it implies that gross contradiction, that the first free act belonging to the affair, is determined by a free act which is before it.

Or if they say that the free acts of the will are determined by some *other act* of the soul, and not an act of will or choice, this also destroys their notion of liberty, consisting in the acts of the will being determined by the will itself;

Part II—Where It Is Considered, whether There Is, or Can Be Any Such Sort of Freedom of Will

or if they hold that the acts of the will are determined by *nothing at all* that is prior to them, but that they are contingent in that sense, that they are determined and fixed by no cause at all; this also destroys their notion of liberty, consisting in the will's determining its own acts.

This being the true state of the Arminian notion of liberty, it hence comes to pass, that the writers that defend it are forced into gross inconsistencies, in what they say upon this subject. To instance in Dr. Whitby; he in his "Discourse on the Freedom of the Will," opposes the opinion of the Calvinists, who place man's liberty "only in a power of doing what he will," as that wherein they plainly agree with Mr. Hobbes.

**Daniel Whitby: Liberty is doing what men will without necessity and consists in power of willing as we please.**

**JE: Liberty is doing what men will from necessity.**

And yet he himself mentions the very same notion of liberty, as the dictate of "the sense and common reason of mankind, and a rule laid down by the light of nature"; viz. that "liberty is a power of acting from ourselves, or DOING WHAT WE WILL."[1] This is indeed, as he says, a thing agreeable to "the sense and common reason of mankind"; and therefore it is not so much to be wondered at, that he unawares acknowledges it against himself: for if liberty doesn't consist in this, what else can be devised that it should consist in?

If it be said, as Dr. Whitby elsewhere[2] insists, that

> it doesn't only consist in liberty of "doing what we will," but also a liberty of willing without necessity; still the question returns, What does that liberty of willing without necessity consist in, but in a power of willing *as we please*, without being impede by a contrary necessity? Or in other words, a liberty for the soul in its willing to act *according to its own choice*?

Yea, this very thing the same author seems to allow, and suppose again and again, in the use he makes of sayings of the fathers, whom he quotes as his vouchers.

Thus he cites these words of Origen, which he produces as a testimony on his side:

> "The soul acts by *HER OWN CHOICE*, and it is free for her to incline to whatever part *SHE WILL*."[3]

And those words of Justin Martyr:

---

1. Whitby, 326.

2. Dis. IV, ch. 3, and in the first part of the sentence just quoted: "That only is voluntary which we lie under no Necessity to do or to forebear, and *what we do being unwilling, we do out of Necessity, Liberty being a Power of Acting from ourselves, or doing what we will*" (p. 326).

3. Whitby, 342.

> "The doctrine of the Christians is this, that nothing is done or suffered according to fate, but that every man doth good or evil ACCORDING TO HIS OWN FREE CHOICE."[4]

And from Eusebius, these words;

> "If fate be established, philosophy and piety are overthrown... all these things depending upon the necessity introduced by the stars, and not upon meditation and exercise proceeding from our own free choice."[5]

And again, the words of Macarius,

> "God, to preserve the liberty of man's will, suffered their bodies to die, that it might be in their choice to turn to good or evil.... They who are acted by the Holy Spirit, are not held under any necessity, but have liberty to turn themselves, and *do what they will* in this life."[6]

***DW: Men do acts of good or evil by their own free choice without preceding the act of will.***

***JE: Men do acts of good or evil not by their own free choice but by preceding act of will, i.e., free choice of will.***

Thus, the Doctor in effect comes into that very notion of liberty, which the Calvinists have; which he at the same time condemns, as agreeing with the opinion of Mr. Hobbes, namely,

> the soul's acting by its own choice, men's doing good or evil according to their own free choice, their being in that exercise which proceeds from their own free choice, having it in their choice to turn to good or evil, and doing what they will. So that if men exercise this liberty in the acts of the will themselves, it must be in exerting acts of will as they will, or "according to their own free choice"; or exerting acts of will "that proceed from their choice."

And if it be so, then let everyone judge

> whether this doesn't suppose a free choice going before the free act of will, or whether an act of choice doesn't go before that act of the will which *proceeds from it*.

And if it be thus with all free acts of the will, then let everyone judge,

---

4. Whitby, 360.

5. Whitby, 363.

6. Whitby, 369–70. Whitby, *A Discourse Concerning the Five Points,* Dis. IV, ch. 5, 369–70. Whitby quotes Macarius' saying that, had the bodies of Christians been suddenly made immortal, "*the World beholding... the Strangeness of the thing, would have been converted to Good... not by their own free Will, but by a kind of Necessity, and therefore God, to preserve the Liberty of Man's Will...*"

> whether it won't follow that there is a free choice or will going before the first free act of the will exerted in the case. And then let everyone judge, whether this be not a contradiction.

And finally, let everyone judge

> whether in the scheme of these writers there be any possibility of avoiding these absurdities.

If liberty consists, as Dr. Whitby himself says, in a man's "doing what he will"; and a man exercises this liberty, not only in external actions, but in the acts of the will themselves; then so far as liberty is exercised in the latter, it consists in *willing what he wills*:

and if any say so, one of these two things must be meant, either

(1) that a man has power to will, as he does will; because what he wills, he wills; and therefore has power to will what he has power to will. If this be their meaning, then all this mighty controversy about freedom of the will and self-determining power, comes wholly to nothing; all that is contended for being no more than this, that the mind of man does what it does, and is the subject of what it is the subject of, or that what is, is; wherein none has any controversy with them. Or

(2) the meaning must be, that a man has power to will as he pleases or chooses to will: that is, he has power by one act of choice, to choose another; by an antecedent act of will to choose a consequent act; and therein to execute his own choice.

And if this be their meaning, it is nothing but shuffling with those they dispute with, and baffling their own reason. For still the question returns,

> wherein lies man's liberty in that antecedent act of will which chose the consequent act?

The answer according to the same principles must be, that his liberty in this also lies in his willing as he would, or as he chose, or agreeable to another act of choice preceding that.

And so the question returns *in infinitum*, and the like answer must be made *in infinitum*: in order to support their opinion, there must be no beginning, but free acts of will must have been chosen by foregoing free acts of will, in the soul of every man, without beginning; and so before he had a being, from all eternity.[7]

---

7. [Ramsey asserts JE's argument might be imported from Locke. See Ramsey's "Introduction," *WJE* 1:63–65.]

# Section 6

## Concerning the Will's Determining in Things Which are Perfectly Indifferent[1], in the View of the Mind

A great argument for self-determining power, is the supposed experience we universally have of an ability to determine our wills, in cases wherein no prevailing motive is presented: the will (as is supposed) has its choice to make between two or more things, that are perfectly equal in the view of the mind; and the will is apparently altogether indifferent; and yet we find no difficulty in coming to a choice; the will can instantly determine itself to one, by a sovereign power which it has over itself, without being moved by any preponderating inducement.

*IW: The will is free from all influence or restraint of any kind and is determined by itself, as a sovereign self-determining power of the soul.*

Thus the aforementioned author of an *Essay on the Freedom of the Will, etc.* (pp. 25, 26, 27),[2] supposes,

> that there are many instances, wherein the will is determined neither by present uneasiness, nor by the greatest apparent good, nor by the last dictate of the understanding, nor by anything else, but merely by itself, as a sovereign self-determining power of the soul"; and that "the soul does not will this or that action, in some cases, by any other influence, but because it will.

Thus (says he),

---

1. [The word "indifferent" means a state of things having no choice or inclination to something and neutral balance and equilibrium, and that is wholly different from the word "disinterested," which means having no desire to do a particular thing. So Locke uses a term, "tabula rasa (blank slate)," which means the blank slate of the mind and heart of a newborn baby.]

2. Watts, *Essay*, sec. 2; *Works* 2:250

> "I can turn my face to the south, or the north; I can point with my finger upward, or downward. [...] And thus, in some cases, the will determines itself in a very sovereign manner, because it will, without a reason borrowed from the understanding: and hereby it discovers its own perfect power of choice, rising from within itself, and free from all influence or restraint of any kind."

And in pp. 66, 70, and 73, 74,[3] this author very expressly supposes the will in many cases to be determined by "no motive at all, and acts altogether without motive, or ground of preference."—Here I would observe,

**IW's First supposition: *The will makes choices in its indifference. That is, the will is in its indifference before it makes a choice or has a preference. That is, the will does not choose until it comes to be indifferent.***

**JE: *The will does not choose at all in its indifference.***

1. The very supposition which is here made, directly contradicts and overthrows itself. For the thing supposed, wherein this grand argument consists, is, that among several things the will actually chooses one before another, at the same time that it is perfectly indifferent; which is the very same thing as to say, the mind has a preference, at the same time that it has no preference. What is meant can't be, that the mind is indifferent before it comes to have a choice, or till it has a preference; or, which is the same thing, that the mind is indifferent until it comes to be not indifferent. For certainly this author did not suppose he had a controversy with any person in supposing this. And then it is nothing to his purpose, that the mind which chooses, was indifferent once; unless it chooses, remaining indifferent; for otherwise, it doesn't choose at all in that case of indifference, concerning which is all the question. Besides, it appears in fact, that the thing which this author supposes, is not that the will chooses one thing before another, concerning which it is indifferent *before* it chooses; but also is indifferent *when* it chooses; and that its being otherwise than indifferent is not till afterwards, in consequence of its choice; that the chosen thing's appearing preferable and more agreeable than another, arises from its choice already made. His words are (p. 30):

> Where the objects which are proposed, appear equally fit or good, the will is left without a guide or director; and therefore must make its own choice, by its own determination; it being properly a self-determining power. And in such cases the will does as it were make a good to itself by its own choice, i.e. creates its own pleasure or delight in this self-chosen good. Even as a man by seizing upon a spot of unoccupied land, in an uninhabited country, makes it his own possession and property, and as such rejoices in it. Where things were indifferent before, the will finds nothing to make them more agreeable, considered merely in themselves; but the pleasure it feels ARISING FROM ITS

---

3. Watts, *Essay*, sec. 6, *obj.* 3, 4; *Works* 6:265–67.

Section 6—Concerning the Will's Determining in Things Which are Perfectly Indifferent

*OWN CHOICE*, and its perseverance therein. We love many things which we have chosen, AND PURELY BECAUSE WE CHOSE THEM.

This is as much as to say, that we first begin to prefer many things, now ceasing any longer to be indifferent with respect to them, purely because we have preferred and chosen them before.

***JE's Point: Choice or Preference does not equal the foundation of itself or the fruit or consequence of itself. Choice equals preferring. Preference does not equal its fruit.***

These things must needs be spoken inconsiderately by this author. Choice or preference can't be before itself, in the same instance, either in the order of time or nature: it can't be the foundation of itself, or the fruit or consequence of itself. The very act of choosing one thing rather than another, is preferring that thing, and that is setting a higher value on that thing. But that the mind sets a higher value on one thing than another, is not, in the first place, the fruit of its setting a higher value on that thing.

***IW: The will is entirely indifferent until it is determined as it pleases.***

[Nevertheless] This author says (p. 36),[4] "The will may be perfectly indifferent, and yet the will may determine itself to choose one or the other." And again in the same page, "I am entirely indifferent to either; and yet my will may determine itself to choose." And again, "Which I shall choose must be determined by the mere act of my will." If the choice is determined by a mere act of will, then the choice is determined by a mere act of choice. And concerning this matter, viz. that the act of the will itself is determined by an act of choice, this writer is express, in p. 72.[5] Speaking of the case, where there is no superior fitness in objects presented, he has these words: "There it must act by its own *CHOICE*, and determine itself as it *PLEASES*."

***JE: The ground of the will's act is called the very determination, that is, an act of choice and preference to more agreeableness and superior pleasedness. The idea of that thing preferred does preponderate, or prevail in the mind, has a prevailing influence on the will.***

Where it is supposed that the very determination, which is the ground and spring of the will's act, is an act of *choice* and *pleasure*, wherein one act is more agreeable, and the mind better pleased in it than another; and this *preference*, and superior *pleasedness* is the ground of all it does in the case. And if so, the mind is not indifferent when it determines itself, but *had rather* do one thing than another, had rather determine itself one way than another. And therefore the will doesn't act at all in indifference; not so much as in the first step it takes, or the first rise and beginning of its acting. If it be possible for the understanding to act in indifference, yet to be sure the will never does; because the will's beginning to act is the very same thing as its beginning to choose

---

4. Watts, *Essay*, sec. 3, *prop.* 8; *Works* 6:253.
5. Watts, *Essay*, sec. 6, *obj.* 3, *ans.* 2; *Works* 6:267.

or prefer. And if in the very first act of the will, the mind prefers something, then the idea of that thing preferred, does at that time preponderate, or prevail in the mind; or, which is the same thing, the idea of it has a prevailing influence on the will.

So that this wholly destroys the thing supposed, viz. that the mind can by a sovereign power choose one of two or more things, which in the view of the mind are, in every respect, perfectly equal, one of which does not at all preponderate, nor has any prevailing influence on the mind above another.

***IW: The will chooses in its indifference; the mind has a choice, so in effect, it supposes that it has a preference.***

***JE: His absurd supposition came to deny itself, yet it allows the view of his opponents.***

So that this author, in his grand argument for the ability of the will to choose one of two, or more things, concerning which it is perfectly indifferent, does at the same time, in effect, deny the thing he supposes, and allows and asserts the point he endeavors to overthrow; even that the will, in choosing, is subject to no prevailing influence of the idea, or view of the thing chosen. And indeed it is impossible to offer this argument without overthrowing it; the thing supposed in it being inconsistent with itself, and that which denies itself. To suppose the will to act at all in a state of perfect indifference, either to determine itself, or to do anything else, is to assert that the mind chooses without choosing. To say that when it is indifferent, it can do as it pleases, is to say that it can follow its pleasure, when it has no pleasure to follow. And therefore if there be any difficulty in the instances of two cakes, or two eggs, etc., which are exactly alike, one as good as another; concerning which this author supposes the mind in fact has a *choice*,[6] and so in effect supposes that it has a *preference*; it as much concerned himself to solve the difficulty, as it does those whom he opposes. For if these instances prove anything to his purpose, they prove that a man chooses without choice. And yet this is not to his purpose; because if this is what he asserts, his own words are as much against him, and do as much contradict him, as the words of those he disputes against can do.

***IW's second supposition: The will chooses a thing in its indifference without any external cause or influence. Its determination is on objects but not to actions.***

***JE: The will acts under a preponderating cause without being moved by any inducement. Its determination is not on objects but on actions.***

***ILL: Casting of a lot on a chessboard looks like an unexpected event without any cause, but it is acted by the subsequent determinations of the mind under some motive and cause.***

2. There is no great difficulty in showing, in such instances as are alleged, not only *that it must needs be so*, that the mind must be influenced in its choice by something

---

6. Watts, *Essay*, sec. 3, *prop.* 8; *Works* 6:253–54.

that has a preponderating influence upon it, but also *how it is so*. A little attention to our own experience, and a distinct consideration of the acts of our own minds in such cases, will be sufficient to clear up the matter.

Thus, supposing I have a chessboard before me; and because I am required by a superior, or desired by a friend, or to make some experiment concerning my own ability and liberty, or on some other consideration, I am determined to touch some one of the spots or squares on the board with my finger; not being limited or directed in the first proposal, or my own first purpose, which is general, to any one in particular; and there being nothing in the squares in themselves considered, that recommends any one of all the sixty-four, more than another:

**JE: *The mind cannot remain in absolute indifference but always under influence of a prevailing inducement or reason.***

in this case, my mind determines to give itself up to what is vulgarly called accident,[7] by determining to touch that square which happens to be most in view, which my eye is especially upon at that moment, or which happens to be then most in my mind,[8] or which I shall be directed to by some other such-like accident. Here are several steps of the mind's proceeding (though all may be done as it were in a moment): the first step is its general determination that it will touch one of the squares. The next step is another *general* determination to give itself up to accident, in some certain way; as to touch that which shall be most in the eye or mind at that time, or to some other such-like accident. The third and last step is a *particular* determination to touch a certain individual spot, even that square, which, by that sort of accident the mind has pitched upon, has actually offered itself beyond others.

Now it is apparent that in none of these several steps does the mind proceed in absolute indifference, but in each of them is influenced by a preponderating inducement. So it is in the first step; the mind's general determination to touch one of the sixty-four spots: the mind is not absolutely indifferent whether it does so or no: it is induced to it, for the sake of making some experiment, or by the desire of a friend, or some other motive that prevails. So it is in the second step, the mind's determining to give itself up to accident, by touching that which shall be most in the eye, or the idea of which shall be most prevalent in the mind, etc. The mind is not absolutely indifferent whether it proceeds by this rule or no; but chooses it, because it appears at that time a convenient and requisite expedient in order to fulfill the general purpose aforesaid. And so it is in the third and last step, its determining to touch that individual spot which actually does prevail in the mind's view. The mind is not indifferent concerning

---

7. I have elsewhere observed [in P. I, sec.3; *FOW*, 155] what that is which is vulgarly called "accident"; that it is nothing akin to the Arminian metaphysical notion of "contingence," something not connected with anything foregoing; but that it is something that comes to pass in the course of things, in some affair that men are concerned in, unforeseen, and not owing to their design.

8. [Guelzo, 69. "Edwards consistently limited his discussion to what was happening at the precise moment of choice."]

this; but is influenced by a prevailing inducement and reason; which is, that this is a prosecution of the preceding determination, which appeared requisite, and was fixed before in the second step.

Accident will ever serve a man, without hindering him a moment, in such a case. It will always be so among a number of objects in view, one will prevail in the eye, or in idea beyond others. When we have our eyes open in the clear sunshine, many objects strike the eye at once, and innumerable images may be at once painted in it by the rays of light; but the attention of the mind is not equal to several of them at once; or if it be, it doesn't continue so for any time.

And so it is with respect to the ideas of the mind in general: several ideas are not in equal strength in the mind's view and notice at once; or at least, don't remain so for any sensible continuance. There is nothing in the world more constantly varying, than the ideas of the mind: they don't remain precisely in the same state for the least perceivable space of time: as is evident by this, that all perceivable time is judged and perceived by the mind only by the succession or the successive changes of its own ideas. Therefore while the views or perceptions of the mind remain precisely in the same state, there is no perceivable space or length of time, because no sensible succession at all.

*JE: Many things may be seen as if they do not have a cause.*

As the acts of the will, in each step of the aforementioned procedure, don't come to pass without a particular cause, every act is owing to a prevailing inducement; so the accident, as I have called it, or that which happens in the unsearchable course of things, to which the mind yields itself, and by which it is guided, is not anything that comes to pass without a cause; and the mind in determining to be guided by it, is not determined by something that has no cause; any more than if it determined to be guided by a lot, or the casting of a die. For though the die's falling in such a manner be accidental to him that casts it, yet none will suppose that there is no cause why it falls as it does. The involuntary changes in the succession of our ideas, though the cause may not be observed, have as much a cause, as the changeable motions of the motes that float in the air, or the continual, infinitely various, successive changes of the unevennesses on the surface of the water.

There are two things especially, which are probably the occasions of confusion in the minds of them who insist upon it, that the will acts in a proper indifference, and without being moved by any inducement, in its determinations in such cases as have been mentioned.

*IW's first fallacy: Whitby forgot that a man cannot be indifferent but always prefers a particular thing before another. ILL: How do you choose between two eggs or two cakes which appear equally good?*

1. They seem to mistake the point in question, or at least not to keep it distinctly in

view. The question they dispute about, is, Whether the mind be indifferent about the *objects* presented, one of which is to be taken, touched, pointed to, etc., as two eggs, two cakes, which appear equally good. Whereas the question to be considered, is, Whether the person be indifferent with respect to his own *actions*; whether he doesn't, on some consideration or other, prefer one act with respect to these objects before another.

The mind in its determination and choice, in these cases, is not most immediately and directly conversant about the *objects presented*; but the *acts to be done* concerning these objects. The objects may appear equal, and the mind may never properly make any choice between them: but the next act of the will being about the external actions to be performed, taking, touching, etc., these may not appear equal, and one action may properly be chosen before another. In each step of the mind's progress, the determination is not about the objects, unless indirectly and improperly, but about the actions, which it chooses for other reasons than any preference of the objects, and for reasons not taken at all from the objects.

There is no necessity of supposing, that the mind does ever at all properly choose one of the objects before another; either before it has taken, or afterwards. Indeed the man chooses to *take* or *touch* one rather than another; but not because it chooses the *thing* taken, or touched; but from foreign considerations. The case may be so, that of two things offered, a man may, for certain reasons, choose and prefer the taking of that which he *undervalues*, and choose to neglect to take that which his mind *prefers*. In such a case, choosing the thing taken, and choosing to take, are diverse: and so they are in a case where the things presented are equal in the mind's esteem, and neither of them preferred. All that fact and experience make evident, is, that the mind chooses one action rather than another. And therefore the arguments which they bring, in order to be to their purpose, ought to be to prove that the mind chooses the action in perfect indifference, with respect to that *action*; and not to prove that the mind chooses the action in perfect indifference with respect to the *object*; which is very possible, and yet the will not act at all without prevalent inducement, and proper preponderation.

### IW's second fallacy: Whitby failed to differentiate between the mind's general indifference and its particular one, and he forgot the fact that a man cannot be indifferent in particular and present circumstances, in which he/she is acting.

2. Another reason of confusion and difficulty in this matter, seems to be, not distinguishing between a *general* indifference, or an indifference with respect to what is to be done in a more distant and general view of it, and a *particular* indifference, or an indifference with respect to the next immediate act, viewed with its particular and present circumstances. A man may be perfectly indifferent with respect to his own actions, in the former respect; and yet not in the latter. Thus, in the foregoing instance

of touching one of the squares of a chessboard; when it is first proposed that I should touch one of them, I may be perfectly indifferent which I touch; because as yet I view the matter remotely and generally, being but in the first step of the mind's progress in the affair. But yet, when I am actually come to the last step, and the very next thing to be determined is, which is to be touched, having already determined that I will touch that which happens to be most in my eye or mind, and my mind being now fixed on a particular one, the act of touching that, considered thus immediately, and in these particular present circumstances, is not what my mind is absolutely indifferent about.

# Section 7

## Concerning the Notion of Liberty of Will Consisting in Indifference

What has been said in the foregoing section, has a tendency in some measure to evince the absurdity of the opinion of such as place liberty in indifference, or in that equilibrium whereby the will is without all antecedent determination or bias, and left hitherto free from any prepossessing inclination to one side or the other; that the determination of the will to either side may be entirely from itself, and that it may be owing only to its own power, and that sovereignty which it has over itself, that it goes this way rather than that.

But inasmuch as this has been of such long standing, and has been so generally received, and so much insisted on by Pelagians, semi-Pelagians, Jesuits, Socinians, Arminians, and others, it may deserve a more full consideration. And therefore I shall now proceed to a more particular and thorough inquiry into this notion.

Now lest some should suppose that I don't understand those that place liberty in indifference, or should charge me with misrepresenting their opinion, I would signify, that I am sensible,

*Arminian defenders of free will claim that the liberty of the will consists in indifference. Yet revisionists claim that the liberty of the will shall be composed in the indifference of the soul's power of willing or choosing.*

there are some, who when they talk of the liberty of the will as consisting in indifference, express themselves as though they would not be understood of the indifference of the inclination or tendency of the will, but of, I know not what, indifference of the soul's power of willing; or that the will, with respect to its power or ability to choose, is indifferent, can go either way indifferently, either to the right hand or left, either act or forbear to act, one as well as the other. Though this seems to be a refining only of some particular writers, and newly invented, and which will by no means consist with the manner of expression used by the defenders of liberty of indifference in general.

And I wish such refiners would thoroughly consider, whether they distinctly know their own meaning, when they make a distinction between indifference of the soul as to its *power* or *ability* of willing or choosing, and the soul's indifference as to the preference or choice itself; and whether they don't deceive themselves in imagining that they have any distinct meaning at all. The indifference of the soul as to its ability or power to will, must be the same thing as the indifference of the state of the power or faculty of the will, or the indifference of the state which the soul itself, which has that power or faculty, hitherto remains in, as to the exercise of that power, in the choice it shall by and by make.

***Ar: Indifference is essential to freedom of will. The will is free from predetermination, and it has room for the exercise of its self-determining power.***

But not to insist any longer on the abstruseness and inexplicableness of this distinction; let what will be supposed concerning the meaning of them that make use of it, thus much must at least be intended by Arminians, when they talk of indifference as essential to liberty of will, if they intend anything, in any respect to their purpose, viz. that it is such an indifference as leaves the will not determined already; but free from actual possession, and vacant of predetermination, so far, that there may be room for the exercise of the *self-determining power* of the will; and that the will's freedom consists in, or depends upon this vacancy and opportunity that is left for the will itself to be the determiner of the act that is to be the free act.

***JE: A soul or will must not be indifferent or free because it is already under antecedent preponderation or inclination.***

And here I would observe in the first place, that to make out this scheme of liberty, the indifference must be *perfect* and *absolute*; there must be a perfect freedom from all antecedent preponderation or inclination. Because if the will be already inclined, before it exerts its own sovereign power on itself, then its inclination is not wholly owing to itself: if when two opposites are proposed to the soul for its choice, the proposal doesn't find the soul wholly in a state of indifference, then it is not found in a state of liberty for mere self- determination.

The least degree of antecedent bias must be inconsistent with their notion of liberty. For so long as prior inclination possesses the will, and is not removed, it binds the will, so that it is utterly impossible that the will should act otherwise than agreeably to it. Surely the will can't act or choose contrary to a remaining prevailing inclination of the will. To suppose otherwise, would be the same thing as to suppose, that the will is inclined contrary to its present prevailing inclination, or contrary to what it is inclined to. That which the will chooses and prefers, that, all things considered, it preponderates and inclines to. It is equally impossible for the will to choose contrary to its own remaining and present preponderating inclination, as it is to prefer contrary to its own present preference, or choose contrary to its own present choice. The will therefore, so long as it is under the influence of an old preponderating inclination, is not at liberty for a new free act, or any act that shall now be an act of self-determination. The act which is a self-determined free act, must be an act which the will determines in the possession and use of such a liberty, as consists in a freedom from everything, which, if it were there, would make it impossible that the will, at that time, should be otherwise than that way to which it tends.

*Ar: Will is adamant and opposes its antecedent inclination.*

*JE: Will is not so adamant enough to oppose its antecedent, but it follows it.*

If anyone should say, there is no need that the indifference should be perfect; but although a former inclination and preference still remains, yet, if it is not very strong and violent, possibly the strength of the will may oppose and overcome it—This is grossly absurd; for the strength of the will, let it be never so great, does not at all enable it to act one way, and act the contrary way,[1] both at the same time. It gives it no such sovereignty and command, as to cause itself to prefer and not to prefer at the same time, or to choose contrary to its own present choice.

Therefore, if there be the least degree of antecedent preponderation of the will, it must be perfectly abolished, before the will can be at liberty to determine itself the contrary way. And if the will determines itself the same way, it was not a free determination, because the will is not wholly at liberty in so doing: its determination is not altogether from itself, but it was partly determined before, in its prior inclination: and all the freedom the will exercises in the case, is in an increase of inclination, which it gives itself, over and above what it had by foregoing bias; so much is from itself, and so much is from perfect indifference.

*Ar: The will can act in indifference or equilibrium, and it is free.*

*JE: The will acts after the preceding inclination, and it cannot remain in absolute indifference, and so it is not free.*

For though the will had a previous tendency that way, yet as to that additional degree of inclination, it had no tendency. Therefore, the previous tendency is of no consideration, with respect to the act wherein the will is free. So that it comes to the same thing which was said at first, that as to the act of the will, wherein the will is free, there must be *perfect* indifference, or equilibrium.

*ILL: The celestial body moves by an antecedent bias, moves by the universal gravity, and then works by its self-moving power.*

To illustrate this; if we should suppose a sovereign self-moving power in a natural body: but that the body is in motion already, by an antecedent bias;[2] for instance,

1. [Corrected, from "and not the contrary way."]

2. [JE borrows the three laws of motion first compiled by Isaac Newton. These laws describe how common objects move under the influence of forces. The first builds on Galileo's concept of inertia;

gravitation towards the center of the earth;[3] and has one degree of motion already, by virtue of that previous tendency; but by its self-moving power it adds one degree more to its motion, and moves so much more swiftly towards the center of the earth than it would do by its gravity only: it is evident, that all that is owing to a self-moving power in this case, is the additional degree of motion; and that the other degree of motion which it had from gravity, is of no consideration in the case, doesn't help the effect of the free self-moving power in the least; the effect is just the same, as if the body had received from itself one degree of motion from a state of perfect rest.

**ILL: As the scale is tipped towards one side by a self-moving power of self-preponderating power, men's will cannot act at all if it is free from an antecedent bias and in absolute indifference.**

So if we should suppose a self-moving power given to the scale of a balance, which has a weight of one degree beyond the opposite scale; and we ascribe to it an ability to add to itself another degree of force the same way, by its self-moving power; this is just the same thing as to ascribe to it a power to give itself one degree of preponderation from a perfect equilibrium; and so much power as the scale has to give itself an overbalance from a perfect equipoise, so much self-moving self-preponderating power it has, and no more. So that its free power this way is always to be measured from perfect equilibrium.

I need say no more to prove, that, if indifference be essential to liberty, it must be perfect indifference; and that so far as the will is destitute of this, so far it is destitute of that freedom by which it is its own master, and in a capacity of being its own determiner, without being at all passive, or subject to the power and sway of something else, in its motions and determinations.

Having observed these things, let us now try whether this notion of the liberty of will consisting in indifference and equilibrium, and the will's self-determination in such a state, be not absurd and inconsistent.

*Ar: An act of the will can be exerted in a state of freedom.*

And here I would lay down this as an axiom of undoubted truth; that every free act is done *in* a state of freedom, and not only *after* such a state. If an act of the will be an act wherein the soul is free, it must be exerted in a *state* of freedom, and in the *time*

---

the second describes the relation between force, mass, and acceleration; and the third explains how forces always happen in pairs. See Isaac Newton, *Philosophiæ Naturalis Principia Mathematica* (Mathematical Principles of Natural Philosophy, 1687); Jonathan Edwards, Original Sin, *WJE* 3:399.]

3. [JE declares that "infinite wisdom must be exercised in order that gravity and motion be perfectly harmonious," and that "it is universally allowed that gravity depends immediately on the divine influence;" and "it may be proved that solidity and gravity are in a good sense the same, and resolvable into each other; and because solidity has been proved to be the very being of a body: therefore we may infallibly conclude that the very being, and the manner of being, and the whole of bodies depends immediately on the divine power." See "Of Atoms," *WJE* 6:230, 235.]

of freedom. It will not suffice, that the act immediately follows a state of liberty; but liberty must yet continue, and coexist with the act; the soul remaining in possession of liberty. Because that is the notion of a free act of the soul, even an act wherein the soul uses or exercises liberty. But if the soul is not, in the very time of the act, in the possession of liberty, it can't at that time be in the use of it.

***Arminian Absurdity: A soul chooses a thing before another even if it is free and indifferent.***

***JE: The will and its freedom are contrary and destroy each other, and the latter does not exist.***

Now the question is, whether ever the soul of man puts forth any act of will, while it yet remains in a state of liberty, in that notion of a state of liberty, viz. as implying a state of indifference; or whether the soul ever exerts an act of choice or preference, while at that very time the will is in a perfect equilibrium, not inclining one way more than another. The very putting of the question is sufficient to show the absurdity of the affirmative answer: for how ridiculous would it be for anybody to insist, that the soul chooses one thing before another, when at the very same instant it is perfectly indifferent with respect to each! This is the same thing as to say, the soul prefers one thing to another, at the very same time that it has no preference. Choice and preference can no more be in a state of indifference, than motion can be in a state of rest, or than the preponderation of the scale of a balance can be in a state of equilibrium. Motion may be the next moment after rest; but can't coexist with it, in *any*, even the *least* part of it. So choice may be immediately after a state of indifference, but has no coexistence with it: even the very beginning of it is not in a state of indifference. And therefore if this be liberty, no act of the will, in any degree, is ever performed in a state of liberty, or in the time of liberty. Volition and liberty are so far from agreeing together, and being essential one to another, that they are contrary one to another, and one excludes and destroys the other, as much as motion and rest, light and darkness, or life and death. So that the will acts not at all, does not so much as begin to act in the time of such liberty: freedom is perfectly at an end, and has ceased to be, at the first moment of action; and therefore liberty can't reach the action, to affect, or qualify it, or give it a denomination, or any part of it, any more than if it had ceased to be twenty years before the action began. The moment that liberty ceases to be, it ceases to be a qualification of anything. If light and darkness succeed one another instantaneously, light qualifies nothing after it is gone out, to make anything lightsome or bright, any more at the first moment of perfect darkness, than months or years after.

Life denominates nothing *vital* at the first moment of perfect death. So freedom, if it consists in, or implies indifference, can denominate nothing free, at the first moment of preference or preponderation. Therefore, it is manifest, that no liberty which the soul is possessed of, or ever uses, in any of its acts of volition, consists in indifference; and that the opinion of such as suppose, that indifference belongs to the very essence of liberty, is to the highest degree absurd and contradictory.

If anyone should imagine, that this manner of arguing is nothing but trick and delusion; and to evade the reasoning, should say, that "the thing wherein the will exercises its liberty, is not in the act of choice or preponderation itself, but in *determining* itself to a certain choice or preference; that the act of the will wherein it is free, and uses its own sovereignty, consists in its *causing* or determining the change or *transition* from a state of indifference to a certain preference, or determining to give a certain turn to the balance, which has hitherto been even; and that this act the will exerts in a state of liberty, or while the will yet remains *in equilibrium*, and perfect master of itself." I say, if anyone chooses to express his notion of liberty after this, or some such manner, let us see if he can make out his matters any better than before.

**Ar: *The will remains in a state of perfect freedom and indifference and equilibrium, without preference.***

**JE: *Nevertheless it determines to put itself out of that state, and if it determines in itself, its freedom cannot be exerted in the determination.***

What is asserted is, that the will, while it yet remains in perfect equilibrium, without preference, determines to change itself from that state, and excite in itself a certain choice or preference. Now let us see whether this doesn't come to the same absurdity we had before. If it be so, that the will, while it yet remains perfectly indifferent, determines to put itself out of that state, and give itself a certain preponderation; then I would inquire, whether the soul doesn't determine this of choice; or whether the will's coming to a determination to do so, be not the same thing as the soul's coming to a choice to do so. If the soul doesn't determine this of choice, or in the exercise of choice, then it doesn't determine it voluntarily. And if the soul doesn't determine it voluntarily, or of its own will, then in what sense does its will determine it? And if the will doesn't determine it, then how is the liberty of the will exercised in the determination? What sort of liberty is exercised by the soul in those determinations, wherein there is no exercise of choice, which are not voluntary, and wherein the will is not concerned? But if it be allowed, that this determination is an act of choice, and it be insisted on, that the soul, while it yet remains in a state of perfect indifference, chooses to put itself out of that state, and to turn itself one way; then the soul is already come to a choice, and chooses that way.

**Ar: *A soul chooses itself in a state of perfect indifference without preference, and it acts without choice.***

And so we have the very same absurdity which we had before. Here is the soul in a state of choice, and in a state of equilibrium, both at the same time: the soul already choosing one way, while it remains in a state of perfect indifference, and has no choice of one way more than the other. And indeed this manner of talking, though it may a little hide the absurdity, in the obscurity of expression, is more nonsensical, and increases the inconsistence. To say, the free act of the will, or the act which the will exerts in a state of freedom and indifference, does not imply preference in it, but is what the will does in order to causing or producing a preference, is as much as to say, the soul chooses (for to will and to choose are the same thing) without choice, and prefers without preference, in order to cause or produce the beginning of a preference, or the first choice. And that is, that the first choice is exerted without choice, in order to produce itself.

### *Ar: The will's freedom and indifference are the same, and liberty and acts come from the indifference.*

### *JE: If the will is in indifference, it cannot exert anything due to its choice and determination and act.*

If any, to evade these things, should own, that a state of liberty, and a state of indifference are not the same, and that the former may be without the latter; but should say, that indifference is still essential to the freedom of an act of will, in some sort, namely, as it is necessary to go immediately before it; it being essential to the freedom of an act of will that it should directly and immediately arise out of a state of indifference: still this will not help the cause of Arminian liberty, or make it consistent with itself. For if the act springs immediately out of a state of indifference, then it does not arise from antecedent choice or preference. But if the act arises directly out of a state of indifference, without any intervening choice to choose and determine it, then the act not being determined by choice, is not determined by the will; the mind exercises no free choice in the affair, and free choice and free will have no hand in the determination of the act. Which is entirely inconsistent with their notion of the freedom of volition.

If any should suppose,[4] that these difficulties and absurdities may be avoided, by saying, that the liberty of the mind consists in a power to suspend the act of the will, and so to keep it in a state of indifference, till there has been opportunity for consideration; and so shall say, that however indifference is not essential to liberty in such a manner, that the mind must make its choice in a state of indifference, which is an inconsistency, or that the act of will must spring immediately out of indifference;

yet indifference may be essential to the liberty of acts of the will in this respect; viz. that liberty consists in a power of the mind to forbear or suspend the act of volition, and keep the mind in a state of indifference for the present, till there has been opportunity for proper deliberation: I say, if anyone imagines that this helps the matter, it is a great mistake: it reconciles no inconsistency, and relieves no difficulty which the affair is attended with. For here the following things must be observed,

### *Ar: To choose and determine the act or suspend volition are acts of the volition.*

---

4. [John Locke's supposition, see Locke, *Essay*, bk. II, ch.21, no. 47, 53, 57.]

1. That this *suspending* of volition, if there be properly any such thing, is itself an act of volition. If the mind determines to suspend its act, it determines it voluntarily; it chooses, on some consideration, to suspend it. And this choice or determination, is an act of the will: and indeed it is supposed to be so in the very hypothesis; for it is supposed, that the liberty *of the will* consists in its power to do thus, and that its doing it is the very thing wherein *the will* exercises its liberty. But how can the will exercise liberty in it, if it isn't an act of the will? The liberty of the will is not exercised in anything but what the will does.

**Ar: *To determine or lead to a suspending acting (that is, =to keep the mind in a state of indifference) is not only a free act of the will but also its power.***

2. This determining to suspend acting is not only an act of the will, but it is supposed to be the only free act of the will; because it is said, that *this* is the thing wherein the liberty of the will consists. Now if this be so, then this is all the act of will that we have to consider in this controversy, about the liberty of will, and in our inquiries, wherein the liberty of man consists. And now the aforementioned difficulties remain: the former question returns upon us; viz. wherein consists the freedom of the will *in those acts* wherein it is free? And if this act of determining a suspension be the only act in which the will is free, then wherein consists the will's freedom with respect to this act of suspension? And how is indifference essential to this act? The answer must be, according to what is supposed in the evasion under consideration, that the liberty of the will in this act of suspension, consists in a power to suspend even this act, till there has been opportunity for thorough deliberation. But this will be to plunge directly into the grossest nonsense: for it is the act of suspension itself that we are speaking of; and there is no room for a space of deliberation and suspension, in order to determine whether we will suspend or no. For that supposes, that even suspension itself may be deferred: which is absurd; for the very deferring the determination of suspension, to consider whether we will suspend or no, will be actually suspending.

For during the space of suspension, to consider whether to suspend, the act is *ipso facto* suspended. There is no medium between suspending to act, and immediately acting; and therefore no possibility of avoiding either the one or the other one moment; and so no room for deliberation before we do either of them.

## Section 7—Concerning the Notion of Liberty of Will Consisting in Indifference

*Ar: The liberty is an act of suspension, and it consists in the power of a determination of suspension; it is in the volition to suspend the act. There is no medium between suspending to act and immediately acting, and no time to consider whether or not to suspend that.*

*JE: There is no such a liberty. Even if yes, it is in the act but not in the volition. Whether suspension or act, there is no medium nor time to consider.*

And besides, this is attended with ridiculous absurdity another way: for now it is come to that, that liberty consists wholly in the mind's having power to suspend its determination whether to suspend or no; that there may be time for consideration, whether it be best to suspend. And if liberty consists in this only, then this is the liberty under consideration: we have to inquire now, how liberty with respect to this act of suspending a determination of suspension, consists in indifference, or how indifference is essential to it. The answer, according to the hypothesis we are upon, must be, that it consists in a power of suspending even this last mentioned act, to have time to consider whether to suspend that. And then the same difficulties and inquiries return over again with respect to that; and so on forever. Which, if it would show anything, would show only that there is no such thing as a free act. It drives the exercise of freedom back *in infinitum*; and that is to drive it out of the world.

And besides all this, there is a delusion, and a latent gross contradiction in the affair another way; inasmuch as in explaining how, or in what respect the will is free with regard to a particular act of volition, it is said, that its liberty consists in a power to determine to suspend *that act*, which places liberty not in that act of volition which the inquiry is about, but altogether in another antecedent act. Which contradicts the thing supposed in both the question and answer. The question is, wherein consists the mind's liberty *in any particular act* of volition? And the answer, in pretending to show wherein lies the mind's liberty *in that act*, in effect says, it doesn't lie in that act at all, but in another, viz. a volition *to suspend that act*. And therefore the answer is both contradictory, and altogether impertinent and beside the purpose. For it doesn't show wherein the liberty of the will consists in the act in question; instead of that, it supposes it doesn't consist in that act at all, but in another distinct from it, even a volition to suspend that act, and take time to consider of it. And no account is pretended to be given wherein the mind is free with respect to that act, wherein this answer supposes the liberty of the mind indeed consists, viz. the act of suspension, or of determining the suspension.

On the whole, it is exceeding manifest, that the liberty of the mind does not consist in indifference, and that indifference is not essential or necessary to it, or at all belonging to it, as the Arminians suppose; that opinion being full of nothing but absurdity and self-contradiction.

# Section 8

## Concerning the Supposed Liberty of the Will, as Opposite to All Necessity

It is a thing chiefly insisted on by Arminians, in this controversy, as a thing most important and essential in human liberty, that volitions, or the acts of the will, are *contingent* events;[1] understanding contingence as opposite, not only to constraint, but to all necessity. Therefore, I would particularly consider this matter.

*Ar: Volitions or acts of the will are contingent, and they both are contradictory.*

*JE: There are no contingent volitions. The effect cannot take place without any cause or reason.*

And

1. I would inquire, whether there is, or can be any such thing, as a volition which is contingent in such a sense, as not only to come to pass without any necessity of constraint or coaction,[2] but also without a *necessity of consequence*, or an infallible connection with anything foregoing.

2. Whether, if it were so, this would at all help the cause of liberty.

**I. I would consider whether volition is a thing that e'er does, or can come to pass, in this manner, contingently.**

And here it must be remembered, that it has been already shown, that nothing can ever come to pass without a cause, or reason why it exists in this manner rather than another; and the evidence of this has been particularly applied to the acts of the will. Now if this be so, it will demonstrably follow, that the acts of the will are never

---

1. [Volitional contingency: a primary tenet of Arminianism, which Richard Muller stated elsewhere.]

2. [Whitby well defines the "coaction" by an ILL of "a Dog tied to a Cart's Tail; he may follow without being drawn, but if he doth not, he must follow by being drawn." (*Dis.* IV, ch. 4, no. 2; p. 355).]

contingent, or without necessity, in the sense spoken of; inasmuch as those things which have a cause, or reason of their existence, must be connected with their cause. This appears by the following considerations.

***JE: An event has a cause and ground of its existence, they are connected, and the event depends on a cause.***

1. For an event to have a cause and ground of its existence, and yet not to be connected with its cause, is an inconsistence. For if the event is not connected with the cause, it is not dependent on the cause;

> its existence is as it were loose from its influence, and may attend it, or may not; it being a mere contingence, whether it follows or attends the influence of the cause, or not: and that is the same thing as not to be dependent on it. And to say, the event is not dependent on its cause, is absurd: it is the same thing as to say, it is not its cause, nor the event the effect of it: for dependence on the influence of a cause, is the very notion of an effect.

If there be no such relation between one thing and another, consisting in the connection and dependence of one thing on the influence of another, then it is certain there is no such relation between them as is signified by the terms "cause" and "effect." So far as an event is dependent on a cause, and connected with it, so much causality is there in the case, and no more. The cause does, or brings to pass no more in any event, than is dependent on it. If we say, the connection and dependence is not total, but partial, and that the effect, though it has some connection and dependence, yet is not entirely dependent on it; that is the same thing as to say, that not all that is in the event is an effect of that cause, but that only part of it arises from thence, and part some other way.

***Arminian Supposition: An event and thing can contingently rise without cause.***

***JE: An event is necessarily connected with a cause. It does not follow the influence of the same cause and state and circumstance.***

2. If there are some events which are not necessarily connected with their causes, then it will follow, that there are some things which come to pass without any cause, contrary to the supposition. For if there be any event which was not necessarily connected with the influence of the cause under such circumstances, then it was contingent whether it would attend or follow the influence of the cause, or no; it might have followed, and it might not, when the cause was the same, its influence the same, and under the same circumstances. And if so, why did it follow, rather than not follow? There is no cause or reason of this. Therefore, here is something without any cause or reason why it is, viz. the following of the effect on the influence of the cause, with which it was not necessarily connected. If there be not a necessary connection of the effect on anything

antecedent, then we may suppose that sometimes the event will follow the cause, and sometimes not, when the cause is the same, and in every respect in the same state and circumstances. And what can be the cause and reason of this strange phenomenon, even this diversity, that in one instance, the effect should follow, in another not? It is evident by the supposition, that this is wholly without any cause or ground. Here is something in the present manner of the existence of things, and state of the world, that is absolutely without a cause. Which is contrary to the supposition, and contrary to what has been before demonstrated.

**Arminian Supposition: *There are some events which have a cause and ground of their existence that yet are not necessarily connected with their cause.***

**JE: *If there is a significant cause even at the same time and circumstance, an effect always rises in any case.***

3. To suppose there are some events which have a cause and ground of their existence, that yet are not necessarily connected with their cause, is to suppose that they have a cause which is not their cause. Thus, if the effect be not necessarily connected with the cause, with its influence, and influential circumstances; then, as I observed before, it is a thing possible and supposable, that the cause may sometimes exert the same influence, under the same circumstances, and yet the effect not follow. And if this actually happens in any instance, this instance is a proof, in fact, that the influence of the cause is not sufficient to produce the effect. For if it had been sufficient, it would have done it. And yet, by the supposition, in another instance, the same cause, with perfectly the same influence, and when all circumstances which have any influence, are the same, it *was followed* with the effect. By which it is manifest, that the effect in this last instance was not owing to the influence of the cause, but must come to pass some other way. For it was proved before, that the influence of the cause was not sufficient to produce the effect. And if it was not sufficient to produce it, then the production of it could not be owing to that influence, but must be owing to something else, or owing to nothing. And if the effect be not owing to the influence of the cause, then it is not the cause. Which brings us to the contradiction, of a cause, and no cause, that which is the ground and reason of the existence of a thing, and at the same time is not the ground and reason of its existence, nor is sufficient to be so.

If the matter be not already so plain as to render any further reasoning upon it impertinent, I would say, that that which seems to be the cause in the supposed case, can be no cause; its power and influence having, on a full trial, proved insufficient to produce such an effect: and if it be not sufficient to produce it, then it doesn't produce it. To say otherwise, is to say, there is power to do that which there is not power to do. If there be in a cause sufficient power exerted, and in circumstances sufficient to produce an effect, and so the effect be actually produced at *one time*; these things all concurring, will produce the effect at *all times*. And so we may turn it the other way; that which proves not sufficient at one time, cannot be sufficient at another, with precisely the same influential circumstances. And therefore if the effect follows, it is not owing to that cause; unless the different time be a circumstance which has influence: but that is contrary to the supposition; for it is supposed that all circumstances that have influence, are the same.

And besides, this would be to suppose the time to be the cause; which is contrary to the supposition of the other thing's being the cause. But if merely diversity of time has no influence, then it is evident that it is as much of an absurdity to say, the cause was sufficient to produce the effect at one time, and not at another; as to say, that it is sufficient to produce the effect at a certain time, and yet not sufficient to produce the same effect at that same time.

On the whole, it is clearly manifest, that every effect has a necessary connection with its cause, or with that which is the true ground and reason of its existence. And therefore if there be no event without a cause, as was proved before, then no event whatsoever is contingent in the manner that Arminians suppose the free acts of the will to be contingent.

# Section 9

## Of the Connection of the Acts of the Will with the Dictates of the Understanding[1]

***JE: It is true that every act of the will is in some way connected with the understanding.***

It is manifest, that the acts of the will are none of them contingent in such a sense as to be without all necessity, or so as not to be necessary with a necessity of consequence and connection; because every act of the will is some way connected with the understanding, and is as the greatest apparent good is, in the manner which has already been explained; namely, that the soul always wills or chooses that which, in the present view of the mind, considered in the whole of that view, and all that belongs to it, appears most agreeable. Because, as was observed before, nothing is more evident than that, when men act voluntarily, and do what they please, then they do what appears most agreeable to them; and to say otherwise, would be as much as to affirm, that men don't choose what appears to suit them best, or what seems most pleasing to them; or that they don't choose what they prefer. Which brings the matter to a contradiction.

***JE: Arminians allow some connection and yet disallow the necessity.***

As it is very evident in itself, that the acts of the will have some connection with the dictates or views of the understanding, so this is allowed by some of the chief of the Arminian writers: particularly by Dr. Whitby and Dr. Samuel Clarke. Dr. Turnbull, though a great enemy to the doctrine of necessity, allows the same thing. In his *Christian Philosophy* (p. 196) he with much approbation cites another philosopher, as of the same mind, in these words:

---

1. [In this section JE presents intellectualism, which regards the intellect as superior to the will, and that the intellect is the basic factor, both in the universe and in human conduct.]

### Section 9—Of the Connection of the Acts of the Will with the Dictates of the Understanding

> No man (says an excellent philosopher) sets himself about anything, but upon some view or other, which serves him for a reason for what he does; and whatsoever faculties he employs, the understanding, with such light as it has, well or ill informed, constantly leads; and by that light, true or false, all her operative powers are directed. The will itself, how absolute and incontrollable soever it may be thought, never fails in its obedience to the dictates of the understanding. Temples have their sacred images; and we see what influence they have always had over a great part of mankind; but in truth, the ideas and images in men's minds are the invisible powers that constantly govern them; and to these they all pay universally a ready submission.[2]

But whether this be in a just consistence with themselves, and their own notions of liberty, I desire may now be impartially considered.

**Whitby's Supposition: All we need is that the Holy Spirit should illuminate our understanding, and not that He act on our will. And we are able to choose good and to refuse evil.**

Dr. Whitby plainly supposes, that the acts and determinations of the will always follow the understanding's apprehension or view of the greatest good to be obtained, or evil to be avoided; or in other words, that the determinations of the will constantly and infallibly follow these two things in the understanding:

1. The degree of good to be obtained, and evil to be avoided, proposed to the understanding, and apprehended, viewed, and taken notice of by it.

2. The degree of the understanding's view, notice or apprehension of that good or evil; which is increased by attention and consideration. That this is an opinion he is exceeding peremptory in [as he is in every opinion which he maintains in his controversy with the Calvinists], with disdain of the contrary opinion, as absurd and self-contradictory, will appear by the following words of his, in his *Discourse on the Five Points*.

> Now, it is certain, that what naturally makes the understanding to perceive, is evidence proposed, and apprehended, considered or adverted to: for nothing else can be requisite to make us come to the knowledge of the truth.... Again, what makes the will choose, is something approved by the understanding; and consequently appearing to the soul as good.
>
> And whatsoever it refuses, is something represented by the understanding, and so appearing to the will, as evil. Whence all that God requires of us is, and can be only this; to refuse the evil, and choose the good. Wherefore, to say that evidence proposed, apprehended and considered, is not sufficient to make the understanding approve; or that the greatest good proposed, the greatest

---

2. [George Turnbull, *The Principles of Moral and Christian Philosophy* (London, 1740), 2 vols. 2 (containing *Christian Philosophy*), 196.]

evil threatened, when equally believed and reflected on, is not sufficient to engage the will to choose the good and refuse the evil, is in effect to say, *that which alone doth move the will to choose or to refuse*, is not sufficient to engage it so to do; which being contradictory to itself, must of necessity be false. Be it then so, that we naturally have an aversation to the truths proposed to us in the gospel; that only can make us indisposed to attend to them, but cannot hinder our conviction, when we do apprehend them, and attend to them. . . . Be it, that there is in us also a renitency to the good we are to choose; that only can indispose us to believe it is, and to approve it as our chiefest good. Be it, that we are prone to the evil that we should decline; that only can render it the more difficult for us to believe it is the worst of evils. But yet, *what we do really believe to be our chiefest good, will still be chosen; and what we apprehend to be the worst of evils, will, whilst we do continue under that conviction, be refused by us*. It therefore can be only requisite, in order to these ends, that the good Spirit should so illuminate our understandings, that we attending to, and considering what lies before us, should apprehend, and be convinced of our duty; and that the blessings of the gospel should be so propounded to us, as that we may discern them to be our chiefest good; and the miseries it threatens, so as we may be convinced they are the worst of evils; that we may choose the one, and refuse the other.[3]

### JE: It is wrong to suppose that while following the illumination, conviction, and notice of the understanding, the will chooses the greatest good and refuses the greatest evil.

Here let it be observed, how plainly and peremptorily it is asserted, that the greatest good proposed, and the greatest evil threatened, when equally believed and reflected on. This is sufficient to engage the will to choose the good, and refuse the evil, and is that alone which doth move the will to choose or to refuse; and that it is contradictory to itself to suppose otherwise; and therefore must of necessity be false; and then what we do really believe to be our chiefest good will still be chosen, and what we apprehend to be the worst of evils, will, whilst we continue under that conviction, be refused by us.

Nothing could have been said more to the purpose, fully to signify and declare, that the determinations of the will must evermore follow the illumination, conviction, and notice of the understanding, with regard to the greatest good and evil proposed, reckoning both the degree of good and evil understood, and the degree of understanding, notice, and conviction of that proposed good and evil; and that it is thus necessarily, and can be otherwise in no instance: because it is asserted, that it implies a contradiction, to suppose it ever to be otherwise.

---

3. Whitby, *Discourse on the Five Points*, pp. 211, 212, 213 (Dis. III, ch. 1).

## Section 9—Of the Connection of the Acts of the Will with the Dictates of the Understanding

**DW: *There is no need of any physical operation of the Spirit of God on the will to change and determine that to a good choice.***

I am sensible, the Doctor's aim in these assertions is against the Calvinists; to show, in opposition to them, that there is no need of any physical operation of the Spirit of God on the will, to change and determine that to a good choice, but that God's operation and assistance is only moral, suggesting ideas to the understanding; which he supposes to be enough, if those ideas are attended to, infallibly to obtain the end. But whatever his design was, nothing can more directly and fully prove, that every determination of the will, in choosing and refusing, is necessary; directly contrary to his own notion of the liberty of the will. For if the determination of the will, evermore, in this manner, follows the light, conviction, and view of the understanding, concerning the greatest good and evil, and this be that alone which moves the will, and it be a contradiction to suppose otherwise; then it is *necessarily* so, the will necessarily follows this light or view of the understanding, not only in some of its acts but in every act of choosing and refusing. So that the will doesn't determine itself in any one of its own acts; but all its acts, every act of choice and refusal, depends on, and is necessarily connected with some antecedent cause; which cause is not the will itself, nor any act of its own, nor anything pertaining to that faculty, but something belonging to another faculty, whose acts go before the will, in all its acts, and govern and determine them every one.

**DW: *The act of the will just depends on its preceding act and the understanding, and yet the act is not necessary.***

Here, if it should be replied, that although it be true, that according to the Doctor, "the final determination of the will always depends upon, and is infallibly connected with the understanding's conviction, and notice of the greatest good; yet the acts of the will are not necessary; because that conviction and notice of the understanding is first dependent on a preceding act of the will, in determining to attend to, and take notice of the evidence exhibited; by which means the mind obtains that degree of conviction which is sufficient and effectual to determine the consequent and ultimate choice of the will;

and that the will with regard to that preceding act, whereby it determines whether to attend or no, is not necessary; and that in this, the liberty of the will consists, that when God holds forth sufficient objective light, the will is at liberty whether to command the attention of the mind to it" —

Nothing can be more weak and inconsiderate than such a reply as this. For that preceding act of the will, in determining to attend and consider, still is an act of the will [it is so to be sure, if the liberty of the will consists in it, as is supposed]; and if it be an act of the will, it is an act of choice or refusal. And therefore, if what the Doctor asserts be true, it is determined by some antecedent light in the understanding concerning the greatest apparent good or evil.

### DW: The light in the understanding alone moves the will.

For he asserts, it is that light "which alone doth move the will to choose or refuse." And therefore the will must be moved by that in choosing to attend to the objective light offered, in order to another consequent act of choice: so that this act is no less necessary than the other. And if we suppose another act of the will, still preceding both these mentioned, to determine both, still that also must be an act of the will, and an act of choice; and so must, by the same principles, be infallibly determined by some certain degree of light in the understanding concerning the greatest good.

### JE: If Whitby argues as such, that consequently would indicate that he says the will is not free and admits its necessity.

And let us suppose as many acts of the will, one preceding another, as we please, yet they are every one of them necessarily determined by a certain degree of light in the understanding, concerning the greatest and most eligible good in that case; and so, not one of them free according to Dr. Whitby's notion of freedom. And if it be said, the reason why men don't attend to light held forth, is because of ill habits contracted by evil acts committed before, whereby their minds are indisposed to attend to, and consider of the truth held forth to them by God, the difficulty is not at all avoided: still the question returns, What determined the will in those preceding evil acts? It must, by Dr. Whitby's principles, still be the view of the understanding concerning the greatest good and evil. If this view of the understanding be "that alone which doth move the will to choose or refuse," as the Doctor asserts, then every act of choice or refusal, from a man's first existence, is moved and determined by this view; and this view of the understanding exciting and governing the act, must be before the act: and therefore the will is necessarily determined, in every one of its acts, from a man's first existence, by a cause beside the will, and a cause that doesn't proceed from, or depend on any act of the will at all.

### JE: 1) Whitby destroyed the base of his argument;

### 2) Rather, he hindered anti-Calvinists.

Which at once utterly abolishes the Doctor's whole scheme of liberty of will; and he, at one stroke, has cut the sinews of all his arguments from the goodness, righteousness, faithfulness and sincerity of God, in his commands, promises, threatenings, calls, invitations, expostulations; which he makes use of, under the heads of reprobation, election, universal redemption, sufficient and effectual grace, and the freedom of the will of man; and has enervated and made vain all those exclamations against the doctrine of the Calvinists, as charging God with manifest unrighteousness, unfaithfulness, hypocrisy, fallaciousness, and cruelty; which he has over, and over, and over again, numberless times in his book.

Section 9—Of the Connection of the Acts of the Will with the Dictates of the Understanding

***Clark's Supposition: The determination of the will or choice is made by the dictate of the understanding. The last dictate of the understanding is the same as the act of the will.***

***JE: If so, that means that such determination is not the determination of the will; liberty of choice has no influence in it, and the dictate of the understanding existed before the will determines.***

Dr. Samuel Clarke, in his *Demonstration of the Being and Attributes of God*,[4] to evade the argument to prove the necessity of volition, from its necessary connection with the last dictate of the understanding, supposes the latter *not to be diverse from* the act of the will itself. But if it be so, it will not alter the case as to the evidence of the necessity of the act of the will.

***JE: Like Whitby holds the view of the understanding alone moves the will, Clarke says the dictate of it is the determination of volition itself.***

If the dictate of the understanding be the very same with the determination of the will or choice, as Dr. Clarke supposes, then this determination is no *fruit* or *effect* of choice: and if so, no liberty of choice has any hand in it: as to volition or choice, it is necessary; that is, choice can't prevent it. If the last dictate of the understanding be the same with the determination of volition itself, then the existence of that determination must be necessary as to volition; inasmuch as volition can have no opportunity to determine whether it shall exist or no, it having existence already before volition has opportunity to determine anything. It is itself the very rise and existence of volition. But a thing, after it exists, has no opportunity to determine as to its own existence; it is too late for that.

***Clarke: Liberty is what soul or mind chooses as the dictate of the understanding and is that which it pleases.***

If liberty consists in that which Arminians suppose, viz. in the will's determining its own acts, having free opportunity, and being without all necessity; this is the same as to say, that liberty consists in the soul's having power and opportunity to have what determinations of the will it pleases or chooses. And if the determinations of the will, and the last dictates of the understanding be the same thing, then liberty consists in the mind's having power to have what dictates of the understanding it pleases, having opportunity to choose its own dictates of understanding. But this is absurd; for it is to make the determination of choice prior to the dictate of understanding, and the ground of it; which can't consist with the dictate of understanding's being the determination of choice itself.

Here is no way to do in this case, but only to recur to the old absurdity, of one determination before another, and the cause of it; and another before that, determining

---

4. Edit 6. [London, 1725] p. 93.

that; and so on *in infinitum*. If the last dictate of the understanding be the determination of the will itself, and the soul be free with regard to that dictate, in the Arminian notion of freedom; then the soul, before that dictate of its understanding exists, voluntarily and according to its own choice determines, in every case, what that dictate of the understanding shall be; otherwise that dictate, as to the will, is necessary; and the acts determined by it, must also be necessary. So that here is a determination of the mind prior to that dictate of the understanding, an act of choice going before it, choosing and determining what that dictate of the understanding shall be: and this preceding act of choice, being a free act of will, must also be the same with another last dictate of the understanding: and if the mind also be free in that dictate of understanding, that must be determined still by another; and so on forever.

**JE: *The understanding and the will are different faculties of soul.*[5]**

**Arminian Notion of Liberty**

Besides, if the dictate of the understanding, and determination of the will be the same, this confounds the understanding and will, and makes them the same. Whether they be the same or no, I will not now dispute; but only would observe, that if it be so, and the Arminian notion of liberty be just, then all

> liberty consists in a self-determining power in the understanding, free of all necessity; being independent, undetermined by anything prior to its own acts and determinations; and the more the understanding is thus independent, and sovereign over its own determinations, the more free. By this therefore the freedom of the soul, as a moral agent, must consist in the independence of the understanding on any evidence or appearance of things, or anything whatsoever that stands forth to the view of the mind, prior to the understanding's determination. And what a sort of liberty is this! Consisting in an ability, freedom and easiness of judging, either according to evidence, or against it; having a sovereign command over itself at all times, to judge, either agreeably or disagreeably to what is plainly exhibited to its own view.

**Ar: *Liberty is independence from moral means and power of the understanding and reason.***

**JE: *If so, in vain are all applications to the understanding and all moral instructions.***

Certainly, it is no liberty that renders persons the proper subjects of persuasive reasoning, arguments, expostulations, and suchlike moral means and inducements. The use of which with mankind, is a main argument of the Arminians, to defend their notion of liberty without all necessity. For according to this,

---

5. [See *Religious Affections*, WJE 2:96.]

the more free men are, the less they are under the government of such means, less subject to the power of evidence and reason, and more independent on their influence, in their determinations.

And whether the understanding and will are the same or no, as Dr. Clarke seems to suppose, yet in order to maintain the Arminian notion of liberty without necessity,

> the free will is not determined by the understanding, nor necessarily connected with the understanding; and the further from such connection, the greater the freedom. And when the liberty is full and complete, the determinations of the will have no connection at all with the dictates of the understanding.

And if so, in vain are all applications to the understanding, in order to induce to any free virtuous act; and so in vain are all instructions, counsels, invitations, expostulations, and all arguments and persuasives whatsoever: for these are but applications to the understanding, and a clear and lively exhibition of the objects of choice to the mind's view. But if, after all, the will must be self-determined, and independent on the understanding, to what purpose are things thus represented to the understanding, in order to determine the choice?

# Section 10

## Volition Necessarily Connected with the Influence of Motives; with Particular Observations on the Great Inconsistence of Mr. Chubb's[1] Assertions and Reasonings, About the Freedom of the Will

***JE: Every act of the will has some motive which is a cause of the act.***

***Ar: The will wills and chooses without any motive or inducement.***

That every act of the will has some cause, and consequently (by what has been already proved) has a necessary connection with its cause, and so is necessary by a necessity of connection and consequence, is evident by this, that every act of the will whatsoever, is excited by some motive: which is manifest, because, if the will or mind, in willing and choosing after the manner that it does, is excited so to do by no motive or inducement, then it has no end which it proposes to itself, or pursues in so doing; it aims at nothing, and seeks nothing. And if it seeks nothing, then it doesn't go after anything, or exert any inclination or preference towards anything. Which brings the matter to a contradiction; because for the mind to will something, and for it to go after something by an act of preference and inclination, are the same thing.

But if every act of the will is excited by a motive, then that motive is the cause of the act of the will. If the acts of the will are excited by motives, then motives are the causes of their being excited; or, which is the same thing, the cause of their being put forth into act and existence. And if so, the existence of the acts of the will is properly the effect of their motives. Motives do nothing as motives or inducements, but by their

---

1. [Thomas Chubb (1679—1747) was one of three antagonists and was known as a Deist. Deism of the age was rational doctrine of the religion in the era of 17th and 18th Century's Enlightenment, which is a theological theory concerning the relationship between the Creator and the natural world, and insists that God has created the universe but remains apart from it and permits his creation to administer itself through natural laws. So this theory denies God as the sovereigner and that made JE to believe the Arminian notion of free will based on such Deism.]

influence; and so much as is done by their influence, is the effect of them. For that is the notion of an effect, something that is brought to pass by the influence of another thing.

***JE: Necessary connection: motive (cause of act of will) volition (effect of motive) act of will.***

And if volitions are properly the effects of their motives, then they are necessarily connected with their motives. Every effect and event being, as was proved before, necessarily connected with that which is the proper ground and reason of its existence. Thus it is manifest, that volition is necessary, and is not from any self-determining power in the will:

***JE: Volition merely follows after the previous motive and yet it is not caused by the will; rather, the motive biases the will.***

***Ar: The will itself chooses a certain inclination in a state of indifference.***

the volition which is caused by previous motive and inducement, is not caused by the will exercising a sovereign power over itself, to determine, cause and excite volitions in itself. This is not consistent with the will's acting in a state of indifference and equilibrium, to determine itself to a preference; for the way in which motives operate, is by biasing the will, and giving it a certain inclination or preponderance one way.

***Thomas Chubb: The will acts by motive and excitement, that is the previous ground and reason. When various motives are presented, the will chooses or rejects one. The will chooses prior to motive.***

Here it may be proper to observe, that Mr. Chubb, in his collection of *Tracts on Various Subjects*,[2] has advanced a scheme of liberty, which is greatly divided against itself, and thoroughly subversive of itself; and that many ways.

***TC: Motive and excitement is the previous ground and reason of all the will's acts.***

I. He is abundant in asserting, that the will, in all its acts, is influenced by motive and excitement; and that this is the previous ground and reason of all its acts, and that it is never otherwise in any instance. He says (p. 262), "No action can take place without some motive to excite it." And in p. 263: "Volition cannot take place without some PREVIOUS reason or motive to induce it." And in p. 310: "Action would not take place without some reason or motive to induce it; it being absurd to suppose, that the active faculty would be exerted without some PREVIOUS reason to dispose the mind to action." So also p. 257. And he speaks of these things [motive and excitement] as what we may be absolutely certain of, and which are the foundation, the only foundation

---

2. [Thomas Chubb, *A Collection of Tracts on Various Subjects* (London, 1730). Hereafter cited as *Tracts*.]

we have of a certainty of the moral perfections of God (pp. 252, 253, 254, 255, 261, 262, 263, 264).

***TC: The will or mind first chooses to comply with or reject the motive proposing to it, for it has liberty and power to do so.***

And yet at the same time, by his scheme, the influence of motives upon us to excite to action, and to be actually a ground of volition, is *consequent* on the volition or choice of the mind. For he very greatly insists upon it, that in all free actions, before the mind is the subject of those volitions which motives excite, it chooses to be so. It chooses whether it will comply with the motive, which presents itself in view, or not; and when various motives are presented, it chooses which it will yield to, and which it will reject. So p. 256: "Every man has power to act, or to refrain from acting agreeably with, or contrary to, any motive that presents." P. 257: "Every man is at liberty to act, or refrain from acting agreeably with, or contrary to, what each of these motives, considered singly, would excite him to.. . . Man has power, and is as much at liberty to reject the motive that does prevail, as he has power, and is at liberty to reject those motives that do not."

And so pp. 310, 311: "In order to constitute a moral agent, it is necessary, that he should have power to act, or to refrain from acting, upon such moral motives as he pleases." And to the like purpose in many other places. According to these things, the will acts first, and chooses or refuses to comply with the motive that is presented, before it falls under its prevailing influence: and it is first determined by the mind's pleasure or choice, what motives it will be induced by, before it is induced by them.

***TC: The mind or will first act and determine what motives shall be the ground and reason of its volition and choice.***

***TC's Supposition: The choice is already made before the motive has its effect, and the influence of the motive is also the consequence of that very choice.***

Now, how can these things hang together? How can the mind first act, and by its act of volition and choice determine what motives shall be the ground and reason of its volition and choice? For this supposes,

> the choice is already made, before the motive has its effect; and that the volition is already exerted, before the motive prevails, so as actually to be the ground of the volition; and makes the prevailing of the motive, the consequence of the volition, which yet it is the ground of. If the mind has already chosen to comply with a motive, and to yield to its excitement, it doesn't need to yield to it after this: for the thing is effected already, that the motive would excite to, and the will is beforehand with the excitement; and the excitement comes in too late, and is needless and in vain afterwards. If the mind has already chosen to yield to a motive which invites to a thing, that implies and in fact is choosing the thing invited to; and the very act of choice is before the influence of the

motive which induces, and is the ground of the choice; the son is beforehand with the father that begets him: the choice is supposed to be the ground of that influence of the motive, which very influence is supposed to be the ground of the choice. And so *vice versa*, the choice is supposed to be the consequence of the influence of the motive, which influence of the motive is the consequence of that very choice.

### JE: If the motive prevails over the will, then how can the motive be a previous ground and reason of the act and choice of the will?

And besides, if the will acts first towards the motive before it falls under its influence, and the prevailing of the motive upon it to induce it to act and choose, be the fruit and consequence of its act and choice, then how is the motive "a PREVIOUS ground and reason of the act and choice," so that "in the nature of the things, volition cannot take place without some PREVIOUS reason and motive to induce it"; and that this act is consequent upon, and follows the motive? Which things Mr. Chubb often asserts, as of certain and undoubted truth. So that the very same motive is both *previous* and *consequent*, both before and after, both the ground and fruit of the very same thing!

### TC: The will is excited and acts by motive, which is "the passive ground or reason of that action."

II. Agreeable to the aforementioned inconsistent notion of the will's first acting towards the motive, choosing whether it will comply with it, in order to its becoming a ground of the will's acting, before any act of volition can take place, Mr. Chubb frequently calls motives and excitements to the action of the will, "the passive ground or reason of that action."[3] Which is a remarkable phrase; than which I presume there is none more unintelligible, and void of distinct and consistent meaning, in all the writings of Duns Scotus, or Thomas Aquinas. When he represents the motive to action or volition as passive, he must mean — passive in that affair, or passive with respect to that action which he speaks of; otherwise it is nothing to his purpose, or relating to the design of his argument: he must mean (if that can be called a meaning) that the motive to volition is first acted *upon* or *towards* by the volition, choosing to yield to it, making it a ground of action, or determining to fetch its influence from thence; and so to make it a previous ground of its own excitation and existence.

### JE: The soul acts by the cause of its existence, which is the passive ground of that existence.

Which is the same absurdity, as if one should say, that the soul of man, or any other thing should, previous to its existing, choose what cause it would come into existence by, and should act upon its cause, to fetch influence from thence, to bring it into being; and so its cause should be a passive ground of its existence!

3. Chubb, *Tracts*, 257, 258, 263, 264.

Part II—Where It Is Considered, whether There Is, or Can Be Any Such Sort of Freedom of Will

**JE: TC allows that the volition does not take place without motive, and ironically asserts that the latter is a passive ground of an act of the will.**

Mr. Chubb does very plainly suppose motive or excitement to be the ground of the being of volition. He speaks of it as the ground or reason of the EXERTION of an act of the will (pp. 391 and 392); and expressly says, that "volition cannot TAKE PLACE without some previous ground or motive to induce it" (p. 263).[4] And he speaks of the act as FROM the motive, and FROM THE INFLUENCE of the motive (p. 352); and from the influence that the motive has on the man, for the PRODUCTION of an action (p. 317). Certainly, there is no need of multiplying words about this; it is easily judged, whether motive can be the ground of volition's being exerted and taking place, so that the very production of it is from the influence of the motive, and yet the motive, before it becomes the ground of the volition, is passive, or acted upon by the volition.

But this I will say, that a man who insists so much on clearness of meaning in others, and is so much in blaming their confusion and inconsistence, ought, if he was able, to have explained his meaning in this phrase of "passive ground of action," so as to show it not to be confused and inconsistent.

**TC's wrong supposition: Motive is a passive ground of action because (1) a motive just invites a volition to choose something; (2) a motive is just a "previous ground" of its existence.**

If any should suppose, that Mr. Chubb, when he speaks of motive as a "passive ground of action," doesn't mean passive with regard to that volition which it is the ground of, but some other antecedent volition (though his purpose and argument, and whole discourse, will by no means allow of such a supposition) yet it would not help the matter in the least. For (1) if we suppose there to be an act of volition or choice, by which the soul chooses to yield to the invitation of a motive to another volition, by which the soul chooses something else; both these supposed volitions are in effect the very same. A volition, or choosing to yield to the force of a motive inviting to choose something, comes to just the same thing as choosing the thing which the motive invites to, as I observed before. So that here can be no room to help the matter, by a distinction of two volitions. (2) If the motive be passive with respect, not to the same volition that the motive excites to, but one truly distinct and prior; yet, by Mr. Chubb, that prior volition can't take place, without a motive or excitement, as a "previous ground" of its existence. For he insists, that it is absurd to suppose any volition should take place, "without some previous [. . .] motive to induce it."

**JE: Technically speaking, the motive to the volition to which the former influenced can be passive, and yet it is not so to preceding motives.**

---

4. [*Tracts*, 257, 258, 263, 264.]

So that at last it comes to just the same absurdity: for if *every* volition must have a previous motive, then the very *first* in the whole series must be excited by a previous motive; and yet the motive to that first volition is passive; but can't be passive with regard to another antecedent volition, because, by the supposition, it is the very first: therefore if it be passive with respect to any volition, it must be so with regard to that very volition that it is the ground of, and that is excited by it.

**TC: *Volition does not always follow the strongest motive but rather the weakest one.***

**JE: *That means the will acts wholly without motive, without any previous reason to dispose the mind to it. If so, it is contradictory to what he said.***

III. Though Mr. Chubb asserts, as above, that every volition has some motive, and that, in the nature of the thing, no volition can take place "without some [. . .] motive to induce it"; yet he asserts, that volition does not always follow the strongest motive; or in other words, is not governed by any superior strength of the motive that is followed, beyond motives to the contrary, previous to the volition itself. His own words, p. 258, are as follows: "Though with regard to physical causes, that which is strongest always prevails, yet it is otherwise with regard to moral causes. Of these, sometimes the stronger, sometimes the weaker, prevails. And the ground of this difference is evident, namely, that what we call moral causes, strictly speaking, are no causes at all, but barely passive reasons of, or excitements to the action, or to the refraining from acting: which excitements we have power, or are at liberty to comply with or reject, as I have showed above."

**TC: *The will is not always determined by the motive which is strongest or by any strength previous to the volition itself.***

And so throughout the paragraph, he, in a variety of phrases, insists, that the will is not always determined by the strongest motive, unless by strongest we preposterously mean actually prevailing in the event;[5] which is not in the motive, but in the will; but that the will is not always determined by the motive which is strongest, by any strength previous to the volition itself. And he elsewhere does abundantly assert, that the will is determined by no superior strength or advantage that motives have, from any constitution or state of things, or any circumstances whatsoever, previous to the actual determination of the will. And indeed his whole discourse on human liberty implies it, his whole scheme is founded upon it.

**JE: *There is a diversity of strength in motives to choice and they have it in certain limited degrees.***

But these things cannot stand together. There is such a thing as a diversity of strength in motives to choice, previous to the choice itself. Mr. Chubb himself supposes, that

---

5. i.e. unless by the motive prevailing because it was strongest, we mean to say "that it prevailed, because it *did prevail*" (Chubb, *Tracts,* 258).

they do "previously invite," "induce," "excite" and "dispose the mind to action." This implies, that they have something in themselves that is *inviting*, some tendency to *induce* and *dispose* to volition, previous to volition itself. And if they have in themselves this nature and tendency, doubtless they have it in certain limited degrees, which are capable of diversity; and some have it in greater degrees, others in less; and they that have most of this tendency, considered with all their nature and circumstances, previous to volition, they are the strongest motives; and those that have least, are the weakest motives.

### TC: Volitions sometimes don't follow the strongest motive but the weakest.

Now if volitions sometimes don't follow the motive which is strongest, or has most previous tendency or advantage, all things considered, to induce or excite it, but follows the weakest, or that which as it stands previously in the mind's view, has least tendency to induce it; herein the will apparently acts wholly without motive, without any previous reason to dispose the mind to it, contrary to what the same author supposes. The act wherein the will must proceed without previous motive to induce it, is the act of preferring the weakest motive. For how absurd is it to say, the mind sees previous reason in the motive, to prefer that motive before the other; and at the same time to suppose, that there is nothing in the motive, in its nature, state, or any circumstances of it whatsoever, as it stands in the previous view of the mind, that gives it any preference; but on the contrary, the other motive that stands in competition with it, in all these respects, has most belonging to it, that is inviting and moving, and has most of a tendency to choice and preference?

### JE: Two rival motives compete to be preferred and chosen, appearing with superior strength and all appearing preferableness.

### TC: There is no previous reason for the act of preference. The motive is not in the act which is preferred, but wholly in the other.

This is certainly as much as to say, there is previous ground and reason in the motive for the act of preference, and yet no previous reason for it. By the supposition, as to all that is in the two rival motives which tends to preference, previous to the act of preference, it is not in that which is preferred, but wholly in the other: because appearing superior strength, and all appearing preferableness is in that;

### TC: There is previous ground in a thing for an event that takes place, and it follows another without any previous reason.

and yet Mr. Chubb supposes, that the act of preference is from "previous ground and reason" in the motive which is preferred. But are these things consistent? Can there be previous ground in a thing for an event that takes place, and yet no previous tendency in it to that event? If one thing follows another, without any previous tendency to its following, then I should think it very plain, that it follows it without any manner of previous reason why it should follow.

*TC: The mind prefers the weaker motive to the other one.*

*JE: All the preferableness, or previous tendency to preference, is on the other side, with the strongest motive to the weaker one. Any preference to comparative neglect, rejection, or undervaluing does not affect the motive which is already preferred.*

Yea, in this case, Mr. Chubb supposes, that the event follows an antecedent or a previous thing, as the ground of its existence, not only that has *no tendency* to it, but *a contrary tendency*. The event is the preference which the mind gives to that motive which is weaker, as it stands in the previous view of the mind; the immediate antecedent is the view the mind has of the two rival motives conjunctly; in which previous view of the mind, all the preferableness, or previous tendency to preference, is supposed to be on the other side, or in the contrary motive; and all the unworthiness of preference, and so previous tendency to comparative neglect, rejection or undervaluing, is on that side which is preferred: and yet in this view of the mind is supposed to be the "previous ground or reason" of this act of preference, "exciting it, and disposing the mind to it."

Which, I leave the reader to judge, whether it be absurd or not. If it be not, then it is not absurd to say, that the previous tendency of an antecedent to a consequent, is the ground and reason why that consequent does not follow; and the want of a previous tendency to an event, yea, a tendency to the contrary, is the true ground and reason why that event does follow.

*JE: An act of choice or preference is a comparative act, which the mind chooses or prefers one among two or more rival things in the mind's view.*

An act of choice or preference is a comparative act, wherein the mind acts with reference to two or more things that are compared, and stand in competition in the mind's view.

*TC: The mind prefers what appears inferior because it acts absolutely without any motive or inducement.*

*JE: ILL: 1) Is it possible for a hungry man to choose that which he has least appetite to and to refuse that to which he has the strongest appetite?*

If the mind, in this comparative act, prefers that which appears inferior in the comparison, then the mind herein acts absolutely without motive, or inducement, or any temptation whatsoever. Thus,[6] if a hungry man has the offer of two sorts of food, both which he finds an appetite to, but has a stronger appetite to one than the other; and there be no circumstances or excitements whatsoever in the case to induce him to

---

6. [Corrected, from "Then."]

take either one or the other, but merely his appetite: if in the choice he makes between them, he chooses that which he has least appetite to, and refuses that to which he has the strongest appetite, this is a choice made absolutely without previous motive, excitement, reason or temptation, as much as if he were perfectly without all appetite to either: because his volition in this case is a comparative act, attending and following a comparative view of the food which he chooses, viewing it as related to, and compared with the other sort of food, in which view his preference has absolutely no previous ground, yea, is against all previous ground and motive. And if there be any principle in man from whence an act of choice may arise after this manner, from the same principle, volition may arise wholly without motive on either side. If the mind in its volition can go beyond motive, then it can go without motive: for when it is beyond the motive, it is out of the reach of the motive, out of the limits of its influence, and so without motive. If volition goes beyond the strength and tendency of motive, and especially if it goes against its tendency, this demonstrates the independence of volition on[7] motive. And if so, no reason can be given for what Mr. Chubb so often asserts, even that "in the nature of things volition cannot take place without a motive to induce it."

### ILL: 2) Is it possible a balance scale descends which has the least weight, and so to raise the greater weight?

If the Most High should endow a balance with agency or activity of nature, in such a manner, that when unequal weights are put into the scales, its agency could enable it to cause that scale to descend which has the least weight, and so to raise the greater weight; this would clearly demonstrate, that the motion of the balance does not depend on weights in the scales, at least as much, as if the balance should move itself, when there is no weight in either scale.

And the activity of the balance which is sufficient to move itself against the greater weight, must certainly be more than sufficient to move it when there is no weight at all.

### TC's Supposition: The will cannot stir at all without some motive, and so it is dependent on the latter.

### JE's Objection: Though TC says the will is dependent on it, it is wholly independent of it because the will is not determined by any previous superior strength of the motive but determines its motive.

Mr. Chubb supposes, that the will can't stir at all without some motive; and also supposes, that if there be a motive to one thing, and none to the contrary, volition will infallibly follow that motive. This is virtually to suppose an entire dependence of the will on motives: if it were not wholly dependent on them, it could surely help itself

---

7. [Corrected, from "or."]

a little without them, or help itself a little against a motive, without help from the strength and weight of a contrary motive. And yet his supposing that the will, when it has before it various opposite motives, can use them as it pleases, and choose its own influence from them, and neglect the strongest, and follow the weakest, supposes it to be wholly independent on motives.

It further appears, on Mr. Chubb's supposition, that volition must be without any previous ground in any motive, thus: if it be as he supposes, that the will is not determined by any previous superior strength of the motive, but determines and chooses its own motive, then, when the rival motives are exactly equal in strength and tendency to induce, in all respects, it may follow either; and may in such a case, sometimes follow one, sometimes the other. And if so, this diversity which appears between the acts of the will, is plainly without previous ground in either of the motives; for all that is previously in the motives, is supposed precisely and perfectly the same, without any diversity whatsoever. Now perfect identity, as to all that is previous in the antecedent, can't be the ground and reason of diversity in the consequent. Perfect identity in the ground can't be a reason why it is not followed with the same consequence. And therefore the source of this diversity of consequence must be sought for elsewhere.

***TC's Insistence: No volition can take place without some motive, yet the mind itself picks and chooses its motive to follow without any previous strength of motives.***

And lastly, it may be observed, that however Mr. Chubb does much insist that no volition can take place without some motive to induce it, which previously disposes the mind to it; yet, as he also insists that the mind without reference to any previous superior strength of motives, picks and chooses for its motive to follow; he himself herein plainly supposes, that with regard to the mind's preference of one motive before another, it is not the motive that disposes the will, but the will disposes itself to follow the motive.

***TC: Necessity cannot consist with agency or freedom. Man's will has in him a power or liberty of doing either good or evil, and so that he might choose otherwise if he pleases.***

***IV. Mr. Chubb supposes necessity to be utterly inconsistent with agency; and that to suppose a being to be an agent in that which is necessary, is a plain contradiction (p. 311).***

And throughout his discourses on the subject of liberty, he supposes, that necessity cannot consist with agency or freedom; and that to suppose otherwise, is to make liberty and necessity, action and passion, the same thing. And so he seems to suppose, that there is no action strictly speaking, but volition; and that as to the effects of volition in body or mind, in themselves considered, being necessary, they are said to be free, only as they are the effects of an act that is not necessary.[8]

And yet, according to him, volition itself is the *effect of volition*; yea, every act of free volition: and therefore every act of free volition must, by what has now been observed from him, be necessary. That every act of free volition is itself the effect of volition, is abundantly supposed by him. In p. 341, he says,

> "If a man is such a creature as I have above proved him to be, that is, if he has in him a power or liberty of doing either good or evil, and either of these is the subject of his own free choice, so that he might, *IF HE HAD PLEASED*, have *CHOSEN* and done the contrary."

Here he supposes, all that is good or evil in man is the effect of his choice; and so that his good or evil choice itself is the effect of his pleasure or choice, in these words, "he might if he had *PLEASED*, have *CHOSEN* the contrary."

So in p. 386: "Though it be highly reasonable, that a man should always choose the greater good . . . yet he may, if he *PLEASE, CHOOSE* otherwise."

Which is the same thing as if he had said, he may, if he *chooses, choose* otherwise. And then he goes on, "that is, he may, *if he pleases, choose* what is good for himself, etc."

And again in the same page,

> "The will is not confined by the understanding to any particular sort of good, whether greater or less; but is at liberty to *choose* what kind of good *it pleases*."

If there be any meaning in these last words, the meaning must be this, that *the will is at liberty to choose what kind of good it chooses to choose*; supposing the act of choice itself determined by an antecedent choice.

The liberty Mr. Chubb speaks of, is not only a man's having power to move his body agreeably to an antecedent act of choice, but to use or exert the faculties of his soul. Thus, in p. 379, speaking of the faculties of his mind, he says,

> "Man [. . .] has power, and is at liberty to neglect these faculties, to use them aright, or to abuse them, *as he pleases*."

### TC: *An act of man is not a necessity of nature but a produce of free choice.*

And that he supposes an Act of Choice, or Exercise of Pleasure, properly distinct from, and antecedent to those acts thus chosen, directing, commanding, and producing the chosen acts, and even the acts of choice themselves, is very plain

in p. 283,

---

8. [Ramsey, moral *actions* — "As to the word *free*, which is commonly added in this case, this term is wholly superfluous; because every agent is free . . . so far as he is an agent; a necessary agent being a plain contradiction" (Chubb, *Tracts*, 311).]

> "He can *command his actions*; and herein consists his liberty; he can give or deny himself that pleasure *as he pleases*."

And p. 377,

> "If the actions of men . . . are not the *Produce of a free Choice*, or Election, but spring from a Necessity of Nature . . . he cannot in reason be the object of reward or punishment on their account. Whereas, if action in man, whether good or evil, is *the Produce of Will or free Choice*; so that a man in either case, had it in his power, and was at liberty to have CHOSEN the contrary, he is the proper object of reward or punishment, according as he CHOOSES to behave himself."

Here in these last words, he speaks of liberty of CHOOSING, ACCORDING AS HE CHOOSES. So that the behavior which he speaks of as subject to his choice, is his *choosing* itself, as well as his external conduct consequent upon it. And therefore it is evident, he means not only external actions, but the acts of choice themselves, when he speaks of "all free actions, as the PRODUCE of free choice."

And this is abundantly evident in what he says in pp. 372, and 373. Now these things imply a twofold great absurdity and inconsistence.

### JE: Chubb supposes every free act of choice is the produce of free choice which would be identified with the other cause.

1. To suppose, as Mr. Chubb plainly does, that every free act of choice is "commanded by," and is the "produce of free choice," is to suppose the first free act of choice belonging to the case, yea, the first free act of choice that ever man exerted, to be "the produce" of an antecedent act of choice. But I hope I need not labor at all to convince my readers, that it is an absurdity to say, the very *first* act is the produce of another act that went *before* it.

### JE: As every act of choice is the effect of a prior act, it would be necessarily connected with that other cause and would be not free but necessary.

2. If it were both possible and real, as Mr. Chubb insists, that every free act of choice was the produce or the effect of a free act of choice; yet even then, according to his principles, no one act of choice would be free, but everyone necessary; because, every act of choice being the effect of a foregoing act, every act would be necessarily connected with that foregoing cause. For Mr. Chubb himself says (p. 389), "When the self-moving power is exerted, it becomes the necessary cause of its effects." So that his notion of a free act, that is rewardable or punishable, is a heap of contradictions. It is a free act, and yet, by his own notion of freedom, is necessary; and therefore by him it is a contradiction, to suppose it to be free.

According to him, every free act is the produce of a free act; so that there must be an infinite number of free acts in succession, without any beginning, in an agent that has a beginning. And therefore here is an infinite number of free acts, every one of them free; and yet not any one of them free, but every act in the whole infinite chain a necessary effect. All the acts are rewardable or punishable, and yet the agent cannot, in reason, be the object of reward or punishment, on account of any one of these actions. He is active in them all, and passive in none; yet active in none, but passive in all, etc.

***TC: Motives are not "causes" of the acts of the will, and they are merely passive and have no causality in the production of action.***

***JE: Motives are "causes" of the acts of the will, and they are merely positive and have causality in the production of action.***

**V. Mr. Chubb does most strenuously deny, that motives are "causes" of the acts of the will; or that the moving principle in man is "*moved,*" or "*caused to be exerted*" by motives. His words (p. 388) are,**

> If the moving principle in man is MOVED, or CAUSED TO BE EXERTED, by something external to man, which all motives are, then it would not be a self-moving principle, seeing it would be moved by a principle external to itself. And to say, that a self-moving principle is MOVED, or CAUSED TO BE EXERTED, by a cause external to itself, is absurd and a contradiction, etc.

And in the next page, it is particularly and largely insisted, that motives are causes in no case, that

> "they are merely passive in the production of action, and have no causality in the production of it . . . no causality, to be the cause of the exertion of the will."

Now I desire it may be considered, how this can possibly consist with what he says in other places. Let it be noted here,

***JE: 1) Chubb speaks with a forked tongue; he says in other places that motives are cause of the acts of the will.***

1. Mr. Chubb abundantly speaks of motives as "excitements of the acts of the will"; and says, that "motives do excite volition, and induce it," and that they are necessary to this end; that "in the reason and nature of things, volition cannot take place without motives to excite it." But now if motives *excite* the will, they *move* it; and yet he says, it is absurd to say, the will is moved by motives. And again (if language is of any significance at all) if motives excite volition, then they are the cause of its being excited; and to cause volition to be excited, is to cause it to be put forth or exerted. Yea, Mr. Chubb says himself (p. 317), motive is necessary to the "exertion" of the active faculty. To excite, is positively to *do* something; and certainly that which does something, is the cause of the thing *done* by it. To create, is to cause to be created; to make, is to cause

to be made; to kill, is to cause to be killed; to quicken, is to cause to be quickened; and *to excite*, is *to cause to be excited*.⁹

To excite, is to be a cause, in the most proper sense, not merely a negative occasion, but a ground of existence by positive influence. The notion of exciting, is exerting influence to cause the effect to arise or come forth into existence.

***JE: 2) Chubb himself admits motives as a prevalent influence and consequently he acknowledges them to be a cause.***

2. Mr. Chubb himself (p. 317) speaks of motives as the ground and reason of action BY "INFLUENCE," and BY "PREVAILING INFLUENCE." Now, what can be meant by a cause, but something that is the ground and reason of a thing by its influence, an influence that is *prevalent* and so effectual?

***JE: 3) Chubb reverses his word; he says that motives are "influence as prevailing for the production of an action," and yet that it is absurd to call them causes.***

3. This author not only speaks of motives as the ground and reason of action, by prevailing influence; but expressly of their "influence as prevailing FOR THE PRODUCTION of an action," in the same p. 317: which makes the inconsistency still more palpable and notorious. The *production* of an effect is certainly the *causing* of an effect; and productive influence is causal influence, if anything is; and that which has this influence prevalently, so as thereby to become the ground of another thing, is a cause of that thing, if there be any such thing as a cause. This influence, Mr. Chubb says, motives have to produce an action; and yet he says, it is absurd and a contradiction, to say they are causes.

***JE: 4) Chubb repeats the same idea, rather he agrees on my point. Motive, which takes place in the understanding and previous reason to dispose the mind, is necessary to action.***

4. In the same page, he once and again speaks of motives as "disposing" the agent to action, "by their influence." His words are these:

> As motive, which takes place in the understanding, and is the product of intelligence, is NECESSARY to action, that is, to the EXERTION of the active faculty, because that faculty would not be exerted without some PREVIOUS REASON to DISPOSE the mind to action; so from hence it plainly appears, that when a man is said to be *disposed* to one action rather than another, [. . .] this properly signifies the PREVAILING INFLUENCE that one motive has upon a man FOR THE PRODUCTION of an action, or for the being at rest,

---

9. [Chubb, *Tracts*, 263.]

before all other motives, for the production of the contrary. For as motive is the ground and reason of any action, so the motive that prevails, *disposes* the agent to the performance of that action.[10]

Now, if motives dispose the mind to action, then they *cause* the mind to be disposed; and to cause the mind to be disposed, is to cause it to be willing; and to cause it to be willing, is to cause it to will;

and that is the same thing as to be the cause of an act of the will. And yet this same Mr. Chubb holds it to be absurd, to suppose motive to be a cause of the act of the will.

### *Conclusion: Chubb rejects JE's position: "Motives are the previous ground and reason" of the acts of the will.*

And if we compare these things together, we have here again a whole heap of inconsistences. "Motives are the previous ground and reason" of the acts of the will; yea, the "necessary" ground and reason of "their exertion, without which they will not be exerted, and cannot in the nature of things take place"; and they do "excite" these acts of the will, and do this by a "prevailing influence"; yea, "an influence which prevails for the production of the act" of the will, and for "the disposing of the mind to it": and yet it is "absurd," to suppose "motive to be a cause" of an act of the will, or that "a principle of will is moved or caused to be exerted by it," or that it has "any causality in the production of it, or any causality to be the cause of the exertion of the will."

A due consideration of these things which Mr. Chubb has advanced, the strange inconsistences which the notion of liberty consisting in the will's power of self-determination void of all necessity, united with that dictate of common sense, that there can be no volition without a motive, drove him into, may be sufficient to convince us, that it is utterly impossible ever to make that notion of liberty consistent with the influence of motives in volition. And as it is in a manner self-evident, that there can be no act of will, choice or preference of the mind, without some motive or inducement, something in the mind's view, which it aims at, seeks, inclines to, and goes after; so it is most manifest, there is no such liberty in the universe as *Arminians* insist on; nor any such thing possible, or conceivable.

---

10. "To say that motive prevailed, because it was strongest, is the same as to say, that it prevailed, because it *did prevail*." (Chubb, *Tracts,* 258).

# Section 11

## The Evidence of God's Certain Foreknowledge of the Volitions of Moral Agents

*JE: God foreknows what volitions men have and what actions they would take.*

That the acts of the wills of moral agents are not contingent events, in that sense, as to be without all necessity, appears by God's certain foreknowledge of such events.

In handling this argument, I would in the first place prove, that God has a certain foreknowledge of the voluntary acts of moral agents; and secondly, show the consequence, or how it follows from hence, that the volitions of moral agents are not contingent, so as to be without necessity of connection and consequence.

First, I am to prove, that God has an absolute and certain foreknowledge of the free actions of moral agents.

One would think, it should be wholly needless to enter on such an argument with any that profess themselves Christians: but so it is; God's certain foreknowledge of the free acts of moral agents, is denied by some that pretend to believe the Scriptures to be the Word of God; and especially of late. I therefore shall consider the evidence of such a prescience in the most High, as fully as the designed limits of this essay will admit of; supposing myself herein to have to do with such as own the truth of the Bible.

*Argument I: God foreknows and so He can predict.*

*Arg. I. My first argument shall be taken from God's prediction of such events. Here I would in the first place lay down these two things as axioms.*

*JE: (1) God foreknows, and so He can foretell.*

(1) If God doesn't foreknow, he can't foretell such events; that is, he can't peremptorily and certainly foretell them. If God has no more than an uncertain guess concerning events of this kind, then he can declare no more than an uncertain guess. Positively to

### JE: (2) God foreknows the future volitions of men, and so He can foretell their acts.

(2) If God doesn't certainly foreknow the future volitions of moral agents, then neither can he certainly foreknow those events which are consequent and dependent on these volitions. The existence of the one depending on the existence of the other, the knowledge of the existence of the one depends on the knowledge of the existence of the other; and the one can't be more certain than the other.

### Ar: God is unable to know men's volitions and their consequences.

Therefore, how many, how great, and how extensive so ever the consequences of the volitions of moral agents may be; though they should extend to an alteration of the state of things through the universe, and should be continued in a series of successive events to all eternity, and should in the progress of things branch forth into an infinite number of series, each of them going on in an endless line or chain of events; God must be as ignorant of all these consequences, as he is of the volition whence they first take their rise: all these events, and the whole state of things depending on them, how important, extensive and vast so ever, must be hid from him.

### JE: The world's history is a succession of volitions of moral agents.

These positions being such as I suppose none will deny, I now proceed to observe the following things.

### 1. God's Prediction of Moral Conduct and Qualities

1. Men's moral conduct and qualities, their virtues and vices, their wickedness and good practice, things rewardable and punishable, have often been foretold by God.

**Pharaoh**'s moral conduct, in refusing to obey God's command, in letting his people go, was foretold. God says to Moses (Ex. 3:19), "I am sure, that the king of Egypt will not let you go." Here God professes not only to guess at, but to know Pharaoh's future disobedience. In Ch. Ex. 7:4, God says, "But Pharaoh shall not hearken unto you; that I may lay mine hand upon Egypt," etc. And Ch. Ex. 9:30: Moses says to Pharaoh, "As for thee, and thy servants, I KNOW that ye will not fear the Lord." See also Ch. Ex. 9:9.

The moral conduct of **Josiah**, by name, in his zealously exerting himself in opposition to idolatry, in particular acts of his, was foretold above three hundred years before he was born, and the prophecy sealed by a miracle, and renewed and confirmed by the words of a second prophet, as what surely would not fail (I Kgs. 13:1–6, 32). This prophecy was also in effect a prediction of the moral conduct of the people, in upholding their schismatical and idolatrous worship till that time, and the idolatry of those priests of the high places, which it is foretold Josiah should offer upon that altar of Bethel.

Micaiah foretold the foolish and sinful conduct of **Ahab**, in refusing to hearken to the word of the Lord by him, and choosing rather to hearken to the false prophets, in going to Ramoth-Gilead to his ruin (I Kings 21:20–22).

The moral conduct of **Hazael** was foretold, in that cruelty he should be guilty of; on which Hazael says, "What, is thy servant a dog, that he should do this thing!" The Prophet speaks of the event as what he knew, and not what he conjectured.

II Kings 8:12: "I know the evil thou wilt do unto the children of Israel: thou wilt dash their children, and rip up their women with child."

The moral conduct of **Cyrus** is foretold, long before he had a being, in his mercy to God's people, and regard to the true God, in turning the captivity of the Jews, and promoting the building of the Temple (Isaiah 44:28 and Isaiah 45:13; compare II Chronicles 36:22, II Chronicles 36:23 and Ezra 1:1–4).

How many instances of the moral conduct of the kings of the north and south, particular instances of the wicked behavior of the **kings of Syria and Egypt**, are foretold in the eleventh chapter of Daniel? Their corruption, violence, robbery, treachery, and lies.

And particularly, how much is foretold of the horrid wickedness of **Antiochus Epiphanes**, called there a "vile person," instead of "Epiphanes," or illustrious. In that chapter, and also in Daniel 8:9–14, 23, to the end, are foretold his flattery, deceit and lies, his having "his heart set to do mischief," and set "against the holy Covenant," his "destroying and treading under foot the holy people," in a marvelous manner, his "having indignation against the holy Covenant, setting his heart against it," and "conspiring against it," his "polluting the sanctuary of strength, treading it under foot, taking away the daily sacrifice, and placing the abomination that maketh desolate"; his great pride, "magnifying himself against God," and "uttering marvelous blasphemies against Him," till God in "indignation should destroy him."

Withal the moral conduct of the **Jews**, on occasion of his persecution, is predicted. It is foretold, that "he should corrupt many by flatteries" (Daniel 11:32–34). But that others should behave with a glorious constancy and fortitude, in opposition to him (v. 32). And that some good men should fall, and repent (v. 35).

Christ foretold **Peter**'s sin, in denying his Lord, with its circumstances, in a peremptory manner.

And so, that great sin of **Judas**, in betraying his master, and its dreadful and eternal punishment in hell, was foretold in the like positive manner (Matthew 26:21–25 and parallel places in the other Evangelists).

## 2. God's Prediction of Man's Moral Events

2. Many events have been foretold by God, which were consequent and dependent on the moral conduct of particular persons, and were accomplished, either by their virtuous or vicious actions.

Thus, the children of **Israel's going down into Egypt** to dwell there, was foretold to Abraham (Genesis 15), which was brought about by the wickedness of Joseph's brethren in selling him, and the wickedness of Joseph's mistress, and his own signal virtue in resisting her temptation.

The accomplishment of the thing prefigured in Joseph's dream, depended on the same moral conduct.

Jotham's parable and prophecy (Judges 9:15–20), was accomplished by the **wicked conduct of Abimelech, and the men of Shechem**.

The prophecies against the house of Eli (I Samuel 2–3) were accomplished by **the wickedness of Doeg the Edomite**, in accusing the priests;

and the great impiety, and extreme **cruelty of Saul** in destroying the priests at Nob (I Samuel 22).

Nathan's prophecy against David (II Samuel 12:11–12) was fulfilled by the horrible **wickedness of Absalom**, in rebelling against his father, seeking his life, and lying with his concubines in the sight of the sun.

The prophecy against Solomon (I Kings 11:11–13) was fulfilled by **Jeroboam's rebellion and usurpation**, which are spoken of as his wickedness (II Chronicles. 13:5–6; compare v. 18).

The prophecy against Jeroboam's family (I Kings 14) was fulfilled by the **conspiracy, treason, and cruel murders of Baasha** (I Kings 15:27, etc.).

The predictions of the prophet Jehu against the house of Baasha (I Kings 16 at the beginning) were fulfilled by the **treason and parricide of Zimri** (I Kings 16:9–13, 20).

### 3. God's Prediction of Man's Future Moral Conducts and Events

3. How often has God foretold the future moral conduct of nations and peoples, of numbers, bodies, and successions of men; with God's judicial proceedings, and many other events consequent and dependent on their virtues and vices; which could not be foreknown, if the volitions of men, wherein they acted as moral agents, had not been foreseen?

The **future cruelty of the Egyptians** in oppressing Israel, and God's judging and punishing them for it, was foretold long before it came to pass (Genesis 15:13–14).

The continuance of the **iniquity of the Amorites**, and the increase of it until it "should be full," and they ripe for destruction, was foretold above four hundred years beforehand (Genesis 15:16; Acts 7:6–7).

The prophecies of the **destruction of Jerusalem, and the land of Judah**, were absolute (II Kings 20:17–19; Ch. 22:15 to the end). It was foretold in Hezekiah's time, and was abundantly insisted on in the book of the prophet Isaiah, who wrote nothing after Hezekiah's days. It was foretold in Josiah's time, in the beginning of a great reformation (II Kings 22). And it is manifest by innumerable things in the predictions of the prophets, relating to this event, its time, its circumstances, its continuance and end; the return from the captivity, the restoration of the Temple, city and land, and many circumstances, and consequences of that; I say, these show plainly, that the prophecies of this great event were *absolute*.

### JE: Man's wickedness was predicted and yet it was an efficient cause for God's punishment.

And yet this event was connected with, and dependent on two things in men's moral conduct: first, the injurious rapine and violence of the king of Babylon and his people, as the efficient cause[1]; which God often speaks of as what he highly resented, and would severely punish; and secondly, the final obstinacy of the Jews. That great event is often spoken of as suspended on this (Jeremiah 4:1; 5:1; 7:1–7; 11:1–6; 17:24 to the end; 25:1–7; 26:1–8, 13; and 38:17–18). Therefore, this destruction and captivity could not be foreknown, unless such a moral conduct of the Chaldeans and Jews had been foreknown. And then it was foretold, that the people "should be finally obstinate," to the destruction and utter desolation of the city and land (Isaiah 6:9–11; Jeremiah 1:18, 1:19; 7:27–29; Ezekiel 3:7; and 24:13–14).

### God's Prediction of Israel's Future Corruption

The final obstinacy of those Jews who were left in the land of Israel, and who afterwards went down into Egypt, in their idolatry and rejection of the true God, was foretold by God, and the prediction confirmed with an oath (Jeremiah 44:26–27). And God tells the people (Isaiah 48:3, 4–8) that he had predicted those things which should be consequent on their treachery and obstinacy, because he knew they would be obstinate; and that he had declared these things beforehand, for their conviction of his being the only true God, etc.

### God's Prediction of Babylon's Future Destruction and Judgment

The destruction of Babylon, with many of the circumstances of it, was foretold, as the judgment of God for the exceeding pride and haughtiness of the heads of that monarchy, Nebuchadnezzar, and his successors, and their wickedly destroying other nations, and particularly for their exalting themselves against the true God and his people, before any of these monarchs had a being (Isaiah, chs. 13, 14, 47; compare Habakkuk 2:5 to the end, and Jeremiah 50 and 51). That Babylon's destruction was to be a recompense, according to the works of their own hands, appears by Jeremiah 25:14. The immorality which the people of Babylon, and particularly her princes and

---

1. [As Aristotle had developed and improved the doctrine of Plato, he regards nature as an adaptation of means to ends, and four *causes* – material cause, moving or efficient cause, formal cause, final cause – as contributing to the production of any object.]

great men, were guilty of, that very night that the city was destroyed, their reveling and drunkenness at Belshazzar's idolatrous feast, was foretold (Jeremiah 51:39, 57).

### *God's Prediction of the Return of the Jews from the Babylonian Captivity*

The return of the Jews from the Babylonish captivity is often very particularly foretold, with many circumstances, and the promises of it are very peremptory (Jeremiah 31:35–40; and 32:6–15, 41–44; and 33:24–26). And the very time of their return was prefixed (Jeremiah 25:11–12; and 29:10, 29:11; II Chronicles 36:21; Ezekiel 4:5–6; and Daniel 9:2). And yet the prophecies represent their return as consequent on their repentance.

And their repentance itself is very expressly and particularly foretold (Jeremiah 29:12–14; 31:8–9, 31:18–31; 33:8; 50:4–5; Ezekiel 6:8–10; 7:16; 14:22, 14:23; and 20:43, 20:44).

### *The Old Testament's Prediction of Christ's Sufferings*

It was foretold under the Old Testament, that the Messiah should suffer greatly through the malice and cruelty of men; as is largely and fully set forth (Psalm 22, applied to Christ in the New Testament, Matthew 27:35, 43; Luke 23:34; John 19:24; Hebrews 2:12). And likewise in Psalm 69, which, it is also evident by the New Testament, is spoken of Christ (John 15:25; 7:5, etc.; and John 2:17; Romans 15:3; Matthew 27:34, 48; Mark 15:23; John 19:29). The same thing is also foretold, Isaiah 53 and 50:6; and Micah 5:1. This cruelty of men was their sin, and what they acted as moral agents. It was foretold, that there should be an union of heathen and Jewish rulers against Christ (Psalm 2:1–2, compared with Acts 4:25–28). It was foretold, that the Jews should generally reject and despise the Messiah (Isaiah 49:5–6, 49:7 and 53:1–3; Psalm 22:6–7 and 69:4, 8, 69:19, 69:20). And it was foretold, that the body of that nation should be rejected in the Messiah's days, from being God's people, for their obstinacy in sin (Isaiah 49:4–7 and 8:14–16, compared with Romans 10:19; and Isaiah 65 at the beginning, compared with Romans 10:20–21). It was foretold, that Christ should be rejected by the chief priests and rulers among the Jews (Psalm 118:22, compared with Matthew 21:42; Acts 4:11; I Peter 2:4, 7).

### *Christ's Own Prediction of His Sufferings*

Christ himself foretold his being delivered into the hands of the elders, chief priests and scribes, and his being cruelly treated by them, and condemned to death; and that he by them should be delivered to the Gentiles; and that he should be mocked, and scourged, and crucified (Matthew 16:21 and 20:17–19; Luke 9:22; John 8:28), and that the people should be concerned in and consenting to his death (Luke 20:13–18), especially the inhabitants of Jerusalem (Luke 13:33–35). He foretold, that the disciples should all be offended because of him that night that he was betrayed, and should forsake him (Matthew 26:31; John 16:32). He foretold that he should be rejected of that generation, even the body of the people, and that they should continue obstinate, to their ruin (Matthew 12:45, 21:33–42 and 22:1–7; Luke 13:25–35, 17:25, 19:14, 27, 19:41–44; 20:13–18 and 23:34–39).

As it was foretold in both Old Testament and New, that the Jews should reject the Messiah, so it was foretold that the Gentiles should receive him, and so be admitted to the privileges of God's people; in places too many to be now particularly mentioned.

### Bible's Prediction of Gentiles' Conversion and Jews' Envy

It was foretold in the Old Testament, that the Jews should envy the Gentiles on this account (Deuteronomy 32:21 compared with Romans 10:19). Christ himself often foretold, that the Gentiles would embrace the true religion, and become his followers and people (Matthew 8:10–12, 21:41–43 and 22:8–10; Luke 13:28, 14:16–24 and 20:16; John 10:16). He also foretold the Jews' envy of the Gentiles on this occasion (Matthew 20:12–16, Luke 15:26 to the end). He foretold, that they should continue in this opposition and envy, and should manifest it in cruel persecutions of his followers, to their utter destruction (Matthew 21:33–42, 22:6 and 23:34–39; Luke 11:49–51). The Jews' obstinacy is also foretold (Acts 22:18). Christ often foretold the great persecutions his followers should meet with, both from Jews and Gentiles (Matthew 10:16–18, 21, 22, 34–36 and 24:9; Mark 13:9; Luke 10:3, 12:11, 12:49–53; and Luke 21:12, 16–17; John 15:18–21; and 16:1–4, 20–22, 16:33). He foretold the martyrdom of particular persons (Matthew 20:23; John 13:36; and John 21:18, 21:19, 22). He foretold the great success of the gospel in the city of Samaria, as near approaching; which afterwards was fulfilled by the preaching of Philip (John 4:35–38). He foretold the rising of many deceivers, after his departure (Matthew 24:4–5, 11), and the apostasy of many of his professed followers (Matthew 24:10–12).

### Apostle Paul's Prediction of his own Persecutions

The persecutions, which the Apostle Paul was to meet with in the world, were foretold (Acts 9:16–23 and 21:11). The Apostle says to the Christian Ephesians (Acts 20:29–30), "I know, that after my departure shall grievous wolves enter in among you, not sparing the flock: also of your own selves shall men arise, speaking perverse things, to draw away disciples after them." The Apostle says, he knew this; but he did not know it, if God did not know the future actions of moral agents.

## 4. God's Foreknowledge of Men's Future Moral Conducts and Events

4. Unless God foreknows the future acts of moral agents, all the prophecies we have in Scripture concerning the great Antichristian apostasy; the rise, reign, wicked qualities and deeds of the Man of Sin[2], and his instruments and adherents; the extent and long continuance of his dominion, his influence on the minds of princes and others, to corrupt them, and draw them away to idolatry, and other foul vices; his great and cruel persecutions; the behavior of the saints under these great temptations, etc., etc.: I say, unless the volitions of moral agents are foreseen, all these prophecies are uttered without knowing the things foretold.

The predictions relating to this great apostasy are all of a moral nature,[3] relating to men's virtues and vices, and their exercises, fruits and consequences, and events depending on them; and are very particular; and most of them often repeated, with many precise characteristics, descriptions, and limitations of qualities, conduct, influence, effects, extent, duration, periods, circumstances, final issue, etc., which it would be very long to mention particularly.

And to suppose, all these are predicted by God without any certain knowledge of the future moral behavior of free agents, would be to the utmost degree absurd.

### 5. God's Foreknowledge and Predictions of Eschatological Events

5. Unless God foreknows the future acts of men's wills, and their behavior as moral agents, all those great things which are foretold in both Old Testament and New concerning the erection, establishment, and universal extent of the kingdom of the Messiah, were predicted and promised while God was in ignorance whether any of these things would come to pass or no, and did but guess at them. For that kingdom is not of this world, it doesn't consist in things external, but is within men, and consists in the dominion of virtue in their hearts, in righteousness, and peace, and joy in the Holy Ghost; and in these things made manifest in practice, to the praise and glory of God. The Messiah came to save men from their sins, and deliver them from their spiritual enemies; that they might serve him in righteousness and holiness before him: he gave himself for us, that he might redeem us from all iniquity, and purify unto himself a peculiar people, zealous of good works. And therefore his success consists in gaining men's hearts to virtue, in their being made God's willing people in the day of his power. His conquest of his enemies consists in his victory over men's corruptions and vices. And such success, such victory, and such a reign and dominion is often expressly foretold: that his kingdom shall fill the earth; that all people, nations and languages should serve and obey him; and so, that all nations should go up to the mountain of the house of the Lord, that he might teach them his ways, and that they might walk in his paths: and that all men should be drawn to Christ, and the earth be full of the knowledge of the Lord (by which, in the style of

---

2. ["The Man of Sin" signifies "Man of Lawlessness," i.e., Anti-Christ. 2 The. 2:3–10.]
3. [In this JE affirms that world history is of moral history of moral events.]

Scripture, is meant true virtue and religion) as the waters cover the seas; that God's law should be put into men's inward parts, and written in their hearts; and that God's people should be all righteous, etc.

## OT Predictions of the Universal Prevalence of His Kingdom of the Messiah and True Religion of Jesus Christ

A very great part of the prophecies of the Old Testament is taken up in such predictions as these. And here I would observe, that the prophecies of the universal prevalence of the kingdom of the Messiah, and true religion of Jesus Christ, are delivered in the most peremptory manner, and confirmed by the oath of God.

> Isaiah 45:22 to the end: "Look to me, and be ye saved, all the ends of the earth; for I am God, and there is none else. I have *SWORN* by myself, the word is gone out of my mouth in righteousness, and shall not return, that unto me every knee shall bow; and every tongue shall swear. *SURELY*, shall one say, in the Lord have I righteousness and strength: even to him shall men come," etc.

But here this peremptory declaration, and great oath of the Most High, are delivered with such mighty solemnity, to things which God did not know, if he did not certainly foresee the volitions of moral agents.

## Parables and Predictions of the Restoration of the Jews and Conversion of Gentiles

And all the predictions of Christ and his apostles, to the like purpose, must be without knowledge: as those of our Savior comparing the kingdom of God to a grain of mustard seed, growing exceeding great, from a small beginning; and to leaven, hid in three measures of meal, till the whole was leavened, etc. And the prophecies in the Epistles concerning the restoration of the nation of the Jews to the true church of God, and the bringing in the fullness of the Gentiles; and the prophecies in all the Revelation concerning the glorious change in the moral state of the world of mankind, attending the destruction of Antichrist, the kingdoms of the world becoming the kingdoms of our Lord and of his Christ; and its being granted to the Church to be arrayed in that fine linen, white and clean, which is the righteousness of saints, etc.

## Corol. 1. If God had no pre-knowledge, the promise would be based on uncertainties.

*Corol. 1.* Hence that great promise and oath of God to Abraham, Isaac and Jacob, so much celebrated in Scripture, both in the Old Testament and New, namely, that in their seed all the nations and families of the earth should be blessed, must be made on uncertainties, if God doesn't certainly foreknow the volitions of moral agents. For the fulfillment of this promise consists in that success of Christ in the work of redemption, and that setting up of his spiritual kingdom over the nations of the world, which has been spoken of. Men are blessed in Christ no otherwise than as they are brought to acknowledge him, trust in him, love and serve him, as is represented and predicted in

Psalm 72:11: "All kings shall fall down before him; all nations shall serve him."

With v. 17: "Men shall be blessed in him; all nations shall call him blessed."

This oath to Jacob and Abraham is fulfilled in subduing men's iniquities; as is implied in that of the prophet Micah (Micah 7:19-20).

### Corol. 2. If God had no pre-knowledge, it would be based on conjecture.

*Corol.* 2. Hence also it appears, that first gospel promise that ever was made to mankind, that great prediction of the salvation of the Messiah, and his victory over Satan, made to our first parents (Genesis 3:15), if there be no certain prescience of the volitions of moral agents, must have no better foundation than conjecture. For Christ's victory over Satan consists in men's being saved from sin, and in the victory of virtue and holiness, over that vice and wickedness, which Satan by his temptation has introduced, and wherein his kingdom consists.

### 6. God predicts of men's events through his prescience and foreknowledge, which is connected with and depends on their volitions and voluntary actions.

6. If it be so, that God has not a prescience of the future actions of moral agents, it will follow, that the prophecies of Scripture in general are without foreknowledge. For Scripture-Prophecies, almost all of them, if not universally without any exception, are either predictions of the actings and behaviors of moral agents, or of events depending on them, or some way connected with them; judicial dispensations, judgments on men for their wickedness, or rewards of virtue and righteousness, remarkable manifestations of favor to the righteous, or manifestations of sovereign mercy to sinners, forgiving their iniquities, and magnifying the riches of divine grace; or dispensations of providence, in some respect or other, relating to the conduct of the subjects of God's moral government, wisely adapted thereto; either providing for what should be in a future state of things, through the volitions and voluntary actions of moral agents, or consequent upon them, and regulated and ordered according to them. So that all events that are foretold, are either moral events, or other events which are connected with, and accommodated to moral events.

### God, who foresees the volitions of men, can predict the future world history.

That the predictions of Scripture in general must be without knowledge, if God doesn't foresee the volitions of men, will further appear, if it be considered, that almost all events belonging to the future state of the world of mankind, the changes and revolutions which come to pass in empires, kingdoms, and nations, and all societies, depend innumerable ways on the acts of men's wills; yea, on an innumerable multitude of millions of millions of volitions of mankind. Such is the state and course of things in the world of mankind, that one single event, which appears in itself exceeding inconsiderable, may in the progress and series of things, occasion a succession of the greatest and most important and extensive events; causing the state of mankind to be vastly different from what it would otherwise have been, for all succeeding generations

### ILL: World conquerors followed innumerable acts of their parents' wills.

For instance, the coming into existence of those particular men, who have been the great conquerors of the world, which under God have had the main hand in all the consequent state of the world, in all after-ages; such as Nebuchadnezzar, Cyrus, Alexander, Pompey, Julius Caesar, etc.; undoubtedly depended on many millions of acts of the will, which followed, and were occasioned one by another, in their parents. And perhaps most of these volitions depended on millions of volitions of hundreds and thousands of others, their contemporaries of the same generation; and most of these on millions of millions of volitions of others in preceding generations. As we go back, still the number of volitions, which were some way the occasion of the event, multiply as the branches of a river, till they come at last, as it were, to an infinite number.

### JE: Innumerable preceding circumstances and occurrences bring out the things, and the latter occasions men's volitions.

This will not seem strange, to anyone who well considers the matter; if we recollect what philosophers tell us of the innumerable multitudes of those things which are as it were the *principia*, or *stamina vitae*, concerned in generation; the *animalcula* in *semine masculo*, and the *ova* in the womb of the female; the impregnation, or animating of one of these in distinction from all the rest, must depend on things infinitely minute, relating to the time and circumstances of the act of the parents, the state of their bodies, etc., which must depend on innumerable foregoing circumstances and occurrences; which must depend, infinite ways, on foregoing acts of their wills; which are occasioned by innumerable things that happen in the course of their lives, in which their own, and their neighbor's behavior, must have a hand, an infinite number of ways. And as the volitions of others must be so many ways concerned in the conception and birth of such men; so, no less, in their preservation, and circumstances of life, their particular determinations and actions, on which the great revolutions they were the occasions of, depended.

### ILL: The proposal that he whose horse neighed first should be a king came into a man's mind, and his volitions were concerned with it, and consequently, Dario I was chosen.

As for instance, when the conspirators in Persia, against the Magi, were consulting about a succession to the empire, it came into the mind of one of them, to propose, that he whose horse neighed first, when they came together the next morning, should be king. Now such a thing's coming into his mind, might depend on innumerable incidents, wherein the volitions of mankind had been concerned. But in consequence of this accident, Darius, the son of Histaspes, was king. And if this had not been, probably his successor would not have been the same, and all the circumstances of the Persian Empire might have been far otherwise. And then perhaps Alexander might never have conquered that empire. And then probably the circumstances of the world in all succeeding ages, might have been vastly otherwise.

### ILL: Alexander's preservation, the preservation and success of the Roman people, and the mighty revolutions depend on other foregoing occurrences so do depending on men's foregoing volitions.

I might further instance in many other occurrences; such as those on which depended Alexander's preservation, in the many critical junctures of his life, wherein a small trifle would have turned the scale against him; and the preservation and success of the Roman people, in the infancy of their kingdom and commonwealth, and afterwards; which all the succeeding changes in their state, and the mighty revolutions that afterwards came to pass in the habitable world, depended upon. But these hints may be sufficient for every discerning considerate person, to convince him, that the whole state of the world of mankind, in all ages, and the very being of every person who has ever lived in it, in every age, since the times of the ancient prophets, has depended on more volitions, or acts of the wills of men, than there are sands on the seashore.

### JE: God does exactly foresee the future acts of will and so does see their future events.

And therefore, unless God does most exactly and perfectly foresee the future acts of men's wills, all the predictions which he ever uttered concerning David, Hezekiah, Josiah, Nebuchadnezzar, Cyrus, Alexander; concerning the four monarchies, and the revolutions in them; and concerning all the wars, commotions, victories, prosperities and calamities, of any of the kingdoms, nations, or communities of the world, have all been without knowledge.

### Deistic Understanding of God: God does not foresee the volitions and free actions of men.

So that, according to this notion of God's not foreseeing the volitions and free actions of men, God could foresee nothing pertaining to the state of the world of mankind in future ages; not so much as the being of one person that should live in it; and could foreknow no events, but only such as he would bring to pass himself by the extraordinary interposition of his immediate power; or things which should come to pass in the natural material world, by the laws of motion, and course of nature, wherein that is independent on the actions or works of mankind: that is, as he might, like a very able mathematician and astronomer, with great exactness calculate the revolutions of the heavenly bodies, and the greater wheels of the machine of the external creation.

### Ar: He could not foresee anything.

And if we closely consider the matter, there will appear reason to convince us, that he could not with any absolute certainty foresee even these.

**Reason 1: Because God could not foresee the time of his interposition and the state of the moral world.**

As to the first, namely things done by the immediate and extraordinary interposition of God's power, these can't be foreseen, unless it can be foreseen when there shall be occasion for such extraordinary interposition. And that can't be foreseen, unless the state of the moral world can be foreseen. For whenever God thus interposes, it is with regard to the state of the moral world, requiring such divine interposition.

Thus God could not certainly foresee the universal deluge, the calling of Abraham, the destruction of Sodom and Gomorrah, the plagues on Egypt, and Israel's redemption out of it, the expelling the seven nations of Canaan, and the bringing Israel into that land; for these all are represented as connected with things belonging to the state of the moral world. Nor can God foreknow the most proper and convenient time of the day of judgment, and general conflagration; for that chiefly depends on the course and state of things in the moral world.

**Reason 2: Because God could not know men's volitions and the future state of the moral world.**

Nor, secondly, can we on this supposition reasonably think, that God can certainly foresee what things shall come to pass, in the course of things, in the natural and material world, even those which in an ordinary state of things might be calculated by a good astronomer. For the moral world is the end of the natural world; and the course of things in the latter, is undoubtedly subordinate to God's designs with respect to the former.[4] Therefore he has seen cause, from regard to the state of things in the moral world, extraordinarily to interpose, to interrupt and lay an arrest on the course of things in the natural world; and even in the greater wheels of its motion; even so as to stop the sun in its course. And unless he can foresee the volitions of men, and so know something of the future state of the moral world, he can't know but that he may still have as great occasion to interpose in this manner, as ever he had: nor can he foresee how, or when, he shall have occasion thus to interpose.

**Corol. 1. Consequently, if God does not foresee men's volitions, all his word would be false.**

Corol. 1. It appears from the things which have been observed, that unless God foresees the volitions of moral agents, that cannot be true which is observed by the apostle James, Acts 15:18, "Known unto God are all his works from the beginning of the world."

---

4. [Corrected from "former" and "latter."]

***Corol. 2. If God does not foresee men's volitions, all his prophecies would be mere conjecture.***

*Corol.* 2. It appears from what has been observed, that unless God foreknows the volitions of moral agents, all the prophecies of Scripture have no better foundation than mere conjecture; and that, in most instances, a conjecture which must have the utmost uncertainty; depending on an innumerable, and as it were infinite, multitude of volitions, which are all, even to God, uncertain events: however, these prophecies are delivered as absolute predictions, and very many of them in the most positive manner, with asseverations; and some of them with the most solemn oaths.

***Corol. 3. If the Arminians' notion is true, Christ would be a liar.***

*Corol.* 3. It also follows from what has been observed, that if this notion of God's ignorance of future volitions be true, in vain did Christ say (after uttering many great and important predictions, concerning God's moral kingdom, and things depending on men's moral actions), Matthew 24:35, "Heaven and earth shall pass away; but my words shall not pass away."

***Corol. 4. If God is ignorant, there would be no distinction from all other beings.***

*Corol.* 4. From the same notion of God's ignorance, it would follow, that in vain has God himself often spoken of the predictions of his Word, as evidences of his foreknowledge; and so as evidences of that which is his prerogative as GOD, and his peculiar glory, greatly distinguishing him from all other beings; as in Isaiah 41:22–26, 43:9–10, 44:8, 45:21, 46:10 and 48:14.

***Argument II. JE's Supralapsarianism: God foreknew the fall of man and angels and its results.*** [5]

---

5. [*FOW*, 267, 285–87, in "292. SUPRALAPSARIANS," *The "Miscellanies," WJE* 13:384, JE had pains to clear his position concerning what Francis Turretine (1623–1687) asks: Is the object of predestination "homo creabilis, aut labilis" (supralapsarianism), or is it "homo conditus, & lapsus" (infralapsarianism)? In Franciscus Turretinus, Loc. IV (*De prædestinatione*), *quæstio* 9 (1, 376–86). For JE it referred to "Turretinus, "De prædestinatione," q. 9, and Mastricht, "De prædestinatione," § 12," Lib. III, cap. 2 *Theoretico-practica theologia*, pp. 284–85, In that, Harry S. Stout argues that Turretine affirms infralapsarianism and yet Mastricht holds supralapsarianism, in which God predestined the elect and reprobate before creation and fall. Following after Petrus van Mastricht, JE declares so clearly his supralapsarianism in his MSC no. 292 and *FOW* that he could maintain consistency with his other doctrines.

Among the twentieth-century scholars, Conrad Cherry and Stephen Holmes demonstrated Edwards is supralapsarian. See Conrad Cherry, *The Theology of Jonathan Edwards: A Reappraisal* (Garden City, N.Y., 1966), 101, 102, 104, 189; Stephen R. Holmes, *God of grace & God of glory: An account of the theology of Jonathan Edwards* (A&C Black, 2000). Oliver Crisp was neutral, but now changed to this. See Oliver D. Crisp, *Revisioning Christology: Theology in the Reformed Tradition* (Ashgate Publishing, Ltd., 2011), 65.

On the contrary, John Gerstner, Michael McClymond, and Gerald McDermott identify JE as an infralapsarian. See John Gerstner, *The Rational Biblical Theology of Jonathan Edwards* (Ligonier: 1992), 2:161, 164; Michael J. McClymond and Gerald R. McDermott, *The Theology of Jonathan Edwards*

*Arg. II.* **If God doesn't foreknow the volitions of moral agents, then he did not foreknow the** *fall* **of man, nor of angels, and so could not foreknow the great things which are** *consequent* **on these events; such as**

*JE: God foreknew before the fall the great things which are consequent on the fall.*

his sending his Son into the world to die for sinners, and all things pertaining to the great work of redemption; all the things which were done for four thousand years before Christ came, to prepare the way for it; and the incarnation, life, death, resurrection and ascension of Christ; and the setting him at the head of the universe, as king of heaven and earth, angels and men; and the setting up his church and kingdom in this world, and appointing him the judge of the world; and all that Satan should do in the world in opposition to the kingdom of Christ: and the great transactions of the day of judgment, that men and devils shall be the subjects of, and angels concerned in;

*Supralapsarianism: Bible verses to attest.*

they are all what God was ignorant of before the fall. And if so, the following scriptures, and others like them, must be without any meaning, or contrary to truth:

Ephesians 1:4, "According as he hath chosen us in him before the foundation of the world."

I Peter 1:20: "Who verily was foreordained before the foundation of the world."

II Timothy 1:9, "Who hath saved us, and called us with an holy calling; not according to our works, but according to his own purpose, and grace, which was given us in Christ Jesus before the world began."

So, Ephesians 3:11 (speaking of the wisdom of God in the work of redemption), "According to the eternal purpose which he purposed in Christ Jesus."

Titus 1:2, "In hope of eternal life, which God, that cannot lie, promised before the world began."

Romans 8:29, "Whom he did foreknow, them he also did predestinate," etc.

I Peter 1:2, "Elect, according to the foreknowledge of God the Father."

*God foreknew the volitions of man after the fall.*

If God did not foreknow the fall of man, nor the redemption by Jesus Christ, nor the volitions of man since the fall; then he did not foreknow the saints in any sense; neither as particular persons, nor as societies or nations; either by election, or mere foresight of their virtue or good works; or any foresight of anything about them relating to their salvation; or any benefit they have by Christ, or any manner of concern of theirs with a Redeemer.

---

(New York: Oxford University Press, 2012), 335.

For further debate, see Douglas A. Sweeney, *Nathaniel Taylor, New Haven Theology, and the Legacy of Jonathan Edwards* (Oxford University Press, 2002), 214–16.]

Part II—Where It Is Considered, whether There Is, or Can Be Any Such Sort of Freedom of Will

### *Argument III. God seems to regret, yet eventually he could not regret but rule perfectly.*

Arg. III. On the supposition of God's ignorance of the future volitions of free agents, it will follow, that God must in many cases truly repent what he has done, so as properly to wish he had done otherwise: by reason that the event of things, in those affairs which are most important, viz. the affairs of his moral kingdom, being uncertain and contingent, often happens quite otherwise than he was aware beforehand. And there would be reason to understand that, in the most literal sense, in Genesis 6:6: "It repented the Lord, that he had made man on the earth, and it grieved him at his heart." And that, I Sam. 15:11, contrary to that, Numbers 23:19: "God is not the son of man, that he should repent." And, I Samuel 15:15, 29: "Also the Strength of Israel will not lie, nor repent: for he is not a man that he should repent."

Yea, from this notion it would follow, that God is liable to repent and be grieved at his heart, in a literal sense, continually; and is always exposed to an infinite number of real disappointments, in his governing the world; and to manifold, constant, great perplexity and vexation: but this is not very consistent with his title of "God over all, blessed for evermore"; which represents him as possessed of perfect, constant and uninterrupted tranquility and felicity, as God over the universe, and in his management of the affairs of the world, as supreme and universal ruler. See Romans 1:25, 9:5; II Corinthians 11:31; I Timothy 6:15.

### *Argument IV. God does neither repent nor alter, but he is immutable.*

Arg. IV. It will also follow from this notion, that

### *Ar: Due to the contingency and uncertainty of all things, God always changes his designs.*

as God is liable to be continually repenting what he has done; so he must be exposed to be constantly changing his mind and intentions, as to his future conduct; altering his measures, relinquishing his old designs, and forming new schemes and projections. For his purposes, even as to the main parts of his scheme, namely, such as belong to the state of his moral kingdom, must be always liable to be broken, through want of foresight; and he must be continually putting his system to rights, as it gets out of order, through the contingence of the actions of moral agents: he must be a being, who, instead of being absolutely immutable, must necessarily be the subject of infinitely the most numerous acts of repentance, and changes of intention, of any being whatsoever; for this plain reason, that his vastly extensive charge comprehends an infinitely greater number of those things which are to him contingent and uncertain.

In such a situation, he must have little else to do, but to mend broken links as well as he can, and be rectifying his disjointed frame and disordered movements, in the best manner the case will allow. The supreme Lord of all things must needs be under great and miserable disadvantages, in governing the world which he has made, and has the care of, through his being utterly unable to find out things of chief importance, which hereafter shall befall his system; which if he did but know, he might make seasonable provision for. In many cases, there may be very great necessity that he should make provision, in the manner of his ordering and disposing things, for some great events which are to happen, of vast and extensive influence, and endless consequence to the universe; which he may see afterwards, when it is too late, and may wish in vain that he had known beforehand, that he might have ordered his affairs accordingly. And it is in the power of man, on these principles, by his devices, purposes and actions, thus to disappoint God, break his measures, make him continually to change his mind, subject him to vexation, and bring him into confusion.

### JE: From the beginning to now, God accomplishes perfectly his plan.

But how do these things consist with reason, or with the Word of God? Which represents, that all God's works, all that he has ever to do, the whole scheme and series of his operations, are from the beginning perfectly in his view; and declares, that

> whatever "devices" and designs "are in the hearts of men, the counsel of the Lord is that which shall stand," and "the thoughts of his heart to all generations" (Proverbs 19:21, Psalm 33:10–11).
>
> "And that which the Lord of Hosts hath purposed, none shall disannul" (Isaiah 14:27).
>
> And that he cannot be frustrated "in one design or thought" (Job 42:2).
>
> "And that what God doth, it shall be forever, that nothing can be put to it, or taken from it" (Ecclesiastes 3:14).

The stability and perpetuity of God's counsels are expressly spoken of as connected with the foreknowledge of God (Isaiah 46:10),

> "Declaring the end from the beginning, and from ancient times the things that are not yet done; saying, my counsel shall stand, and I will do all my pleasure."

And how are these things consistent with what the Scripture says of God's immutability, which represents him as "without variableness, or shadow of turning"[6]; and speaks of him most particularly as unchangeable with regard to his purposes.

> Malachi 3:6, "I am the Lord; I change not; therefore ye sons of Jacob are not consumed." Exodus 3:14, "I AM THAT I AM."
>
> Job 23:13–14, "He is in one mind; and who can turn him? And what his soul desireth, even that he doth: for he performeth the thing that is appointed for me."

---

6. [James 1:17]

## Argument V. God foresaw the creation and fall and he performs the redemption of angels and men.

**Arg. V. If this notion of God's ignorance of the future volitions of moral agents be thoroughly considered in its consequences, it will appear to follow from it, that**

> God, after he had made the world, was liable to be wholly *frustrated of his end* in the creation of it; and so has been in like manner liable to be frustrated of his end in all the great works he hath wrought. It is manifest, the moral world is the end of the natural: the rest of the creation is but an house which God hath built, with furniture, for moral agents: and the good or bad state of the moral world depends on the improvement they make of their moral[7] agency, and so depends on their volitions. And therefore, if these can't be foreseen by God, because they are contingent, and subject to no kind of necessity, then the affairs of the moral world are liable to go wrong, to any assignable degree; yea, liable to be utterly ruined.

As on this scheme, it may well be supposed to be literally said, when mankind, by the abuse of their moral agency, became very corrupt before the flood, "that the Lord repented that he had made man on the earth, and it grieved him at his heart"; so, when he made the universe, he did not know but that he might be so disappointed in it, that it might grieve him at his heart that he had made it.

It actually proved, that all mankind became sinful, and a very great part of the angels apostatized:

> and how could God know beforehand, that all of them would not? And how could God know but that all mankind, notwithstanding means used to reclaim them, being still left to the freedom of their own will, would continue in their apostasy, and grow worse and worse, as they of the old world before the flood did?

**Ar: *Owing to the free will of angels and men, their moral agency was abused and corrupted, and so even God could not foreknow and he was totally disappointed.***

According to the scheme I am endeavoring to confute, neither the fall of men nor angels, could be foreseen, and God must be greatly disappointed in these events; and so the grand scheme and contrivance for our redemption, and destroying the works of the devil, by the Messiah, and all the great things God has done in the prosecution of these designs, must be only the fruits of his own disappointment, and contrivances of his to mend and patch up, as well as he could, his system, which originally was all very good, and perfectly beautiful; but was marred, broken and confounded by the free of angels and men.

---

7. [Corrected from "natural."]

And still he must be liable to be totally disappointed a second time: he could not know, that he should have his desired success, in the incarnation, life, death, resurrection and exaltation of his only begotten Son, and other great works accomplished to restore the state of things: he could not know after all, whether there would actually be any tolerable measure of restoration; for this depended on the free will of man.

***JE: How could God, without foreseeing men's volitions, know their repentance or not?***

There has been a general great apostasy of almost all the Christian world, to that which was worse than heathenism; which continued for many ages. And how could God, without foreseeing men's volitions, know whether ever Christendom would return from this apostasy? And which way could he tell beforehand how soon it would begin? The Apostle says, it began to work in his time; and how could it be known how far it would proceed in that age? Yea, how could it be known that the gospel, which was not effectual for the reformation of the Jews, would ever be effectual for the turning of the heathen nations from their heathen apostasy, which they had been confirmed in for so many ages?

It is represented often in Scripture, that God who made the world for himself, and created it for his pleasure, would infallibly obtain his end in the creation, and in all his works; that as all things are of him, so they would all be to him; and that in the final issue of things, it would appear that he is the first, and the last. Revelation 21:6: "And he said unto me, it is done. I am Alpha and Omega, the beginning and the end, the first and the last." But these things are not consistent with God's being so liable to be disappointed in all his works, nor indeed with his failing of his end in anything that he has undertaken, or done.

# Section 12

## God's Certain Foreknowledge of the Future Volitions of Moral Agents, Inconsistent with Such a Contingence of Those Volitions, as Is Without All Necessity

*JE: Men's volition or act or event is not contingent but foreknown by God and so it is necessary.*

Having proved, that God has a certain and infallible prescience of the acts of the will of moral agents, I come now, in the second place, to show the consequence; to show how it follows from hence, that these events are *necessary*, with a necessity of connection or consequence.

The chief Arminian divines, so far as I have had opportunity to observe, deny this consequence; and affirm, that if such foreknowledge be allowed, it is no evidence of any necessity of the event foreknown. Now I desire, that this matter may be particularly and thoroughly inquired into. I cannot but think, that on particular and full consideration, it may be perfectly determined, whether it be indeed so, or not.

In order to a proper consideration of this matter, I would observe the following things.

### I. *The existence of all things is necessary.*

I. It is very evident, with regard to a thing whose existence is infallibly and indissolubly connected with something which already hath, or has had existence, the existence of that thing is necessary. Here may be noted,

#### 1. *All things at present have existed from the past.*

1. I observed before, in explaining the nature of necessity, that in things which are past, their past existence is now necessary: having already made sure of existence, it

is too late for any possibility of alteration in that respect: it is now impossible, that it should be otherwise than true, that that thing has existed.

## 2. *The divine foreknowledge has also existed from the past.*

2. If there be any such thing as a divine foreknowledge of the volitions of free agents, that foreknowledge, by the supposition, is a thing which already has, and long ago had existence; and so, now its existence is necessary; it is now utterly impossible to be otherwise, than that this foreknowledge should be, or should have been.

## 3. *Those things which are indissolubly connected with other things that are necessary could not exist but are necessary.*

3. 'This also very manifest, that those things which are indissolubly connected with other things that are necessary, are themselves necessary.

As that proposition whose truth is necessarily connected with another proposition, which is necessarily true, is itself necessarily true. To say otherwise, would be a contradiction; it would be in effect to say, that the connection was indissoluble, and yet was not so, but might be broken. If that, whose existence is indissolubly connected with something whose existence is now necessary, is itself not necessary, then it may *possibly not exist*, notwithstanding that indissoluble connection of its existence.

Whether the absurdity is not glaring, let the reader judge.

## 4. *If there be an infallible foreknowledge of men's volitions, their events occur necessarily.*

4. It is no less evident, that if there be a full, certain and infallible foreknowledge of the future existence of the volitions of moral agents, then there is a certain infallible and indissoluble connection between those events and that foreknowledge; and that therefore, by the preceding observations, those events are necessary events; being infallibly and indissolubly connected with that whose existence already is, and so is now necessary, and can't but have been.

To say, the foreknowledge is certain and infallible, and yet the connection of the event with that foreknowledge is not indissoluble, but dissoluble and fallible, is very absurd. To affirm it, would be the same thing as to affirm, that there is no necessary connection between a proposition's being infallibly known to be true, and its being true indeed. So that it is perfectly demonstrable, that if there be any infallible knowledge of future volitions, the event is *necessary*; or, in other words, that it is *impossible* but the event should come to pass. For if it is not impossible but that it may be otherwise, then it is not impossible that the proposition which affirms its future coming to pass, may not now be true. But how absurd is that, on the supposition that there is now an infallible knowledge [i.e. knowledge which it is impossible should fail] that it is true. There is this absurdity in it, that it is not impossible but that there now should be no truth in that proposition, which is now infallibly known to be true.

***II. JE's objection against Arminians' supposition that it is a contradiction if a future event is possible to be foreknown and necessary, it must have evidence, and yet there is not anything.***

II. That (supposition) no future event can be certainly foreknown, whose existence is contingent, and without all necessity, may be proved thus;

***Ar: Any intellect comes to know things evidently with evidence: It is natural for it to be known as there it is.***

> it is impossible for a thing to be certainly known to any intellect without *evidence*. To suppose otherwise, implies a contradiction: because for a thing to be certainly known to any understanding, is for it to be *evident* to that understanding: and for a thing to be evident to any understanding, is the same thing, as for that understanding to *see evidence* of it:

> but no understanding, created or increated, can see evidence where there is none: for that is the same thing, as to see that to be, which is not. And therefore, if there be any truth which is absolutely without evidence, that truth is absolutely unknowable, insomuch that it implies a contradiction to suppose that it is known.

***JE: If a future event is contingent and unnecessary, neither self-evidence or proof is impossible, and yet it is necessary, then it is possible and now possible to foreknow it.***

But if there be any future event, whose existence is contingent, without all necessity, the future existence of that event is absolutely *without evidence*. If there be any evidence of it, it must be one of these two sorts, either *self-evidence*, or proof; for there can be no other sort of evidence but one of these two; an evident thing must be either evident *in itself*, or evident *in something else*; that is, evident by connection with something else. But a future thing, whose existence is without all necessity, can have neither of these sorts of evidence. It can't be self-evident: for if it be, it may be now known by what is now to be seen in the thing itself; either its present existence, or the necessity of its nature: but both these are contrary to the supposition. It is supposed, both that the thing has no present existence to be seen; and also that it is not of such a nature as to be necessarily existent for the future: so that its future existence is not self-evident. And secondly, neither is there any proof, or evidence in anything else, or evidence of connection with something else that is evident; for this also is contrary to the supposition. It is supposed, that there is now nothing existent, with which the future existence of the *contingent* event is connected. For such a connection destroys its contingence, and supposes necessity. Thus it is demonstrated, that there is in the nature of things absolutely no evidence at all of the future existence of that event, which is contingent, without all necessity (if any such event there be); neither self-evidence nor proof. And therefore the thing in reality is not evident; and so can't be seen to be evident, or, which is the same thing, can't be known.

*Ar: God's creation is in absolute contingence.*

Let us consider this in an example. Suppose that five thousand seven hundred and sixty years ago, there was no other being but the divine Being; and then this world, or some particular body or spirit, all at once starts out of nothing into being, and takes on itself a particular nature and form; all in *absolute contingence*, without any concern of God, or any other cause, in the matter; without any manner of ground or reason of its existence; or any dependence upon, or connection at all with anything foregoing:

*JE: It is fair that there is no any evidence in an event: If an event did not happen yet, there would not be any evidence.*

I say, that if this be supposed, there was no evidence of that event beforehand. There was no evidence of it to be seen *in the thing itself*; for the thing itself, as yet, was not. And there was no evidence of it to be seen *in anything else*; for evidence in something else, is *connection with* something else: but such connection is contrary to the supposition. There was no evidence before, that this thing *would happen*; for by the supposition,

*Ar's sophistry: The reason why there is no evidence is that there is no reason why a certain thing should happen; why the thing happens without cause is that all things are same.*

> there was no reason why it *should happen*, rather than something else, or rather than nothing. And if so, then all things before were exactly equal, and the same, with respect to that and other possible things; there was no preponderation, no superior weight or value; and therefore nothing that could be of any weight or value to determine any understanding. The thing was absolutely without evidence, and absolutely unknowable.

*JE's Objection: Even if men's understanding and discerning and sight are unlimited and they might discern evidence, they would not be perfectly able to do so.*

An increase of understanding, or of the capacity of discerning, has no tendency, and makes no advance, to a discerning any signs or evidences of it, let it be increased never so much; yea, if it be increased infinitely. The increase of the strength of sight may have a tendency to enable to discern the evidence which is far off, and very much hid, and deeply involved in clouds and darkness; but it has no tendency to enable to discern evidence where there is none. If the sight be infinitely strong, and the capacity of discerning infinitely great, it will enable a being to see all that there is, and to see it perfectly, and with ease; yet it has no tendency at all to enable a being to discern that evidence which is not; but on the contrary, it has a tendency to enable to discern with great certainty that there is none.

### III. Ar's Supposition: *The future volitions of men are not necessary and that they may not happen, and yet God certainly foreknows them.*

### JE's Objection: *That is to say that God's foreknowledge is inconsistent with itself.*

### III. To suppose the future volitions of moral agents not to be necessary events;

### Ar: *Events may not happen.*

or, which is the same thing, events which it is not impossible but that they may not come to pass; and yet to suppose that God certainly foreknows them, and knows all things; is to suppose God's knowledge to be inconsistent with itself.

### Ar: *A thing will infallibly be, or it may possibly not be.*

For to say, that God certainly, and without all conjecture, knows that a thing will infallibly be, which at the same time he knows to be so contingent, that it may possibly not be, is to suppose his knowledge inconsistent with itself; or that one thing that he knows is utterly inconsistent with another thing that he knows. It is the same thing as to say, he now knows a proposition to be of certain infallible truth, which he knows to be of contingent uncertain truth.

### Ar's Uncertain Proposition: *As a future volition is so without all necessity, there is nothing to hinder men's volition, but later it may not be so.*

If a future volition is so without all necessity, that there is nothing hinders but that it may not be, then the proposition which asserts its future existence, is so uncertain, that there is nothing hinders but that the truth of it may entirely fail. And if God knows all things, he knows this proposition to be thus uncertain.

### Ar's Inconsistent Proposition: *Such an uncertain proposition is inconsistent with God's knowing that it is infallibly true.*

And that is inconsistent with his knowing that it is infallibly true; and so inconsistent with his infallibly knowing that it is true. If the thing be indeed contingent, God views it so, and judges it to be contingent, if he views things as they are. If the event be not necessary, then it is possible it may never be: and if it be possible that it may never be, God knows it may possibly never be; and that is to know that the proposition which affirms its existence, may possibly not be true; and that is to know that the truth of it is uncertain; which surely is inconsistent with his knowing it as a certain truth.

Section 12—God's Certain Foreknowledge of the Future Volitions of Moral Agents

***Ar's Absurd Contradiction: God may have ways of knowing unexpected events; God may know contradiction to be true; he may know a thing to be certain, and at the same time he knows it not to be certain.***

If volitions are in themselves contingent events, without all necessity, then it is no argument of perfection of knowledge in any being to determine peremptorily that they will be; but on the contrary, an argument of ignorance and mistake: because it would argue, that he supposes that proposition to be certain, which in its own nature, and all things considered, is uncertain and contingent. To say in such a case, that God may have ways of knowing contingent events which we can't conceive of, is ridiculous; as much so, as to say, that God may know contradictions to be true, for ought we know, or that he may know a thing to be certain, and at the same time know it not to be certain, though we can't conceive how; because he has ways of knowing, which we can't comprehend.

***JE: Though, human freedom is not restricted by the absolute decree and foreknowledge of God.***

*Corol. 1.* From what has been observed it is evident, that the absolute *decrees* of God are no more inconsistent with human liberty, on account of any necessity of the event which follows from such decrees, than the absolute *foreknowledge* of God. Because the connection between the event and certain foreknowledge, is as infallible and indissoluble, as between the event and an absolute decree. That is, it is no more impossible that the event and decree should not agree together, than that the event and absolute knowledge should disagree. The connection between the event and foreknowledge is absolutely perfect, by the supposition: because it is supposed, that the certainty and infallibility of the knowledge is absolutely perfect. And it being so, the certainty can't be increased; and therefore the connection between the knowledge and thing known, can't be increased; so that if a decree be added to the foreknowledge, it doesn't at all increase the connection, or make it more infallible and indissoluble. If it were not so, the certainty of knowledge might be increased by the addition of a decree; which is contrary to the supposition, which is, that the knowledge is absolutely perfect, or perfect to the highest possible degree.

There is as much of an impossibility but that the things which are infallibly foreknown, should be, or (which is the same thing) as great a necessity of their future existence, as if the event were already written down, and was known and read by all mankind, through all preceding ages, and there were the most indissoluble and perfect connection possible, between the writing, and the thing written. In such a case, it would be as impossible the event should fail of existence, as if it had existed already; and a decree can't make an event surer or more necessary than this.

***JE: The necessity does not restrict human freedom.***

And therefore, if there be any such foreknowledge, as it has been proved there is, then necessity of connection and consequence, is not at all inconsistent with any liberty which man, or any other creature enjoys. And from hence it may be inferred, that absolute decrees of God, which don't at all increase the necessity, are not at all inconsistent with the liberty which man enjoys, on any such account, as that they make the event decreed necessary, and render it utterly impossible but that it should come to pass. Therefore, if absolute decrees are inconsistent with man's liberty as a moral agent, or his liberty in a state of probation, or any liberty whatsoever that he enjoys, it is not on account of any necessity which absolute decrees infer.

**DW: *God's foreknowledge does not influence his actions nor diminish that freedom, and yet his decree is active and unfrustrably produces its end.***

Dr. Whitby supposes, there is a great difference between God's foreknowledge, and his decrees, with regard to necessity of future events. In his *Discourse on the Five Points*, p. 474, etc.[1] he says,

> God's prescience has no influence at all on our actions. . . . Should God (says he) by immediate revelation, give me the knowledge of the event of any man's state or actions, would my knowledge of them have any influence upon his actions? Surely none at all. . . . Our knowledge doth not affect the things we know, to make them more certain, or more future, than they would be without it. Now foreknowledge in God is knowledge. As therefore knowledge has no influence on things that are, so neither has foreknowledge on things that shall be. And consequently, the foreknowledge of any action that would be otherwise free, cannot alter or diminish that freedom. Whereas God's decree of election is powerful and active, and comprehends the preparation and exhibition of such means, as shall unfrustrably produce the end. Hence, God's prescience renders no actions necessary.

**DW: *Agreeing with Origen and Blanc and Clarke, God's prescience is not the cause of future things.***

And to this purpose [p. 473], he cites Origen[2], where he says, "God's prescience is not the cause of things future, but their being future is the cause of God's prescience that they will be": and Le Blanc[3], where he says, "This is the truest resolution of this

---

1. Whitby, *Discourse on the Five Points*, Dis. VI, ch. 1, pp. 474–75. As Ramsey found, Whitby cites Cicero, *De* divination, 1. 2. n. 14.

2. [Origen (Origenes Adamantius) C.185-c.254, born in Alexandria, Egypt): As a Neoplatonic, he maintained that the soul is divided into the rational and the irrational, while the former, immaterial, possesses the freedom of the will, and the power to reascend to purer life. To him the freedom of the will is an essential fact of the reason, notwithstanding the foreknowledge of God. See Michael Frede, *A Free Will: Origins of the Notion in Ancient Thought* (University of California Press, 2011), 102–11.]

3. [Louis le Blanc de Beaulieu (1614-1675), a French professor at the Academy of Sedan, was born

difficulty, that prescience is not the cause that things are future; but their being future is the cause they are foreseen." In like manner Dr. Clarke[4], in his *Demonstration of the Being and Attributes of God* [pp. 95–99], and the author (Isaac Watts) of *The Freedom of Will, in God and the Creature*, speaking to the like purpose[5] with Dr. Whitby, represents foreknowledge as having no more influence on things known, to make them necessary, than after-knowledge, or to that purpose.[6]

**Ar's Evasion: *God's absolute fore/preknowledge may prove the necessity of an event, and yet not be a cause to influence the event.***

To all which I would say; that what is said about knowledge, its not having influence on the thing known to make it necessary, is nothing to the purpose, nor does it in the least affect the foregoing reasoning. Whether prescience be the thing that *makes* the event necessary or no, it alters not the case. Infallible foreknowledge may *prove* the necessity of the event foreknown, and yet not be the thing which *causes* the necessity. If the foreknowledge be absolute, this proves the event known to be necessary, or proves that it is impossible but that the event should be, by some means or other, either by a decree, or some other way, if there be any other way: because, as was said before, it is absurd to say, that a proposition is known to be certainly and infallibly true, which yet may possibly prove not true.

**Ar's Evasion: *God's absolute foreknowledge is not a cause of the necessity of an event, nor proves the necessity.***

The whole of the seeming force of this evasion lies in this; that, inasmuch as certain foreknowledge doesn't *cause* an event to be necessary, as a decree does; therefore it doesn't *prove* it to be necessary, as a decree does. But there is no force in this arguing:

---

at Beaulieu. He offered a plan for the union of Catholics and Protestants, but his negotiations did not succeed. He left, Sermons, a Traite de l'Oigin aie la Sainte Ecriture (London, 1660), and a collection entitled Theses Sedanenses (Sedan, 1675). See Hoefer, Nouv. Biog. Generale, s. v. http://www.biblical-cyclopedia.com/B/beaulieu-louis-le-blanc-de.html]

4. [Samuel Clarke (1675–1729) was influenced most by Isaac Newton, and held natural religion is contrary to naturalism, and Christian faith is so to Deism, and yet he was charged an enemy of JE for his doctrine of the will.]

5. [In JE's view these three authors represent the so called "Open Theism," also known as "openness theology" and the "openness of God," that is the typical Arminian supposition that God does not control the universe but leaves it "open" for men to make significant choices.]

6. [Ramsey's footnote is revised by *WJE Online* editor as follows: In these pages of *Freedom of Will*, Watts is treating difficulties that arise from the hypothesis that all things are determined by "superior fitness" (p. 94). The phrases JE provides are perhaps not direct quotes, for there are no passages resembling them in Watts' treatise. It is possible that JE has more immediately in mind Clarke's *Demonstration*, not pp. 95–99, as cited here (which discuss ideas such as the trinity and substance), but pp. 209–18, which deal precisely with "The Certainty of Divine Foreknowledge not inconsistent with the Liberty of Men's Actions." See also Turnbull, *Principles*, 2:135–38, who takes the same position as the authors JE quotes at this point: "knowledge of no kind, neither knowledge of present, past, nor to come, can have any productive efficiency" (p. 135), and suchlike statements.]

Part II—Where It Is Considered, whether There Is, or Can Be Any Such Sort of Freedom of Will

***Ar's Evasion: A thing cannot prove the necessity, there is no an evidence to prove it, but the evidence of a causal influence alone can make it so.***

for it is built wholly on this supposition, that nothing can prove, or be an evidence of a thing's being necessary, but that which has a causal influence to make it so. But this can never be maintained.

***JE: God's foreknowledge can prove the possibility and impossibility of an event and can be a cause of the (im)possibilities.***

If certain foreknowledge of the future existing of an event, be not the thing which first *makes* it impossible that it should fail of existence; yet it may, and certainly does *demonstrate*, that it is impossible it should fail of it, however that impossibility comes. If foreknowledge be not the cause, but the effect of this impossibility, it may prove that there is such an impossibility, as much as if it were the cause.

***JE: It is impossible that a thing infallibly foreknown would not occur.***

It is as strong arguing from the effect to the cause, as from the cause to the effect. It is enough, that an existence which is infallibly foreknown, cannot fail, whether that impossibility arises from the foreknowledge, or is prior to it. It is as evident, as it is possible anything should be, that it is impossible a thing which is infallibly known to be true, should prove not to be true: therefore there is a necessity that it should not be otherwise;[7] whether the knowledge be the cause of this necessity, or the necessity the cause of the knowledge.

***JE: All certain knowledge, whether it be foreknowledge or after-knowledge, proves the truth of the proposition, consisting in the impossibility of the nonexistence of the event.***

All certain knowledge, whether it be foreknowledge or after-knowledge, or concomitant knowledge, proves the thing known now to be necessary, by some means or other; or proves that it is impossible it should now be otherwise than true. I freely allow, that foreknowledge doesn't prove a thing to be necessary any more than after-knowledge: but then after-knowledge which is certain and infallible, proves that it is now become impossible but that the proposition known should be true. Certain after-knowledge proves that it is now, in the time of the knowledge, by some means or other, become impossible but that the proposition which predicates *past* existence on the event, should be true. And so does certain foreknowledge prove, that now, in the time of the knowledge, it is by some means or other, become impossible but that the proposition which predicates *future* existence on the event, should be true. The necessity of the

---

7. [*WJE Online* adds a footnote as follows: This slight correction of the text (1754 ed., p. 124) is needed to restore JE's meaning. The Worcester ed. reads, "Therefore there is a *Necessity* connected with such knowledge"; and here for once the Dwight edition sticks closer to the original by repeating the error, which must simply have been a slip on JE's part, or his printer's.]

truth of the propositions, consisting in the present impossibility of the nonexistence of the event affirmed, in both cases, is the immediate ground of the certainty of the knowledge; there can be no certainty of knowledge without it.

***JE's arguing from the effect to the cause: Certainty of knowledge is from the certainty that is in the things themselves which are known; observing the things known is discerning whether foreknowledge is true or not.***

There must be a certainty in things themselves, before they are certainly known, or (which is the same thing) known to be certain. For certainty of knowledge is nothing else but knowing or discerning the certainty there is in the things themselves which are known. Therefore, there must be a certainty in things to be a ground of certainty of knowledge, and to render things capable of being known to be certain. And this is nothing but the necessity of the truth known, or its being impossible but that it should be true; or, in other words, the firm and infallible connection between the subject and predicate of the proposition that contains that truth.

***JE's propositional logic consists of a subject and predicate, in which the subject is that the event is possible, and the predicate is that the event will occur (exist) in the future. Therefore, the event will occur necessarily in the future.***

All certainty of knowledge consists in the view of the firmness of that connection. So God's certain foreknowledge of the future existence of any event, is his view of the firm and indissoluble connection of the subject and predicate of the proposition that affirms its future existence. The subject is that possible event; the predicate is its future existing: but if future existence be firmly and indissolubly connected with that event, then the future existence of that event is necessary. If God certainly knows the future existence of an event which is wholly contingent, and may possibly never be, then he sees a firm connection between a subject and predicate that are not firmly connected; which is a contradiction.

***JE: "Mere" knowledge doesn't affect the thing known, to make it more certain or more future. But "certain" knowledge supposes certain future, and the thing proves it true.***

I allow what Dr. Whitby says to be true, that mere "knowledge doesn't affect the thing known, to make it more certain or more future." But yet, I say, it supposes and proves the thing to be *already*, both future, and certain; i.e. necessarily future. Knowledge of futurity, supposes futurity; and a *certain knowledge* of futurity, supposes *certain futurity*, antecedent to that certain knowledge. But there is no other certain futurity of a thing, antecedent to certainty of knowledge, than a prior impossibility but that the thing should prove true; or (which is the same thing) the necessity of the event.

***Ar: As the cause, the future existence of the event has produced an effect, viz. prescience.***

I would observe one thing further concerning this matter, and it is this; that if it be as those aforementioned writers suppose, that God's foreknowledge is not the cause, but the effect of the existence of the event foreknown; this is so far from showing that this foreknowledge doesn't infer the necessity of the existence of that event, that it rather shows the contrary the more plainly. Because it shows the existence of the event to be so settled and firm, that it is as if it had already been; inasmuch as *in effect* it actually exists already; its future existence has already had actual influence and efficiency, and has *produced an effect*, viz. prescience: the effect exists already; and as the effect supposes the cause, is connected with the cause, and depends entirely upon it, therefore it is as if the future event, which is the cause, had existed already. The effect is firm as possible, it having already the possession of existence, and has made sure of it. But the effect can't be more firm and stable than its cause, ground and reason. The building can't be firmer than the foundation.

**ILL: *The prescience as the cause has produced an effect, viz. the event's future existence: When the heavenly bodies as the cause are to be projected in the telescope, their images are caught as the effect. The images are the antecedent effects because the perfect ideas of the images are in the divine mind.***

To illustrate this matter, let us suppose the appearances and images of things in a glass; for instance, a reflecting telescope, to be the real effects of heavenly bodies (at a distance, and out of sight) which they resemble: if it be so, then, as these images in the telescope have had a past actual existence, and it is become utterly impossible now that it should be otherwise than that they have existed; so they being the true effects of the heavenly bodies they resemble, this proves the existing of those heavenly bodies to be as real, infallible, firm and necessary, as the existing of these effects; the one being connected with, and wholly depending on the other.

**JE: *The future existence of things is a cause and influences necessary images to be an effect.***

Now let us suppose future existences some way or other to have influence back, to produce effects beforehand, and cause exact and perfect images of themselves in a glass, a thousand years before they exist, yea, in all preceding ages; but yet that these images are real effects of these future existences, perfectly dependent on, and connected with their cause; these effects and images, having already had actual existence, rendering that matter of their existing perfectly firm and stable, and utterly impossible to be otherwise; this proves in like manner as in the other instance, that the existence of the things which are their causes, is also equally sure, firm and necessary; and that it is alike impossible but that they should be, as if they had been already, as their effects have. And if instead of images in a glass, we suppose the antecedent effects to be perfect ideas of them in the divine mind, which have existed there from all eternity, which are as properly effects, as truly and properly connected with their cause, the case is not altered.

***Ar: The foreknowledge of God is irrational, and he had the most perfect knowledge of all events but he no longer has it.***

Another thing which has been said by some Arminians, to take off the force of what is urged from God's prescience, against the contingence of the volitions of moral agents, is to this purpose; "That when we talk of foreknowledge in God, there is no strict propriety in our so speaking; and that although it be true, that there is in God the most perfect knowledge of all events from eternity to eternity, yet there is no such thing as *before* and *after* in God, but he sees all things by one perfect unchangeable view, without any succession."

***JE: 1. His foreknowledge proves that the known truth came to pass and it exists.***

To this I answer, 1. It has been already shown, that all certain knowledge proves the necessity of the truth known; whether it be before, after, or at the same time. Though it be true, that there is no succession in God's knowledge, and the manner of his knowledge is to us inconceivable, yet thus much we know concerning it, that there is no event, past, present, or to come, that God is ever uncertain of; he never is, never was, and never will be without infallible knowledge of it; he always sees the existence of it to be certain and infallible.

***JE: There is never anything contingent. The reason why the foreknowledge seems to be not in God is because things and events look like future to men and past and present to him.***

And as he always sees things just as they are in truth; hence there never is in reality anything contingent in such a sense, as that possibly it may happen never to exist. If, strictly speaking, there is no foreknowledge in God, it is because those things which are future to us, are as present to God, as if they already had existence: and that is as much as to say, that future events are always in God's view as evident, clear, sure and necessary, as if they already were. If there never is a time wherein the existence of the event is not present with God, then there never is a time wherein it is not as much impossible for it to fail of existence, as if its existence were present, and were already come to pass.

***JE: God, who views things perfectly, knows the actions of men.***

God's viewing things so perfectly and unchangeably as that there is no succession in his ideas or judgment, doesn't hinder but that there is properly now, in the mind of God, a certain and perfect knowledge of the moral actions of men, which to us are an hundred years hence: yea, the objection supposes this; and therefore it certainly doesn't hinder but that, by the foregoing arguments, it is now impossible these moral actions should not come to pass.

**JE: If God's foreknowledge of actions of men and their events is infallible, they will occur necessarily. Thus, there is an infallible necessary connection between both the foreknowledge and actions or events.**

We know, that God knows the future voluntary actions of men in such a sense beforehand,[8] as that he is able particularly to declare, and foretell them, and write them, or cause them to be written down in a Book, as he often has done; and that therefore the necessary connection which there is between God's knowledge and the event known, does as much prove the event to be necessary beforehand, as if the divine knowledge were in the same sense before the event, as the prediction or writing is. If the knowledge be infallible, then the expression of it in the written prediction is infallible; that is, there is an infallible connection between that written prediction and the event. And if so, then it is impossible it should ever be otherwise, than that that prediction and the event should agree: and this is the same thing as to say, it is impossible but that the event should come to pass: and this is the same as to say, that its coming to pass is necessary. So that it is manifest, that there being no proper succession in God's mind, makes no alteration as to the necessity of the existence of the events which God knows. Yea,

**JE: 2. His foreknowledge proves that it is perfect, and it is impossible for things to not exist.**

2. This[9] is so far from weakening the proof, which has been given of the impossibility of the not coming to pass of future events known, as that it establishes that wherein the strength of the foregoing arguments consists, and shows the clearness of the evidence. For,

**JE's Objection: God's foreknowledge is perfectly certain, and its change is impossible.**

(1) The very reason why God's knowledge is without succession, is, because it is absolutely perfect, to the highest possible degree of clearness and certainty:

all things, whether past, present or to come, being viewed with equal evidence and fullness; future things being seen with as much clearness, as if they were present; the view is always in absolute perfection; and absolute constant perfection admits of no alteration, and so no succession; the actual existence of the thing known, doesn't at all increase, or add to the clearness or certainty of the thing known: God calls the things that are not, as though they were; they are all one to him as if they had already

---

8. [JE clearly states supralapsarianism.]

9. ["This" indicates Arminians' argument mentioned before "1." of this section: *Ar: The foreknowledge of God is irrational, and He had the most perfect knowledge of all events but He no longer has it.*]

existed. But herein consists the strength of the demonstration before given, of the impossibility of the not existing of those things whose existence God knows; that it is as impossible they should fail of existence, as if they existed already. This objection, instead of weakening this argument, sets it in the clearest and strongest light; for it supposes it to be so indeed, that the existence of future events is in God's view so much as if it already had been, that when they come actually to exist, it makes not the least alteration or variation in his view or knowledge of them.

### *JE's Objection: As God himself is immutable, so his knowledge is immutable and its change is impossible.*

(2) The objection is founded on the *immutability* of God's knowledge: for it is the immutability of knowledge [that] makes his knowledge to be without succession. But this most directly and plainly demonstrates the thing I insist on, viz. that it is utterly impossible the known events should fail of existence. For if that were possible, then it would be possible for there to be a change in God's knowledge and view of things. For if the known event should fail of existence, and not come into being, as God expected, then God would see it, and so would change his mind, and see his former mistake; and thus there would be change and succession in his knowledge. But as God is immutable, and so it is utterly and infinitely impossible that his view should be changed; so it is, for the same reason, just so impossible that the foreknown event should not exist: and that is to be impossible in the highest degree: and therefore the contrary is necessary. Nothing is more impossible than that the immutable God should be changed, by the succession of time; who comprehends all things, from eternity to eternity, in one, most perfect, and unalterable view; so that his whole eternal duration is *vitae interminabilis, tota, simul*, and *perfecta possessio*.

On the whole, I need not fear to say, that there is no geometrical theorem or proposition whatsoever, more capable of strict demonstration, than that God's certain prescience of the volitions of moral agents is inconsistent with such a contingence of these events, as is without all necessity; and so is inconsistent with the Arminian notion of liberty.

### *Corol. 2. Calvinist doctrine of decrees is different from Arminian fatalism.*

*Corol. 2.* Hence the doctrine of the Calvinists, concerning the absolute decrees of God, does not at all infer any more fatality in things, than will demonstrably follow from the doctrine of most Arminian divines, who acknowledge God's omniscience, and universal prescience. Therefore, all objections they make against the doctrine of the Calvinists, as implying Hobbes' doctrine of necessity, or the Stoical doctrine of fate, lie no more against the doctrine of Calvinists, than their own doctrine: and therefore it doesn't become those divines, to raise such an outcry against the Calvinists, on this account.

***Corol. 3.** Calvinists assert that unregenerate men are unable to perform the conditions of salvation and are not under any coaction, yet under necessity. But Arminians object it by insisting that Calvinistic doctrines are inconsistent with human liberty, because they infer necessity.*

*Corol.* 3. Hence all arguing from necessity, against the doctrine of the inability of unregenerate men to perform the conditions of salvation, and the commands of God requiring spiritual duties, and against the Calvinistic doctrine of efficacious grace; I say, all arguings of Arminians (such of them as own God's omniscience) against these things, on this ground, that these doctrines, though they don't suppose men to be under any constraint or coaction, yet suppose them under necessity, with respect to their moral actions, and those things which are required of them in order to their acceptance with God;

and their arguing against the necessity of men's volitions, taken from the reasonableness of God's commands, promises, and threatenings, and the sincerity of his counsels and invitations;

and all objections against any doctrines of the Calvinists as being inconsistent with human liberty, because they infer necessity;

I say, all these arguments and objections must fall to the ground, and be justly esteemed vain and frivolous, as coming from them; being maintained in an inconsistence with themselves, and in like manner leveled against their own doctrine, as against the doctrine of the Calvinists.

# Section 13

## Whether We Suppose the Volitions of Moral Agents to be Connected with Anything Antecedent, or Not, Yet They Must be Necessary in Such a Sense as to Overthrow Arminian Liberty

***JE: The will itself is a cause of all acts of the will, and its effects are necessary and consequent and passive.***

Every act of the will has a cause, or it has not.

If it has a cause, then, according to what has already been demonstrated, it is not contingent, but necessary; the effect being necessarily dependent and consequent on its cause; and that, let the cause be what it will. If the cause is the will itself, by antecedent acts choosing and determining; still the *determined* and *caused* act must be a necessary effect. The act that is the determined effect of the foregoing act which is its cause, can't prevent the efficiency of its cause; but must be wholly subject to its determination and command, as much as the motions of the hands and feet: the consequent commanded acts of the will are as passive and as necessary,[1] with respect to the antecedent determining acts, as the parts of the body are to the volitions which determine and command them.

***JE: The free acts of the will are determined by the will itself, and so they are free; likewise, they are determined by an antecedent act, and so they are necessary; therefore the free acts are necessary.***

And therefore, if all the free acts of the will are thus, if they are all determined effects, determined by the will itself, that is, determined by antecedent choice, then they are

---

1. ["EFFICACIOUS GRACE. We are not merely passive in it, nor yet does God do some and we do the rest, but God does all and we do all. God produces all and we act all. For that is what he produces, our own acts. God is the only proper author and fountain; we only are the proper actors. We are in different respects wholly passive and wholly active." *WJE* 21:251.]

all necessary; they are all subject to, and decisively fixed by the foregoing act, which is their cause: yea, even the determining act itself; for that must be determined and fixed by another act, preceding that, if it be a free and voluntary act; and so must be necessary. So that by this all the free acts of the will are necessary, and can't be free unless they are necessary: because they can't be free, according to the Arminian notion of freedom, unless they are determined by the will; which is to be determined by antecedent choice; which being their cause, proves them necessary. And yet they say, necessity is utterly inconsistent with liberty. So that, by their scheme, the acts of the will can't be free unless they are necessary, and yet cannot be free if they be necessary![2]

### *Ar: The will is the subject, and so it does not need any cause but is free.*

### *JE: Contrary to what it insists, the will is not active in determining but passive.*

But if the other part of the dilemma be taken, and it be affirmed that the free acts of the will have no cause, and are connected with nothing whatsoever that goes before them and determines them, in order to maintain their proper and absolute contingence, and this should be allowed to be possible; still it will not serve their turn. For if the volition comes to pass by perfect contingence, and without any cause at all, then it is certain, no act of the will, no prior act of the soul was the cause, no determination or choice of the soul, had any hand in it. The will, or the soul, was indeed the subject of what happened to it accidentally, but was not the cause. The will is not active in causing or determining, but purely the passive subject; at least according to their notion of action and passion.

### *Ar: The will determines as it pleases, and its act is not necessary but contingent, for there is no cause or order in its determination.*

In this case, contingence does as much to prevent the determination of the will, as a proper cause; and as to the will, it was necessary, and could be no otherwise. For to suppose that it could have been otherwise, if the will or soul had pleased, is to suppose that the act is dependent on some prior act of choice or pleasure; contrary to what now is supposed: it is to suppose that it might have been otherwise, if its cause had made it or ordered it otherwise. But this doesn't agree to its having no cause or orderer at all. That must be necessary as to the soul, which is dependent on no free act of the soul: but that which is without a cause, is dependent on no free act of the soul: because, by the supposition, it is dependent on nothing, and is connected with nothing.

### *What does the liberty mean by Arminians?*

In such a case, the soul is necessarily subjected to what accident brings to pass, from time to time, as much as the earth, that is inactive, is necessarily subjected to what falls upon it. But this doesn't consist with the Arminian notion of liberty, which is the

2. [Corrected as "if they be not necessary."]

will's power of determining itself in its own acts, and being wholly active in it, without passiveness, and without being subject to necessity. Thus, contingence belongs to the Arminian notion of liberty, and yet is inconsistent with it.

I would here observe, that the author of the *Essay on the Freedom of Will, in God and the Creature* (pp. 76, 77)[3] says as follows,

### What does the chance mean by Arminians?

> "The word 'chance' always means something done without design. Chance and design stand in direct opposition to each other: and chance can never be properly applied to the acts of the will, which is the spring of all design, and which designs to choose whatsoever it doth choose, whether there be any superior fitness in the thing which it chooses, or no; and it designs to determine itself to one thing, where two things perfectly equal are proposed, merely because it will."

### Isaac Watts: *The will is the spring of all design to choose and determine, and sometimes its act occurs without any spring and by chance.*

### JE: *The design regresses to a foregoing design determining that and then to another.*

But herein appears a very great inadvertence in this author. For if "the will be the spring of all design," as he says, then certainly it is not always the effect of design; and the acts of the will themselves must sometimes come to pass when they don't *spring from* design; and consequently come to pass by chance, according to his own definition of chance. And if "the will designs to choose whatsoever it does choose, and designs to determine itself," as he says, then it designs to determine all its designs. Which carries us back from one design to a foregoing design determining that, and to another determining that; and so on *in infinitum*. The very first design must be the effect of foregoing design, or else it must be by chance, in his notion of it.

### JE: *The acts of the will are connected with their foregoing cause, and its liberty comes from the volitions being necessarily connected with the views of the understanding.*

Here another alternative may be proposed, relating to the connection of the acts of the will with something foregoing that is their cause, not much unlike to the other; which is this: either human liberty is such that it may well stand with volitions being necessarily connected with the views of the understanding, and so is consistent with necessity; or it [the latter] is inconsistent with, and contrary to such a connection and necessity. The former is directly subversive of the Arminian notion of liberty, consisting in freedom from all necessity.

### Arminian Notion of Liberty: *It is freedom from any necessity of the will.*

---

3. [Isaac Watts, *Essay*, sec. 6, *ans.* to *obj.* 5; reprinted in *Works* 6:268.]

***JE's Notion of Liberty: Giving up to contingency is unintelligent. It is coming from necessary connection of volition with preceding views and dictates of the understanding, and it is of human right.***

And if the latter be chosen, and it be said, that liberty is inconsistent with any such necessary connection of volition with foregoing views of the understanding, it consisting in freedom from any such necessity of the will as that would imply; then the liberty of the soul consists (in part at least) in the freedom from restraint, limitation and government, in its actings, by the understanding, and in liberty and liableness to act contrary to the understanding's views and dictates: and consequently the more the soul has of this disengagedness, in its acting, the more liberty. Now let it be considered what this brings the noble principle of human liberty to, particularly when it is possessed and enjoyed in its perfection, viz. a full and perfect freedom and liableness to act altogether at random, without the least connection with, or restraint or government by, any dictate of reason, or anything whatsoever apprehended, considered or viewed by the understanding; as being inconsistent with the full and perfect sovereignty of the will over its own determinations. The notion mankind have conceived of liberty, is some dignity or privilege, something worth claiming. But what dignity or privilege is there, in being given up to such a wild contingence as this, to be perfectly and constantly liable to act unintelligently and unreasonably, and as much without the guidance of understanding, as if we had none, or were as destitute of perception as the smoke that is driven by the wind!

# PART III

Wherein Is Inquired, Whether Any Such Liberty of Will as Arminians Hold, Be Necessary to Moral Agency, Virtue and Vice, Praise, and Dispraise, Etc.

# Section 1

## God's Moral Excellency Necessary, Yet Virtuous and Praiseworthy

***The Question: Is it requisite to moral agency any such kind of freedom that excludes the necessity of the will?***

Having considered the first thing that was proposed to be inquired into, relating to that freedom of will which Arminians maintain; namely, whether any such thing does, ever did, or ever can exist, or be conceived of; I come now to the second thing proposed to be the subject of inquiry, viz. whether any such kind of liberty be requisite to moral agency, virtue and vice, praise and blame, reward and punishment, etc.

I shall begin with some consideration of the virtue and agency of the supreme moral Agent, and fountain of all agency and virtue.

***JE: The acts of God and men are necessary and yet they are deserved to be praised if they are virtuous.***

***DW: If the acts are needed, they cannot be praised or blamed, for they do them inevitably without freedom.***

Dr. Whitby, in his *Discourse on the Five Points* (p. 14), says, "If all human actions are necessary, virtue and vice must be empty names; we being capable of nothing that is blameworthy, or deserves praise; for who can blame a person for doing only what he could not help, or judge that he deserves praise only for what he could not avoid?"[1] To the like purpose he speaks in places innumerable; especially in his discourse on the freedom of the will; constantly maintaining, that a "freedom not only from coaction, but from necessity," is absolutely requisite, in order to actions being either worthy of blame, or deserving of praise.[2] And to this agrees, as is well known, the current doc-

---

1. [Whitby, *Discourse on the Five Points*, Dis. I, ch. 1, p. 14.]
2. [Whitby, *Discourse on the Five Points*, Dis. I, ch. 1, p. 328.]

trine of Arminian writers; who in general hold, that there is no virtue or vice, reward or punishment, nothing to be commended or blamed, without this freedom. And yet Dr. Whitby, p. 300, allows, that God is without this freedom; and Arminians, so far as I have had opportunity to observe, generally acknowledge, that God is necessarily holy, and his will necessarily determined to that which is good.

### JE: God is the holy and virtuous being and so he is worthy to be praised. And he is the most perfect pattern and foundation of virtue.

So that, putting these things together, the infinitely holy God, who always used to be esteemed by God's people, not only virtuous, but a being in whom is all possible virtue, and every virtue[3] in the most absolute purity and perfection, and in infinitely greater brightness and amiableness than in any creature; the most perfect pattern of virtue, and the fountain from whom all others' virtue is but as beams from the sun; and who has been supposed to be, on the account of his virtue and holiness, infinitely more worthy to be esteemed, loved, honored, admired, commended, extolled and praised, than any creature; and he who is thus everywhere represented in Scripture;

### DW and Ar: God is necessarily holy and good and virtuous, and he is not worthy to be praised and given thanks.

I say, this being, according to this notion of Dr. Whitby, and other Arminians, has no virtue at all;

> virtue, when ascribed to him, is but "an empty name"; and he is deserving of no commendation or praise; because he is under necessity, he can't avoid being holy and good as he is; therefore no thanks to him for it. It seems, the holiness, justice, faithfulness, etc., of the Most High, must not be accounted to be of the nature of that which is virtuous and praiseworthy.

### Ar: God is necessarily good but did not become so by his self-determining power, and so he is not virtuous.

They will not deny, that these things in God are good; but then we must understand them, that they are no more virtuous, or of the nature of anything commendable, than the good that is in any other being that is not a moral agent; as the brightness of the sun, and the fertility of the earth are good, but not virtuous, because these properties are necessary to these bodies, and not the fruit of self-determining power.

There needs no other confutation of this notion of God's not being virtuous or praiseworthy, to Christians acquainted with the Bible, but only stating and particularly representing of it. To bring texts of Scripture, wherein God is represented as in every respect, in the highest manner virtuous, and supremely praiseworthy, would be

---

3. [Virtue (ἀρετή, *arétē*) is defined to be any excellence of a person (in body or mind) or of a thing, an eminent endowment, property or quality, and it is used of the human mind and in an ethical sense, in Thayer's Greek Lexicon.]

endless, and is altogether needless to such as have been brought up under the light of the gospel.

***DW and Ar: Men are worthy of that esteem, and yet God is not worthy of it.***

It were to be wished, that Dr. Whitby, and other divines of the same sort, had explained themselves, when they have asserted that that which is necessary, is "not deserving of praise"; at the same time that they have owned God's perfection to be necessary, and so in effect represented God as not deserving praise. Certainly, if their words have any meaning at all, by "praise," they must mean the exercise or testimony of some sort of esteem, respect, or honorable regard.

And will they then say, that men are worthy of that esteem, respect, and honor for their virtue, small and imperfect as it is, which yet God is not worthy of, for his infinite righteousness, holiness, and goodness?

***Ar: The virtuous man had some sort of peculiar excellent dignity and he is worthy to be praised.***

If so, it must be because of some sort of peculiar excellency in the virtuous man, which is his prerogative, wherein he really has the preference; some dignity, that is entirely distinguished from any excellency, amiableness or honorableness in God; not in imperfection and dependence, but in pre-eminence; which therefore he doesn't receive from God, nor is God the fountain or pattern of it; nor can God, in that respect, stand in competition with him, as the object of honor and regard; but man may claim a peculiar esteem, commendation and glory, that God can have no pretension to. Yea, God has no right, by virtue of his necessary holiness, to intermeddle with that grateful respect and praise, due to the virtuous man, who chooses virtue, in the exercise of a freedom *ad utrumque*;[4] any more than a precious stone, which can't avoid being hard and beautiful.

***JE: The respect of the virtuous man is entirely different from that of God. God is worthy of all praises: esteem, love, admiration, honor, praise, or gratitude.***

And if it be so, let it be explained what that peculiar respect is, that is due to the virtuous man, which differs in nature and kind, in some way of pre-eminence, from all that is due to God. What is the name or description of that peculiar affection? Is it esteem, love, admiration, honor, praise, or gratitude? The Scripture everywhere represents God as the highest object of all these: there we read of the "soul's magnifying the Lord," or "loving him with all the heart, with all the soul, with all the mind, and with all the strength"; admiring him, and his righteous acts, or greatly regarding them as marvelous and wonderful; honoring, glorifying, exalting, extolling, blessing,

---

4. [Ramsey: Freedom to choose either of two things, or to act in either way or direction, *whichever one pleases*, which is deleted in *WJE Online* edition, to which the editor added a note: "On both sides"; *ad utrumque* was a variant of *ad utrumque,* denoting the freedom to choose either of two things, or to act in either way or direction or on either side.]

thanking, and praising him; "giving unto him all the glory" of the good which is done or received, rather than unto men; "that no flesh should glory in his presence"; but that he should be regarded as the being to whom all glory is due. What then is that respect? What passion, affection, or exercise is it, that Arminians call "praise," diverse from all these things, which men are worthy of for their virtue, and which God is not worthy of, in any degree?

**Ar: *If God does not do good acts from his liberty or good will, but by the necessity and from mere compulsion, why should we praise him? So he must not be good.***

If that necessity which attends God's moral perfections and actions, be as inconsistent with a being worthy of praise, as a necessity of coaction; as is plainly implied in or inferred from Dr. Whitby's discourse; then why should we thank God for his goodness, any more than if he were forced to be good, or any more than we should thank one of our fellow creatures who did us good, not freely, and of good will, or from any kindness of heart, but from mere compulsion, or extrinsical necessity? Arminians suppose, that God is necessarily a good and gracious being: for this they make the ground of some of their main arguments against many doctrines maintained by Calvinists: they say, these are "certainly" false, and it is "impossible" they should be true, because they are not consistent with the goodness of God. This supposes, that it is impossible but that God should be good: for if it be possible that he should be otherwise, then that impossibility of the truth of these doctrines ceases, according to their own argument.

**JE: *Most strictly speaking, it is our duty, and yet it cannot fully praise and appreciate him, and so it cannot properly reward his virtue.***

That virtue in God is not, in the most proper sense, *rewardable*, is not for want of merit in his moral perfections and actions, sufficient to deserve rewards from his creatures; but because he is infinitely above all capacity of receiving any reward or benefit from the creature: he is already infinitely and unchangeably happy, and we can't be profitable unto him. But still he is worthy of our supreme benevolence for his virtue; and would be worthy of our beneficence, which is the fruit and expression of benevolence, if our goodness could extend to him. If God deserves to be thanked and praised for his goodness, he would for the same reason, deserve that we should also requite his kindness, if that were possible. "What shall I render to the Lord for all his benefits?" is the natural language of thankfulness: and so far as in us lies, it is our duty to recompense God's goodness, and *render again according to benefits received*. And that we might have opportunity for so natural an expression of our gratitude to God, as beneficence, notwithstanding his being infinitely above our reach; he has appointed others to be his receivers, and to stand in his stead, as the objects of our beneficence; such are especially our indigent brethren.

# Section 2

## The Acts of the Will of the Human Soul of Jesus Necessarily Holy, Yet Truly Virtuous, Praiseworthy, Rewardable, etc.

**DW: *A freedom, not from coaction but from necessity, is requisite to a moral agent.***

**JE: *He/she needs not the freedom but necessity. Jesus also was a perfect holy subject of the law and became virtuous, and he was worthy of praise.***

I have already considered how Dr. Whitby insists upon it, that a freedom, not only from coaction, but necessity, is "requisite to either virtue or vice, praise or dispraise, reward or punishment." He also insists on the same freedom as absolutely requisite to a person's being the subject of a law, of precepts or prohibitions; in the book before mentioned (pp. 301, 314, 328, 339–42, 347, 361, 373, 410). And of promises and threatenings (pp. 298, 301, 305, 311, 339–40, 363). And as requisite to a state of trial (p. 297, etc.).

Now therefore, with an eye to these things, I would inquire into the moral conduct and practice of our Lord Jesus Christ, which he exhibited in his human nature here, in his state of humiliation. And first, I would show, that his holy behavior was necessary; or that it was impossible it should be otherwise, than that he should behave himself holily, and that he should be perfectly holy in each individual act of his life. And secondly, that his holy behavior was properly of the nature of virtue, and was worthy of praise; and that he was the subject of law, precepts or commands, promises and rewards; and that he was in a state of trial.

**JE: *I. The acts of the will of Christ should be not otherwise than holy.***

I. It was impossible, that the acts of the will of the human soul of Christ should, in any instance, degree or circumstance, be otherwise than holy, and agreeable to God's nature and will. The following things make this evident.

### JE—1. Christ was promised by God to preserve him from sin, and he did act holy.

1. God had promised so effectually to preserve and uphold him by his Spirit, under all his temptations, that he should not fail of reaching the end for which he came into the world; which he would have failed of, had he fallen into sin. We have such a promise (Isaiah 42:1–4), "Behold my servant, whom I uphold; mine elect, in whom my soul delighteth: I have put my Spirit upon him: he shall bring forth judgment to the Gentiles: he shall not cry, nor lift up, nor cause his voice to be heard in the street . . . He shall bring forth judgment unto truth. He shall not fail, nor be discouraged, till he hath set judgment in the earth; and the isles shall wait for his law."

This promise of Christ's having God's Spirit put upon him, and his not crying and lifting up his voice etc., relates to the time of Christ's appearance on earth; as is manifest from the nature of the promise, and also the application of it in the New Testament (Matthew 12:18). And the words imply a promise of his being so upheld by God's Spirit, that he should be preserved from sin; particularly from pride and vainglory, and from being overcome by any of the temptations he should be under to affect the glory of this world; the pomp of an earthly prince, or the applause and praise of men: and that he should be so upheld, that he should by no means fail of obtaining the end of his coming into the world, of bringing forth judgment unto victory, and establishing his kingdom of grace in the earth.

And in the following verses, this promise is confirmed, with the greatest imaginable solemnity:

> "Thus saith the LORD, he that created the heavens, and stretched them out; he that spread forth the earth, and that which cometh out of it; he that giveth breath unto the people upon it, and spirit to them that walk therein: I the Lord have called thee in righteousness, and will hold thine hand; and will keep thee, and give thee for a covenant of the people, for a light of the Gentiles, to open the blind eyes, to bring out the prisoners from the prison, and them that sit in darkness out of the prison-house. I am JEHOVAH, that is my name," etc.[1]

Very parallel with these promises is that (Isaiah 49:7–9) which also has an apparent respect to the time of Christ's humiliation on earth:

> "Thus saith the Lord, the Redeemer of Israel, and his Holy One, to him whom man despiseth, to him whom the nation abhorreth, to a servant of rulers, Kings shall see and arise, princes also shall worship; because of the Lord that is faithful, and the Holy One of Israel, and he shall choose thee. Thus saith the Lord, in an acceptable time have I heard thee; in a day of salvation have I helped thee; and I will preserve thee, and give thee for a covenant of the people, to establish the earth, &c. [That thou mayest say to the prisoners, Go

---

1. [Isaiah 42:5–8, JE prefers the name JEHOVAH to LORD and he used the former. See *WJE* 1:390.]

forth; to them that are in darkness, Shew yourselves. They shall feed in the ways, and their pastures shall be in all high places]."[2]

And in Isaiah 50:5-9, we have the Messiah expressing his assurance, that God would help him, by so opening his ear, or inclining his heart to God's commandments, that he should not be rebellious, but should persevere, and not apostatize, or turn his back: that through God's help, he should be immovable, in a way of obedience, under the great trials of reproach and suffering he should meet with; setting his face like a flint: so that he knew he should not be ashamed, or frustrated in his design; and finally should be approved and justified, as having done his work faithfully:

> The Lord hath opened mine ear; so that I was not rebellious, neither turned away my back: I gave my back to the smiters, and my cheeks to them that plucked off the hair; I hid not my face from shame and spitting. For the Lord God will help me; therefore shall I not be confounded: therefore have I set my face as a flint, and I know that I shall not be ashamed. He is near that justifieth me: who will contend with me? Let us stand together. Who is mine adversary? Let him come near to me. Behold the Lord God will help me: who is he that shall condemn me? Lo, they shall all wax old as a garment, the moth shall eat them up.

### JE—2. Due to the absolute certainty of God's promise, the absolute impossibility of Christ's sin was guaranteed.

2. The same thing is evident from all the promises which God made to the Messiah, of his future glory, kingdom and success, in his office and character of a mediator: which glory could not have been obtained, if his holiness had failed, and he had been guilty of sin. God's absolute promise of any things makes the things promised *necessary*, and their failing to take place absolutely *impossible*: and in like manner it makes those things necessary, on which the thing promised depends, and without which it can't take effect. Therefore, it appears, that it was utterly impossible that Christ's holiness should fail, from such absolute promises as those

> (Psalms 110:4), "The Lord hath sworn, and will not repent, thou art a priest forever, after the order of Melchizedek."

And from every other promise in that psalm, contained in each verse of it.

> And Psalms 2:6, Psalms 2:7, "I will declare the decree: the Lord hath said unto me, thou art my Son, this day have I begotten thee: ask of me, and I will give thee the heathen for thine inheritance," etc.

> Psalms 45:3, Psalms 45:4, etc., "Gird thy sword on thy thigh, O most mighty, with thy glory and thy majesty; and in thy majesty ride prosperously."

---

2. [JE refers to Isaiah 49:7-9, but verse 9 is omitted, so this edition added it.]

And so everything that is said from thence to the end of the psalm. And those promises, Isaiah 52:13–15; and Isaiah 53:10–12.

And all those promises which God makes to the Messiah, of success, dominion and glory in the character of redeemer, in Ch. 49.

### JE—3. It is because God promised that he would send a righteous, sinless Savior.

3. It was often promised to the church of God of old, for their comfort, that God would give them a righteous, sinless Savior.

> Jeremiah 23:5–6, "Behold, the days come, saith the Lord, that I will raise up unto David a righteous branch; and a king shall reign and prosper, and shall execute judgment and justice in the earth. In his days shall Judah be saved, and Israel shall dwell safely. And this is the name whereby he shall be called, The Lord our Righteousness." So,
>
> Jeremiah 33:15, "I will cause the branch of righteousness to grow up unto David; and he shall execute judgment and righteousness in the land."
>
> Isaiah 9:6–7, "For unto us a child is born . . . upon the throne of David and of his kingdom, to order it, and to establish it with judgment and justice, from henceforth, even forever: the zeal of the Lord of hosts will do this."
>
> Ch. Isaiah 11, at the beginning: "There shall come forth a rod out of the stem of Jesse, and a branch shall grow out of his roots; and the Spirit of the Lord shall rest upon him. . . the spirit of knowledge, and of the fear of the Lord. . . with righteousness shall he judge the poor, and reprove with equity . . . righteousness shall be the girdle of his loins, and faithfulness the girdle of his reins."
>
> Ch. 52:13, "My servant shall deal prudently"
>
> Ch. 53:9, "Because he had done no violence, neither was guile found in his mouth."

If it be impossible, that these promises should fail, and it be easier for heaven and earth to pass away, than for one jot or tittle of these promises of God to pass away, then it was impossible that Christ should commit any sin. Christ himself signified that it was impossible but that the things which were spoken concerning him should be fulfilled.

> Luke 24:44, "That all things must be fulfilled, which were written in the law of Moses, and in the prophets, and in the Psalms concerning me."
>
> Matthew 26:54, "But how then shall the Scripture be fulfilled, that thus it must be?"
>
> Mark 14:49, "But the Scriptures must be fulfilled."

And so the Apostle, Acts 1:16–17, "This Scripture must needs have been fulfilled."

### JE—4. It is because it is impossible for God to fail to keep his promise sworn and made to the church of old.

4. All the promises which were made to the church of old, of the Messiah as a future Savior, from that made to our first parents in paradise, to that which was delivered by the prophet Malachi, show it to be impossible that Christ should not have persevered in perfect holiness. The ancient predictions given to God's church, of the Messiah as a Savior, were of the nature of promises; as is evident by the predictions themselves, and the manner of delivering them. But they are expressly and very often called promises in the New Testament; as in Luke 1:54–55, Luke 1:72–73; Acts 13:32–33; Romans 1:1–3; and Ch. 15:8; Hebrews 6:13, etc.

These promises were often made with great solemnity, and confirmed with an oath; as in

> Genesis 22:16–17, "By myself have I sworn, saith the Lord, that in blessing, I will bless thee, and in multiplying, I will multiply thy seed, as the stars of heaven, and as the sand which is upon the seashore: . . . and in thy seed shall all the nations of the earth be blessed."

Compare Luke 1:72–73 and Galatians 3:8, 15–16. The Apostle in Hebrews 6:17–18 speaking of this promise to Abraham, says,

> "Wherein God willing more abundantly to show to the heirs of promise the immutability of his counsel, confirmed it by an oath; that by two IMMUTABLE things, in which it was IMPOSSIBLE for God to lie, we[3] might have strong consolation."

In which words, the *necessity* of the accomplishment, or [which is the same thing] the *impossibility* of the contrary, is fully declared. So God confirmed the promise of the great salvation of the Messiah, made to David, by an oath

> [Psalms 89:3, Psalms 89:4], "I have made a covenant with my chosen, I have sworn unto David my servant; thy seed will I establish forever, and build up thy throne to all generations."

There is nothing that is so abundantly set forth in Scripture, as sure and irrefragable, as this promise and oath to David. See Psalms 89:34–36; II Samuel 23:5; Isaiah 55:3; Acts 2:29–30; and Acts 13:34. The Scripture expressly speaks of it as utterly impossible that this promise and oath to David, concerning the everlasting dominion of the Messiah of his seed, should fail.

---

3. [Corrected from "he."]

Jeremiah 33:15, etc., "In those days, and at that time, I will cause the branch of righteousness to grow up unto David. . ... For thus saith the Lord, David shall never want a man to sit upon the throne of the house of Israel."

Vv. 20–21, "If you can break my covenant of the day, and my covenant of the night, and that there should not be day and night in their season; then may also my covenant be broken with David my servant, that he should not have a son to reign upon his throne."

So in vv. 25–26. Thus abundant is the Scripture in representing how impossible it was, that the promises made of old concerning the great salvation and kingdom of the Messiah should fail: which implies, that it was impossible that this Messiah, the second Adam, the promised seed of Abraham, and of David, should fall from his integrity, as the first Adam did.

### JE—5. As the Father promised and swore to the Messiah, he perfected the work of redemption without failing or committing sin.

5. All the promises that were made to the church of God under the old testament, of the great enlargement of the church, and advancement of her glory, in the days of the gospel, after the coming of the Messiah; the increase of her light, liberty, holiness, joy, triumph over her enemies, etc., of which so great a part of the Old Testament consists; which are repeated so often, are so variously exhibited, so frequently introduced with great pomp and solemnity, and are so abundantly sealed with typical and symbolical representations; I say, all these promises imply, that the Messiah should perfect the work of redemption; and this implies, that he should persevere in the work which the Father had appointed him, being in all things conformed to his will.

These promises were often confirmed by an oath [see Isaiah 54:9 with the context; Ch. 62:8]. And it is represented as utterly impossible that these promises should fail [Isaiah 49:15 with the context; Ch. 54:10 with the context; Ch. 51:4–8; Ch. 40:8 with the context]. And therefore it was impossible, that the Messiah should fail, or commit sin.

### JE—6. It is because the promise made to the Messiah was supported by the promise to his direct parents.

6. It was *impossible*, that the Messiah should fail of persevering in integrity and holiness, as the first Adam did, because this would have been inconsistent with the promises which God made to the blessed Virgin, his mother, and to her husband; implying, that "he should save his people from their sins," that "God would give him the throne of his father David," that "he should reign over the house of Jacob forever"; and that "of his kingdom there should be no end." These promises were sure, and it was impossible they should fail. And therefore the Virgin Mary, in trusting fully to them, acted reasonably, having an immovable foundation of her faith; as Elizabeth observes,

Section 2—The Acts of the Will of the Human Soul of Jesus Necessarily Holy, Yet Truly Virtuous

[Luke 1,] v. 45, "And blessed is she that believeth; for there shall be a performance of those things which were told her from the Lord."

### JE—7. It is because Christ should not sin and fail in the work of our redemption, which is necessary for our salvation.

7. That it should have been possible that Christ should sin, and so fail in the work of our redemption, does not consist with the eternal purpose and decree of God, revealed in the Scriptures, that he would provide salvation for fallen man in and by Jesus Christ, and that salvation should be offered to sinners through the preaching of the gospel. Such an absolute decree as this Arminians don't deny. This much at least [out of all controversy] is implied in such scriptures, as I Corinthians 2:7; Ephesians 1:4-5 and Ch. 3:9-11; I Peter 1:19-20. Such an absolute decree as this, Arminians allow to be signified in these texts. And the Arminians' election of nations and societies, and general election of the Christian church, and conditional election of particular persons, imply this. God could not decree before the foundation of the world, to save all that should believe in, and obey Christ, unless he had absolutely decreed that salvation should be provided, and effectually wrought out by Christ. And since [as the Arminians themselves strenuously maintain] a decree of God infers necessity; hence it became necessary that Christ should persevere, and actually work out salvation for us, and that he should not fail by the commission of sin.

### JE—8. It is because the promise is made by God, who cannot lie.

8. That it should have been possible for Christ's holiness to fail, is not consistent with what God promised to his Son before all ages. For, that salvation should be offered to men through Christ, and bestowed on all his faithful followers, is what is at least implied in that certain and infallible promise spoken of by the Apostle (Titus 1:2), "In hope of eternal life; which God, that cannot lie, promised before the world began." This doesn't seem to be controverted by Arminians.[4]

### JE—9. It is because Christ's promise made to the Father before the creation was certain and immovable.

9. That it should be possible for Christ to fail of doing his Father's will, is inconsistent with the promise made to the Father by the Son, by the *Logos* that was with the Father from the beginning, before he took the human nature: as may be seen in Psalms 40:6, Psalms 40:7-8 (compared with the Apostle's interpretation, Hebrews 10:5-9),

> "Sacrifice and offering thou didst not desire: mine ears hast thou opened (or bored); burnt-offering and sin-offering thou hast not required. Then said I, Lo, I come: in the volume of the book it is written of me, I delight to do thy will, O my God, and thy law is within my heart."

4. See Whitby, *Discourse on the Five Points*, pp. 48, 49, 50.

Where is a manifest allusion to the covenant which the willing servant, who loved his master's service, made with his master, to be his servant forever, on the day wherein he had his ear bored; which covenant was probably inserted in the public records, called the "volume of the book," by the judges, who were called to take cognizance of the transaction (Exodus 21). If the *Logos*, who was with the Father, before the world, and who made the world, thus engaged in covenant to do the will of the Father in the human nature, and the promise, was as it were recorded, that it might be made sure, doubtless it was *impossible* that it should fail; and so it was *impossible* that Christ should fail of doing the will of the Father in the human nature.

### *JE—10. If Christ were not morally perfect, our salvation would come to nothing.*

10. If it was possible for Christ to have failed of doing the will of his Father, and so to have failed of effectually working out redemption for sinners, then the salvation of all the saints, who were saved from the beginning of the world, to the death of Christ, was not built on a firm foundation. The Messiah, and the redemption which he was to work out by his obedience unto death, was the foundation of the salvation of all the posterity of fallen man, that ever were saved. Therefore, if when the Old Testament saints had the pardon of their sins, and the favor of God promised them, and salvation bestowed upon them, still it was possible that the Messiah, when he came, might commit sin, then all this was on a foundation that was not firm and stable, but liable to fail; something which it was possible might never be.

God did as it were trust to what his Son had engaged and promised to do in future time; and depended so much upon it, that he proceeded actually to save men on the account of it, as though it had been already done. But this trust and dependence of God, on the supposition of Christ's being liable to fail of doing his will, was leaning on a staff that was weak, and might possibly break. The saints of old trusted on the promises of a future redemption to be wrought out and completed by the Messiah, and built their comfort upon it: Abraham saw Christ's day and rejoiced; and he and the other patriarchs died in the faith of the promise of it (Hebrews 11:13). But on this supposition, their faith and their comfort, and their salvation, was built on a movable fallible foundation; Christ was not to them a tried stone, a sure foundation; as in Isaiah 28:16. David entirely rested on the covenant of God with him, concerning the future glorious dominion and salvation of the Messiah, of his seed; says, it was "all his salvation, and all his desire"; and comforts himself that this covenant was an "everlasting covenant, ordered in all things and sure" (II Samuel 23:5).

But if Christ's virtue might fail, he was mistaken: his great comfort was not built so sure, as he thought it was, being founded entirely on the determinations of the free will of Christ's human soul; which was subject to no necessity, and might be determined either one way or the other. Also the dependence of those who looked for redemption in Jerusalem, and waited for the consolation of Israel (Luke 2:25 and Luke 2:38), and the confidence of the disciples of Jesus, who forsook all and followed him, that they might enjoy the benefits of his future kingdom, was built on a sandy foundation.

***JE—11. Christ predicted and finished all of his course of obedience and overcame all temptations and trials. If it had been not so, and he had failed in his work, Christ himself would have been guilty of presumption, in so abounding in peremptory promises of great things.***

11. The man Christ Jesus, before he had finished his course of obedience, and while in the midst of temptations and trials, was abundant in positively predicting his own future glory in his kingdom, and the enlargement of his church, the salvation of the Gentiles through him, etc., and in promises of blessings he would bestow on his true disciples in his future kingdom; on which promises he required the full dependence of his disciples (John 14). But the disciples would have had no ground for such dependence, if Christ had been liable to fail in his work: and Christ himself would have been guilty of presumption, in so abounding in peremptory promises of great things, which depended on a mere contingency; viz. the determinations of his free will, consisting in a freedom *ad utrumque*, to either sin or holiness, standing in indifference, and incident, in thousands of future instances, to go either one way or the other.

Thus it is evident, that it was *impossible* that the acts of the will of the human soul of Christ should be otherwise than holy, and conformed to the will of the Father; or, in other words, they were necessarily so conformed.

I have been the longer in the proof of this matter, it being a thing denied by some of the greatest Arminians, by Episcopius[5] in particular; and because I look upon it as a point clearly and absolutely determining the controversy between Calvinists and Arminians, concerning the necessity of such a freedom of will as is insisted on by the latter, in order to moral agency, virtue, command or prohibition, promise or threatening, reward or punishment, praise or dispraise, merit or demerit. I now therefore proceed,

### Was Christ really the holy moral agent?

II. To consider whether Christ, in his holy behavior on earth, was not thus a moral agent, subject to commands, promises, etc.:

***DW: Men need only the freedom ad utrumlibet without necessity. If promise becomes motive in their acts, there would be no liberty in the will.***

***JE: Christ made his promises offered as motives to disciples to do their moral acts, as his Father did so to him. Christ's will was determined not by a freedom ad utrumlibet but by necessity committed to holiness and good alone, and it was always holy.***

---

5. [Ramsey, Simon Episcopius (1583–1643), a Dutch theologian who studied under Arminius and Gomarus at Leyden and succeeded Gomarus as professor there, was one of the leaders of the Remonstrants before the Synod of Dort (1618–19). Banished for a time, he later returned to Holland and headed the newly founded Remonstrant seminary in Amsterdam.]

Dr. Whitby very often speaks of what he calls a freedom *ad utrumlibet*[6] without necessity, as requisite to law and commands; and speaks of necessity as entirely inconsistent with injunctions and prohibitions.

**JE: *Christ, too, received commandments from his Father and in necessity obeyed and he was promised to be given a reward.***

But yet we read of Christ's being the subject of the commands of his Father [John 10:18 and John 15:10]. And Christ tells us, that everything that he said, or did, was in compliance with commandments he had received of the Father [John 12:49–50 and John 14:31]. And we often read of Christ's obedience to his Father's commands [Romans 5:19, Philippians 2:8, Hebrews 5:8].

**DW: *Promises to reward were offered only to induce motives to obey, which is not dependent upon necessary determination.***

The aforementioned writer represents promises offered as motives to persons to do their duty, or as being moved and induced by promises, as utterly inconsistent with a state wherein persons have not a liberty *ad utrumlibet*, but are necessarily determined to one. [See particularly, pp. 298 and 311].

**JE: *If the Bible and Christian religion were not false, it is normal that the Father promised rewards to Christ who had good will and good choice.***

But the thing which this writer asserts, is demonstrably false, if the Christian religion be true. If there be any truth in Christianity or the holy Scriptures, the man Christ Jesus had his will infallibly, unalterably and unfrustrably determined to good, and that alone; but yet he had promises of glorious rewards made to him, on condition of his persevering in, and perfecting the work which God had appointed him [Isaiah 53:10–12; Psalms 2 and Psalms 110; Isaiah 49:7–9].

### Christ's Promises of Reward to His Disciples

In Luke 22:28–29, Christ says to his disciples,

> "Ye are they which have continued with me in my temptations; and I appoint unto you a kingdom, as my Father hath appointed unto me."

The word most properly signifies to appoint by covenant, or promise. The plain meaning of Christ's words is this:

> "As you have partaken of my temptations and trials, and have been steadfast, and have overcome; I promise to make you partakers of my reward, and to give you a kingdom; as the Father has promised me a kingdom for continuing steadfast, and overcoming in those trials."

---

6. [*WJE Online* 1, freedom *to choose either of two things*, or *to act in either way or direction*, whichever one pleases.]

Section 2—The Acts of the Will of the Human Soul of Jesus Necessarily Holy, Yet Truly Virtuous

And the words are well explained by those in Revelation 3:21,

> "To him that over cometh, will I grant to sit with me in my throne; even as I also overcame, and am set down with my Father in his throne."

### The Father's Promises of Reward to Christ

And Christ had not only promises of glorious success and rewards made to his obedience and sufferings, but the Scriptures plainly represent him as using these promises for motives and inducements to obey and suffer; and particularly that promise of a kingdom which the Father had appointed him, or sitting with the Father on his throne; as in Hebrews 12:1–2,

> "Let us lay aside every weight, and the sin which doth easily beset us, and let us run with patience the race that is set before us, looking unto Jesus, the author and finisher of our faith; who for the joy that was set before him, endured the cross, despising the shame, and is set down on the right hand of the throne of God."

**DW: Jesus obeyed in his will not free ad utrumque but necessarily by compulsion, and so there is no virtue and no worth to be rewarded.**

And how strange would it be to hear any Christian assert, that the holy and excellent temper and behavior of Jesus Christ, and that obedience which he performed under such great trials, was not virtuous or praiseworthy; because his will was not free *ad utrumque*, to either holiness or sin, but was unalterably determined to one; that upon this account, there is no virtue at all, in all Christ's humility, meekness, patience, charity, forgiveness of enemies, contempt of the world, heavenly-mindedness, submission to the will of God, perfect obedience to his commands (though he was obedient unto death, even the death of the cross), his great compassion to the afflicted, his unparalleled love to mankind, his faithfulness to God and man, under such great trials; his praying for his enemies, even when nailing him to the cross; that "virtue," when applied to these things, "is but an empty name"; that there was no merit in any of these things; that is, that Christ was "worthy" of nothing at all on the account of them, worthy of no reward, no praise, no honor or respect from God or man; because his will was not indifferent, and free either to these things, or the contrary; but under such a strong inclination or bias to the things that were excellent, as made it *impossible* that he should choose the contrary; that upon this account (to use Dr. Whitby's language) "it would be sensibly unreasonable" that the human nature should be rewarded for any of these things![7]

According to this doctrine, that Creature who is evidently set forth in Scripture as the "first born of every creature," as having "in all things the preeminence" , and

---

7. [Whitby, *Discourse*, Dis. I, ch. 1, no. 3; p. 15.]

as the highest of all creatures in virtue, honor, and worthiness of esteem, praise and glory, on the account of his virtue, is less worthy of reward or praise, than the very least of saints; yea, no more worthy than a clock or mere machine, that is purely passive, and moved by natural necessity.

**JE: Is there any reason why Jesus could not be praised for he obeyed necessarily by compulsion? The Father and angels praised him, but Arminians did not so and they seem to not have faith in God.**

If we judge by scriptural representations of things, we have reason to suppose, that Christ took on him our nature, and dwelt with us in this world, in a suffering state, not only to satisfy for our sins; but that he, being in our nature and circumstances, and under our trials, might be our most fit and proper example, leader and captain, in the exercise of glorious and victorious virtue, and might be a visible instance of the glorious end and reward of it; that we might see in him the beauty[8], amiableness, and true honor and glory, and exceeding benefit of that virtue, which it is proper for us human beings to practice; and might thereby learn, and be animated, to seek the like glory and honor, and to obtain the like glorious reward. See Hebrews 2:9–14, with Hebrews 5:8–9 and Hebrews 12:1–3; John 15:10; Romans 8:17; II Timothy 2:11–12; I Peter 2:19–20 and I Peter 4:13.

But if there was nothing of any virtue or merit, or worthiness of any reward, glory, praise or commendation at all, in all that he did, because it was all necessary, and he could not help it; then how is here anything so proper to animate and incite us, free creatures, by patient continuance in well doing, to seek for honor, glory, and virtue?

*God spoke well of Christ and testified.*

God speaks of himself as peculiarly well pleased with the righteousness of this servant of his (Is. 42:21), "The Lord is well pleased for his righteousness' sake." The sacrifices of old are spoken of as a sweet savor to God, but the obedience of Christ as far more acceptable than they.

> Psalms 40:6–8, "Sacrifice and offering thou didst not desire: mine ear hast thou opened (as thy servant performing willing obedience); burnt-offering and sin-offering hast thou not required: then said I, Lo, I come (as a servant that cheerfully answers the calls of his master): I delight to do thy will, O my God, and thy law is within mine heart."

---

8. [JE first theologized the beauty of God to articulate his ethics, and in the 20th century the following scholars did groundwork of it by applying aesthetic view of JE. See Roland A. Delattre, "Aesthetics and Ethics: Jonathan Edwards and the Recovery of Aesthetics for Religious Ethics," *The Journal of Religious Ethics* 31 (2), 277–97; Clyde A. Holbrook, *The Ethics of Jonathan Edwards: Morality and Aesthetics* (Ann Arbor: University of Michigan, 1973).]

Matthew 17:5, "This is my beloved Son, in whom I am well pleased." And Christ tells us expressly, that the Father loves him for that wonderful instance of his obedience, his voluntarily yielding himself to death, in compliance with the Father's command.

John 10:17–18, "Therefore doth my Father love me, because I lay down my life: . . . no man taketh it from me; but I lay it down of myself. . . . This commandment received I of my Father."

### *Angels, too, spoke well of Christ and testified.*

And if there was no merit in Christ's obedience unto death, if it was not worthy of praise, and of the most glorious rewards, the heavenly hosts were exceedingly mistaken, by the account that is given of them, in

Revelation 5:8–12. "The four beasts and the four and twenty elders fell down before the Lamb, having every one of them harps, and golden vials full of odors . . . and they sung a new song, saying, thou art WORTHY to take the book, and to open the seals thereof; for thou wast slain . . . and I beheld, and I heard the voice of many angels round about the throne, and the beasts, and the elders, and the number of them was ten thousand times ten thousand, and thousands of thousands, saying with a loud voice, WORTHY is the Lamb that was slain, to receive power, and riches, and wisdom, and strength, and honor, and glory, and blessing."

Christ speaks of the eternal life which he was to receive, as the reward of his obedience to the Father's commandments.

John 12:49–50, "I have not spoken of myself; but the Father which sent me, he gave me a commandment what I should say, and what I should speak: and I know that his commandment is life everlasting: whatsoever I speak therefore, even as the Father said unto me, so I speak."

God promises to divide him a portion with the great, etc., for his being his righteous servant, for his glorious virtue under such great trials and sufferings.

Isaiah 53:11–12, "He shall see of the travail of his soul and be satisfied: by his knowledge shall my righteous servant justify many; for he shall bear their iniquities. Therefore will I divide him a portion with the great, and he shall divide the spoil with the strong, because he hath poured out his soul unto death."

### *God rewards Christ far above all His other servants.*

The Scriptures represent God as rewarding him far above all his other servants.

Philippians 2:7–9, "He took on him the form of a servant, and was made in the likeness of men: and being found in fashion as a man, he humbled himself, and became obedient unto death, even the death of the cross: wherefore God also hath highly exalted him, and given him a name above every name."

Psalms 45:7, "Thou lovest righteousness, and hatest wickedness; therefore God, thy God, hath anointed thee with the oil of gladness above thy fellows."

### Christ was bestowed the benefits as reward for His obedience.

There is no room to pretend, that the glorious benefits bestowed in consequence of Christ's obedience, are not properly of the nature of a reward. What is a reward, in the most proper sense, but a benefit bestowed in consequence of something morally excellent in quality or behavior, in testimony of well-pleasedness in that moral excellency, and respect and favor on that account? If we consider the nature of a reward most strictly, and make the utmost of it, and add to the things contained in this description, proper merit or worthiness, and the bestowment of the benefit in consequence of a promise; still it will be found, there is nothing belonging to it, but that the Scripture is most express as to its belonging to the glory bestowed on Christ, after his sufferings; as appears from what has been already observed: there was a glorious benefit bestowed in consequence of something morally excellent, being called "righteousness" and "obedience"; there was great favor, love and well-pleasedness, for this righteousness and obedience, in the bestower; there was proper merit, or worthiness of the benefit, in the obedience; it was bestowed in fulfillment of promises, made to that obedience; and was bestowed *therefore*, or because he had performed that obedience.

### Christ met with the difficulties and afflictions in the course of His obedience, which are called his trials, but He overcame them well and was rewarded.

I may add to all these things, that Jesus Christ, while here in the flesh, was manifestly in a state of trial. The last Adam, as Christ is called (I Corinthians 15:45, Romans 5:14), taking on him the human nature, and so the form of a servant, and being under the law, to stand and act for us, was put into a state of trial, as the first Adam was. Dr. Whitby mentions these three things as evidences of persons being in a state of trial (*On the Five Points*, pp. 298, 299): namely, their afflictions being spoken of as their trials or temptations, their being the subjects of promises, and their being exposed to Satan's temptations. But Christ was apparently the subject of each of these. Concerning promises made to him, I have spoken already. The difficulties and afflictions he met with in the course of his obedience, are called his temptations or trials.

> Luke 22:28, "Ye are they which have continued with me in my temptations," or trials. Hebrews 2:18, "For in that he himself hath suffered, being tempted [or tried] he is able to succor them that are tempted." And Hebrews 4:15, "We have not an high priest, which cannot be touched with the feeling of our infirmities; but was in all points tempted like as we are, yet without sin."

And as to his being tempted by Satan, it is what none will dispute.

# Section 3

## The Case of Such as are Given Up of God to Sin, and of Fallen Man in General, Proves Moral Necessity and Inability to be Consistent with Blameworthiness

*DW: Men are not responsible for their sins committed necessarily.*

*JE: The freedom of the will participates in their sins, and so they must be blameworthy.*

Dr. Whitby asserts freedom, not only from coaction, but necessity, to be essential to anything deserving the name of "sin," and to an action's being culpable: in these words (*Discourse on Five Points*, ed. 3, p. 348),

> "If they be thus necessitated, then neither their sins of omission or commission could deserve that name; it being essential to the nature of sin, according to St. Austin's[1] definition, that it be an action, *a quo liberum est abstinere* [from which the sinner might abstain].[2] Three things seem plainly necessary to make an action or omission culpable:
>
> (1.) That it be in our power to perform or forbear it: for, as Origen, and all the fathers say, (ἀδεὶς ἀδύνατον μὴ ποιήσας ψεχτός ἐςι), 'no man is blameworthy for not doing what he could not do.' "[3]

---

1. [This quotation is not of JE, but of DW, who quoted it from "St. Austin," to whom means St. Augustine (Aurelius Augustinus) of Hippo, and certainly formed his view in reading Augustine's *De gratia et libero arbitrio* (On Grace and Free Will).]

2. [JE quoted this from DW "*a quo liberum est abstinere,*" but he omitted his liberal English translation "from which the sinner might abstain."]

3. [JE quotes Whitby, but he omits the Greek sentence, ἀδεὶς ἀδύνατον μὴ ποιήσας ψεχτός ἐςι, for the English-translated one is in parallel in it.]

(2.) [And elsewhere the Doctor insists,] that "when any do evil of necessity, what they do is no vice, that they are guilty of no fault,[4] are worthy of no blame, dispraise,[5] or dishonor,[6] but are unblameable."

### Men are given up of God to sin, yet they must be still blameworthy.

If these things are true, in Dr. Whitby's sense of necessity,

(3.) they will prove all such to be blameless, who are given up of God to sin, in what they commit after they are thus given up. That there is such a thing as men's being judicially given up to sin, is certain, if the Scripture rightly informs us;[7] such a thing being often there spoken of: as in

Psalms 81:12, "So I gave them up to their own hearts' lust, and they walked in their own counsels." Acts 7:42, "Then God turned, and gave them up to worship the host of heaven." Romans 1:24, "Wherefore, God also gave them up to uncleanness, through the lusts of their own hearts, to dishonor their own bodies between themselves." V. 26, "For this cause God gave them up to vile affections." V. 28, "And even as they did not like to retain God in their knowledge, God gave them over to a reprobate mind, to do those things that are not convenient."

### What is God's giving men up to their sins?

It is needless to stand particularly to inquire, what God's "giving men up to their own hearts' lusts" signifies: it is sufficient to observe, that hereby is certainly meant God's so ordering or disposing things, in some respect or other, either by doing or forbearing to do, as that the consequence should be men's continuing in their sins. So much as men are given up *to*, so much is the consequence of their being given up; whether that be less or more.

If God doesn't order things so, by action or permission, that sin will be the consequence, then the event proves that they are not given up to that consequence.

If good be the consequence, instead of evil, then God's mercy is to be acknowledged in that good; which mercy must be contrary to God's judgment in giving up to evil.

If the event must prove that they are given up to evil as the consequence, then the persons who are the subjects of this judgment, must be the subjects of such an event, and so the event is necessary.

4. Whitby, *Discourse on the Five Points*, Dis. IV, ch. 3, no. 3, p. 347; ch. 4, no. 3, pp. 360 f.; ch. 5, no. 2, p. 377.

5. Dis. IV, ch. 1, no. 3, p. 303; no. 8, p. 326; ch. 2, p. quotation is 329; etc.

6. Dis. IV, ch. 5, no. 2, p. 371.

7. [JE states the Double Predestination that God predestined some to election but others to reprobation, which was originated by Augustine and then was formulated by John Calvin and yet refuted by Jacobus Arminius.]

## Section 3—The Case of Such as are Given Up of God to Sin, and of Fallen Man in General

**JE: *Sins are committed even in co-action or necessity, yet they are not blameless. ILL: Jews' unbelief at Egypt; Judas' betrayal.***

If not only *coaction*, but *all necessity*, will prove men blameless, then Judas was blameless, after Christ had given him over, and had already declared his certain damnation, and that he should *verily* betray him. he was guilty of no sin in betraying is master, on this supposition; though his so doing is spoken of by Christ as the most aggravated sin, more heinous than the sin of Pilate in crucifying him. And the Jews in Egypt, in Jeremiah's time, were guilty of no sin, in their not worshipping the true God, after God had "sworn by his great name, that his name should be no more named in the mouth of any man of Judah, in all the land of Egypt" (Jeremiah 44:26).

**DW: *Due to moral impossibility or inability, persons cannot avoid sinning. The greater moral difficulty is, the more difficult is to prevent it, and the less blamable the omission is.***

**JE: *The giving up to sin is also the judgment of God and so the avoiding of sin is impossible. Moral or natural impossibility cannot excuse persons in not doing or not avoiding anything.***

Dr. Whitby (*Discourse on Five Points*, pp. 302–3) denies, that men, in this world, are ever so given up by God to sin, that their wills should be necessarily determined to evil; though he owns, that hereby it may become "exceeding difficult" for men to do good, having a strong bent, and powerful inclination to what is evil.

But if we should allow the case to be just as he represents, the judgment of giving up to sin will no better agree with his notions of that liberty, which is essential to praise or blame, than if we should suppose it to render the avoiding of sin *impossible*.

For if an impossibility of avoiding sin wholly excuses a man; then, for the same reason, its being difficult to avoid it excuses him in part; and this just in proportion to the degree of difficulty.

If the influence of *moral* impossibility or inability be the same, to excuse persons in not doing, or not avoiding anything, as that of *natural* inability (which is supposed), then undoubtedly, in like manner, *moral difficulty* has the same influence to excuse with *natural difficulty*.

But all allow, that natural impossibility wholly excuses, and also that natural difficulty excuses in part, and makes the act or omission less blamable, in proportion to the difficulty. All natural difficulty, according to the plainest dictates of the light of nature, excuses in some degree, so that the neglect is not so blamable, as if there had been no difficulty in the case: and so the greater the difficulty is, still the more excusable, in proportion to the increase of the difficulty. And as natural impossibility wholly excuses and excludes all blame, so the nearer the difficulty approaches to impossibility, still the nearer a person is to blamelessness, in proportion to that approach. And if the case of moral impossibility or necessity, be just the same with natural necessity or coaction, as to influence to excuse a neglect, then also, for the same reason, the case of natural difficulty doesn't differ in influence, to excuse a neglect, from moral difficulty, arising from a strong bias or bent to evil, such as Dr. Whitby owns in the case of those that are given up to their own hearts' lusts.

So that the fault of such persons must be lessened, in proportion to the difficulty, and approach to impossibility. If ten degrees of moral difficulty make the action quite impossible, and so wholly excused, then if there be nine degrees of difficulty, the person is in great part excused, and is nine degrees in ten, less blameworthy, than if there had been no difficulty at all; and he has but one degree of blameworthiness.

**DW: *The action or omission is the matter of the man who commits sin with his liberty, and it is not owing to the increase of moral inclination or difficulty.***

The reason is plain, on Arminian principles; viz. because as difficulty, by antecedent bent and bias on the will, is increased, liberty of indifference, and self-determination in the will, is diminished: so much hindrance and impediment is there, in the way of the will's acting freely, by mere self-determination. And if ten degrees of such hindrance take away all such liberty, then nine degrees take away nine parts in ten, and leave but one degree of liberty. And therefore there is but one degree of blamableness, *caeteris paribus*,[8] in the neglect; the man being no further blamable in what he does, or neglects, than he has liberty in that affair: for blame or praise (say they) arises wholly from a good use or abuse of liberty.

From all which it follows, that a strong bent and bias one way, and difficulty of going the contrary, never causes a person to be at all more exposed to sin, or anything blamable: because as the difficulty is increased, so much the less is required and expected. Though in one respect, exposedness to sin or fault is increased, viz. by an increase of exposedness to the evil action or; yet it is diminished in another respect, to balance it; namely, as the sinfulness or blamableness of the action or omission is diminished in the same proportion. So that, on the whole, the affair, as to exposedness to guilt or blame, is left just as it was.

**JE: *Even if a free agent like a balance scale is induced with a self-moving power and neglects and fails due to its newly faced difficulty, she/he must be blamable.***

---

8  [*Caeteris paribus* means that if all other relevant things, factors, or elements remain unaltered.]

## Section 3—The Case of Such as are Given Up of God to Sin, and of Fallen Man in General

To illustrate this, let us suppose a scale of a balance to be intelligent, and a free agent, and induced with a self-moving power,[9] by virtue of which it could act and produce effects to a certain degree; *ex gratia*[10] to move itself up or down with a force equal to a weight of ten pounds; and that it might therefore be required of it, in ordinary circumstances, to move itself down with that force; for which it has power and full liberty, and therefore would be blameworthy if it failed of it.

But then let us suppose a weight of ten pounds to be put in the opposite scale, which in force entirely counterbalances its self-moving power, and so renders it impossible for it to move down at all; and therefore wholly excuses it from any such motion.

But if we suppose there to be only nine pounds in the opposite scale, this renders its motion not impossible, but yet more difficult; so that it can now only move down with the force of one pound: but however, this is all that is required of it under these circumstances; it is wholly excused from nine parts of its motion: and if the scale, under these circumstances, neglects to move, and remains at rest, all that it will be blamed for, will be its neglect of that one tenth part of its motion; which it had as much liberty and advantage for, as in usual circumstances, it has for the greater motion, which in such a case would be required. So that this new difficulty, doesn't at all increase its exposedness to anything blameworthy.[11]

And thus the very supposition of difficulty in the way of a man's duty, or proclivity to sin, through a being given up to hardness of heart, or indeed by any other means whatsoever, is an inconsistence, according to Dr. Whitby's notions of liberty, virtue and vice, blame and praise. The avoiding sin and blame, and the doing what is virtuous and praiseworthy, must be always equally easy.[12]

**DW: *A person is given up and becomes unable to avoid sins and commits them, and so he/she would not be blamed.***

**JE: *It is just that a person who is entirely depraved and has no ability to avoid them should be condemned.***

---

9. [Plato identifies a self-moving mover as a god because he believes a soul has the unique characteristic of self-movement, the autonomous initiation of movement. See *Laws*, X, 895–9, Jowett's translation; J.C.A. Gaskin, "Philosophy and the Existence of God," *An Encyclopedia of Philosophy*, ed. G.H.R. Parkinson (UK: Routledge, 2012 ), 335, and also Henri Pemberton, *A View of Sir Isaac Newton* (1728), 34, 35: "For suppose a body by the structure or disposition of its parts or by any other circumstance in its make was induced with a *power* of moving itself; this *self-moving* principle, which should be thus inherent in the body, and not depend on anything external, must change the direction wherein it would act, as often as the position of the body was changed."]

10 [*Ex gratia* means "as a favor, not by legal necessity, voluntarily, out of kindness or grace."]

11. [Edwards's description in this ILL is not of his position but of Whitby's.]

12. [This sentence represents not Edwards's view but Whitby's.]

Dr. Whitby's notions of liberty, obligation, virtue, sin, etc., lead him into another great inconsistence. He abundantly insists, that necessity is inconsistent with the nature of sin or fault. He says in the aforementioned treatise (p. 14),

> "Who can blame a person for doing what he could not help?"

And (p. 15),

> "It being sensibly unjust, to punish any man for doing that which it was never in his power to avoid."[13]

And in p. 341 to confirm his opinion, he quotes one of the fathers, saying,

> "Why doth God command, if man hath not free will and power to obey?"

And again in the same and the next page,

> "Who will not cry out, that it is folly to command him, that hath not liberty to do what is commanded; and that it is unjust to condemn him, that has it not in his power to do what is required?"[14]

And in p. 373, he cites another saying,

> "A law is given to him that can turn to both parts; i.e. obey or transgress it: but no law can be against him who is bound by nature."[15]

And yet the same Dr. Whitby asserts, that fallen man is not able to perform perfect obedience. In p. 165 he has these words:

> "The nature of Adam had power to continue innocent, and without sin; whereas it is certain, our nature never had so."[16]

But if we have not power to continue innocent and without sin, then sin is consistent with necessity, and we may be sinful in that which we have not power to avoid; and those things can't be true, which he asserts elsewhere, namely,

> "That if we be necessitated, neither sins of omission nor commission, would deserve that name" (p. 348).[17]

If we have it not in our power to be innocent, then we have it not in our power to be blameless: and if so, we are under a necessity of being blameworthy. And how does this consist with what he so often asserts, that necessity is inconsistent with blame or praise?

---

13. Whitby, *Discourse on the Five Points*, Dis. I, Ch. 1, no. 3.
14. Whitby, *Discourse*, Dis. IV, Ch. 2, no. 4.
15. Whitby, *Discourse*, Dis. IV, Ch. 5, no. 2, quoting St. Macarius of Egypt (4th c. CE), Homily 26.
16. Whitby, *Discourse*, Dis. II, Ch. 6, no. 7. See above, Intro., pt. 5, no. 9.
17. Whitby, *Discourse*, Dis. IV, Ch. 3, no. 3.

## Section 3—The Case of Such as are Given Up of God to Sin, and of Fallen Man in General

If we have it not in our power to perform perfect obedience to all the commands of God, then we are under a necessity of breaking some commands, in some degree; having no power to perform so much as is commanded. And if so, why does he cry out of the unreasonableness and folly of commanding beyond what men have power to do?

***Ar: It is unjust that God requires anything of us beyond our power; imperfect obedience is not blameworthy under a new law of Christ.***

And Arminians in general are very inconsistent with themselves in what they say of the inability of fallen man in this respect. They strenuously maintain, that

> it would be unjust in God, to require anything of us beyond our present power and ability to perform;

and also hold, that

> we are now unable to perform perfect obedience, and that Christ died to satisfy for the imperfections of our obedience, and has made way that our imperfect obedience might be accepted instead of perfect: wherein they seem insensibly to run themselves into the grossest inconsistence.

For [as I have observed elsewhere], they hold

> "that God in mercy to mankind has abolished that rigorous constitution or law, that they were under originally; [...] and instead of it, has introduced a more mild constitution, and put us under a new law, which requires no more than imperfect sincere obedience, in compliance with our poor infirm impotent circumstances since the fall."[18]

***Ar: Under Christ's new law, our imperfect obedience is not a sin.***

***JE: Did Christ die in vain for our imperfect obedience that is not a sin?***

Now, how can these things be made consistent? I would ask what law these imperfections of our obedience are a breach of?

If they are a breach of no law that we were ever under, then they are not sins.

And if they be not sins, what need of Christ's dying to satisfy for them?

But if they are sins, and the breach of some law, what law is it? They can't be a breach of their new law; for that requires no other than imperfect obedience, or obedience with imperfections: and therefore to have obedience attended with imperfections, is no breach of it; for it is as much as it requires. And they can't be a breach of their old law; for that, they say, is entirely abolished, and we never were under it. They say, it would not be just in God to require of us perfect obedience, because it would not be just to require more than we can perform, or to punish us for failing of it. And

18. ["Justification by Faith Alone (delivered in 1734, published in 1738), *WJE* 19:165–66.]

therefore, by their own scheme, the imperfections of our obedience don't deserve to be punished.

> What need therefore of Christ's dying, to satisfy for them?
>
> What need of his suffering, to satisfy for that which is no fault, and in its own nature deserves no suffering?
>
> What need of Christ's dying, to purchase, that our *imperfect* obedience should be accepted, when according to their scheme, it would be unjust in itself, that any other obedience than *imperfect* should be required?
>
> What need of Christ's dying to make way for God's accepting such an obedience, as it would be unjust in him not to accept?
>
> Is there any need of Christ's dying, to prevail with God not to do unrighteously?

If it be said, that Christ died to satisfy that old law for us, that so we might not be under it, but that there might be room for our being under a more mild law; still I would inquire,

what need of Christ's dying that we might not be under a law, which (by their principles) it would be in itself unjust that we should be under, whether Christ had died or no, because in our present state we are not able to keep it?

**Henry Stebbing: Owing to original sin, we are utterly physically challenged to perform the condition of pardon and to obey the new law, without grace, that God requires. and it is ridiculous.**

**JE: Whether God requires or withholds his grace, we cannot make a complaint of that, for we cannot perform the condition without it, and it is like a total debt.**

So the Arminians are inconsistent with themselves, not only in what they say of the need of Christ's satisfaction to atone for those imperfections which we cannot avoid, but also in what they say of the grace of God, granted to enable men to perform the sincere obedience of the new law.

> "I grant (says Dr. Stebbing)[19] indeed, that by reason of original sin, we are utterly disabled for the performance of the condition, without new grace from God. But I say then, that he gives such grace to all of us, by which the performance of the condition is truly possible: and upon this ground he may, and doth most righteously require it."

If Dr. Stebbing intends to speak properly, by "grace" he must mean, that assistance which is of grace, or of free favor and kindness. But yet in the same place he

---

19. [Henry Stebbing, *A Treatise Concerning the Operations of the Holy Spirit, Being the Substance of the late Reverend and Learned Dr. William Clagett's Discourse upon That Subject, with Large Additions* (London, 1719; 2nd, ed., 1725), 112–13. [Stebbing abstracted the words of Dr. William Clagett, in his book against Dr. Owen. See "Book of Minutes on the Arminian Controversy" (Gazeteer Notebook), in *WJE* 37:34.]

speaks of it as very "unreasonable, unjust and cruel," for God to require that, as the condition of pardon, that is become impossible by original sin.

If it be so,

> what *grace* is there in giving assistance and ability to perform the condition of pardon?

> Or why is that called by the name of grace, that is an absolute debt, which God is bound to bestow, and which it would be unjust and cruel in him to withhold, seeing he requires that, *as the condition of pardon*, which we cannot perform without it?

# Section 4

## Command, and Obligation to Obedience, Consistent with Moral Inability to Obey

*Why should men be required to obey, though they are unable?*

*Why are they responsible, though they cannot hold from disobeying?*

*Ar: Necessity is inconsistent with law or command; natural and moral inability are the same.*

*JE: Necessity is consistent with law or command; natural and moral inability are diverse.*

It being so much insisted on by Arminian writers, that necessity is inconsistent with law or command, and particularly, that it is absurd to suppose God by his command should require that of men which they are unable to do; not allowing in this case for any difference that there is between natural and moral inability; I would therefore now particularly consider this matter.[1]

And for the greater clearness, I would distinctly lay down the following things.

---

1. [In the late 1770s Sutcliff, Fuller, and Ryland of Old England read JE's *FOW* and his distinction between moral and natural inability helped them solve their question of duty faith, and Ryland loaned a book from John Newton, *The Consistency of the Sinner's Inability to comply with the Gospel. . . . On John 6:44* (1769, by John Smalley, a disciple of Edwards and Bellamy). In the end Ryland declared that owing to the natural inability, sinners could be freely invited to respond to the gospel because they were under no natural inability to comply with its terms, and it rather affected William Carey and Andrew Fuller to activism in mission. See D. Bruce Hindmarsh, "The Reception of Jonathan by Early Evangelicals in England," in *Jonathan Edwards at Home and Abroad: Historical Memories, Cultural Movements, Global Horizons*, ed., David William Kling, and Douglas A. Sweeney (University of South Carolina Press, 2003), 207–08.]

### I. *The soul only is directly the subject of receiving or perceiving commands, the body is subject to the former, and the will is the object of the former.*

I. The will itself, and not only those actions which are the effects of the will, is the proper object of precept or command. That is, such or such a state or acts of men's wills, is in many cases, properly required of them by command; and not only those alterations in the state of their bodies or minds that are the consequences of volition. This is most manifest; for it is the soul only, that is properly and directly the subject of precepts or commands; that only being capable of receiving or perceiving commands. The motions or state of the body are matter of command, only as they are subject to the soul, and connected with its acts.

But now the soul has no other faculty whereby it can, in the most direct and proper sense, consent, yield to, or comply with any command, but the faculty of the will; and it is by this faculty only, that the soul can directly disobey, or refuse compliance: for the very notions of "consenting," "yielding," "accepting," "complying," "refusing," "rejecting," etc., are, according to the meaning of the terms, nothing but certain acts of the will.

Obedience, in the primary nature of it, is the submitting and yielding of the will of one to the will of another. Disobedience is the not consenting, not complying of the will of the commanded to the manifested will of the commander. Other acts that are not the acts of the will, as certain motions of the body and alterations in the soul, are obedience or disobedience only indirectly, as they are connected with the state or actions of the will, according to an established law of nature.

So that it is manifest, the will itself may be required: and the being of a good will is the most proper, direct and immediate subject of command; and if this can't be prescribed or required by command or precept, nothing can; for other things can be required no otherwise than as they depend upon, and are the fruits of a good will.

### *The first one in a series of acts determines the following acts, and as the subject of command, it either obeys or disobeys.*

*Corol.* 1. If there be several acts of the will, or a series of acts, one following another, and one the effect of another, the *first and determining act* is properly the subject of command, and not only the consequent acts, which are dependent upon it. Yea, it is this more especially which is that which command or precept has a proper respect to; because it is this act that determines the whole affair: in this act the obedience or disobedience lies, in a peculiar manner; the consequent acts being all subject to it, and governed and determined by it. This determining governing act must be the proper subject of precept, or none.

### *Ar: The soul acts prior to the will and determines all the acts and volitions of the will.*

### *JE: The acts of the soul are not the same the acts of the will; command is matter of will, and so the soul cannot be subject to it.*

*Corol.* 2. It also follows from what has been observed, that if there be any sort of act, or exertion of the soul, prior to all free acts of the will or acts of choice in the case, directing and determining what the acts of the will shall be; that act or exertion of the soul can't properly be subject to any command or precept, in any respect whatsoever, either directly or indirectly, immediately or remotely. Such acts can't be subject to commands *directly*, because they are no acts of the will; being by the supposition prior to all acts of the will, determining and giving rise to all its acts: they not being acts of the will, there can be in them no consent to, or compliance with any command. Neither can they be subject to command or precept *indirectly* or *remotely*; for they are not so much as the effects or consequences of the will, being prior to all its acts. So that if there be any obedience in that original act of the soul, determining all volitions, it is an act of obedience wherein the will has no concern at all; it preceding every act of will. And therefore, if the soul either obeys or disobeys in this act, it is wholly involuntarily; there is no willing obedience or rebellion, no compliance or opposition of the will in the affair: and what sort of obedience or rebellion is this!

**Ar: *The freedom of the will implies the soul's determining all its own acts of will.***

And thus the Arminian notion of the freedom of the will consisting in the soul's determining its own acts of will, instead of being essential to moral agency, and to men's being the subjects of moral government,[2] is utterly inconsistent with it. For if the soul determines *all* its acts of will, it is therein subject to no command or moral government, as has been now observed;

**JE: *A preceding one of the will's acts plays a role of the subject of commend, and so it is necessary.***

because its original determining act is no act of will or choice, it being prior, by the supposition, to *every act* of will. And the soul can't be the subject of command in the act of the will itself, which depends on the foregoing determining act, and is determined by it; inasmuch as this is necessary, being the necessary consequence and effect of that prior determining act, which is not voluntary. Nor can the man be the subject of command or government in his external actions; because these are all necessary, being the necessary effects of the acts of the will themselves. So that mankind, according to this scheme, are subjects of command or moral government in nothing at all; and all their moral agency is entirely excluded, and no room left for virtue or vice in the world.

---

2. [The term "moral government" was first used by Hugo Grotius (1583–1645), then by Edwards. N.W. Taylor's definition of it is the most similar to Edwards as followings: 1. A moral government is an influence on moral beings, or on beings capable of moral action 2. A perfect moral government implies a moral governor 3. The influence of a perfect moral government is designed so to control the action of moral beings, as to secure the great end of action on their part See Nathaniel W. Taylor, *Lectures on the Moral Government of God*, vol. 1 (New York: Clark, Austin & Smith, 1859), 7–10.]

## Section 4—Command, and Obligation to Obedience, Consistent with Moral Inability to Obey

**JE: *If, as Arminians hold, events occur by pure accident and men act from their freedom of indifference, law and commands would be of no use.***

So that it is the Arminian scheme, and not the scheme of the Calvinists, that is utterly inconsistent with moral government, and with all use of laws, precepts, prohibitions, promises, or threatenings. Neither is there any way whatsoever to make their principles consist with these things. For if it be said, that there is no prior determining act of the soul, preceding the acts of the will, but that volitions are events that come to pass by pure accident, without any determining cause, this is most palpably inconsistent with all use of laws and precepts; for nothing is more plain than that laws can be of no use to direct and regulate perfect accident; which by the supposition of its being pure accident, is in no case regulated by anything preceding; but happens this way or that perfectly by chance, without any cause or rule. The perfect uselessness of laws and precepts also follows from the Arminian notion of indifference, as essential to that liberty which is requisite to virtue or vice. For the end of laws is to *bind to one side*; and the end of commands is to turn the will one way: and therefore they are of no use unless they turn or bias the will that way. But if liberty consists in indifference, then their biasing the will one way only, destroys liberty; as it puts the will out of equilibrium. So that the will, having a bias, through the influence of binding law, laid upon it, is not wholly left to itself, to determine itself which way it will, without influence from without.

**JE: *The opposition or defect of the will to the given commands implies that a man is in a moral inability to that thing.***

II. Having shown that the will itself, especially in those acts which are original, leading and determining in any case, is the proper subject of precept and command, and not only those alterations in the body, etc., which are the effects of the will; I now proceed in the second place, to observe that the very opposition or defect of the will itself, in that act which is its *original and determining act* in the case,

I say the will's opposition in this act to a thing proposed or commanded, or its failing of compliance, implies a moral inability to that thing: or in other words, whenever a command requires a certain state or act of the will, and the person commanded, notwithstanding the command and the circumstances under which it is exhibited, still finds his will opposite or wanting, in *that*, belonging to its state or acts, *which is original and determining in the affair*, that man is morally unable to obey that command.

**JE: *Man is morally unable to obey, not only under the influence or prevalence of a contrary inclination, but also under a want of inclination.***

This is manifest from what was observed in the first part, concerning the nature of *moral* inability, as distinguished from natural: where it was observed, that a man may then be said to be morally unable to do a thing, when he is under the influence or prevalence of a contrary inclination, or has a want of inclination, under such circumstances and views. It is also evident from what has been before proved, that the will is always, and in every individual act, necessarily determined by the strongest motive; and so is always unable to go against the motive, which all things considered, has now the greatest strength and advantage to move the will. But not further to insist on these things, the truth of the position now laid down, viz. that when the will is opposite *to*, or failing of a compliance with a thing *in its original determining inclination or act*, it is not able to comply, appears by the consideration of these two things.

### 1. The will acts after the inclination, and it cannot alter its present choice but its future one.

1. The will in the time of that diverse or opposite leading act or inclination, and when actually under the influence of it, is not able to exert itself to the contrary, to make an alteration, in order to a compliance. The inclination is unable to change itself; and that for this plain reason, that it is unable to incline to change itself. Present choice can't at present choose to be otherwise: for that would be at present to choose something diverse from what is at present chosen. If the will, all things now considered, inclines or chooses to go that way, then it can't choose, all things now considered, to go the other way, and so can't choose to be made to go the other way. To suppose that the mind is now sincerely inclined to change itself to a different inclination, is to suppose the mind is now truly inclined otherwise than it is now inclined. The will may oppose some future remote act that it is exposed to, but not its own present act.

### 2. The will cannot comply with the command by any act of its own when it is already under the opposite leading act.

2. As it is impossible that the will should comply with the thing commanded with respect to its *leading act*, by any act of its own, in the time of that diverse or opposite leading and original act, or after it is actually come under the influence of that determining *choice or inclination*; so it is impossible it should be determined to a compliance by any foregoing act; for by the very supposition, there is no foregoing act; the opposite or noncomplying act being that act which is *original* and *determining* in the case.

Therefore, it must be so, that if this *first determining act* be found noncomplying, on the proposal of the command, the mind is morally unable to obey. For to suppose it to be able to obey, is to suppose it to be able to determine and cause its *first determining act* to be otherwise, and that it has power better to govern and regulate its *first governing and regulating act*, which is absurd; for it is to suppose a prior act of the will, determining its first determining act; that is, an act prior to the first, and leading and governing the original and governing act of all; which is a contradiction.

Here if it should be said, that although the mind has not any ability to will contrary to what it does will, in the original and leading act of the will, because there is

## Section 4—Command, and Obligation to Obedience, Consistent with Moral Inability to Obey

supposed to be no prior act to determine and order it otherwise, and the will can't immediately change itself, because it can't at present incline to a change; yet the mind has an ability for the present *to forebear* to proceed to action, and take time for deliberation; which may be an occasion of the change of the inclination—

*(1) JE: An act of the will is all the act of the mind, which exercises all that be commanded.*

I answer,

(1) In this objection that seems to be forgotten which was observed before, viz. that the determining to take the matter into consideration, is itself an act of the will:

and if this be all the act wherein the mind exercises ability and freedom, then this, by the supposition, must be all that can be commanded or required by precept.

And if this act be the commanded act, then all that has been observed concerning the commanded act of the will remains true, that the very want of it is a moral inability to exert it, etc.

*(2) JE: There is another act before the first and leading act of the will, that determines the latter.*

(2) We are speaking concerning the first and leading act of the will in the case, or about the affair; and if a determining to deliberate, or on the contrary, to proceed immediately without deliberating, be the first and leading act; or whether it be or no, if there be another act before it, which determines that; or whatever be the original and leading act; still the foregoing proof stands good, that the noncompliance of the leading act implies moral inability to comply.

If it should be objected, that these things make all moral inability equal, and suppose men morally unable to will otherwise than they actually do will, in all cases, and equally so, in every instance —

In answer to this objection, I desire two things may be observed,

*JE: The will acts by moral necessity and is morally unable to do otherwise. Depending on the case and the person, the inability may be greater than others.*

First, that if by being *equally* unable, be meant as *really* unable; then so far as the inability is merely moral, it is true, the will, in every instance, acts by moral necessity, and is morally unable to act otherwise, as truly and properly in one case as another; as, I humbly conceive, has been perfectly and abundantly demonstrated by what has been said in the preceding part of this essay. But yet, in some respect, the inability may be said to be greater in some instances than others: though the man may be truly unable (if moral inability can truly be called inability), yet he may be further from being able to do some things than others. As it is in things which men are naturally unable to do.

**ILL:** *As a person whose strength is only enough to lift the weight of 100 pounds is unable to lift 101 pounds, so is he to do things contrary to his present inclination or motive.*

A person whose strength is no more than sufficient to lift the weight of one hundred pounds, is as truly and really unable to lift one hundred and one pounds, as ten thousand pounds; but yet he is further from being able to lift the latter weight than the former; and so, according to common use of speech, has a greater inability for it. So it is in moral inability.

A man is truly morally unable to choose contrary to a present inclination, which in the least degree prevails; or contrary to that motive, which, all things considered, has strength and advantage now to move the will, in the least degree, superior to all other motives in view: but yet he is further from ability to resist a very strong habit, and a violent and deeply rooted inclination, or a motive vastly exceeding all others in strength. And again, the inability may in some respects be called greater, in some instances than others, as it may be *more general* and *extensive to all acts of that kind*.

So men may be said to be unable in a different sense, and to be further from moral ability, who have that moral inability which is *general* and *habitual*, than they who have only that inability which is *occasional* and *particular*.[3]

Thus in cases of natural inability; he that is born blind may be said to be unable to see, in a different manner, and is in some respects further from being able to see, than he whose sight is hindered by a transient cloud or mist.

**JE:** *The present volition or choice is brought out from an old habit, and so men cannot resist or avoid the former.*

And besides, that which was observed in the first part of this discourse concerning the inability which attends a *strong and settled habit*, should be here remembered; viz. that fixed habit is attended with this peculiar moral inability, by which it is distinguished from *occasional volition*, namely, that endeavors to avoid future volitions of that kind, which are agreeable to such a habit, much more frequently and commonly prove vain and insufficient.

For though it is impossible there should be any true sincere desires and endeavors against a present volition or choice, yet there may be against volitions of that kind, when viewed at a distance.

A person may desire and use means to prevent future exercises of a certain inclination; and in order to it, may wish the habit might be removed; but his desires and endeavors may be ineffectual.

The man may be said in some sense to be unable; yea, even as the word "unable" is a *relative term*, and has relation to ineffectual endeavors; yet not with regard to present, but remote endeavors.

---

3. [See Pt. I, sec. 4 for the distinction of moral inability.]

***JE: It is impossible to quit an old habit; the opposite desires and endeavors just look contrary to present volitions but not so, nor is alien but homogeneous.***

Secondly, it must be borne in mind, according to what was observed before, that indeed no inability whatsoever which is merely moral, is properly called by the name of "inability"; and that in the strictest propriety of speech, a man may be said to have a thing in his power, if he has it at his election; and he can't be said to be unable to do a thing, when he can if he now pleases, or whenever he has a proper, direct and immediate desire for it.

As to those desires and endeavors that may be against the exercises of a strong habit, with regard to which men may be said to be unable to avoid those exercises, they are remote desires and endeavors in two respects. First, as to *time*; they are never against present volitions, but only against volitions of such a kind, when viewed at a distance. Secondly, as to their *nature*; these opposite desires are not directly and properly against the habit and inclination itself, or the volitions in which it is exercised; for these, in themselves considered, are agreeable; but against something else, that attends them, or is their consequence; the opposition of the mind is leveled entirely against this; the inclination or volitions themselves are not at all opposed directly, and for their own sake; but only indirectly, and remotely on the account of something alien and foreign.

### III. *JE: Though men are morally unable, a good state or act of will can be properly required by the command.*

III. Though the opposition of the will itself, or the very want of will to a thing commanded, implies a moral inability to that thing; yet, if it be as has been already shown, that the being of a good state or act of will, is a thing most properly required by command; then, in some cases such a state or act of will may properly be required, which at present is not, and which may also be wanting after it is commanded. And therefore those things may properly be commanded, which men have a moral inability for.

Such a state or act of the will, may be required by command, as does not already exist. For if that volition only may be commanded to be which already is, there could be no use of precept; commands in all cases would be perfectly vain and impertinent.

### *Ar: Who shall not disobey the rightful command?*

### *JE: Consequently, that means men always obey it necessarily.*

And not only may such a will be required as is wanting before the command is given, but also such as may possibly be wanting afterwards; such as the exhibition of the command may not be effectual to produce or excite.

Otherwise, no such thing as disobedience to a proper and rightful command is possible in any case; and there is no case supposable or possible, wherein there can be an inexcusable or faulty disobedience. Which Arminians cannot affirm, consistently with their principles: for this makes obedience to just and proper commands always *necessary*, and disobedience impossible.

And so the Arminian would overthrow himself, yielding the very point we are upon, which he so strenuously denies, viz. that law and command are consistent with necessity. If merely that inability will excuse disobedience, which is implied in the opposition or defect of inclination, remaining after the command is exhibited, then wickedness always carries that in it which excuses it.

***Ar: Men's moral inability is not related to their wickedness.***

***JE: Men are morally unable in terms of their evil inclination and wickedness.***

It is evermore so, that by how much the more wickedness there is in a man's heart, by so much is his inclination to evil the stronger, and by so much the more therefore has he of moral inability to the good required. His moral inability, consisting in the strength of his evil inclination, is the very thing wherein his wickedness consists; and yet according to Arminian principles, it must be a thing inconsistent with wickedness; and by how much the more he has of it, by so much is he the further from wickedness.

***Moral inability: Men cannot excuse their moral inability, for it is from their evil inclination and wickedness. Natural inability: Men cannot excuse their inability, for it is arisen from the want of natural capacity or external hindrance.***

Therefore, on the whole, it is manifest, that moral inability alone (which consists in disinclination) never renders anything improperly the subject matter of precept or command, and never can excuse any person in disobedience, or want of conformity to a command.[4] Natural inability, arising from the want of natural capacity, or external hindrance (which alone is properly called inability) without doubt wholly excuses, or makes a thing improperly the matter of command. If men are excused from doing or acting any good thing, supposed to be commanded, it must be through some defect or obstacle that is not in the will itself, but extrinsic to it; either in the capacity of understanding, or body, or outward circumstances.

Here two or three things may be observed,

***Excusable acts are arisen from the want of capacity in the natural faculty of understanding.***

***Inexcusable acts are arisen from the moral state of the will or inclination itself.***

1. As to spiritual duties or acts, or any good thing in the state of immanent acts of the will itself, or of the affections (which are only certain modes of the exercise of the will) if persons are justly excused, it must be through want of capacity in the natural faculty of understanding.

---

4. [See also *FOW*, 159, 305.]

Thus the same spiritual duties, or holy affections and exercises of heart, can't be required of men, as may be of angels; the capacity of understanding being so much inferior. So men can't be required to love those amiable persons whom they have had no opportunity to see, or hear of, or come to the knowledge of, in any way agreeable to the natural state and capacity of the human understanding. But the insufficiency of motives will not excuse; unless their being insufficient arises not from the moral state of the will or inclination itself, but from the state of the natural understanding.

The great kindness and generosity of another may be a motive insufficient to excite gratitude in the person that receives the kindness, through his vile and ungrateful temper: in this case, the insufficiency of the motive arises from the state of the will or inclination of heart, and don't at all excuse. But if this generosity is not sufficient to excite gratitude, being unknown, there being no means of information adequate to the state and measure of the person's faculties, this insufficiency is attended with a natural inability, which entirely excuses.

**JE: *Motions of the body or exercises of mind are not the immanent acts of the will itself but are required as effects of the will. This will do his duty in full compliance with a given command. On the contrary, men can be perfectly excused if their wills do not comply and they have no volition but natural inability.***

2. As to such motions of body, or exercises and alterations of mind, which don't consist in the immanent acts or state of the will itself, but are supposed to be required as effects of the will; I say, in such supposed effects of the will, in cases wherein there is no want of a capacity of understanding; that inability, and that only excuses, which consists in want of connection between them and the will. If the will fully complies, and the proposed effects don't prove, according to the laws of nature, to be connected with his volition, the man is perfectly excused; he has a natural inability to the thing required. For the will itself, as has been observed, is all that can be directly and immediately required by command; and other things only indirectly, as connected with the will. If therefore there be a full compliance of will, the person has done his duty; and if other things don't prove to be connected with his volition, that is not owing to him.

***Natural and moral inabilities would be inexcusable obstacles if they were arisen from the want of understanding and strength.***

3. Both these kinds of natural inability that have been mentioned, and so all inability that excuses, may be resolved into one thing; namely, want of natural capacity or strength; either capacity of understanding, or external strength. For when there are external defects and obstacles, they would be no obstacles, were it not for the imperfection and limitations of understanding and strength.

**JE: *God's command is more proper to moral inability of fallen men than his invitation.***

*Corol.* If things for which men have a moral inability, may properly be the matter of precept or command, then they may also of invitation and counsel. Commands, and invitations come very much to the same thing; the difference is only circumstantial: commands are as much a manifestation of the will of him that speaks, as invitations, and as much testimonies of expectation of compliance. The difference between them lies in nothing that touches the affair in hand. The main difference between command and invitation consists in the enforcement of the will of him who commands or invites. In the latter it is his *kindness*, the goodness which his will arises from: in the former it is his *authority*. But whatever be the ground of the will of him that speaks, or the enforcement of what he says, yet seeing neither his will nor expectation is any more testified in the one case than the other; therefore a person's being known to be morally unable to do the thing to which he is directed *by invitation*, is no more an evidence of insincerity in him that directs, in manifesting either a will, or expectation which he has not, than his being known to be morally unable to do what he is directed to *by command*. So that all this grand objection of Arminians against the inability of fallen men to exert faith in Christ, or to perform other spiritual gospel duties, from the sincerity of God's counsels and invitations, must be without force.

# Section 5

## That Sincerity of Desires and Endeavors, Which is Supposed to Excuse in the Nonperformance of Things in Themselves Good, Particularly Considered

*Can men excuse that they commit sin and disobey to do good, even though they desire and endeavor to do it? Is it proper to do good without any right end?*

*JE: Nonbelievers do as such, and sincere desire and endeavor is good and virtuous.*

*Ar: We are not guilty if we had sincere desire and endeavor but did not perform well.*

It is what is much insisted on by many, that some men, though they are not able to perform spiritual duties, such as repentance of sin, love to God, a cordial acceptance of Christ as exhibited and offered in the gospel, etc., yet they may sincerely desire and endeavor these things; and therefore must be excused; it being unreasonable to blame them for the omission of those things which they sincerely desire and endeavor to do, but can't do.

Concerning this matter, the following things may be observed.

***1. Arminian Absurdity: It is absurd that men desire spiritual duties and yet are not able to perform them.***

1. What is here supposed, is a great mistake, and gross absurdity; even that men may sincerely choose and desire those spiritual duties of love, acceptance, choice, rejection, etc., consisting in the exercise of the will itself, or in the disposition and inclination of the heart; and yet not be able to perform or exert them. This is absurd, because it is absurd to suppose that a man should directly, properly and sincerely incline to have an inclination, which at the same time is contrary to his inclination: for that is to suppose him not to be inclined to that which he is inclined to.

If a man, in the state and acts of his will and inclination, does properly and directly fall in with those duties, he therein performs them: for the duties themselves consist in that very thing; they consist in the state and acts of the will being so formed and directed.

If the soul properly and sincerely falls in with a certain proposed act of will or choice, the soul therein makes that choice its own. Even as when a moving body falls in with a proposed direction of its motion, that is the same thing as to move in that direction.

### 2. Arminian Absurdity: *It is absurd that men don't perform inward duties and yet say they desire to do them.*

2. That which is called a "desire" and "willingness" for those inward duties, in such as don't perform them, has respect to these duties only indirectly and remotely, and is improperly represented as a willingness for them; not only because (as was observed before) it respects those good volitions only in a distant view, and with respect to future time; but also because evermore, not these things themselves, but something else, that is alien and foreign, is the object that terminates these volitions and desires.

### ILL: *A drunkard tried to stop drinking but failed, for he had no sincere desire.*

A drunkard, who continues in his drunkenness, being under the power of a love, and violent appetite to strong drink, and without any love to virtue; but being also extremely covetous and close, and very much exercised and grieved at the diminution of his estate, and prospect of poverty, may in a sort "desire" the virtue of temperance: and though his present will is to gratify his extravagant appetite, yet he may wish he had a heart to forbear future acts of intemperance, and forsake his excesses, through an unwillingness to part with his money: but still he goes on with his drunkenness; his wishes and endeavors are insufficient and ineffectual: such a man has no proper, direct, sincere willingness to forsake this vice, and the vicious deeds which belong to it: for he acts voluntarily in continuing to drink to excess: his desire is very improperly called a willingness to be temperate; it is no true desire of that virtue; for it is not that virtue that terminates his wishes; nor have they any direct respect at all to it. It is only *the saving his money*, and avoiding poverty, that terminates, and exhausts the whole strength of his desire. The virtue of temperance is regarded only very indirectly and improperly, even as a necessary means of gratifying the vice of covetousness.

### ILL: *A wicked man wishes holiness, but he has no sincere willingness, like a sick man desires a dose that he greatly abhors, to save his life.*

So, a man of an exceeding corrupt and wicked heart, who has no love to God and Jesus Christ, but on the contrary, being very profanely and carnally inclined, has the greatest distaste of the things of religion, and enmity against them; yet being of a family, that from one generation to another, have most of them died in youth of an hereditary consumption; and so having little hope of living long; and having been instructed in the necessity of a supreme love to Christ, and gratitude for his death and sufferings, in order to his salvation from eternal misery; if under these circumstances he should, through fear of eternal torments, wish he had such a disposition: but his profane and carnal heart remaining, he continues still in his habitual distaste of, and enmity to God and religion, and wholly without any exercise of that love and gratitude (as doubtless the very devils themselves, notwithstanding all the devilishness of their temper, would wish for a holy heart, if by that means they could get out of hell): in this case, there is no sincere willingness to love Christ and choose him as his chief good:

these holy dispositions and exercises are not at all the direct object of the will: they truly share no part of the inclination or desire of the soul; but all is terminated on deliverance from torment: and these graces and pious volitions, notwithstanding this forced consent, are looked upon as undesirable; as when a sick man desires a dose he greatly abhors, to save his life. — From these things it appears:

### 3. Indirect willingness is not that exercise of the will which the command requires, but it is entirely a different one.

3. That this indirect willingness which has been spoken of, is not that exercise of the will which the command requires; but is entirely a different one; being a volition of a different nature, and terminated altogether on different objects; wholly falling short of that virtue of will, which the command has respect to.

### 4. This different volition is indirectly concerned with the duty required, and it is want of the will, and is wholly destitute of the virtue.

4. This other volition, which has only some indirect concern with the duty required, can't excuse for the want of that good will itself, which is commanded; being not the thing which answers and fulfills the command, and being wholly destitute of the virtue which the command seeks.

### ILL: An evil son hates his good and rich father but apprehends his future and takes his indirect willingness from his dishonest motive to honor him, but he cannot be excused for his disobedience to God's commands and dispositions.

Further to illustrate this matter: If a child has a most excellent father, that has ever treated him with fatherly kindness and tenderness, and has every way in the highest degree merited his love and dutiful regard, being withal very wealthy; but the son is of so vile a disposition, that he inveterately hates his father; and yet, apprehending that his hatred of him is like to prove his ruin, by bringing him finally to poverty and abject circumstances, through his father's disinheriting him, or otherwise; which is exceeding cross to his avarice and ambition; he therefore wishes it were otherwise: but yet remaining under the invincible power of his vile and malignant disposition, he continues still in his settled hatred of his father. Now if such a son's indirect willingness

to have love and honor towards his father, at all acquits or excuses before God, for his failing of actually exercising these dispositions towards him which God requires,
it must be on one of these two accounts.

(1) Either that it answers and fulfills the command. But this it does not, by the supposition; because the thing commanded is love and honor to his worthy parent. If the command be proper and just, as is supposed, then it obliges to the thing commanded; and so nothing else but that can answer the obligation. Or

(2) it must be at least because there is that virtue or goodness in his indirect willingness, that is equivalent to the virtue required; and so balances or countervails it, and makes up for the want of it. But that also is contrary to the supposition.

The willingness the son has merely from a regard to money and honor, has no goodness in it, to countervail the want of the pious filial respect required.

**JE: Even though there is a sincere desire to do bad, there would not always be a virtue.**

Sincerity and reality, in that indirect willingness which has been spoken of, don't make it the better. That which is real and hearty is often called sincere; whether it be in virtue or vice. Some persons are sincerely *bad*; others are sincerely *good*; and others may be sincere and hearty in things which are in their own nature *indifferent*; as a man may be sincerely desirous of eating when he is hungry. But a being sincere, hearty and in good earnest, is no virtue, unless it be in a thing that is virtuous. A man may be sincere and hearty in joining a crew of pirates, or a gang of robbers. When the devils cried out, and besought Christ not to torment them, it was no mere pretense; they were very hearty in their desires not to be tormented: but this did not make their will or desires virtuous. And if men have sincere desires, which are in their kind and nature no better, it can be no excuse for the want of any required virtue.

**JE: If there is not real goodness in all endeavors and desires, they are nothing.**

And as a man's being sincere in such an indirect desire or *willingness* to do his duty, as has been mentioned, can't excuse for the want of performance; so it is with *endeavors* arising from such a willingness. The endeavors can have no more goodness in them, than the will which they are the effect and expression of. And therefore, however sincere and real, and however great a person's endeavors are; yea, though they should be to the utmost of his ability; unless the will which they proceed from be truly good and virtuous, they can be of no avail, influence or weight to any purpose whatsoever, in a moral sense or respect. That which is not truly virtuous in God's sight, is looked upon by him as good for nothing: and so can be of no value, weight or influence in his account, to recommend, satisfy, excuse or make up for any moral defect. For nothing can counterbalance evil, but good.

***ILL: If a thing in a scale is not real, the scale does not descend. Real goodness is like a real weight.***

If evil be in one scale, and we put a great deal into the other, sincere and earnest desires, and many and great endeavors; yet if there be no real goodness in all, there is no weight in it; and so it does nothing towards balancing the real weight which is in the opposite scale.

***ILL: 00000000000000000000000000001 = 1***

It is only like the subtracting a thousand naughts from before a real number, which leaves the sum just as it was.

***JE: The endeavors without pure virtue have no good influence and can't help to avoid evils.***

Indeed, such endeavors may have a *negatively* good influence. Those things which have no positive virtue[1], have no positive moral influence; yet they may be an occasion of persons avoiding some positive evils.

***ILL: If a man saved his debtor from water for money, that is nothing good.***

As if a man were in the water with a neighbor that he had ill will to, who could not swim, holding him by his hand; which neighbor was much in debt to him; and should be tempted to let him sink and drown; but should refuse to comply with the temptation; not from love to his neighbor, but from the love of money, and because by his drowning he should lose his debt; that which he does in preserving his neighbor from drowning, is nothing good in the sight of God: yet hereby he avoids the greater guilt that would have been contracted, if he had designedly let his neighbor sink and perish.

***Ar: The reason why men are excused on the account of sincere honest endeavors is because in them is a positive moral weight or influence.***

But when Arminians in their disputes with Calvinists insist so much on sincere desires and endeavors, as what must excuse men, must be accepted of God, etc., it is manifest they have respect to some positive moral weight or influence of those desires and endeavors. Accepting, justifying, or excusing on the account of sincere honest endeavors (as they are called) and men's doing what they can, etc., has relation to some moral value, something that is accepted as good, and as such, countervailing some defect.

***Ambiguous definition of "sincere" raises confusion: Men's thinking would be virtuous if only there are sincere desires and endeavors.***

---

1. [Positive virtue means the virtue to exercise the duty required.]

But there is a great and unknown deceit, arising from the ambiguity of the phrase, "sincere endeavors." Indeed, there is a vast indistinctness and unfixedness in most, or at least very many of the terms used to express things pertaining to moral and spiritual matters. Whence arise innumerable mistakes, strong prejudices, inextricable confusion, and endless controversy.

The word "sincere" is most commonly used to signify something that is good: men are habituated to understand by it the same as "honest" and "upright"; which terms excite an idea of something good in the strictest and highest sense; good in the sight of him who sees not only the outward appearance, but the heart.[2] And therefore men think that if a person be sincere, he will certainly be accepted. If it be said that anyone is sincere in his endeavors, this suggests to men's minds as much, as that his heart and will is good, that there is no defect of duty, as to virtuous inclination; he honestly and uprightly desires and endeavors to do as he is required; and this leads them to suppose that it would be very hard and unreasonable to punish him, only because he is unsuccessful in his endeavors, the thing endeavored being beyond his power. — Whereas it ought to be observed, that the word "sincere" has these different significations:

### *"Sincerity" is reality of will and endeavor towards anything that is professed or pretended.*

1. "Sincerity," as the word is sometimes used, signifies no more than *reality of will and endeavor*, with respect to anything that is professed or pretended; without any consideration of the nature of the principle or aim, whence this real will and true endeavor arises.

If a man has some real desire to obtain a thing, either direct or indirect, or does really endeavor after a thing, he is said sincerely to desire or endeavor it; without any consideration of the goodness or virtuousness of the principle he acts from, or any excellency or worthiness of the end he acts for.

### *ILL: A man who sincerely helps his neighbor's wife for adultery.*

Thus a man that is kind to his neighbor's wife, who is sick and languishing, and very helpful in her case, makes a show of desiring and endeavoring her restoration to health and vigor; and not only makes such a show, but there is a reality in his pretense, he does heartily and earnestly desire to have her health restored, and uses his true and utmost endeavors for it; he is said sincerely to desire and endeavor it, because he does so truly or really; though perhaps the principle he acts from, is no other than a vile and scandalous passion; having lived in adultery with her, he earnestly desires to have her health and vigor restored, that he may return to his criminal pleasures with her. Or,

### *"True sincerity" has the reality of will and endeavor, which is pure and virtuous.*

2. [Cf. I Sam. 16:7]

2. By "sincerity" is meant, not merely a *reality* of will and endeavor of some sort or other, and from some consideration or other, but a *virtuous sincerity*. That is, that in the performance of those particular acts that are the matter of virtue or duty, there be not only the matter, but the form and essence of virtue, consisting in the aim that governs the act, and the principle exercised in it. There is not only the reality of the act, that is as it were the *body* of the duty; but also the *soul*, which should properly belong to such a body. In this sense, a man is said to be sincere, when he acts with a *pure intention*; not from sinister views, or by-ends: he not only in reality desires and seeks the thing to be done, or qualification to be obtained, for some end or other; but he wills the thing directly and properly, as neither forced nor bribed; the virtue of the thing is properly the object of the will.

In the former sense, a man is said to be sincere, in opposition to a mere pretense, and show of the *particular thing* to be done or exhibited, without any real desire or endeavor at all. In the latter sense, a man is said to be sincere, in opposition to that show of *virtue* there is in merely doing the matter of duty, without the reality of the virtue itself in the soul, and the essence of it, which there is a show of. A man may be sincere in the former sense, and yet in the latter be in the sight of God, who searches the heart, a vile hypocrite.

In the latter kind of sincerity, only, is there anything truly valuable or acceptable in the sight of God. And this is the thing which in Scripture is called sincerity, uprightness, integrity, truth in the inward parts, and a being of a perfect heart.

### Two Kinds of Sincerity: Objectionable and Acceptable

And if there be such a sincerity, and such a degree of it as there ought to be, and there be anything further that the man is not able to perform, or which don't prove to be connected with his sincere desires and endeavors, the man is wholly excused and acquitted in the sight of God; his will shall surely be accepted for his deed: and such a sincere will and endeavor is all that in strictness is required of him, by any command of God. But as to the other kind of sincerity of desires and endeavors, it having no virtue in it (as was observed before), can be of no avail before God, in any case, to recommend, satisfy, or excuse, and has no positive moral weight or influence whatsoever.

### Men's endeavors are worthless without true virtue or holiness in their hearts.

*Corol. 1.* Hence it may be inferred, that nothing in the reason and nature of things appears, from the consideration of any moral weight of that former kind of sincerity, which has been spoken of, at all obliging us to believe, or leading us to suppose, that God has made any positive promises of salvation, or grace, or any saving assistance, or any spiritual benefit whatsoever, to any desires, prayers, endeavors, striving, or obedience of those, who hitherto have no true virtue or holiness in their hearts; though we should suppose all the sincerity, and the utmost degree of endeavor, that is possible to be in a person without holiness.

***JE: Holy dispositions and exercises, such as honor to Christ, love to God, and loving holiness, are not the terms but the condition of salvation.***

Some object against God's requiring, as the condition of salvation, those holy exercises, which are the result of a supernatural renovation; such as a supreme respect to Christ, love to God, loving holiness for its own sake, etc., that these inward dispositions and exercises are above men's power, as they are by nature; and therefore that we may conclude, that when men are brought to be sincere in their endeavors, and do as well as they can, they are accepted; and that this must be all that God requires in order to men's being received as the objects of his favor, and must be what God has appointed as the condition of salvation.

***JE: If their such doing be not arisen from some good principle, disposition, or exercise of heart, like a windmill's doing, some virtuous inclination or act of the will, men's acts are not virtuous.***

Concerning which I would observe, that in such a manner of speaking of men's being accepted, because they are sincere, and do as well as they can, there is evidently a supposition of some virtue, some degree of that which is truly good; though it doesn't go so far as were to be wished. For if men "do what they can," unless their so doing be from some good principle, disposition, or exercise of heart, some virtuous inclination or act of the will; their so doing what they can, is in some respects not a whit better than if they did nothing at all. In such a case, there is no more positive moral goodness in a man's doing what he can, than in a windmill's doing what it can; because the action does no more proceed from virtue;

and there is nothing in such sincerity of endeavor, or doing what we can, that should render it any more a proper or fit recommendation to positive favor and acceptance, or the condition of any reward or actual benefit, than doing nothing; for both the one and the other are alike nothing, as to any true moral weight or value.

***JE: Jehovah's salvation is not consistent with the sincere endeavors of heathens.***

*Corol.* 2. Hence also it follows, there is nothing that appears in the reason and nature of things, which can justly lead us to determine, that God will certainly give the necessary means of salvation, or some way or other bestow true holiness and eternal life on those heathen, who are sincere (in the sense above explained) in their endeavors to find out the will of the deity, and to please him, according to their light, that they may escape his future displeasure and wrath, and obtain happiness in their future state, through his favor.

# Section 6

Liberty of Indifference, Not Only Not Necessary to Virtue, but Utterly Inconsistent with It; and All, Either Virtuous or Vicious Habits or Inclinations, Inconsistent with Arminian Notions of Liberty and Moral Agency

*Ar: Virtuous acts are arisen in a state of indifference.*

*JE: In the will can be no indifference nor equilibrium, but inclination to actions.*

To suppose such a freedom of will, as Arminians talk of, to be requisite to virtue and vice, is many ways contrary to common sense.

*Ar: Indifference is essential to virtue and vice.*

If indifference belongs to liberty of will, as Arminians suppose, and it be essential to a virtuous action that it be performed in a state of liberty, as they also suppose; it will follow, that it is essential to a virtuous action that it be performed in a state of indifference: and if it be performed in a *state* of indifference, then doubtless it must be performed in the *time* of indifference. And so it will follow, that in order to the virtuousness of an act, the heart must be indifferent in the time of the performance of that act, and the more indifferent and cold the heart is with relation to the act which is performed, so much the better; because the act is performed with so much the greater liberty.

*JE: Virtue is not in indifference but in the inclination of the heart to virtuous action.*

But is this agreeable to the light of nature? Is it agreeable[1] to the notions which mankind, in all ages, have of virtue, that it lies in that which is contrary to indifference,

---

1. [WJE Online 1, "In his copy of the Inquiry, JE Jr. inserted 'not,' though this change is not in the printed errata sheet." He changed it wrong.]

even in the tendency and inclination of the heart to virtuous action; and that the stronger the inclination, and so the further from indifference, the more virtuous the *heart*, and so much the more praiseworthy the *act* which proceeds from it?

**Ar: Only in a state of indifference or equilibrium, the will acts.**

**JE: No, it doesn't, because it is no longer in such a state and then its acts follow.**

If we should suppose (contrary to what has been before demonstrated) that there may be an act of will in a state of indifference; for instance, this act, viz. the will's determining to put itself out of a state of indifference, and give itself a preponderance one way, then it would follow, on Arminian principles, that this act or determination of the will is that alone wherein virtue consists, because this only is performed while the mind remains in a state of indifference, and so in a state of liberty:

for when once the mind is put out of its equilibrium, it is no longer in such a state; and therefore all the acts which follow afterwards, proceeding from bias, can have the nature neither of virtue nor vice. Or if the thing which the will can do, while yet in a state of indifference, and so of liberty, be only to suspend acting, and determine to take the matter into consideration, then this determination is that alone wherein virtue consists, and not proceeding to action after the scale is turned by consideration.

So that it will follow from these principles, all that is done after the mind, by any means, is once out of its equilibrium and already possessed by an inclination, and arising from that inclination, has nothing of the nature of virtue or vice, and is worthy of neither blame nor praise.

**JE: Sincerely virtuous actions arise not from indifference but from the good principle or disposition in the heart.**

But how plainly contrary is this to the universal sense of mankind, and to the notion they have of sincerely virtuous actions? Which is, that they are actions which proceed from a heart *well disposed* and *inclined*; and the *stronger*, and the more *fixed* and *determined* the good disposition of the heart, the greater the sincerity of virtue, and so the more of the truth and reality of it. But if there be any acts which are done in a state of equilibrium, or spring immediately from perfect indifference and coldness of heart, they cannot arise from any good principle or disposition in the heart; and consequently, according to common sense, have no sincere goodness in them, having no virtue of heart in them. To have a virtuous heart, is to have a heart that favors virtue, and is friendly to it, and not one perfectly cold and indifferent about it.

**JE: In a state of indifference cannot the will act or determine, it does not need to distinguish good and evil, and it cannot be virtuous or vicious.**

And besides the actions that are done in a state of indifference, or that arise immediately out of such a state, can't be virtuous, because, by the supposition, they are not determined by any preceding choice. For if there be preceding choice, then choice intervenes between the act and the state of indifference; which is contrary to the supposition of the acts arising immediately out of indifference. But those acts which are not determined by preceding choice, can't be virtuous or vicious by Arminian principles, because they are not determined by the will.

***Ar: If the action is determined by a preceding act of choice and can be done without freedom of indifference, we must not distinguish between virtue and vice.***

So that neither one way, nor the other, can any actions be virtuous or vicious according to Arminian principles. If the action *be determined* by a preceding act of choice it can't be virtuous; because the action is not done in a state of indifference, nor does immediately arise from such a state; and so is not done in a state of liberty. If the action be *not determined* by a preceding act of choice, then it can't be virtuous; because then the will is not self-determined in it. So that it is made certain, that neither virtue nor vice can ever find any place in the universe.

***JE: Remaining in indifference, even for a moment, without doing good or rejecting bad, would be highly vicious. ILL: My dying friend.***

Moreover, that it is necessary to a virtuous action that it be performed in a state of indifference, under a notion of that's being a state of liberty, is contrary to common sense; as it is a dictate of common sense, that indifference itself, in many cases, is vicious, and so to a high degree. As if when I see my neighbor or near friend, and one who has in the highest degree merited of me, in extreme distress, and ready to perish, I find an indifference in my heart with respect to anything proposed to be done, which I can easily do, for his relief. So if it should be proposed to me, to blaspheme God, or kill my father, or to do numberless other things which might be mentioned; the being indifferent, for a moment, would be highly vicious and vile.

***Risk of Arminian supposition that this liberty of indifference is essential to virtue and vice; that eliminates the different guilt of crimes and their heinousness.***

And it may be further observed, that to suppose this liberty of indifference is essential to virtue and vice, destroys the great difference of degrees of the guilt of different crimes, and takes away the heinousness of the most flagitious horrid iniquities; such as adultery, bestiality, murder, perjury, blasphemy, etc. For according to these principles, there is no harm at all in having the mind in a state of perfect indifference with respect to these crimes; nay, it is absolutely necessary in order to any virtue in avoiding them, or vice in doing them.

***JE: The state of indifference is the being ready to do and being infinitely near to do; equilibrium of mind is to be full as likely to do.***

But for the mind to be in a state of indifference with respect to them, is to be next door to doing them: it is then infinitely near to choosing, and so committing the fact:

for equilibrium is the next step to a degree of preponderation; and one, even the least degree of preponderation [all things considered] is choice. And not only so, but for the will to be in a state of perfect equilibrium with respect to such crimes, is for the mind to be in such a state, as to be full as likely to choose them as to refuse them, to do them as to omit them.

And if our minds must be in such a state wherein it is as near to choosing as refusing, and wherein it must of necessity, according to the nature of things, be as likely to commit them, as to refrain from them; where is the exceeding heinousness of choosing and committing them?

If there be no harm in often being in such a state, wherein the probability of doing and forbearing are exactly equal, there being an equilibrium, and no more tendency to one than the other; then according to the nature and laws of such a contingence, it may be expected, as an *inevitable* consequence of such a disposition of things, that we should choose them as often as reject them:

that it should generally so fall out is necessary, as equality in the effect is the natural consequence of the equal tendency of the cause, or of the antecedent state of things from which the effect arises: why then should we be so exceedingly to blame, if it does so fall out?

**JE: Arminians insist that liberty is necessary for acts and yet they deny the being of moral inclination, which is contrary to indifference and under which indeed they are.**

It is many ways apparent, that the Arminian scheme of liberty is utterly inconsistent with the being of any such things as either virtuous or vicious habits or dispositions. If liberty of *indifference* be essential to moral agency, then there can be no virtue in any habitual inclinations of the heart; which are contrary to indifference, and imply in their nature the very destruction and exclusion of it. They suppose nothing can be virtuous, in which no liberty is exercised; but how absurd is it to talk of exercising indifference under bias and preponderation.

**Ar: Men must be praised or blamed for their free acts, which are determined by their wills themselves.**

And if *self-determining power* in the will be necessary to moral agency, praise, blame, etc., then nothing done by the will can be any further praise or blameworthy, than so far as the will is moved, swayed and determined by itself, and the scales turned by the sovereign power the will has over itself. And therefore the will must not be put out of its balance already, the preponderation must not be determined and effected beforehand; and so the self-determining act anticipated.

**Ar: Habitual bias impedes liberty, and they itself cannot be either virtuous or vicious.**

**JE: The bias and inclination may be so strong that men must do all in necessity.**

## Section 6—Liberty of Indifference, Not Only Not Necessary to Virtue, but Utterly Inconsistent with It

Thus it appears another way, that habitual bias is inconsistent with that liberty which Arminians suppose to be necessary to virtue or vice; and so it follows, that habitual bias itself cannot be either virtuous or vicious. The same thing follows from their doctrine concerning the inconsistence of necessity with liberty, praise, dispraise, etc. None will deny, that bias and inclination may be so strong as to be invincible, and leave no possibility of the will's determining contrary to it; and so be attended with necessity. This Dr. Whitby allows concerning the will of God, angels and glorified saints, with respect to good; and the will of devils with respect to evil.[2]

Therefore, if necessity be inconsistent with liberty; then when fixed inclination is to such a degree of strength, it utterly excludes all virtue, vice, praise or blame. And if so, then the nearer habits are to this strength, the more do they impede liberty, and so diminish praise and blame.

If very strong habits destroy liberty, the lesser ones proportionably hinder it, according to their degree of strength. And therefore it will follow, that then is the act most virtuous or vicious, when performed without any inclination or habitual bias at all; because it is then performed with most liberty.

***Ar: A fixed bias causes a degree of moral inability and hinders for the contrary act, and so moral acts shall not be judged good or bad and the inability is inconsistent with moral agency.***

***JE: If so, the just praise or blame[3] cannot be given to any moral act.***

Every prepossessing fixed bias on the mind brings a degree of moral inability for the contrary; because so far as the mind is biased and prepossessed, so much hindrance is there of the contrary.[4] And therefore if moral inability be inconsistent with moral agency, or the nature of virtue and vice, then so far as there is any such thing as evil disposition of heart, or habitual depravity of inclination; whether covetousness, pride, malice, cruelty, or whatever else; so much the more excusable persons are; so much the less have their evil acts of this kind, the nature of vice. And on the contrary, whatever excellent dispositions and inclinations they have, so much are they the less virtuous.

***Ar: Habitual disposition of heart cannot be in any degree virtuous or vicious, and it can take away all good ability and self-determining power or hinder the latter.***

It is evident, that no habitual disposition of heart, whether it be to a greater or lesser degree, can be in *any degree* virtuous or vicious; or the actions which proceed from them *at all* praise or blameworthy. Because, though we should suppose the habit not to be of such strength as wholly to take away all moral ability and self-determining

---

2. [Referring to Whitby, *Discourse*, p. 300.]

3. [See Pt. IV, St. 3, or *FOW*, 350.]

4. [JE seems to state the moral inability on the basis of Matthew 26:41, "The spirit indeed *is* willing, but the flesh *is* weak." and Romans 7:19, "The good that I would I do not: but the evil which I would not, that I do."]

power; or hinder but that, although the act be partly from bias, yet it may be in part from self-determination;

***Ar: Keep in mind not of antecedent bias but self-determining power.***

yet in this case, all that is from antecedent bias must be set aside, as of no consideration; and in estimating the degree of virtue or vice, no more must be considered than what arises from self-determining power, without any influence of that bias, because liberty is exercised in no more:

***Ar: The exercise of habitual inclination is not linked to the morality of the action.***

so that all that is the exercise of habitual inclination, is thrown away, as not belonging to the morality of the action. By which it appears, that no exercise of these habits, let them be stronger or weaker, can ever have anything of the nature of either virtue or vice.

***Ar: Human habits are natural and innate, and so they cannot be either virtuous or vicious.***

***JE: They are the effects of those acts wherein the mind exercised liberty and have been acquired and established by repeated free acts, and so in them are the nature of virtue and vice.***

Here if anyone should say, that notwithstanding all these things, there may be the nature of virtue and vice in habits of the mind; because these habits may be the effects of those acts wherein the mind exercised liberty; that however the forementioned reasons will prove that no habits which are natural, or that any are born or created with,[5] can be either virtuous or vicious; yet they will not prove this of habits, which have been acquired and established by repeated free acts —

To such an objector I would say, that this evasion will not at all help the matter.

***JE: Even though men try to live in their freedom, consequently they would live in their necessity.***

For if freedom of will be essential to the very *nature* of virtue and vice, then there is no virtue or vice but only in that very thing, wherein this liberty is exercised. If a man in one or more thing that he does, exercises liberty, and then by those acts is brought into such circumstances, that his liberty ceases, and there follows a long series of acts or events that come to pass necessarily; those consequent acts are not virtuous or vicious, rewardable or punishable; but only the free acts that established this necessity; for in them alone was the man free.

---

5. [Corrected, from "with us."]

## Section 6—Liberty of Indifference, Not Only Not Necessary to Virtue, but Utterly Inconsistent with It

*Ar: It is fair for man to be judged by his acts performed in his liberty because they are not the effects caused by necessity: e.g. health of body, quality of a clock, taste of fruits; these effects are from the free acts of person, maker, and farmer.*

The following effects that are necessary, have no more of the nature of virtue or vice, than health or sickness of body have properly the nature of virtue or vice, being the effects of a course of free acts of temperance or intemperance; or than the good qualities of a clock are of the nature of virtue, which are the effects of free acts of the artificer; or the goodness and sweetness of the fruits of a garden are moral virtues, being the effects of the free and faithful acts of the gardener.

*Ar: Only actions arisen in freedom and done by cause-free acts can be virtuous or vicious.*

If liberty be absolutely requisite to the morality of actions, and necessity wholly inconsistent with it, as Arminians greatly insist; then no *necessary effects* whatsoever, let the cause be never so good or bad, can be virtuous or vicious; but the virtue or vice must be only in the *free cause*. Agreeably to this, Dr. Whitby supposes, the necessity that attends the good and evil habits of the saints in heaven, and damned in hell, which are the consequence of their free acts in their state of probation, shows they are not rewardable or punishable.

*Ar: Can be there any virtue or vice in the actions arisen from virtuous or vicious habits and dispositions?*

On the whole, it appears, that if the notions of Arminians concerning liberty and moral agency be true, it will follow that there is no virtue in any such habits or qualities as humility, meekness, patience, mercy, gratitude, generosity, heavenly-mindedness; nothing at all praiseworthy in loving Christ above father and mother, wife and children, or our own lives; or in delight in holiness, hungering and thirsting after righteousness, love to enemies, universal benevolence to mankind: and on the other hand, there is nothing at all vicious, or worthy of dispraise, in the most sordid, beastly, malignant, devilish dispositions; in being ungrateful, profane, habitually hating God, and things sacred and holy; or in being most treacherous, envious and cruel towards men. For all these things are dispositions and inclinations of the heart. And in short, there is no such thing as any virtuous or vicious *quality of mind*; no such thing as inherent virtue and holiness, or vice and sin:

*Ar: The stronger men's lusts, habits, or dispositions are, the more fixed their evil actions, and yet the further are they from being blameworthy, because they were born with their lusts.*

and the stronger those habits or dispositions are, which used to be called virtuous and vicious, the further they are from being so indeed; the more violent men's lusts are, the more fixed their pride, envy, ingratitude and maliciousness, still the further are they from being blameworthy.

***According to Arminian principles, we face the inconsistency in JE's Illustrations:***

***ILL 1. No blame for an evil man.***

If there be a man that by his own repeated acts, or by any other means, is come to be of the most hellish disposition, desperately inclined to treat his neighbors with injuriousness, contempt and malignity; the further they should be from any disposition to be angry with him, or in the least to blame him.

***ILL 2. Not any reward for a good man***

So on the other hand, if there be a person, who is of a most excellent spirit, strongly inclining him to the most amiable actions, admirably meek, benevolent, etc., so much is he further from anything rewardable or commendable.

***ILL 3. No praise for Jesus' good acts.***

On which principles, the man Jesus Christ was very far from being praiseworthy for those acts of holiness and kindness which he performed, these propensities being so strong in his heart. And above all, the infinitely holy and gracious God, is infinitely remote from anything commendable, his good inclinations being infinitely strong, and he therefore at the utmost possible distance from being at liberty. And in all cases, the stronger the inclinations of any are to virtue, and the more they love it, the less virtuous they are; and the more they love wickedness, the less vicious. Whether these things are agreeable to Scripture, let every Christian, and every man who has read the Bible, judge: and whether they are agreeable to common sense, let everyone judge, that have human understanding in exercise.

***Ar: There is no virtue or vice either in God and angels or men, and we do not need to differentiate them.***

And if we pursue these principles, we shall find that virtue and vice are wholly excluded out of the world; and that there never was, nor ever can be any such thing as one or the other; either in God, angels or men. No propensity, disposition or habit can be virtuous or vicious, as has been shown; because they, so far as they take place, destroy the freedom of the will, the foundation of all moral agency, and exclude all capacity of either virtue or vice.

***JE: Problems of Arminian principles: Habits and dispositions themselves be not virtuous nor vicious.***

And if habits and dispositions themselves be not virtuous nor vicious, neither can the exercise of these dispositions be so: for the exercise of bias is not the exercise of free self-determining will, and so there is no exercise of liberty in it. Consequently no man is virtuous or vicious, either in being well or ill disposed, nor in acting from a good or bad disposition. And whether this bias or disposition be habitual or not, if it exists but a moment before the act of will, which is the effect of it, it alters not the case, as to the necessity of the effect.

Or if there be no previous disposition at all, either habitual or occasional, that determines the act, then it is not choice that determines it:

it is therefore a contingence, that happens to the man, arising from nothing in him; and is necessary, as to any inclination or choice of his; and therefore can't make him either the better or worse, any more than a tree is better than other trees, because it oftener happens to be lit upon by a swan or nightingale; or a rock more vicious than other rocks, because rattlesnakes have happened oftener to crawl over it. So that there is no virtue nor vice in good or bad dispositions, either fixed or transient; nor any virtue or vice in acting from any good or bad previous inclination; nor yet any virtue or vice in acting wholly without any previous inclination. Where then shall we find room for virtue or vice?

# Section 7

## Arminian Notions of Moral Agency Inconsistent with All Influence of Motive and Inducement, in Either Virtuous or Vicious Actions

*Ar: If moral actions are performed in the freedom of the will, they cannot be virtuous or vicious.*

*JE: The will always acts in all influence of motives, so they can be virtuous or vicious depending upon what motive.*

As Arminian notions of that liberty, which is essential to virtue or vice, are inconsistent with common sense, in their being inconsistent with all virtuous or vicious habits and dispositions; so they are no less so in their inconsistency with all influence of motives in moral actions.

*JE: The circumstances of the mind influence its inclination, which determines its choice.*

It is equally against those notions of liberty of will, whether there be, previous to the act of choice; a preponderancy of the inclination, or a preponderancy of those circumstances, which have a tendency to move the inclination. And indeed it comes to just the same thing: to say, the circumstances of the mind are such as tend to sway and turn its inclination one way, is the same thing as to say, the inclination of the mind, as under such circumstances, tends that way.

*Ar: If motives give the mind an inclination, it destroys its freedom and prohibits it from its self-determination.*

Or if any think it most proper to say, that motives do alter the inclination, and give a new bias to the mind; it will not alter the case, as to the present argument. For if motives operate by giving the mind an inclination, then they operate by destroying the mind's indifference, and laying it under a bias. But to do this, is to destroy the Arminian freedom: it is not to leave the will to its own self-determination, but to bring it into subjection to the power of something extrinsic, which operates upon it, sways and determines it, previous to its own determination. So that what is done from motive, can't be either virtuous or vicious. And besides, if the acts of the will are excited by motives, those motives are the causes of those acts of the will: which makes the acts of the will necessary; as effects necessarily follow the efficiency of the cause. And if the influence and power of the motive causes the volition, then the influence of the motive determines volition, and volition don't determine itself; and so is not free, in the sense of Arminians (as has been largely shown already), and consequently can be neither virtuous nor vicious.

### *Arminian Supposition: The liberty consists in a power of suspending a present action for deliberation of other actions.*

The supposition, which has already been taken notice of as an insufficient evasion in other cases, would be in like manner impertinently alleged in this case; namely, the supposition that liberty consists in a power of suspending action for the present, in order to deliberation.

### *JE: The will compares other motives and then follows necessarily the strongest motive.*

If it should be said, though it be true, that the will is under a necessity of finally following the strongest motive, yet it may for the present forbear to act upon the motive presented, till there has been opportunity thoroughly to consider it, and compare its real weight with the merit of other motives. I answer, as follows:

Here again it must be remembered, that if determining thus to suspend and consider, be that act of the will wherein alone liberty is exercised, then in this all virtue and vice must consist; and the acts that follow this consideration, and are the effects of it, being necessary, are no more virtuous or vicious than some good or bad events which happen when they are fast asleep, and are the consequences of what they did when they were awake. Therefore, I would here observe two things.

### *1. Ar: All virtue and vice consists in determining whether to take time for consideration or not.*

### *JE: They overlook the horrid nature of vices.*

1. To suppose that all virtue and vice, in every case, consists in determining whether to take time for consideration, or not, is not agreeable to common sense. For according to such a supposition, the most horrid crimes, adultery, murder, buggery, blasphemy, etc., do not at all consist in the horrid nature of the things themselves, but only in the neglect of thorough consideration before they were perpetrated: which brings their viciousness to a small matter, and makes all crimes equal.

If it be said, that neglect of consideration, when such heinous evils are proposed to choice, is worse than in other cases: I answer, this is inconsistent, as it supposes the very thing to be, which at the same time is supposed not to be; it supposes all moral evil, all viciousness and heinousness, does not consist merely in the want of consideration.

It supposes some crimes in themselves, in their *own nature*, to be more heinous than others, antecedent to consideration or inconsideration, which lays the person under a previous obligation to consider in some cases more than others.

### 2. Ar: *All virtue and vice consist only in the act of the will, and whereby it determines whether to consider or not.*

### JE: *All virtue and vice consist only in the necessary act of the will which is induced by some motive and follows the strongest motive.*

2. If it were so, that all virtue and vice, in every case, consisted only in the act of the will, whereby it determines whether to consider or no, it would not alter the case in the least, as to the present argument. For still in this act of the will on this determination, it is induced by some motive, and necessarily follows the strongest motive; and so is necessary, even in that act wherein alone it is either virtuous or vicious.

One thing more I would observe, concerning the inconsistence of Arminian notions of moral agency with the influence of motives. I suppose none will deny, that it is possible for motives to be set before the mind so powerful, and exhibited in so strong a light, and under so advantageous circumstances, as to be invincible; and such as the mind cannot but yield to.

### Ar: *If the will is to be determined by motive, liberty would be destroyed.*

In this case, Arminians will doubtless say, liberty is destroyed. And if so, then if motives are exhibited with half so much power, they hinder liberty in proportion to their strength, and go half way towards destroying it. If a thousand degrees of motive abolish all liberty, then five hundred take it half away. If one degree of the influence of motive doesn't at all infringe or diminish liberty, then no more do two degrees; for nothing doubled, is still nothing. And if two degrees don't diminish the will's liberty, no more do four, eight, sixteen, or six thousand. For nothing multiplied never so much, comes to but nothing.

### JE: *A motive does not hurt the liberty if the former has no the nature or moral suasion that is at all opposite to liberty.*

If there be nothing in the nature of motive or moral suasion, that is at all opposite to liberty, then the greatest degree of it can't hurt liberty. But if there be anything in the nature of the thing, that is against liberty, then the least degree of it hurts it in some degree; and consequently hurts and diminishes virtue. If invincible motives to that action which is good, take away all the freedom of the act, and so all the virtue of it; then

Section 7—Arminian Notions of Moral Agency Inconsistent with All Influence of Motive and Inducement

the more forcible the motives are, so much the worse, so much the less virtue; and the weaker the motives are, the better for the cause of virtue; and none is best of all.

**JE: *In acts chosen without any motive there is not any good end or virtue.***

Now let it be considered, whether these things are agreeable to common sense. If it should be allowed, that there are some instances wherein the soul chooses without any motive, what virtue can there be in such a choice? I am sure, there is no prudence or wisdom in it. Such a choice is made for no good end; for it is for no end at all. If it were for any end, the view of the end would be the motive exciting to the act;

and if the act be for no good end, and so from no good aim, then there is no good intention in it: and therefore, according to all our natural notions of virtue, no more virtue in it than in the motion of the smoke, which is driven to and for by the wind, without any aim or end in the thing moved, and which knows not whither, nor why and wherefore, it is moved.

**Ar: *The acts of the will, which are induced by causes like counsels, exhortations, invitations, expostulations, etc., can't be virtuous because they are not of the will's self-determining power.***

**JE: *Are they in vain, all endeavors to draw men to virtue by instruction, or persuasion, precept, or example?***

*Corol.* 1. By these things it appears, that the argument against the Calvinists, taken from the use of counsels, exhortations, invitations, expostulations, etc., so much insisted on by Arminians, is truly against themselves. For these things can operate no other way to any good effect, than as in them is exhibited motive and inducement, tending to excite and determine the acts of the will.

But it follows on their principles, that the acts of will excited by such causes, can't be virtuous; because so far as they are from these, they are not from the will's self-determining power. Hence it will follow, that it is not worth the while to offer any arguments to persuade men to any virtuous volition or voluntary action; it is in vain to set before them the wisdom and amiableness of ways of virtue, or the odiousness and folly of ways of vice.

This notion of liberty and moral agency frustrates all endeavors to draw men to virtue by instruction, or persuasion, precept, or example: for though these things may induce men to what is materially virtuous, yet at the same time they take away the form of virtue, because they destroy liberty; as they, by their own power, put the will out of its equilibrium, determine and turn the scale, and take the work of self-determining power out of its hands. And the clearer the instructions are that are given, the more powerful the arguments that are used, and the more moving the persuasions or examples, the more likely they are to frustrate their own design; because they have so much the greater tendency to put the will out of its balance, to hinder its freedom of self-determination; and so to exclude the very form of virtue, and the essence of whatsoever is praiseworthy.

So it clearly follows from these principles, that God has no hand in any man's virtue, nor does at all promote it, either by a physical or moral influence; that none of the moral methods he uses with men to promote virtue in the world, have tendency to the attainment of that end; that all the instructions which he has given to men, from the beginning of the world to this day, by prophets, or apostles, or by his son Jesus Christ; that all his counsels, invitations, promises, threatenings, warnings and expostulations;

that all means he has used with men, in ordinances, or providences; yea, all influences of his Spirit, ordinary and extraordinary, have had no tendency at all to excite any one virtuous act of the mind, or to promote anything morally good and commendable, in any respect.

### *Take only one of three ways of promoting virtue: (1) Spirit's physical operation on the heart; (2) Offering moral motives to the understanding; (3) Giving the will an opportunity to determine itself.*

For there is no way that these or any other means can promote virtue, but one of these three. Either

(1) by a physical operation on the heart. But all effects that are wrought in men in this way, have no virtue in them, by the concurring voice of all Arminians. Or

(2) morally, by exhibiting motives to the understanding, to excite good acts in the will. But it has been demonstrated, that volitions which are excited by motives, are necessary, and not excited by a self-moving power; and therefore, by their principles, there is no virtue in them. Or

(3) by merely giving the will an opportunity to determine itself concerning the objects proposed, either to choose or reject, by its own uncaused, unmoved, uninfluenced self-determination. And if this be all, then all those means do no more to promote virtue, than vice: for they do nothing but give the will opportunity to determine itself either way, either to good or bad, without laying it under any bias to either: and so there is really as much of an opportunity given to determine in favor of evil, as of good.

### *Negative Consequences of the Arminian Doctrine:*

Thus that horrid blasphemous consequence will certainly follow from the Arminian doctrine, which they charge on others; namely, that God acts an inconsistent part in using so many counsels, warnings, invitations, entreaties, etc., with sinners, to induce them to forsake sin, and turn to the ways of virtue; and that all are insincere and fallacious.

It will follow from their doctrine, that God does these things when he knows at the same time, that they have no manner of tendency to promote the effect he seems to aim at; yea, knows that if they have any influence, this very influence will be inconsistent with such an effect, and will prevent it. But what an imputation of insincerity would this fix on him who is infinitely holy and true!

So that theirs is the doctrine which if pursued in its consequences, does horribly reflect on the Most High, and fix on him the charge of hypocrisy; and not the doctrine of the Calvinist; according to their frequent, and vehement exclamations and invectives.

### JE: Without a good intention or aim, i.e., motive, there can be no virtuous act.

*Corol. 2.* From what has been observed in this section, it again appears, that Arminian principles and notions, when fairly examined, and pursued in their demonstrable consequences, do evidently shut all virtue out of the world, and make it impossible that there should ever be any such thing, in any case; or that any such thing should ever be conceived of.

For by these principles, the very notion of virtue or vice implies absurdity and contradiction. For it is absurd in itself, and contrary to common sense, to suppose a virtuous act of mind without any good intention or aim; and by their principles, it is absurd to suppose a virtuous act with a good intention or aim; for to act for an end, is to act from a motive. So that if we rely on these principles, there can be no virtuous act with a good design and end; and it is self-evident, there can be none without: consequently, there can be no virtuous act at all.

### JE: The act, performed without any inclination, motive, and end, must be carried out without any choice of the will, and so there can be no virtuous or vicious act.

*Corol. 3.* It is manifest, that Arminian notions of moral agency, and the being of a faculty of will, cannot consist together; and that if there be any such thing as, either a virtuous, or vicious act, it can't be an act of will; no will can be at all concerned in it. For that act which is performed without inclination, without motive, without end, must be performed without any concern of the will. To suppose an act of the will without these, implies a contradiction.

If the soul in its act has no motive or end; then in that act (as was observed before) it seeks nothing, goes after nothing, exerts no inclination to anything; and this implies, that in that act it desires nothing, and chooses nothing; so that there is no act of choice in the case: and that is as much as to say, there is no act of will in the case. Which very effectually shuts out all vicious and virtuous acts out of the universe; inasmuch as, according to this, there can be no vicious or virtuous act wherein the will is concerned; and according to the plainest dictates of reason, and the light of nature, and also the principles of Arminians themselves, there can be no virtuous or vicious act wherein the will is not concerned. And therefore there is no room for any virtuous or vicious acts at all.

**JE: Men are influenced by either previous inclination or motive, and they take their moral actions which God can foreknow and foretell in advance.**

*Corol. 4.* If none of the moral actions of intelligent beings are influenced by either previous inclination or motive, another strange thing will follow; and this is, that God not only can't foreknow any of the future moral actions of his creatures, but he can make no conjecture, can give no probable guess concerning them. For, all conjecture in things of this nature, must depend on some discerning or apprehension of these two things, *previous disposition*, and *motive*; which, as has been observed, Arminian notions of moral agency, in their real consequence, altogether exclude.

# PART IV

Wherein the Chief Grounds of the Reasonings of Arminians, in Support and defense of Their Notions of Liberty, Moral Agency, etc. and against the Opposite Doctrine, Are Considered

# Section 1

## The Essence of the Virtue and Vice of Dispositions of the Heart, and Acts of the Will, Lies Not in Their Cause, but Their Nature

*Ar: The virtuousness or viciousness is in the cause of the dispositions or acts of the will.*

*JE: No, it is not in their cause but wholly in their nature.*

One main foundation of the reasons, which are brought to establish the aforementioned notions of liberty, virtue, vice, etc., is a supposition, that the virtuousness of the dispositions or acts of the will consists not in the nature of these dispositions or acts, but wholly in the origin or cause of them: so that if the disposition of the mind or act of the will be never so good, yet if the cause of the disposition or act be not our virtue, there is nothing virtuous or praiseworthy in it; and on the contrary, if the will in its inclination or acts be never so bad, yet unless it arises from something that is our vice or fault, there is nothing vicious or blameworthy in it. Hence their grand objection and pretended demonstration, or self-evidence, against any virtue and commendableness, or vice and blameworthiness, of those habits or acts of the will, which are not from some virtuous or vicious determination of the will itself.

Now, if this matter be well considered, it will appear to be altogether a mistake, yea, a gross absurdity; and that it is most certain, that if there be any such things, as a virtuous, or vicious disposition, or volition of mind, the virtuousness or viciousness of them consists not in the origin or cause of these things, but in the nature of them.

*JE: The essence of virtuousness and viciousness do not lie in their cause but in the nature of the dispositions or acts of mind; yet the cause of vice is some erroneous determination of ours or something in us that is our fault.*

If the essence of virtuousness or commendableness, and of viciousness or fault, don't lie in the nature of the dispositions or acts of mind, which are said to be our virtue or our fault, but in their cause, then it is certain it lies nowhere at all. Thus, for instance, if the vice of a vicious act of will, lies not in the nature of the act, but the cause; so that its being of a bad nature will not make it at all our fault, unless it arises from some faulty determination of ours as its cause, or something in us that is our fault; then for the same reason, neither can the viciousness of that cause lie in the nature of the thing itself, but in its cause: that evil determination of ours is not our fault, merely because it is of a bad nature, unless it arises from some cause in us that is our fault.

And when we are come to this higher cause, still the reason of the thing holds good; though this cause be of a bad nature, yet we are not at all to blame on that account, unless it arises from something faulty in us. Nor yet can blameworthiness lie in the nature of *this cause,* but in the cause of *that.* And thus we must drive faultiness back from step to step, from a lower cause to a higher, *in infinitum:* and that is thoroughly to banish it from the world, and to allow it no possibility of existence anywhere in the universality of things.

### Ar: *Fault does not consist in the nature of things, but in their cause, and so the cause only will be blamed.*

On these principles, vice or moral evil can't consist in anything that is an *effect,* because *fault* doesn't consist in the nature of things, but in their cause; as well as because effects are necessary, being unavoidably connected with their cause: therefore, the cause only is to blame.

### JE: *The essence of faultiness can lie only in its nature but not in its cause.*

And so it follows, that faultiness can lie *only in that cause,* which is a *cause only,* and no effect of anything. Nor yet can it lie in this; for then it must lie in the nature of the thing itself; not in its being from any determination of ours, nor anything faulty in us which is the cause, nor indeed from any cause at all, for by the supposition, it is no effect, and *has no cause.* And thus, he that will maintain, it is not the nature of habits or acts of will that makes them virtuous or faulty, but the cause, must immediately run himself out of his own assertion; and in maintaining it, will insensibly contradict and deny it.

### Ar: *Vicious effects are arisen not from their evil nature or from anything inherent in them but from a bad cause.*

This is certain, that if effects are vicious and faulty, not from their nature, or from anything inherent in them, but because they are from a bad cause, it must be on account of the *badness* of the cause; and so on account of the *nature* of the cause: a bad effect in the will must be bad, because the cause is *bad,* or *of an evil nature,* or *has badness* as a quality inherent in it: and a *good* effect in the will must be *good,* by reason of the *goodness* of the cause, or its being *of a good kind and nature.*

**Ar: Vice lies not in bad cause itself but in bad cause. Virtue and vice are not in their essence but in the nature of things.**

And if this be what is meant, the very supposition of fault and praise lying not in the nature of the thing, but the cause, contradicts itself, and does at last[1] resolve the essence of virtue and vice into the nature of things, and supposes it originally to consist saying, "No, the fault of the thing which is the cause, lies not in this, that the cause itself is *of an evil nature,* but that the cause is evil in that sense, that it is from another bad cause." Still the absurdity will follow him; for if so, then the cause before charged is at once acquitted, and all the blame must be laid to the higher cause, and must consist in that's being *evil,* or *of an evil nature.*

**Ar: Our faultiness isn't from our original sin, but it is determined by no act of ours and caused by nothing faulty in us, being absolutely without any cause.**

So now we are come again to lay the blame of the thing blameworthy, to the nature of the thing, and not to the cause. And if any is so foolish as to go higher still, and ascend from step to step, till he is come to that which is the first cause concerned in the whole affair, and will say, all the blame lies in that; then at last he must be forced to own, that the faultiness of the thing which he supposes alone blameworthy, lies wholly *in the nature* of the thing, and not in the original or cause of it; for the supposition is, that it has no original, it is determined by no act of ours, is caused by nothing faulty in us, being absolutely *without any cause.* And so the race is at an end, but the evader is taken in his flight.

**JE: Moral evil consists in a certain deformity like certain dispositions of the heart and acts of the will, and not in the deformity of something else, diverse from the very thing itself, which deserves abhorrence, supposed to be the cause of it.**

It is agreeable to the natural notions of mankind, that moral evil, with its desert of dislike and abhorrence, and all its other ill-deservings, consists in a certain *deformity* in the *nature* of certain dispositions of the heart, and acts of the will; and not in the deformity of *something else,* diverse from the very thing itself, which deserves abhorrence, supposed to be the cause of it. Which would be absurd, because that would be to suppose, a thing that is innocent and not evil, is truly evil and faulty, because another thing is evil. It implies a contradiction; for it would be to suppose, the very thing which is morally evil and blameworthy, is innocent and not blameworthy; but that something else, which is its cause, is only to blame. To say, that vice doesn't consist in the thing which is vicious, but in its cause, is the same as to say, that vice doesn't consist in vice, but in that which produces it.

1. [Corrected, from "at least."]

***JE:*** *It is not false to say that a vice lies in its cause, yet both the first wickedness in the cause and the second one produced by the cause are in the evil nature of things.*

It is true, a cause may be to blame, for being the cause of vice: it may be wickedness in the cause, that it produces wickedness. But it would imply a contradiction, to suppose that these two are the same individual wickedness. The wicked act of the cause in producing wickedness, is one wickedness; and the wickedness produced, if there be any produced, is another. And therefore the wickedness of the latter doesn't lie in the former, but is distinct from it; and the wickedness of both lies in the *evil nature* of the things which are wicked.

The thing which makes sin hateful, is that by which it deserves punishment; which is but the expression of hatred. And that which renders virtue lovely, is the same with that, on the account of which, it is fit to receive praise and reward which are but the expressions of esteem and love. But that which makes vice hateful, is its hateful nature; and that which renders virtue lovely, is its nature.

***JE:*** *Men's will is inherently good or evil, in which is a certain beauty or deformity, and virtue or vice. If the cause of act of will is hateful, there must be another antecedent evil will that is a sin and deserves punishment.*

It is a certain beauty or deformity that are *inherent* in that good or evil will, which is the *soul* of virtue and vice (and not in the *occasion* of it) which is their worthiness of esteem or disesteem, praise or dispraise, according to the common sense of mankind. If the cause or occasion of the rise of a hateful disposition or act of will, be also hateful; suppose another antecedent evil will; that is entirely another sin, and deserves punishment by itself, under a distinct consideration. There is worthiness of dispraise in the nature of an evil volition, and not wholly in some foregoing act which is its cause; otherwise the evil volition which is the effect, is no moral evil, any more than sickness, or some other natural calamity, which arises from a cause morally evil.

***Instances to show a vice in the nature of things:***

***ILL 1:*** *Ingratitude is hateful in itself by its own inherent deformity.*

Thus for instance, ingratitude is hateful and worthy of dispraise, according to common sense; not because something as bad, or worse than ingratitude, was the cause that produced it; but because it is hateful in itself, by its own inherent deformity. So the love of virtue is amiable, and worthy of praise, not merely because something else went before this love of virtue in our minds, which caused it to take place there;

***ILL 2:*** *The love of virtue is praiseworthy because the choice to love it was produced by a good disposition of heart. That is, the choice was of a good nature.*

for instance, our own choice; we chose to love virtue, and by some method or other wrought ourselves into the love of it; but because of the amiableness and condecency of such a disposition and inclination of heart. If that was the case, that we *did* choose to love virtue, and so produced that love in ourselves, this choice itself could be no otherwise amiable or praiseworthy, than as love to virtue, or some other amiable inclination, was exercised and implied in it. If that choice was amiable at all, it must be so on account of some amiable quality in the nature of the choice. If we chose to love virtue, not in love to virtue, or anything that was good, and exercised no sort of good disposition in the choice, the choice itself was not virtuous, nor worthy of any praise, according to common sense, because the choice was not of a *good nature*.

***John Taylor, antagonist in JE's "Original Sin": Man must first do something righteous, then he becomes righteous.***

It may not be improper here to take notice of something said by an author, that has lately made a mighty noise in America.

> "A necessary holiness (says he) is no holiness. . . . Adam could not be originally created in righteousness and true holiness, because he must *choose* to be righteous, *before* he could be righteous. And therefore he must exist, he must be created, yea, he must exercise thought and reflection, before he was righteous."[2]

***JE: In the actions of choosing to be righteous there is no righteousness or holiness.***

There is much more to the same effect in that place, and also in p. 437, 438, 439, 440. If these things are so, it will certainly follow, that the first choosing to be righteous is no righteous choice; there is no righteousness or holiness in it; because no choosing to be righteous goes before it. For he plainly speaks of *choosing to be righteous,* as *what must go before righteousness*: and that which follows the choice, being the effect of the choice, can't be righteousness or holiness: for an effect is a thing necessary, and can't prevent the influence or efficacy of its cause; and therefore is unavoidably dependent upon the cause: and he says, "a necessary holiness is no holiness." So that neither can a choice of righteousness be righteousness or holiness, nor can anything that is consequent on that choice, and the effect of it, be righteousness or holiness; nor can anything that is without choice, be righteousness or holiness. So that by his scheme, all righteousness and holiness is at once shut out of the world, and no door left open, by which it can ever possibly enter into the world.

***JE: Men's common sense espouses such an inconsistent Arminian notion of internal volitions and outward actions; the essence of their moral good or evil lies in their causes.***

---

2. John Taylor, *The Scripture-Doctrine of Original Sin Proposed to Free and Candid Examination* (London, 1740; 3rd ed. Belfast, 1746), 180.

I suppose, the way that men came to entertain this absurd inconsistent notion, with respect to *internal inclinations and volitions* themselves, (or notions that imply it), viz. that the essence of their moral good or evil lies not in their nature, but their cause; was, that it is indeed a very plain dictate of common sense, that it is so with respect to all *outward actions*, and sensible motions of the body; that the moral good or evil of them don't lie at all in the motions themselves; which taken by themselves, are nothing of a moral nature; and the essence of all the moral good or evil that concerns them, lies in those internal dispositions and volitions which are the cause of them.

### Ar: The internal exercises and external actions are the same in their nature.

Now being always used to determine this, without hesitation or dispute, concerning *external actions*; which are the things that in the common use of language are signified by such phrases, as men's "actions," or their "doings"; hence when they came to speak of volitions, and *internal exercises* of their inclinations, under the same denomination of their "actions," or what they "do," they unwarily determined the case must also be the same with these, as with external actions; not considering the vast difference in the nature of the case.

### Ar: Why would men be worthy of blame or praise unless they were not causes of their acts?

### JE: It is because they are the causes of acts of will or choice and also the authors of external actions.

If any shall still object and say, Why is it not necessary that the cause should be considered, in order to determine whether anything be worthy of blame or praise? Is it agreeable to reason and common sense, that a man is to be praised or blamed for that which he is not the cause or author of, and has no hand in?

I answer, such phrases as "being the cause," "being the author." "having a hand," and the like are ambiguous. They are most vulgarly understood for being the designing voluntary cause, or cause by antecedent choice: and it is most certain that men are not in this sense the causes or authors of the first act of their wills, in any case; as certain as anything is, or ever can be; for nothing can be more certain, than that a thing is not before it is, nor a thing of the same kind before the first thing of that kind; and so no choice before the first choice. As the phrase, "being the author," may be understood, not of being the producer by an antecedent act of will; but as a person may be said to be the author of the act of will itself, by his being the immediate agent, or the being that *is acting, or in exercise* in that act; if the phrase of "being the author," is used to signify this, then doubtless common sense requires men's being the authors of their own acts of will, in order to their being esteemed worthy of praise or dispraise on account of them. And common sense teaches, that they must be the authors of *external* actions, in the former sense, namely, their being the causes of them by an act of will or choice, in order to their being justly blamed or praised: but it teaches no such thing with respect to the acts of the will themselves. But this may appear more manifest by the things which will be observed in the following section.

# Section 2

## The Falseness and Inconsistence of That Metaphysical Notion of Action, and Agency, Which Seems to be Generally Entertained by the Defenders of the Arminian Doctrine Concerning Liberty, Moral Agency, Etc.

*Ar: Volitions of the soul are not excited and determined by some external cause.*

*JE: Its volitions may not be caused by itself but by the preceding cause, and it does some acts necessarily.*

*JE: The Arminian demonstration's ground is a metaphysical notion of agency and action.*

One thing that is made very much a ground of argument and supposed demonstration by Arminians, in defense of the aforementioned principles, concerning moral agency, virtue, vice, etc., is their *metaphysical notion of agency and action*.[1] They say,

> unless the soul has a self-determining power, it has no power of "action"; if its volitions be not caused by itself, but are excited and determined by some extrinsic cause, they can't be the soul's own "acts"; and that the soul can't be "active," but must be wholly "passive," in those effects which it is the subject of necessarily, and not from its own free determination.

*Thomas Chubb: Man is an agent and capable of action by his self-determination.*

---

1. [Metaphysics is named by the 1st century editors of Aristotle's writings because his work was discovered as edited after physics, natural science, second philosophy, and in the 16th century this was developed as a branch of philosophy to investigate the fundamental nature and notion of being and things: "What is it?," "What it is like?," etc. And its central branch is ontology.]

Mr. Chubb lays the foundation of his scheme of liberty, and of his arguments to support it, very much in this position, that man is an agent, and capable of action. Which doubtless is true: but *self-determination* belongs to his notion of "action," and is the very essence of it. Whence he infers that it is impossible for a man to act and be acted upon, in the same thing, at the same time; and that nothing that is an action, can be the effect of the action of another: and he insists, that a "necessary agent," or an agent that is necessarily determined to act, is a "plain contradiction."[2]

### TC: *Action is something wherein is no passion or passiveness.*

But those are a precarious sort of demonstrations, which men build on the meaning that they arbitrarily affix to a word; especially when that meaning is abstruse, inconsistent, and entirely diverse from the original sense of the word in common speech. That the meaning of the word "action," as Mr. Chubb and many others use it, is utterly unintelligible and inconsistent, is manifest, because it belongs to their notion of an action, that it is something wherein is no passion or passiveness;

that is (according to their sense of passiveness) it is under the power, influence or action of no cause. And this implies, that action has no cause, and is no effect: for to be an effect implies passiveness, or the being subject to the power and action of its cause. And yet they hold, that the mind's action is the effect of its own determination, yea, the mind's free and voluntary determination; which is the same with free choice.

### JE: *Action is always the effect of foregoing choice.*

So that action is the effect of something preceding, even a preceding act of choice: and consequently, in this effect the mind is passive, subject to the power and action of the preceding cause, which is the foregoing choice, and therefore can't be active. So that here we have this contradiction, that action is always the effect of foregoing choice; and therefore can't be action; because it is passive to the power of that preceding causal choice; and the mind can't be active and passive in the same thing, at the same time.

### Ar: *In human acts there is contingency only, but not necessity or something preceding, and there are acts only determined by free choice.*

### JE: *Yet they exclude no necessity; rather, they are the significant effects of preceding choice and so they are consequent and dependent.*

Again, they say, necessity is utterly inconsistent with action, and a necessary action is a contradiction; and so their notion of action implies contingence, and excludes all necessity. And therefore their notion of action implies, that it has no necessary dependence or connection with anything foregoing; for such a dependence or connection excludes contingence, and implies necessity. And yet their notion of action implies necessity, and supposes that it is necessary, and can't be contingent. For they suppose, that whatever is properly called action, must be determined by the will and free

2. [Chubb, *Tracts*, p. 311, and see above, p. 234 n2.]

choice; and this is as much as to say, that it must be necessary, being dependent upon, and determined by something foregoing; namely, a foregoing act of choice. Again, it belongs to their notion of action, of that which is a proper and mere act, that it is the beginning of motion, or of exertion of power; but yet it is implied in their notion of action, that it is not the beginning of motion or exertion of power, but is consequent and dependent on a preceding exertion of power, viz. the power of will and choice: for they say there is no proper action but what is freely *chosen*; or, which is the same thing, determined by a foregoing act of free choice. But if any of them shall see cause to deny this, and say they hold no such thing as that every action is chosen, or determined by a foregoing choice; but that the very first exertion of will only, undetermined by any preceding act, is properly called action; then I say, such a man's notion of action implies necessity;

for what the mind is the subject of without the determination of its own previous choice, it is the subject of necessarily, as to any hand that free choice has in the affair; and without any ability the mind has to prevent it, by any will or election of its own: because by the supposition it precludes all previous acts of the will or choice in the case, which might prevent it.

**Ar: *The act is not the effect of a predetermining bias, but it springs immediately out of indifference.***

**JE: *However, if the agent is the author of freely and voluntarily, that would be so by previous choice and design.***

So that it is again, in this other way, implied in their notion of act, that it is both necessary and not necessary. Again, it belongs to their notion of an "act," that it is no effect of a predetermining bias or preponderation, but springs immediately out of indifference; and this implies that it can't be from foregoing choice, which is foregoing preponderation: if it be not habitual, but occasional, yet if it causes the act, it is truly previous, efficacious and determining. And yet, at the same time, it is essential to their notion of an act, that it is what the agent is the author of freely and voluntarily, and that is, by previous choice and design.

**JE: *Even though Arminians make their notion and attempt to disown the other cause of acts, finally they could not keep from acknowledging it.***

So that according to their notion of an act, considered with regard to its consequences, these following things are all essential to it; viz. that it should be necessary, and not necessary; that it should be from a cause, and no cause; that it should be the fruit of choice and design, and not the fruit of choice and design; that it should be the beginning of motion or exertion, and yet consequent on previous exertion; that it should be before it is; that it should spring immediately out of indifference and equilibrium, and yet be the effect of preponderation; that it should be self-originated, and also have its original from something else; that it is what the mind causes itself, of its own will, and can produce or prevent, according to its choice or pleasure, and yet what the mind has no power to prevent, it precluding all previous choice in the affair.

***JE: The Arminians' metaphysical notion of act is something with no idea, a confusion of the mind, and an absolute nonentity.***

So that an act, according to their metaphysical notion of it, is something of which there is no idea; it is nothing but a confusion of the mind, excited by words without any distinct meaning, and is an absolute nonentity; and that in two respects: (1) there is nothing in the world that ever was, is, or can be, to answer the things which must belong to its description, according to what they suppose to be essential to it. And (2) there neither is, nor ever was, nor can be, any notion or idea to answer the word, as they use and explain it. For if we should suppose any such notion, it would many ways destroy itself. But it is impossible, any idea or notion should subsist in the mind, whose very nature and essence, which constitutes it, destroys it —-

***ILL: A philosopher's account of the observations: JE illustrates a wrong Arminian notion of act.***

If some learned philosopher, who had been abroad, in giving an account of the curious observations he had made in his travels, should say, he

> "had been in Tierra del Fuego, and there had seen an animal, which he calls by a certain name, that begat and brought forth itself, and yet had a sire and a dam distinct from itself; that it had an appetite, and was hungry before it had a Being; that his master, who led him, and governed him at his pleasure, was always governed by him, and driven by him where he pleased; that when he moved, he always took a step before the first step; that he went with his head first, and yet always went tail foremost; and this, though he had neither head nor tail":

it would be no impudence at all, to tell such a traveler, though a learned man, that he himself had no notion or idea of such an animal as he gave an account of, and never had, nor ever would have.

***Common Signification of Action: Outward actions such as acting or doing, different from thinking or willing.***

As the aforementioned notion of action is very inconsistent, so it is wholly diverse from the original meaning of the word. The more usual signification of it in vulgar speech, seems to be some motion or exertion of power, that is voluntary, or that is the *effect* of the will; and is used in the same sense as "doing": and most commonly it is used to signify *outward* actions. So thinking is often distinguished from acting; and desiring and willing, from doing.

***Better signification of action of inanimate and physical things: motions or alterations or exertions arisen from some internal cause. Action of human beings: the effects of internal volition, or invisible exertions of will; the exercise of thought, or will and inclination.***

Besides this more usual and proper signification of the word "action," there are other ways in which the word is used that are less proper, which yet have place in common speech.

Oftentimes it is used to signify some motion or alteration in inanimate things, with relation to some object and effect. So the spring of a watch is said to act upon the chain and wheels; the sunbeams, to act upon plants and trees; and the fire, to act upon wood.

Sometimes the word is used to signify motions, alterations, and exertions of power, which are seen in corporeal things, *considered absolutely*; especially when these motions seem to arise from some internal cause which is hidden; so that they have a greater resemblance of those motions of our bodies, which are the effects of internal volition, or invisible exertions of will. So the fermentation of liquor, the operations of the loadstone, and of electrical bodies, are called the action of these things.

And sometimes the word "action" is used to signify the exercise of thought, or of will and inclination: so meditating, loving, hating, inclining, disinclining, choosing and refusing, may be sometimes called acting; though more rarely (unless it be by philosophers and metaphysicians) than in any of the other senses.

***Ar: Action is the self-determinate exercise of the will or an exertion of the soul.***

***JE: Such a sense of it is not consistent with a sense used in vulgar speech.***

But the word is never used in vulgar speech in that sense which Arminian divines use it in, namely, for the self-determinate exercise of the will, or an exertion of the soul that arises without any necessary connection with anything foregoing. If a man does something voluntarily, or as the effect of his choice, then in the most proper sense, and as the word is most originally and commonly used, he is said to act: but whether that choice or volition be self-determined, or no, whether it be connected with foregoing habitual bias, whether it be the certain effect of the strongest motive, or some extrinsic cause, never comes into consideration in the meaning of the word.

***JE: Adding a strange meaning to action, Arminians attempt but fail to demonstrate their metaphysics and moral philosophy and theology.***

And if the word "action" is arbitrarily used by some men otherwise, to suit some scheme of metaphysics or morality, no argument can reasonably be founded on such a use of this term, to prove anything but their own pleasure. For divines and philosophers strenuously to urge such arguments, as though they were sufficient to support and demonstrate a whole scheme of moral philosophy and divinity, is certainly to erect a mighty edifice on the sand, or rather on a shadow. And though it may now perhaps, through custom, have become natural for them to use the word in this sense (if that may be called a sense or meaning, which is so inconsistent with itself) yet this doesn't prove that it is agreeable to the natural notions men have of things, or that there can be anything in the creation that should answer such a meaning. And though they appeal to experience, yet the truth is, that men are so far from experiencing any such thing, that it is impossible for them to have any conception of it.

**Ar: *Action and passion are the same things.***

**JE: *The two things are diverse signification and relation. Action is activeness: some motion or exercise of body or mind, without any relation to any object or effect. Passion is passiveness: a being acted upon by something, exerted by some cause.***

If it should be objected, that "action" and "passion" are doubtless words of a contrary signification; but to suppose that the agent, in its action, is under the power and influence of something extrinsic, is to confound action and passion, and make them the same thing —

I answer, that action and passion are doubtless, as they are sometimes used, words of opposite signification; but not as signifying opposite *existences*, but only opposite *relations*.

The words "cause" and "effect" are terms of opposite signification; but nevertheless, if I assert that the same thing may at the same time, in different respects and relations, be both cause and effect, this will not prove that I confound the terms. The soul may be both active and passive in the same thing in different respects, active with relation to one thing, and passive with relation to another.

The word "passion" when set in opposition to *action* or rather activeness, is merely a relative term: it signifies no effect or cause, nor any proper existence; but is the same with *passiveness*, or a being passive, or a being acted upon by something. Which is a mere relation of a thing to some power or force exerted by some cause, producing some effect in it, or upon it.

And "action," when set properly in opposition to passion, or passiveness, is no real existence; it is not the same with "AN action," but is a mere relation: it is the *activeness* of something on another thing, being the opposite relation to the other, viz. a relation of power, or force exerted by some cause, towards another thing, which is the subject of the effect of that power. Indeed, the word "action" is frequently used to signify something not merely relative, but more absolute, and a real existence; as when we say "an action"; when the word is not used transitively, but absolutely, for some motion or exercise of body or mind, without any relation to any object or effect: and as used thus, it is not properly the opposite of "passion"; which ordinarily signifies nothing absolute, but merely the *relation* of *being acted upon*. And therefore if the word "action" be used in the like relative sense, then action and passion are only two contrary relations. And it is no absurdity to suppose, that contrary relations may belong to the same thing, at the same time, with respect to different things. So to suppose, that there are acts of the soul by which a man voluntarily moves, and acts upon objects, and produces effects, which yet themselves are effects of something else, and wherein the soul itself is the object of something acting upon, and influencing that, don't at all confound "action" and "passion."

The words may nevertheless be properly of opposite signification: there may be as true and real a difference between *acting* and being *caused to act*, though we should suppose the soul to be both in the same volition, as there is between *living*, and *being quickened*, or *made to live*. It is no more a contradiction, to suppose that action may be the effect of some other cause, besides the agent, or being that acts, than to suppose that life may be the effect of some other cause, besides the liver, or the being that lives, in whom life is caused to be.

*Ar: The agent is self-determined in internal action, and that the will should be the cause of it.*

*JE: According to their inconsistent notion, it would be so. Yet according to common sense, men are self-directed only in external actions and their wills are the cause of them.*

The thing which has led men into this inconsistent notion of action, when applied to volition, as though it were essential to this internal action, that the agent should be self-determined in it, and that the will should be the cause of it, was probably this; that according to the sense of mankind, and the common use of language it is so, with respect to men's external actions; which are what originally, and according to the vulgar use and most proper sense of the word, are called "actions." Men in these are self-directed, self-determined, and their wills are the cause of the motions of their bodies, and the external things that are done; so that unless men do them voluntarily, and of choice, and the action be determined by their antecedent volition, it is no action or doing of theirs.

*JE: Some Metaphysicians' Fallacy: Men, in the volition, are self-determined by their will. However, it is right that the volition is determined by antecedent volition, like the motion of the body.*

Hence some metaphysicians have been led unwarily, but exceeding absurdly, to suppose the same concerning volition itself, that that also must be determined by the will; which is to be determined by antecedent volition, as the motion of the body is; not considering the contradiction it implies.

*JE: Some metaphysicians fail to distinguish between action and passion.*

But it is very evident, that in the metaphysical distinction between action and passion (though long since become common and the general vogue), due care has not been taken to conform language to the nature of things, or to any distinct clear ideas. As it is in innumerable other philosophical, metaphysical terms, used in these disputes; which has occasioned inexpressible difficulty, contention, error and confusion.

**JE: *The terms' meanings changed, and necessity is mistaken as inconsistent with actions. Action's original meaning was external voluntary action,→ then volition itself,→ and now is different.***

*Necessity's original meaning was constraint, then certainty of existence,→ and now is different.*

And thus probably it came to be thought, that necessity was inconsistent with action, as these terms are applied to volition. First, these terms "action" and "necessity" are changed from their original meaning, as signifying external voluntary action, and constraint (in which meaning they are evidently inconsistent), to signify quite other things, viz. volition itself, and certainty of existence. And when the change of signification is made, care is not taken to make proper allowances and abatements for the difference of sense; but still the same things are unwarily attributed to "action" and "necessity," in the new meaning of the words, which plainly belonged to them in their first sense; and on this ground, maxims are established without any real foundation, as though they were the most certain truths, and the most evident dictates of reason.

**JE: *Arminians strenuously maintain that a necessary action is a contradiction, yet they will not deny God is the active being and holy agent and he necessarily acts justly and faithfully.***

But however strenuously it is maintained, that what is necessary can't be properly called action, and that a necessary action is a contradiction, yet it is probable there are few Arminian divines, who if thoroughly tried, would stand to these principles. They will allow, that God is in the highest sense an active being, and the highest fountain of life and action; and they would not probably deny, that those that are called God's acts of righteousness, holiness and faithfulness, are truly and properly God's acts, and God is really a holy *agent* in them: and yet I trust, they will not deny, that God necessarily acts justly and faithfully, and that it is impossible for him to act unrighteously and unholy.

# Section 3

## The Reasons Why Some Think It Contrary to Common Sense, to Suppose Those Things which Are Necessary, to be Worthy of Either Praise or Blame

It is abundantly affirmed and urged by Arminian writers, that it is contrary to common sense, and the natural notions and apprehensions of mankind, to suppose otherwise than that necessity (making no distinction between natural and moral necessity) is inconsistent with virtue and vice, praise and blame, reward and punishment. And their arguments from hence have been greatly triumphed in; and have been not a little perplexing to many who have been friendly to the truth, as clearly revealed in the holy Scriptures: it has seemed to them indeed difficult, to reconcile Calvinistic doctrines with the notions men commonly have of justice and equity. And the true reasons of it seem to be these that follow.

***Ar: It is against the dictate of common sense that men are to be of praise or blame for their necessary actions.***

I. It is indeed a very plain dictate of common sense, that natural necessity is wholly inconsistent with just praise or blame. If men do things which in themselves are very good, fit to be brought to pass, and very happy effects, properly against their wills, and can't help it; or do them from a necessity that is without their wills, or with which their wills have no concern or connection; then it is a plain dictate of common sense, that it's none of their virtue, nor any moral good in them; and that they are not worthy to be rewarded or praised; or at all esteemed, honored or loved on that account. And on the other hand, that if from like necessity they do those things which in themselves are very unhappy and pernicious, and do them because they can't help it; the necessity is such, that it is all one whether they will them, or no; and the reason why they are done, is from necessity only, and not from their wills; it is a very plain dictate of common sense that they are not at all to blame; there is no vice, fault, or moral evil at all in the effect done; nor are they who are thus necessitated, in any wise worthy to be punished, hated, or in the least disrespected, on that account.

In like manner, if things in themselves good and desirable are absolutely impossible, with a natural impossibility, the universal reason of mankind teaches, that this *wholly* and *perfectly* excuses persons in their not doing them.

***Ar: If men found very difficult in things with a natural impossibility and difficulty, then a person's neglect or omission will be excused in some measure.***

And it is also a plain dictate of common sense, that if the doing things in themselves good, or avoiding things in themselves evil, is not *absolutely impossible*, with such a natural impossibility, but very *difficult*, with a natural difficulty; that is, a difficulty prior *to*, and not at all consisting *in* will and inclination itself, and which would remain the same, let the inclination be what it will; then a person's neglect or omission is excused *in some measure*, though not wholly; his sin is less aggravated, than if the thing to be done were easy. And if instead of difficulty and hindrance, there be a contrary natural propensity in the state of things, to the thing to be done, or effect to be brought to pass, abstracted from any consideration of the inclination of the heart; though the propensity be not so great as to amount to a natural necessity; yet being some approach to it, so that the doing the good thing be very much from this natural tendency in the state of things, and but little from a good inclination;

***Ar: Natural propensity is an approach to natural necessity, so the latter shuts out all virtue.***

then it is a dictate of common sense, that there is so much the less virtue in what is done; and so it is less praiseworthy and rewardable. The reason is easy, viz. because such a natural propensity or tendency is an approach to natural necessity; and the greater the propensity, still so much the nearer is the approach to necessity. And therefore as natural necessity takes away or shuts out *all* virtue, so this propensity approaches to an abolition of virtue; that is, it *diminishes* it. And on the other hand, natural difficulty in the state of things is an approach to natural impossibility. And as the latter, when it is complete and absolute, *wholly* takes away blame; so such difficulty takes away *some* blame, or diminishes blame; and makes the thing done to be less worthy of punishment.

***JE: We are surrounded by necessary events and words in daily living.***

II. Men in their first use of such phrases as these, "must," "can't," "can't help it," "can't avoid it," "necessary," "unable," "impossible," "unavoidable," "irresistible," etc., use them to signify a necessity of constraint or restraint, a natural necessity or impossibility; or some necessity that the will has nothing to do in; which may be, whether men

Part IV—Wherein the Chief Grounds of the Reasonings of Arminians

will or no; and which may be supposed to be just the same, let men's inclinations and desires be what they will.

**JE: *All men experience and know in early childhood that there are innumerable things that are necessary in their words and actions.***

Such kind of terms in their original use, I suppose among all nations, are relative; carrying in their signification (as was before observed) a reference or respect to some contrary will, desire or endeavor, which, it is supposed, is, or may be in the case. All men find, and begin to find in early childhood, that there are innumerable things that can't be done, which they desire to do; and innumerable things which they are averse to, that must be, they can't avoid them, they will be, whether they choose them or no. It is to express this necessity, which men so soon and so often find, and which so greatly and so early affects them in innumerable cases, that such terms and phrases are first formed; and it is to signify such a necessity, that they are first used, and that they are most constantly used, in the common affairs of life;

**JE: *Common terms are not suitable for metaphysical conception and argument.***

and not to signify any such metaphysical, speculative and abstract notion, as that connection in the nature or course of things, which is between the subject and predicate of a proposition, and which is the foundation of the certain truth of that proposition; to signify which, they who employ themselves in philosophical inquiries into the first origin and metaphysical relations and dependences of things, have borrowed these terms, for want of others. But we grow up from our cradles in a use of such terms and phrases, entirely different from this, and carrying a sense exceeding diverse from that in which they are commonly used in the controversy between Arminians and Calvinists.

**JE: *Even though many try to deny the necessity in things, it is impossible for we all naturally learned in childhood to speak such words: "I can't do it."; "I couldn't help it." In this way, we acknowledge it and excuse ourselves and others.***

And it being, as was said before, a dictate of the universal sense of mankind, evident to us as soon as we begin to think, that the necessity signified by these terms, in the sense in which we first learn them, does excuse persons, and free them from all fault or blame; hence our ideas of excusableness or faultlessness is tied to these terms and phrases by a strong habit, which is begun in childhood as soon as we begin to speak, and grows up with us, and is strengthened by constant use and custom, the connection growing stronger and stronger.

**JE: *Men acknowledge the natural necessity by excusing themselves by using terms signifying it: "I can't do it."; "I could not help it."***

The habitual connection which is in men's minds between blamelessness and those aforementioned terms, "must," "cannot," "unable," "necessary," "impossible," "unavoidable," etc., becomes very strong; because as soon as ever men begin to use reason and speech, they have occasion to excuse themselves, from the natural necessity signified by these terms, in numerous instances. "I can't do it." "I could not help it." And all mankind have constant and daily occasion to use such phrases in this sense, to excuse themselves and others in almost all the concerns of life, with respect to disappointments, and things that happen which concern and affect us and others, that are hurtful, or disagreeable to us or them, or things desirable that we or others fail of.

*JE: Men connect their different ideas from early childhood, and such a habitual connection of ideas grow, and their natural sense as well, by that they necessarily judge and imagine. ILL: A normal man imagines that a mountain is bigger than a nose, yet a man born blind but now opened man does not have that sense.*

That a being accustomed to a union of different ideas, from early childhood, makes the habitual connection exceeding strong, as though such connection were owing to *nature*, is manifest in innumerable instances. It is altogether by such a habitual connection of ideas, that men judge of the bigness or distance of the objects of sight from their appearance. Thus it is owing to such a connection early established, and growing up with a person, that he judges a mountain, which he sees at ten miles' distance, to be bigger than his nose, or further off than the end of it. Having been used so long to join a considerable distance and magnitude with such an appearance, men imagine it is by a dictate of natural sense: whereas it would be quite otherwise with one that had his eyes newly opened, who had been born blind: he would have the same visible appearance, but natural sense would dictate no such thing concerning the magnitude or distance of what appeared.[1]

---

1. [Edwards borrows Molyneux's Problem from Locke to illustrate his theory of habitual connection of ideas, like other philosophers such as Berkeley, Leibniz, Voltaire, Diderot, La Mettrie, Helmholtz and William James. Locke interposed the so-called Molyneux's Problem or Question in his *An Essay Concerning Humane Understanding* (2nd edition, 1694), II.ix.vii.

Suppose a Man born blind, and now adult, and taught by his touch to distinguish between a Cube, and a Sphere of the same metal, and nighly of the same bigness, so as to tell, when he felt one and t'other; which is the Cube, which the Sphere. Suppose then the Cube and Sphere placed on a Table, and the Blind Man to be made to see. Quaere, Whether by his sight, before he touch'd them, he could now distinguish, and tell, which is the Globe, which the Cube?

I answer, not. For, though he has obtained the experience of how a globe, how a cube affects his touch, yet he has not yet obtained the experience, that what affects his touch so or so, must affect his sight so or so; or that a protuberant angle in the cube, that pressed his hand unequally, shall appear to his eye as it does in the cube.

For further, see Degenaar, Marjolein, and G. J. C. Lokhorst. "Molyneux problem." *Stanford Encyclopedia of Philosophy.* http:/plato. stanford. edu/entries/molyneux-problem/. Accessed 01 (2017); Marjolein Degenaar, and J. Scott Hauger. "Molyneux's Problem: Three Centuries of Discussion on the Perception of Forms." *ISIS-International Review Devoted to the History of Science and its Cultural Influence* 88, no. 4 (1997): 701–701.]

Part IV—Wherein the Chief Grounds of the Reasonings of Arminians

*JE: Habitual connection of ideas, e.g., blamelessness, and terms is the effect of mere nature, likewise men hear, learn, and use them in the new and metaphysical sense, to signify a quite different kind of necessity, which is not related to a contrary supposable will and endeavor, nor is blamable.*

III. When men, after they had been so habituated to connect ideas of innocency or blamelessness with such terms, that the union seems to be the effect of mere nature, come to hear the same terms used, and learn to use them themselves in the aforementioned new and metaphysical sense, to signify quite another sort of necessity, which has no such kind of relation to a contrary supposable will and endeavor; the notion of plain and manifest blamelessness, by this means, is by a strong prejudice, insensibly and unwarily transferred to a case to which it by no means belongs: the change of the use of the terms, to a signification which is very diverse, not being taken notice of, or adverted to. And there are several reasons why it is not.

*JE: Yet the connection of the two elements is not so effectual but rather ambiguous even to philosophers.*

1. The terms, as used by philosophers, are not very distinct and clear in their meaning: few use them in a fixed determined sense. On the contrary, their meaning is very vague and confused. Which is what commonly happens to the words used to signify things intellectual and moral, and to express what Mr. Locke calls "mixed modes."[2]

If men had a clear and distinct understanding of what is intended by these metaphysical terms, they would be able more easily to compare them with their original and common sense; and so would not be so easily cheated by them. The minds of men are so easily led into delusion by no sort of terms in the world, as by words of this sort.

*JE: Both the terms and their notions of blamelessness are ambiguous, and men cannot assure that the former are necessarily connected with the latter.*

2. The change of the signification of the terms is the more insensible, because the things signified, though indeed very different, yet do in some generals agree. In "necessity," that which is *vulgarly* so called, there is a strong connection between the thing said to be necessary, and something antecedent to it, in the order of nature; so there is also in "philosophical necessity." And though in both kinds of necessity, the connection can't be called by that name, with relation to an opposite will or endeavor, to which it is *superior*; which is the case in vulgar necessity; yet in both, the connection is

---

2. [Locke, Essay, bk. II, ch. 22; 1:381–89. Locke held that men are born with no innate ideas, which are acquired, learned and obtained from our experience. There are two types of ideas of mode: "Simple modes" are generated by taking a single simple idea and either repeating it or varying it (e.g. "dozen," "infinity," "oval," and "space"); "Mixed modes" are formed by combining the simple ideas of different kinds (e.g. "theft," "obligation," and "beauty"). In contrast to modes, substances are either self-subsisting things (e.g. "a man" and "a sheep") or collections of self-subsisting things (e.g. "an army of men" and "a flock of sheep")]

*prior* to will and endeavor, and so in some respect *superior*. In both kinds of necessity there is a foundation for some certainty of the proposition that affirms the event.

. . . The terms used being the same, and the things signified agreeing in these and some other general circumstances, and the expressions as used by philosophers being not well defined, and so of obscure and loose signification; hence persons are not aware of the great difference; and the notions of innocence or faultlessness, which were so strongly associated with them, and were strictly united in their minds, ever since they can remember, remain united with them still, as if the union were altogether natural and necessary; and they that go about to make a separation, seem to them to do great violence even to nature itself.

**JE: They think it irrational that men should be blamed for actions by a moral necessity because they insist this necessity may be against men's wills and sincere endeavors.**

IV. Another reason why it appears difficult to reconcile it with reason, that men should be blamed for that which is necessary with a moral necessity (which as was observed before is a species of philosophical necessity) is, that for want of due consideration, men inwardly entertain that apprehension, that this necessity may be against men's wills and sincere endeavors. They go away with that notion, that men may truly will and wish and strive that it may be otherwise; but that invincible necessity stands in the way.

And many think thus concerning themselves: some that are wicked men think they wish that they were good, that they loved God and holiness; but yet don't find that their wishes produce the effect. The reasons why men think thus, are as follows:

**JE: It is because they believe their will, willingness, volition, and inclinations are all good and consistent altogether.**

(1) They find what may be called an *indirect willingness* to have a better will, in the manner before observed. For it is impossible, and a contradiction to suppose the will to be directly and properly against itself. And they don't consider, that this indirect willingness is entirely a different thing from properly willing the thing that is the duty and virtue required; and that there is no virtue in that sort of willingness which they have.

They don't consider, that the volitions which a wicked man may have that he loved God, are no acts of the will at all against the moral evil of not loving God; but only some disagreeable consequences. But the making the requisite distinction requires more care of reflection and thought than most men are used to. And men through a prejudice in their own favor, are disposed to think well of their own desires and dispositions, and to account them good and virtuous, though their respect to virtue be only *indirect* and *remote*, and it is nothing at all that is virtuous that truly excites or terminates their inclinations.

Part IV—Wherein the Chief Grounds of the Reasonings of Arminians

***JE: The misconception that necessity hinders their true will and endeavor is because they misunderstand the actual meanings of terms and habitually use them and make such wrong suppositions.***

(2) Another thing that insensibly leads and beguiles men into a supposition that this moral necessity or impossibility is, or may be against men's wills, and true endeavors, is the derivation and formation of the terms themselves, that are often used to express it, which is such as seems directly to point to, and hold this forth.

Such words, for instance, as "unable," "unavoidable," "impossible," "irresistible"; which carry a plain reference to a supposable power exerted, endeavors used, resistance made, in opposition to the necessity: and the persons that hear them, not considering nor suspecting but that they are used in their proper sense: that sense being therefore understood, there does naturally, and as it were necessarily arise in their minds a supposition that it may be so indeed, that true desires and endeavors may take place, but that invincible necessity stands in the way, and renders them vain and to no effect.

***JE: Supposing the threatening and punishment to sin to be unjust is not from a dictate of reason but from unreasonable imagination and supposition and argument.***

V. Another thing which makes persons more ready to suppose it to be contrary to reason, that men should be exposed to the punishments threatened to sin, for doing those things which are morally necessary, or not doing those things morally impossible, is, that imagination strengthens the argument, and adds greatly to the power and influence of the seeming reasons against it, from the greatness of that punishment.

To allow that they may be justly exposed to a small punishment, would not be so difficult. Whereas, if there were any good reason in the case, if it were truly a dictate of reason that such necessity was inconsistent with faultiness, or just punishment, the demonstration would be equally certain with respect to a small punishment, or any punishment at all, as a very great one: but it is not equally easy to the imagination. They that argue against the justice of damning men for those things that are thus necessary, seem to make their argument the stronger, by setting forth the greatness of the punishment in strong expressions: "That a man should be cast into eternal burnings, that he should be made to fry in hell to all eternity, for those things which he had no power to avoid, and was under a fatal, unfrustrable, invincible necessity of doing."

# Section 4

It Is Agreeable to Common Sense, and the Natural Notions of Mankind, to Suppose Moral Necessity to be Consistent with Praise and Blame, Reward and Punishment

*Ar: It is against common sense to praise or blame men, who necessarily did any unavoidable actions.*

*JE: It is common sense that men are worthy to be praised or blamed, although they necessarily did any actions.*

Whether the reasons that have been given, why it appears difficult to some persons to reconcile with common sense the praising or blaming, rewarding or punishing those things which are morally necessary, are thought satisfactory, or not; yet it most evidently appears by the following things, that if this matter be rightly understood, setting aside all delusion arising from the impropriety and ambiguity of terms, this is not at all inconsistent with the natural apprehensions of mankind, and that sense of things which is found everywhere in the common people, who are furthest from having their thoughts perverted from their natural channel, by metaphysical and philosophical subtleties; but on the contrary, altogether agreeable *to*, and the very voice and dictate *of* this natural and vulgar sense.[1]

*JE: The common notion is that if men do or be wrong with their own will and pleasure, they are supposed to be blamed.*

---

1. [See "Science and Freedom in Thomas Reid," in James A. Harris, *Of Liberty and Necessity: The Free Will Debate in Eighteenth-Century British Philosophy* (New York: Oxford University Press, 2005), As Harris outlines, Reid holds 'principles of common sense,' that is, men are free in their choices and actions, and emphasizes the naturalness and universality of it.]

I. This will appear if we consider what the vulgar notion of blameworthiness is. The idea which the common people through all ages and nations have of faultiness, I suppose to be plainly this; a person's being or doing wrong, with his own will and pleasure; containing these two things:

> 1. His doing wrong, when he does as he pleases.
>
> 2. His pleasure's being wrong. Or in other words, perhaps more intelligibly expressing their notion; a person's having his heart wrong, and doing wrong from his heart. And this is the sum total of the matter.

### JE: *Their metaphysical notion of it is different from the vulgar one that common people have and is inconsistent with common sense.*

The common people don't ascend up in their reflections and abstractions, to the metaphysical sources, relations and dependences of things, in order to form their notion of faultiness or blameworthiness. They don't wait till they have decided by their refinings, what first determines the will; whether it be determined by something extrinsic, or intrinsic; whether volition determines volition, or whether the understanding determines the will;

whether there be any such thing as metaphysicians mean by contingence (if they have any meaning); whether there be a sort of a strange unaccountable sovereignty in the will, in the exercise of which, by its own sovereign acts, it brings to pass all its own sovereign acts.

### JE: *The common people as rational creatures begin to form the notion from childhood and take a long time to develop it.*

They don't take any part of their notion of fault or blame from the resolution of any such questions. If this were the case, there are multitudes, yea, the far greater part of mankind, nine hundred and ninety-nine out of a thousand would live and die without having any such notion as that of fault ever entering into their heads, or without so much as once having any conception that anybody was to be either blamed or commended for anything. To be sure, it would be a long time before men came to have such notions. Whereas it is manifest, they are some of the first notions that appear in children; who discover as soon as they can think, or speak, or act at all as rational creatures, a sense of desert. And certainly, in forming their notion of it, they make no use of metaphysics.

### JE: *The Two Foundations of the Notion of the Common People: 1. Experience; 2. Natural Sensation.*

All the ground they go upon consists in these two things; *experience*, and a *natural sensation* of a certain fitness or agreeableness which there is in uniting such moral evil as is above described, viz. *a being or doing wrong with the will*, and resentment in others, and pain inflicted on the person in whom this moral evil is. Which *natural sense* is what we call by the name of "conscience."

### JE: Common People's Notion of an Act: A person's own act and deed is done by him of choice for some cause or reason.

It is true, the common people and children, in their notion of a faulty act or deed of any person, do suppose that it is the person's *own act and deed*. But this is all that belongs to what they understand by a thing's being a person's *own deed* or action; even that it is something done by him of choice. That some exercise or motion should begin of itself, doesn't belong to their notion of an action, or doing. If so, it would belong to their notion of it, that it is something which is the cause of its own beginning: and that is as much as to say, that it is before it begins to be. Nor is their notion of an action some motion or exercise that begins accidentally, without any cause or reason; for that is contrary to one of the prime dictates of common sense, namely, that everything that begins to be, has some cause or reason why it is.

The common people, in their notion of a faulty or praiseworthy deed or work done by anyone, do suppose that the man does it in the exercise of *liberty*. But then their notion of liberty is only a person's having opportunity of doing as he pleases.

### The Common Notion of Liberty: Men do their acts in the exercise of liberty; they do as they please.

### Metaphysical Notion of Liberty: Will's first acting, causing its own determinations, i.e., men's free will; making all the determinations.

They have no notion of liberty consisting in the will's first acting, and so causing its own acts; and determining, and so causing its own determinations; or choosing, and so causing its own choice. Such a notion of liberty is what none have, but those that have darkened their own minds with confused metaphysical speculation, and abstruse and ambiguous terms. If a man is not restrained from acting as his will determines, or constrained to act otherwise; then he has liberty, according to common notions of liberty, without taking into the idea that grand contradiction of all the determinations of a man's free will being the effects of the determinations of his free will.

### JE: Normal men will not regard indifference as freedom, but the latter as full inclination in acting.

Nor have men commonly any notion of freedom consisting in indifference. For if so, then it would be agreeable to their notion, that the greater indifference men act with, the more freedom they act with; whereas the reverse is true. He that in acting, proceeds with the fullest inclination, does what he does with the greatest freedom, according to common sense. And so far is it from being agreeable to common sense, that such liberty as consists in indifference is requisite to praise or blame, that on the contrary, the dictate of every man's natural sense through the world is, that the further he is from being indifferent in his acting good or evil, and the more he does either with full and strong inclination, the more is he esteemed or abhorred, commended or condemned.

***Ar: It is inconsistent with the common sense to be praised for their necessary works and blamed for necessary failures. Thus the higher the moral (and natural) necessity or impossibility, the less they are to be blamable or commendable.***

***JE: Saying so just seems to agree with the reason of mankind, but that can take away all praise and blame.***

II. If it were inconsistent with the common sense of mankind, that men should be either to be blamed or commended in any volitions they have or fail of, in case of moral necessity or impossibility; then it would surely also be agreeable to the same sense and reason of mankind, that the nearer the case approaches to such a moral necessity or impossibility, either through a strong antecedent moral propensity on the one hand, or a great antecedent opposition and difficulty on the other, the nearer does it approach to a being neither blamable nor commendable; so that acts exerted with such preceding propensity would be worthy of proportionally less praise; and when omitted, the act being attended with such difficulty, the omission would be worthy of the less blame. It is so, as was observed before, with natural necessity and impossibility, propensity and difficulty: as it is a plain dictate of the sense of all mankind, that natural necessity and impossibility takes away *all* blame and praise; and therefore, that the nearer the approach is to these through previous propensity or difficulty, so praise and blame are proportionally *diminished*.

***JE: According to human reason alone, all praise and blame would be useless, and they would be diminished in the case of similar necessity and impossibility, and would be excusable wholly in neglecting things. And the difference between natural and moral impossibility (and difficulty) would be ignored.***

And if it were as much a dictate of common sense, that moral necessity of doing, or impossibility of avoiding, takes away *all* praise and blame, as that natural necessity or impossibility does this; then, by a perfect parity of reason, it would be as much the dictate of common sense, that an *approach* to moral necessity of doing, or impossibility of avoiding, diminishes praise and blame, as that an approach to natural necessity and impossibility does so. It is equally the voice of common sense, that persons are *excusable in part*, in neglecting things difficult against their wills, as that they are *excusable wholly* in neglecting things impossible against their wills. And if it made no difference, whether the impossibility was natural and against the will, or moral, lying in the will, with regard to excusableness; so neither would it make any difference, whether the difficulty, or approach to necessity be natural against the will, or moral, lying in the propensity of the will.

## Section 4—It Is Agreeable to Common Sense, and the Natural Notions of Mankind

***JE: Common sense of humanity admits that if by moral necessity man exerts good or bad by the disposition in his will, he would be more praiseworthy or blamable.***

But it is apparent, that the reverse of these things is true. If there be an approach to a moral necessity in a man's exertion of good acts of will, they being the exercise of a strong propensity to good, and a very powerful love to virtue; it is so far from being the dictate of common sense, that he is *less* virtuous, and the *less* to be esteemed, loved and praised; that it is agreeable to the natural notions of all mankind that he is so much the *better* man, worthy of *greater* respect, and higher commendation. And the stronger the inclination is, and the nearer it approaches to necessity in that respect, or to impossibility of neglecting the virtuous act, or of doing a vicious one; still the more virtuous, and worthy of higher commendation. And on the other hand, if a man exerts evil acts of mind; as for instance, acts of pride or malice, from a rooted and strong habit or principle of haughtiness and maliciousness, and a violent propensity of heart to such acts; according to the natural sense of all men, he is so far from being the less hateful and blamable on that account, that he is so much the more worthy to be detested and condemned by all that observe him.

***JE: If men's acts are not determined by the sovereign power of the will itself but by an antecedent bias or motive, they would be more virtuous and praiseworthy or more evil and blamable. It is a common notion.***

Moreover, it is manifest that it is no part of the notion which mankind commonly have of a blamable or praiseworthy act of the will, that it is an act which is not determined by an antecedent bias or motive, but by the sovereign power of the will itself; because if so, the greater hand such causes have in determining any acts of the will, so much the less virtuous or vicious would they be accounted; and the less hand, the more virtuous or vicious. Whereas the reverse is true: men don't think a good act to be the less praiseworthy, for the agent's being much determined in it by a good inclination or a good motive; but the more. And if good inclination or motive has but little influence in determining the agent, they don't think his act so much the more virtuous, but the less. And so concerning evil acts, which are determined by evil motives or inclinations.

***Ar: Man's acts, exerted from his good or evil disposition, shall not be praised nor blamed.***

***JE: It is common sense for humanity to praise or blame the acts done by an antecedent good or evil dispositions and tempers.***

Yea, if it be supposed that good or evil dispositions are implanted in the hearts of men by nature itself (which, it is certain, is vulgarly supposed in innumerable cases) yet it is not commonly supposed that men are worthy of no praise or dispraise for such dispositions; although what is natural is undoubtedly necessary, nature being prior to all acts of the will whatsoever.

### ILL: *A man with a bad temper.*

Thus for instance, if a guy appears to be of a very haughty or malicious disposition, and is supposed to be so by his natural temper, it is no vulgar notion, no dictate of the common sense and apprehension of men, that such dispositions are no vices or moral evils, or that such persons are not worthy of disesteem, odium and dishonor; or that the proud or malicious acts which flow from such natural dispositions, are worthy of no resentment.

Yea, such vile natural dispositions, and the strength of them, will commonly be mentioned rather as an aggravation of the wicked acts that come from such a fountain, than an extenuation of them. Its being natural for men to act thus, is often observed by men in the height of their indignation: they will say, "it is his very nature: he is of a vile natural temper; it is as natural to him to act so, as it is to breathe; he can't help serving the devil," etc.

### JE: *The two kinds of necessity, natural and moral, are different.*

But it is not thus with regard to hurtful mischievous things that any are the subjects or occasions of by *natural necessity*, against their inclinations. In such a case, the necessity by the common voice of mankind, will be spoken of as a full excuse. Thus it is very plain, that common sense makes a vast difference between these two kinds of necessity, as to the judgment it makes of their influence on the moral quality and desert of men's actions.

### JE: *By overlooking dictates of men's minds, Arminians hold their metaphysical notion of liberty but reject necessity.*

And these dictates of men's minds are so natural and necessary, that it may be very much doubted whether the Arminians themselves have ever got rid of them; yea, their greatest doctors, that have gone furthest in defense of their metaphysical notions of liberty, and have brought their arguments to their greatest strength, and as they suppose to a demonstration, against the consistence of virtue and vice with any necessity:

### ILL: *Natural necessity: natural disasters by wind and fire. Moral necessity: wicked man's horrible actions to victims; mental patient's misdeeds done to others.*

### JE: *Man must resent evil actions further than any disasters.*

it is to be questioned, whether there is so much as one of them, but that if he suffered very much from the injurious acts of a man under the power of an invincible haughtiness and malignancy of temper, would not, from the aforementioned natural sense of mind, resent it far otherwise, than if as great sufferings came upon him from the wind that blows, and fire that burns by natural necessity; and otherwise than he would, if he suffered as much from the conduct of a man perfectly delirious; yea, though he first brought his distraction upon him some way by his own fault.

### Ar: No one will be blamed for failing actions because of a necessary impossibility.

Some seem to disdain the distinction that we make between *natural* and *moral* necessity, as though it were altogether impertinent in this controversy:

> "That which is necessary (say they) is necessary; it is that which must be, and can't be prevented. And that which is impossible, is impossible, and can't be done: and therefore none can be to blame for not doing it."

And such comparisons are made use of, as the commanding of a man to walk who has lost his legs, and condemning and punishing him for not obeying; inviting and calling upon a man, who is shut up in a strong prison, to come forth, etc. But in these things Arminians are very unreasonable.

Let common sense determine whether there be not a great difference between those two cases;

### ILL: Natural Impossibility: A man is unable to come out for bars of iron.

the one, that of a man who has offended his prince, and is cast into prison; and after he has lain there a while, the king comes to him, calls him to come forth to him; and tells him that if he will do so, and will fall down before him, and humbly beg his pardon, he shall be forgiven, and set at liberty, and also be greatly enriched, and advanced to honor: the prisoner heartily repents of the folly and wickedness of his offense against his prince, is thoroughly disposed to abase himself, and accept of the king's offer; but is confined by strong walls, with gates of brass, and bars of iron.

### ILL: Moral Impossibility: A rebel is unable to admit his fault and ask his forgiveness.

The other case is, that of a man who is of a very unreasonable spirit, of a haughty, ungrateful, willful disposition; and moreover, has been brought up in traiterious principles; and has his heart possessed with an extreme and inveterate enmity to his lawful sovereign; and for his rebellion is cast into prison, and lies long there, loaden with heavy chains, and in miserable circumstances. At length the compassionate prince comes to the prison, orders his chains to be knocked off, and his prison doors to be set wide open; calls to him, and tells him, if he will come forth to him, and fall down before him, acknowledge that he has treated him unworthily, and ask his forgiveness; he shall be forgiven, set at liberty, and set in a place of great dignity and profit in his court. But he is so stout and stomachful, and full of haughty malignity, that he can't be willing to accept the offer: his rooted strong pride and malice have perfect power over him, and as it were bind him, by binding his heart: the opposition of his heart has the mastery over him, having an influence on his mind far superior to the king's grace and condescension, and to all his kind offers and promises.

Part IV—Wherein the Chief Grounds of the Reasonings of Arminians

***JE: It is consistent with common sense that the two rebels should be blamed for their omissions of actions required by necessity, although they have natural or moral impossibility.***

Now, is it agreeable to common sense, to assert and stand to it, that there is no difference between these two cases, as to any worthiness of blame in the prisoners; because, forsooth, there is a necessity in both, and the required act in each case is impossible? It is true, a man's evil dispositions may be as strong and immovable as the bars of a castle. But who can't see, that when a man, in the latter case, is said to be "unable" to obey the command, the expression is used improperly, and not in the sense it has originally and in common speech? And that it may properly be said to be in the rebel's power to come out of prison, seeing he can easily do it if he pleases; though by reason of his vile temper of heart which is fixed and rooted, it is impossible that it should please him?

***JE: Arminians attempted to demonstrate, not by the commons sense but by some philosophical and metaphysical arguments, that "moral necessity is inconsistent with praise and blame." But they fell under grand delusion and prejudice.***

Upon the whole, I presume there is no person of good understanding, who impartially considers the things which have been observed, but will allow that it is not evident from the dictates of the common sense, or natural notions of mankind, that moral necessity is inconsistent with praise and blame. And therefore, if the Arminians would prove any such inconsistency, it must be by some philosophical and metaphysical arguments, and not common sense.

There is a grand illusion in the pretended demonstration of Arminians from common sense. The main strength of all these demonstrations, lies in that prejudice that arises through the insensible change of the use and meaning of such terms as "liberty," "able," "unable," "necessary," "impossible," "unavoidable," "invincible," "action," etc., from their original and vulgar sense, to a metaphysical sense entirely diverse; and the strong connection of the ideas of blamelessness, etc., with some of these terms, by an habit contracted and established, while these terms were used in their first meaning. This prejudice and delusion is the foundation of all those positions they lay down as maxims, by which most of the scriptures, which they allege in this controversy, are interpreted, and on which all their pompous demonstrations from Scripture and reason depend. From this secret delusion and prejudice, they have almost all their advantages: it is the strength of their bulwarks, and the edge of their weapons.

***JE: Like prisoners who lived in a dark cave and had wrong imagination, Arminians distort the common sense of mankind.***

And this is the main ground of all the right they have to treat their neighbors in so assuming a manner, and to insult others, perhaps as wise and good as themselves, as weak bigots, men that dwell in the dark caves of superstition,[2] perversely set, obstinately shutting their eyes against the noonday light, enemies to common sense, maintaining the first-born of absurdities, etc. But perhaps an impartial consideration of the things which have been observed in the preceding parts of this inquiry, may enable the lovers of truth better to judge, whose doctrine is indeed absurd, abstruse, self-contradictory, and inconsistent with common sense, and many ways repugnant to the universal dictates of the reason of mankind.

**JE: *It is agreeable to common sense to suppose that moral necessity to be consistent with praise and blame. Saints have their full freedom and God himself is the active agent of the highest possible freedom.***

*Corol.* From things which have been observed, it will follow, that it is agreeable to common sense to suppose, that the glorified saints have not their freedom at all diminished, in any respect; and that God himself has the highest possible freedom, according to the true and proper meaning of the term; and that he is in the highest possible respect an agent, and active in the exercise of his infinite holiness; though he acts therein in the highest degree necessarily: and his actions of this kind are in the highest, most absolutely perfect manner virtuous and praiseworthy; and are so, for that very reason, because they are most perfectly necessary.

---

2. [Edwards uses Plato's allegory of the cave, in which he presents that men cannot see the real "idea" of things in a dark den but the shadow, that is, the shadow, which Plato learned from Socrates, *The Republic*, Book VII, 514a—521d.]

# Section 5

Concerning Those Objections, That This Scheme of Necessity Renders All Means and Endeavors for the Avoiding of Sin, or the Obtaining Virtue and Holiness, Vain, and to No Purpose; and That It Makes Men No More than Mere Machines in Affairs of Morality and Religion

***Arminian Objection: If man necessarily acts like a machine, any endeavor or means is useless.***

Arminians say, if it be so, that sin and virtue come to pass by a necessity consisting in a sure connection of causes and effects, antecedents and consequents, it can never be worth the while to use any means or endeavors to obtain the one, and avoid the other; seeing no endeavors can alter the futurity of the event, which is become necessary by a connection already established.

But I desire, that this matter may be fully considered; and that it may be examined with a thorough strictness, whether it will follow that endeavors and means, in order to avoid or obtain any future thing, must be more in vain, on the supposition of such a connection of antecedents and consequents, than if the contrary be supposed.

***JE: Means and endeavors are connected with necessity; the former is not in vain. Only if a means is lousy, could an endeavor not occur.***

For endeavors to be in vain, is for them not to be successful; that is to say, for them not eventually to be the means of the thing aimed at, which can't be, but in one of these two ways; either, first, that although the means are used, yet the event aimed at doesn't follow: or, secondly, if the event does follow, it is not because of the means, or from any connection or dependence of the event on the means, the event would have come to pass, as well without the means, as with them. If either of these two things are the case, then the means are not properly successful, and are truly in vain. The successfulness or unsuccessfulness of means, in order to an effect, or their being in vain or not in vain, consists in those means being connected, or not connected, with the effect, in such a manner as this, viz. that the effect is *with* the means, and not *without* them; or, that the being of the effect is, on the one hand, connected with the means, and the want of the effect, on the other hand, is connected with the want of the means.

If there be such a connection as this between means and end, the means are not in vain: the more there is of such a connection, the further they are from being in vain; and the less of such a connection, the more are they in vain.

**Ar: *A means to any effect is more in vain than it would be otherwise; there is less of the connection between means and effect.***

**JE: *A means is a preceding thing, and effect is a following one; there must be the connection between means and effect.***

Now therefore the question to be answered (in order to determine, whether it follows from this doctrine of the necessary connection between foregoing things and consequent ones, that means used in order to any effect, are more in vain than they would be otherwise) is, whether it follows from it, that there is less of the forementioned connection between means and effect; that is, whether on the supposition of there being a real and true connection between antecedent things and consequent ones, there must be less of a connection between means and effect, than on the supposition of there being no fixed connection between antecedent things and consequent ones: and the very stating of this question is sufficient to answer it. It must appear to everyone that will open his eyes, that this question can't be affirmed, without the grossest absurdity and inconsistence.

Means are foregoing things, and effects are following things: and if there were no connection between foregoing things, and following ones, there could be no connection between means and end; and so all means would be wholly vain and fruitless. For it is by virtue of some connection only, that they become successful: it is some connection observed, or revealed, or otherwise known, between antecedent things and following ones, that is what directs in the choice of means. And if there were no such thing as an established connection, there could be no choice, as to means; one thing would have no more tendency to an effect, than another; there would be no such thing as tendency in the case.

All those things which are successful means of other things, do therein prove connected antecedents of them: and therefore to assert, that a fixed connection between antecedents and consequents makes means vain and useless, or stands in the way to hinder the connection between means and end, is just so ridiculous, as to say, that a connection between antecedents and consequents stands in the way to hinder a connection between antecedents and consequents.

***JE: The connection, once fixed and necessary, cannot be changed by any laws or divine power.***

Nor can any supposed connection of the succession or train of antecedents and consequents, from the very beginning of all things, the connection being made already sure and necessary, either by established laws of nature, or by these together with a decree of sovereign immediate interpositions of divine power, on such and such occasions, or any other way [if any other there be];

***JE: There is the necessary connection between antecedents and consequents, in which means and endeavors cannot hinder, but they bring out the effects and events.***

I say, no such necessary connection of a series of antecedents and consequents can in the least tend to hinder, but that the means we use may belong to the series; and so may be some of those antecedents which are connected with the consequents we aim at, in the established course of things. Endeavors which we use, are things that exist; and therefore they belong to the general chain of events; all the parts of which chain are supposed to be connected: and so endeavors are supposed to be connected with some effects, or some consequent things, or other. And certainly this doesn't hinder but that the events they are connected with, may be those which we aim at, and which we choose, because we judge them most likely to have a connection with those events, from the established order and course of things which we observe, or from something in divine revelation.

***ILL: There is a real connection between man's having his eyes open and seeing, and his attempting to open his eyes and doing it. Attempt, aiming, and means do not break the connection or hinder its effects.***

Let us suppose a real and sure connection between a man's having his eyes open in the clear daylight, with good organs of sight, and seeing; so that seeing is connected with his opening his eyes, and not seeing with his not opening his eyes; and also the like connection between such a man's attempting to open his eyes, and his actually doing it: the supposed established connection between these antecedents and consequents, let the connection be never so sure and necessary, certainly doesn't prove that it is in vain, for a man in such circumstances to attempt to open his eyes, in order to seeing: his aiming at that event, and the use of the means, being the effect of his will, doesn't break the connection, or hinder the success.

***JE: The objection that means and endeavors are in vain for their connection with the necessity is not conflicting against Calvinists but to Arminians; if there is no connection between means and end, endeavors and success, they must be in vain.***

So that the objection we are upon, doesn't lie against the doctrine of the necessity of events by a certainty of connection and consequence: on the contrary, it is truly forcible against the Arminian doctrine of contingence and self-determination; which is inconsistent with such a connection. If there be no connection between those events wherein virtue and vice consist, and anything antecedent; then there is no connection between these events and any means or endeavors used in order to them: and if so, then those means must be in vain. The less there is of connection between foregoing things and following ones, so much the less there is between means and end, endeavors and success; and in the same proportion are means and endeavors ineffectual and in vain.

*Ar: Neither virtue nor vice is not connected with and is from a foregoing event or thing but self-determination.*

*JE: A foregoing event or something as a cause, ground, or means of the existence of virtue or vice influences to the determination of the existence.*

It will follow from Arminian principles, that there is no degree of connection between virtue or vice, and any foregoing event or thing: or in other words, that the determination of the existence of virtue or vice doesn't in the least depend on the influence of anything that comes to pass antecedently, from which the determination of its existence is, as its cause, means, or ground; because, so far as it is so, it is not from self-determination: and therefore, so far there is nothing of the nature of virtue or vice. And so it follows, that virtue and vice are not at all, in any degree, dependent upon, or connected with any foregoing event or existence, as its cause, ground, or means. And if so, then all foregoing means must be totally in vain.

*Ar: Any means and endeavors to escape vice or obtain virtue can be in vain if they are done not by self-determination but by necessity.*

*JE: That is not reasonable, but the following answers can be otherwise:*

> *1. By the natural connection between the end and the means; 2. By any divine constitution of God; 3. Revealed way of God's bestowing to occur, in consequence of any means, endeavors, prayers, or deeds.*

Hence it follows, that there cannot, in any consistence with the Arminian scheme, be any reasonable ground of so much as a conjecture concerning the consequence of any means and endeavors, in order to escaping vice or obtaining virtue, or any choice or preference of means, as having a greater probability of success by some than others; either from any natural connection or dependence of the end on the means, or through any divine constitution, or revealed way of God's bestowing or bringing to pass these things, in consequence of any means, endeavors, prayers or deeds. Conjecture in this latter case depends on a supposition that God himself is the giver, or determining cause of the events sought: but if they depend on self-determination, then God is not the determining or disposing author of them: and if these things are not of his disposal, then no conjecture can be made from any revelation he has given concerning any way or method of his disposal of them.

### Ar: Self-determination is essential to virtue.

### JE: Means and endeavors to obtain virtue or avoid vice will be successful.

Yea, on these principles, it will not only follow that men can't have any reasonable ground of judgment or conjecture, that their means and endeavors to obtain virtue or avoid vice, will be successful, but they may be sure they will not; they may be certain, that they will be in vain; and that if ever the thing which they seek comes to pass, it will not be at all owing to the means they use. For means and endeavors can have no effect at all, in order to obtain the end, but in one of these two ways; either

> (1) through a natural tendency and influence, to prepare and dispose the mind more to virtuous acts, either by causing the disposition of the heart to be more in favor of such acts, or by bringing the mind more into the view of powerful motives and inducements: or (2) by putting persons more in the way of God's bestowment of the benefit. But neither of these can be the case. Not the latter; for as has been just now observed, it doesn't consist with the Arminian notion of self-determination, which they suppose essential to virtue, that God should be the bestower, or (which is the same thing) the determining, disposing author of virtue.

Not the former; for natural influence and tendency supposes causality and connection; and that supposes necessity of event, which is inconsistent with Arminian liberty. A tendency of means, by biasing the heart in favor of virtue, or by bringing the will under the influence and power of motives in its determinations, are both inconsistent with Arminian liberty of will, consisting in indifference, and sovereign self-determination, as has been largely demonstrated.

### Ar: All endeavors are in vain for necessity, and so we oppose the doctrine of necessity.

But for the more full removal of this prejudice against that doctrine of necessity which has been maintained, as though it tended to encourage a total neglect of all endeavors as vain; the following things may be considered.

### Ar: The doctrine gives any just occasion for such an improvement and such a use of it would not be unreasonable.

### JE: Unreasonable Arminian Supposition: All being is already fixed unalterably by necessity; therefore, it is folly for men to use any means to any end.

The question is not, whether men may not thus improve this doctrine: we know that many true and wholesome doctrines are abused: but, whether the doctrine gives any just occasion for such an improvement; or whether, on the supposition of the truth of the doctrine, such a use of it would not be unreasonable? If any shall affirm, that it would not, but that the very nature of the doctrine is such as gives just occasion for it, it must be on this supposition; namely, that such an invariable necessity of all things already settled, must render the interposition of all means, endeavors, conclusions or actions of ours, in order to the obtaining any future end whatsoever, perfectly insignificant; because they can't in the least alter or vary the course and series of things, in any event or circumstance; all being already fixed unalterably by necessity: and that therefore it is folly, for men to use any means for *any* end; but their wisdom, to save themselves the trouble of endeavors, and take their ease.

No person can draw such an inference from this doctrine, and come to such a conclusion, without contradicting himself, and going counter to the very principles he pretends to act upon. For he comes to a conclusion, and takes a course, *in order to an end*, even *his ease*, or the saving himself from trouble; he seeks something future, and uses means in order to a future thing, even in his drawing up that conclusion, that he will seek nothing, and use no means in order to anything future, he seeks his future ease, and the benefit and comfort of indolence. If prior necessity that determines all things, makes vain all actions or conclusions of ours, in order to anything future; then it makes vain all conclusions and conduct of ours, in order to our future ease. The measure of our ease, with the time, manner and every circumstance of it, is already fixed, by all-determining necessity, as much as anything else.

**Ar: Happiness or misery is already determined by the necessity; so I cannot increase my happiness, or diminish my misery, and it is better to take my ease and enjoy the comfort of negligence than to do endeavors.**

**JE: Likewise, they cannot reasonably improve the doctrine of necessity.**

If he says within himself,

> "What future happiness or misery I shall have, is already in effect determined by the necessary course and connection of things; therefore, I will save myself the trouble of labor and diligence, which can't add to my determined degree of happiness, or diminish my misery; but will take my ease, and will enjoy the comfort of sloth and negligence."

Such a man contradicts himself: he says,

> the measure of his future happiness and misery is already fixed, and he won't try to diminish the one, nor add to the other: but yet in his very conclusion, he contradicts this; for he takes up this conclusion, *to add to his future happiness*, by the ease and comfort of his negligence; and to diminish his future trouble and misery, by saving himself the trouble of using means and taking pains.

Therefore, persons can't reasonably make this improvement of the doctrine of necessity, that they will go into a voluntary negligence of means for their own happiness. For the principles they must go upon, in order to this, are inconsistent with their making any improvement at all of the doctrine: for to make some improvement of it, is to be influenced by it, to come to some voluntary conclusion, in regard to their own conduct, with some view or aim: but this, as has been shown, is inconsistent with the principles they pretend to act upon. In short, the principles are such as cannot be acted upon at all, or in any respect, consistently. And therefore in every pretense of acting upon them, or making any improvement at all of them, there is a self-contradiction.

**JE: *The doctrine of necessity does not make men mere machines. Because they still have reason and understanding, and a faculty of will, they are capable of volition and choice, of moral habits and acts, and they deserve praise or blame.***

As to that objection[1] against the doctrine which I have endeavored to prove, that it makes men no more than mere machines; I would say, that notwithstanding this doctrine, man is entirely, perfectly and unspeakably different from a mere machine, in that he has reason and understanding, and has a faculty of will, and so is capable of volition and choice; and in that, his will is guided by the dictates or views of his understanding; and in that his external actions and behavior, and in many respect also his thoughts, and the exercises of his mind, are subject to his will; so that he has liberty to act according to his choice, and do what he pleases; and by means of these things, is capable of moral habits and moral acts, such inclinations and actions as according to the common sense of mankind, are worthy of praise, esteem, love and reward; or on the contrary, of disesteem, detestation, indignation and punishment.[2]

**Ar: *Man's will is different from mere machines and it has a self-determining power, that is, a power of choosing, and in many instances can do as he chooses.***

In these things is all the difference from mere machines, as to liberty and agency, that would be any perfection, dignity or privilege, in any respect: all the difference that can be desired, and all that can be conceived of; and indeed all that the pretensions of the Arminians themselves come to, as they are forced often to explain themselves [though their explications overthrow and abolish the things asserted, and pretended to be explained]. For they are forced to explain a self-determining power of will, by a power in the soul, to determine as it chooses or wills; which comes to no more than this, that a man has a power of choosing, and in many instances, can do as he chooses.

**JE: *According to Arminian scheme, a man of dignity becomes unhappier than a machine because the latter is guided by the skillful hand of the owner, and yet the man is left to the guidance of nothing.***

---

1. [JE's rejoinder in this paragraph is sufficient to elicit such a common accusation that the doctrine of necessity makes men "mere machines," which is reenacted by Strauss. See James D. Strauss, "A Puritan in a Post-Puritan World," in *Grace Unlimited*, ed. Clark H. Pinnock (Minneapolis: Bethany Fellowship, 1975), 243.]

2. ["*Begging the question* (petitio principii, assming the initial point)" is literally to catch a point by forcefully taking a question or point, a form of logical fallacy in which a statement or claim is assumed to be true without evidence other than the statement or claim itself. e.g., "This phone is junk because it looks valueless."]

Which is quite a different thing from that contradiction, his having power of choosing his first act of choice in the case. Or if their scheme makes any other difference than this, between men and machines, it is for the worse: it is so far from supposing men to have a dignity and privilege above machines, that it makes the manner of their being determined still more unhappy. Whereas machines are guided by an understanding cause, by the skillful hand of the workman or owner; the will of man is left to the guidance of nothing, but absolute blind contingence.

# Section 6

## Concerning That Objection against the Doctrine which Has Been Maintained, That It Agrees with the Stoical Doctrine of Fate, and the Opinions of Mr. Hobbes

When Calvinists oppose the Arminian notion of the freedom of will, and contingence of volition, and insist that there are no acts of the will, nor any other events whatsoever, but what are attended with some kind of necessity; their opposers cry out of them, as agreeing with the ancient Stoics in their doctrine of fate, and with Mr. Hobbes in his opinion of necessity.

**JE: *The Stoic philosophers were the greatest, wisest and most virtuous of all the heathen philosophers; their teachings were the nearest to Christianity.***

It would not be worthwhile, to take notice of so impertinent an objection, had it not been urged by some of the chief Arminian writers. There were many important truths maintained by the ancient Greek and Roman philosophers, and especially the Stoics, that are never the worse for being held by them. The Stoic philosophers, by the general agreement of Christian divines, and even Arminian divines, were the greatest, wisest and most virtuous of all the heathen philosophers; and in their doctrine and practice came the nearest to Christianity of any of their sects. How frequently are the sayings of these philosophers, in many of the writings and sermons, even of Arminian divines, produced, not as arguments of the falseness of the doctrines which they delivered, but as a confirmation of some of the greatest truths of the Christian religion, relating to the unity and perfections of the Godhead, a future state, the duty and happiness of mankind, etc., as observing how the light of nature and reason in the wisest and best of the heathen, harmonized with, and confirms the gospel of Jesus Christ.

**DW: *Calvinist doctrine of necessity is similar to Stoics and so it is very heathenish.***

## Section 6—Concerning That Objection against the Doctrine which Has Been Maintained

***JE: No. Arminian doctrine is more similar to them, and does believe man's ability to make himself truly virtuous.***

And it is very remarkable concerning Dr. Whitby, that although he alleges the agreement of the Stoics with us, wherein he supposes they maintained the like doctrine with us, as an argument against the truth of our doctrine; yet this very Dr. Whitby alleges the agreement of the Stoics with the Arminians, wherein he supposes they taught the same doctrine with them, as an argument for the truth of their doctrine.[1]

So that when the Stoics agree with *them*, this [it seems] is a confirmation of their doctrine, and a confutation of ours, as showing that our opinions are contrary to the natural sense and common reason of mankind: nevertheless, when the Stoics agree with *us*, it argues no such thing in our favor; but on the contrary, is a great argument against us, and shows our doctrine to be heathenish.

It is observed by some Calvinistic writers, that the Arminians symbolize with the Stoics, in some of those doctrines wherein they are opposed by the Calvinists; particularly in their denying an original, innate, total corruption and depravity of heart; and in what they held of man's ability to make himself truly virtuous and conformed to God; and in some other doctrines.

***JE: Contrary to their argument, our doctrine is not similar to Stoics, theirs is so to Stoics, because they agree with the very worst of them.***

It may be further observed, it is certainly no better objection against our doctrine, that it agrees in some respects with the doctrine of the ancient Stoic philosophers, than it is against theirs, wherein they differ from us, that it agrees in some respects with the opinion of the very worst of the heathen philosophers, the followers of Epicurus, that father of atheism[2] and licentiousness, and with the doctrine of the Sadducees and Jesuits.

***JE: I don't trust in Stoic notion of fate.***

I am not much concerned to know precisely what the ancient Stoic philosophers held concerning fate, in order to determine what is truth; as though it were a sure way to be in the right, to take good heed to differ from them. It seems that they differed among themselves; and probably the doctrine of fate, as maintained by most of them, was in some respects erroneous.

***JE: Fate is repugnant to any liberty consisting in our doing as we please.***

But whatever their doctrine was, if any of them held such a fate, as is repugnant to any liberty consisting in our doing as we please, I utterly deny such a fate. If they held any such fate, as is not consistent with the common and universal notions that mankind have of liberty, activity, moral agency, virtue and vice; I disclaim any such thing, and

---

1. Whitby, *Discourse*, Dis. IV, ch. 1, no. 8; pp. 325, 326, 327.
2. [*FOW*, 420.]

think I have demonstrated that the scheme I maintain is no such scheme. If the Stoics by fate meant anything of such a nature, as can be supposed to stand in the way of the advantage and benefit of the use of means and endeavors, or make(s) it less worth the while for men to desire, and seek after anything wherein their virtue and happiness consists; I hold no doctrine that is clogged with any such inconvenience, any more than any other scheme whatsoever; and by no means so much as the Arminian scheme of contingence; as has been shown.

### JE: Such a fate is inconsistent with the disposal of the absolute agent and the exercise of his perfect liberty.

If they held any such doctrine of universal fatality, as is inconsistent with any kind of liberty, that is or can be any perfection, dignity, privilege or benefit, or anything desirable, in any respect, for any intelligent creature, or indeed with any liberty that is possible or conceivable; I embrace no such doctrine. If they held any such doctrine of fate as is inconsistent with the world's being in all things subject to the disposal of an intelligent wise agent, that presides, not as the soul of the world, but as the sovereign Lord of the universe, governing all things by proper will, choice and design, in the exercise of the most perfect liberty conceivable, without subjection to any constraint, or being properly under the power or influence of anything before, above or without himself; I wholly renounce any such doctrine.

### JE: All that Hobbes said is not wrong, but there is some truth in it.

As to Mr. Hobbes' maintaining the same doctrine concerning necessity; I confess, it happens I never read Mr. Hobbes.[3] Let his opinion be what it will, we need not reject all truth which is demonstrated by clear evidence, merely because it was once held by some bad man. This great truth, that Jesus is the Son of God, was not spoiled because it was once and again proclaimed with a loud voice by the devil. If truth is so defiled because it is spoken by the mouth, or written by the pen of some ill-minded mischievous man, that it must never be received, we shall never know when we hold any of the most precious and evident truths by a sure tenure. And if Mr. Hobbes has made a bad use of this truth, that is to be lamented: but the truth is not to be thought worthy of rejection on that account. It is common for the corruptions of the hearts of evil men, to abuse the best things to vile purposes.

### JE: Arminians are ,more akin to Hobbes than Calvinists to him.

---

3. [The reason why JE emphasizes that "he never read Mr. Hobbes" is that "In New England, necessity was *regarded as a doctrine not* of the *Calvinists, but of freethinkers*; and when JE produced the *Freedom of the Will*, he was classed, *not* with the Westminster divines, *but* with the Stoics, Hobbes, Leibniz, . . .". Conrad Wright, *The Beginnings of Unitarianism in America* (Boston: Starr King Press, 1955), 93.]

I might also take notice of its having been observed, that the Arminians agree with Mr. Hobbes[4] in many more things than the Calvinists. As, in what he is said to hold concerning original sin, in denying the necessity of supernatural illumination, in denying infused grace, in denying the doctrine of justification by faith alone; and other things.

---

4. [Dr. Gill, in his answer to Dr. Whitby[John Gill, *The Cause of God and Truth, being a Confutation of the Arguments from Reason Used by the Arminians; and Particularly by Dr. Whitby, in his Discourse on the Five Points*, ch. 5, sec. 11, nos. 6 f. (London, 1737), Pt. III, pp. 183 ff.]

# Section 7

## Concerning the Necessity of the Divine Will

***Ar: We hold that the will has its self-determining power but deny that the will is to be determined by motives.***

Some may possibly object against what has been supposed of the absurdity and inconsistence of a self-determining power in the will, and the impossibility of its being otherwise, than that the will should be determined in every case by some motive, and by a motive which [as it stands in the view of the understanding] is of superior strength to any appearing on the other side; that if these things are true, it will follow, that not only the will of created minds, but the will of *God himself* is necessary in all its determinations. Concerning which says the author of the *Essay on the Freedom of Will in God and in the Creature* [p. 85–86],[1]

> What strange doctrine is this, contrary to all our ideas of the dominion of God? Does it not destroy the glory of his liberty of choice, and take away from the creator and governor and benefactor of the world, that most free and sovereign agent, all the glory of this sort of freedom? Does it not seem to make him a kind of mechanical medium of fate, and introduce Mr. Hobbes' doctrine of fatality and necessity, into all things that God hath to do with? Does it not seem to represent the blessed God, as a being of vast understanding, as well as power and efficiency, but still to leave him without a will to choose among all the objects within his view? In short, it seems to make the blessed God a sort of almighty minister of fate, under its universal and supreme influence; [. . .] As it was the professed sentiment of some of the ancients, that fate was above the gods.

---

1. [Watts, *Essay* (London, 1732), sec. 7, *dif.* 1, pp. 85–86; reprinted, *Works* 6:272.]

This is declaiming, rather than arguing; and an application to men's imaginations and prejudices, rather than to mere reason. But I would calmly endeavor to consider whether there be any reason in this frightful representation.

***JE: It is much more difficult to conceive things in the divine understanding and will than in the human mind.***

But before I enter upon a particular consideration of the matter, I would observe this: that it is reasonable to suppose, it should be much more difficult to express or conceive things according to exact metaphysical truth, relating to the nature and manner of the existence of things in the divine understanding and will, and the operation of these faculties (if I may so call them) of the divine mind, than in the human mind; which is infinitely more within our view, and nearer to a proportion to the measure of our comprehension, and more commensurate to the use and import of human speech.

***JE: Words were first formed to express external things, and language is more limited to express things internal and spiritual, particularly of the deity.***

Language is indeed very deficient, in regard of terms to express precise truth concerning our own minds, and their faculties and operations. Words were first formed to express external things; and those that are applied to express things internal and spiritual, are almost all borrowed, and used in a sort of figurative sense. Whence they are most of them attended with a great deal of ambiguity and unfixedness in their signification, occasioning innumerable doubts, difficulties and confusions in inquiries and controversies about things of this nature. But language is much less adapted to express things in the mind of the incomprehensible Deity, precisely as they are.

We find a great deal of difficulty in conceiving exactly of the nature of our own souls. And notwithstanding all the progress which has been made in past and present ages, in this kind of knowledge, whereby our metaphysics, as it relates to these things, is brought to greater perfection than once it was; yet here is still work enough left for future inquiries and researches, and room for progress still to be made, for many ages and generations. But we had need to be infinitely able metaphysicians, to conceive with clearness, according to strict, proper and perfect truth, concerning the nature of the divine essence, and the modes of the action and operation of the powers of the divine mind.

***JE: It is very hard to conceive and speak of things about the divine nature and will, and even if done, there must be less propriety in such depictions than his created beings.***

And it may be noted particularly, that though we are obliged to conceive of some things in God as consequent and dependent on others, and of some things pertaining to the divine nature and will as the foundation of others, and so before others in the order of nature: as, we must conceive of the knowledge and holiness of God as prior in the order of nature to his happiness; the perfection of his understanding, as the foundation of his wise purposes and decrees; the holiness of his nature, as the cause and reason of his holy determinations—: yet[2] when we speak of cause and effect, antecedent and consequent, fundamental and dependent, determining and determined, in the first Being, who is self-existent, independent, of perfect and absolute simplicity and immutability, and the first cause of all things; doubtless there must be less propriety in such representations, than when we speak of derived dependent beings, who are compounded, and liable to perpetual mutation and succession.

**JE: God always determines what is best by his will in the moral necessity.**

**Watts: God is not who cannot choose freely nor who determinates in the present necessity.**

Having premised this, I proceed to observe concerning the aforementioned author's exclamation, about the *necessary* determination of God's will, in all things, by what he sees to be *fittest* and *best*.

That all the seeming force of such objections and exclamations must arise from an imagination, that there is some sort of privilege or dignity in being without such a moral necessity, as will make it impossible to do any other, than always choose what is wisest and best; as though there were some disadvantage, meanness and subjection, in such a necessity; a thing by which the will was confined, kept under, and held in servitude by something, which, as it were, maintained a strong and invincible power and dominion over it, by bonds that held him fast, and that he could by no means deliver himself from. Whereas, this must be all mere imagination and delusion.

**JE: It is not dishonor to men or God to act in the necessity.**

It is no disadvantage or dishonor to a being, necessarily to act in the most excellent and happy manner, from the necessary perfection of his own nature. This argues no imperfection, inferiority or dependence, nor any want of dignity, privilege or ascendancy.[3] It is not inconsistent with the absolute, and most perfect sovereignty of God.

---

2. [Restored from Yale edition as "determinations. And yet" to the first 1754 edition.]

3. "It might have been objected with much more plausibleness, that the supreme cause cannot be free, because he must needs do always what is best in the whole. But this would not at all serve Spinoza's purpose: for this is a necessity, not of nature and fate, but of fitness and wisdom; a necessity consistent with the greatest freedom, and most perfect choice. For the only foundation of this necessity is such an unalterable rectitude of will, and perfection of wisdom, as makes it impossible for a wise being to act foolishly." Samuel Clarke, *A Discourse Concerning the Being and Attributes of God, the Obligations of Natural Religion, and the Truth and Certainty of the Christian Revelation* (6th ed. London, 1725), 64.

"[T]hough God is a most perfectly free agent, yet he cannot but do always what is best and wisest in the whole. The reason is evident; because perfect wisdom and goodness are as steady and certain principles of action, as necessity itself; and an infinitely wise and good being, indued with the most perfect liberty, can no more choose to act in contradiction to wisdom and goodness, than a necessary agent can act contrary to the necessity by which it is acted; it being as great an absurdity and impossibility in choice, for infinite wisdom to choose to act unwisely, or infinite goodness to choose what

## *What is the sovereignty of God?*

is not good, as it would be in nature, for absolute necessity to fail of producing its necessary effect. There was indeed no necessity in nature, that God should at first create such being as he has created, or indeed any being at all; because he is in himself infinitely happy and all-sufficient. There was also no necessity in nature, that he should preserve and continue things in being, after they were created; because he would be self-sufficient without their continuance, as he was before their creation. But it was fit and wise and good, that infinite wisdom should manifest, and infinite goodness communicate itself; and therefore it was necessary, in the sense of necessity I am now speaking of, that things should be made *at such a time,* and continued *so long,* and indeed with various perfections in such degrees, as infinite wisdom and goodness saw it wisest and best that they should." Clarke, *Discourse,* 112–13.

"'Tis not a fault, but a perfection of our nature, to desire, will and act, according to the last result of a fair examination. . .." This is so far from being a restraint or diminution of freedom, that it is the very improvement and benefit of it: 'tis not an abridgment, 'tis the end and use of our liberty; and the further we are removed from such a determination, the nearer we are to misery and slavery. A perfect indifference in the mind, not determinable by its last judgment of the good or evil that is thought to attend its choice, would be so far from being an advantage and excellency of any intellectual nature, that it would be as great an imperfection as the want of indifferency to act, or not to act, till determined by the will, would be an imperfection on the other side.. . . 'Tis as much a perfection, that desire or the power of preferring should be determined by good, as that the power of acting should be determined by the will: and the certainer such determination is, the greater the perfection. Nay, were we determined by anything but the last result of our own minds, judging of the good or evil of any action, we were not free. The very end of our freedom being, that we might attain the good we choose; and therefore every man is brought under a necessity by his constitution, as an intelligent being, to be determined in willing by his own thought and judgment, what is best for him to do; also he would be under the determination of some other than himself, which is want of liberty. And to deny that a man's will, in every determination, follows his own judgment, is to say, that a man wills and acts for an end that he would not have, at the same time that he wills and acts for it. For if he prefers it in his present thoughts, before any other, 'tis plain he then thinks better of it, and would have it before any other; unless he can have, and not have it; will, and not will it, at the same time; a contradiction too manifest to be admitted.

"If we look upon those superior beings above us, who enjoy perfect happiness, we shall have reason to judge, that they are more steadily determined in their choice of good than we; and yet we have no reason to think they are less happy, or less free, than we are. And if it were fit for such poor finite creatures as we are, to pronounce what infinite wisdom and goodness could do, I think we might say, that God himself cannot choose what is not good. *The freedom of the Almighty hinders not his being determined by what is best.* . ..

"But to give a right view of this mistaken part of liberty, let me ask, would anyone be a changeling, because he is less determined by wise determinations [Locke has "considerations"], than a wise man? Is it worth the name of freedom, to be at liberty to play the fool, and draw shame and misery upon a man's self? If to break loose from the conduct of reason, and to want that restraint of examination and judgment, that keeps us from doing or choosing the worse, be liberty, true liberty, mad men and fools are the only free men. Yet I think nobody would choose to be mad, for the sake of such liberty, but he that is mad already." Locke, *Essay,* bk. II, ch. 21, nos. 48–51; 1, 345–47.

"[T]his Being having all things always necessarily in view, must always, and eternally will, according to his infinite comprehension of things; that is, must will all things that are wisest and best to be done. There is no getting free of this consequence. If it can will at all, it must will this way. To be capable of knowing, and not capable of willing, is not to be understood. And to be capable of willing otherwise than what is wisest and best, contradicts that knowledge which is infinite. Infinite knowledge must direct the will without error. *Here then is the origin of moral necessity; and that is really, of freedom.*. . .

Perhaps it may be said, when the divine will is determined, from the consideration of the eternal aptitudes of things, it is as necessarily determined, as if it were physically impelled, if that were possible. But it is unskillfulness, to suppose this an objection. The great principle is once established, vis. that the divine will is determined by the eternal reason and aptitudes of things [By this Baxter means,

The sovereignty of God is his ability and authority to do whatever pleases him; whereby "he doth according to his will in the armies of heaven, and amongst the inhabitants of the earth, and none can stay his hand, or say unto him, what dost thou?" The following things belong to the *sovereignty* of God; viz.

(1) supreme, universal, and infinite *power*; whereby he is able to do what he pleases, without control, without any confinement of that power, without any subjection in the least measure to any other power; and so without any hindrance or restraint, that it should be either impossible, or at all difficult, for him to accomplish his will; and without any dependence of his power on any other power, from whence it should be derived, or which it should stand in any need of: so far from this, that all other power is derived from him, and is absolutely dependent on him.

(2) That he has supreme *authority*; absolute and most perfect right to do what he wills, without subjection to any superior authority, or any derivation of authority from any other, or limitation by any distinct independent authority, either superior, equal, or inferior; he being the head of all dominion, and fountain of all authority; and also without restraint by any obligation, implying either subjection, derivation, or dependence, or proper limitation.

(3) That his *will* is supreme, underived, and independent on anything without himself; being in everything determined by his own counsel, having no other rule but his own wisdom; his will not being subject to, or restrained by the will of any other, and others' wills being perfectly subject to his.

(4) That his *wisdom*, which determines his will, is supreme, perfect, underived, self-sufficient, and independent; so that it may be said as in Isaiah 40:14, "With whom took he counsel? And who instructed him and taught him in the path of judgment, and taught him knowledge, and showed him the way of understanding?"—There is no other divine sovereignty but this:

and this is properly *absolute sovereignty*: no other is desirable; nor would any other be honorable, or happy: and indeed there is no other conceivable or possible. It is the glory and greatness of the divine sovereignty, that God's will is determined by his own infinite all-sufficient wisdom in everything; and in nothing at all is either

---

determined by "the intuition of the eternal relations of its own ideas, which are the archetypes of things"], instead of being physically impelled; and after that, the more strong and necessary this determination is, the more perfect the Deity must be allowed to be: it is this that makes him an amiable and adorable being, whose will and power are constantly, immutably determined, by the consideration of what is wisest and best; instead of a surd being, with power, but without discerning and reason. *It is the beauty of this necessity, that it is strong as fate itself, with all the advantage of reason and goodness..* . . It is strange, to see men contend, that the Deity is not free, because he is necessarily rational, immutably good and wise; when a man is allowed still the perfecter being, the more fixedly and constantly his will is determined by reason and truth."

Andrew Baxter, *An Enquiry into the Nature of the Human Soul, Wherein the Immateriality of the Soul is Evinced from the Principles of Reason and Philosophy*, 2 vols. (London, 1733; 3rd ed., 1745), 2:403–04.

directed by any inferior wisdom, or by no wisdom; whereby it would become senseless arbitrariness, determining and acting without reason, design or end.

**Ar: *Necessary divine will is blasphemy for God, and the only contingency excluding wisdom and motive or command belongs to him.***

**JE: *It is glory for God to act necessarily in his wisdom and holiness, for wisdom is in itself excellent.***

If God's will is steadily and surely determined in everything by *supreme* wisdom, then it is in everything necessarily determined to that which is *most* wise. And certainly it would be a disadvantage and indignity, to be otherwise. For if the divine will was not necessarily determined to that which in every case is wisest and best, it must be subject to some degree of undesigning contingence; and so in the same degree liable to evil.

To suppose the divine will liable to be carried hither and thither at random, by the uncertain wind of blind contingence, which is guided by no wisdom, no motive, no intelligent dictate whatsoever [if any such thing were possible], would certainly argue a great degree of imperfection and meanness, infinitely unworthy of the deity. If it be a disadvantage, for the divine will to be attended with this moral necessity, then the more free from it, and the more left at random, the greater dignity and advantage.

And consequently to be perfectly free from the direction of understanding, and universally and entirely left to senseless unmeaning contingence, to act absolutely at random, would be the supreme glory.

**JE: *Which word is more glorious to God? He is wise, or He is holy?***

It no more argues any dependence of God's will, that his supremely wise volition is necessary, than it argues a dependence of his being, that his existence is necessary. If it be something too low, for the supreme Being to have his will determined by moral necessity, so as necessarily, in every case, to will in the highest degree holily and happily; then why is it not also something too low, for him to have his existence, and the infinite perfection of his nature, and his infinite happiness determined by necessity?

**JE: *God is necessarily wise. It is not dishonorable.***

It is no more to God's dishonor, to be necessarily wise, than to be necessarily holy. And if neither of them be to his dishonor, then it is not to his dishonor necessarily to act holily and wisely. And if it be not dishonorable, to be necessarily holy and wise, in the highest possible degree, no more is it mean or dishonorable, necessarily to act holily and wisely in the highest possible degree; or [which is the same thing] to do that, in every case, which above all other things is wisest and best.

**JE: *God is necessarily holy. It is not dishonorable.***

The reason why it is not dishonorable, to be necessarily *most* holy, is, because holiness in itself is an excellent and honorable thing. For the same reason, it is no dishonor to be necessarily *most* wise, and in every case to act most wisely, or do the thing which is the wisest of all; for wisdom is also in itself excellent and honorable.

### IW: The doctrine of necessity makes God a kind of minister and medium of fate.

The aforementioned author of the *Essay on the Freedom of Will*, etc., as has been observed, represents that doctrine of the divine will's being in everything necessarily determined by superior fitness, as making the blessed God a kind of almighty minister and mechanical medium of fate: and he insists (pp. 93–94),[4] that this moral necessity and impossibility is in effect the same thing with physical and natural necessity and impossibility: and in pp. 54–55[5] he says,

> The scheme which determines the will always and certainly by the understanding, and the understanding by the appearance of things, seems to take away the true nature of vice and virtue. For the sublimest of virtues, and the vilest of vices, seem rather to be matters of fate and necessity, flowing naturally and necessarily from the existence, the circumstances, and present situation of persons and things: for this existence and situation necessarily makes such an appearance to the mind; from this appearance flows a necessary perception and judgment, concerning these things; this judgment necessarily determines the will: and thus by this chain of necessary causes, virtue and vice would lose their nature, and become natural ideas, and necessary things, instead of moral and free actions.

### JE: Yet Watts allows that God is a perfectly wise being and chooses the fittest and best and acts it.

And yet this same author allows (pp. 30–31),[6] that a perfectly wise being will constantly and certainly choose what is most fit; and says (pp. 102–3),[7]

> "I grant, and always have granted, that wheresoever there is such an antecedent superior fitness of things, God acts according to it, so as never to contradict it; and particularly, in all his judicial proceedings, as a governor, and distributer of rewards and punishments."

---

4. [Watts, *Essay*, sec. 7, *dif.* 3, pp. 93–94; reprinted, *Works* 6:275. "[I]n philosophical strictness and the truth of things, this moral necessity and impossibility, and this metaphysical necessity and impossibility will appear to be very near akin: and though there may be some difference between these two necessaries, viz. moral and metaphysical, as to the immediate and proxime cause and reason of their necessity, yet the necessity of both of them is a physical or natural necessity, they are both equally strong and unalterable, and the original cause and reason why both of them are necessary, lies in the very nature of things" (p. 93).]

5. [Watts, *Essay*, sec. 5, *adv.* 4, pp. 54–55; reprinted, *Works* 6:260.]
6. Watts, *Essay*, sec. 3, *prop.* 4, pp. 30–31; reprinted, *Works* 6:251.
7. Watts, *Essay*, sec. 7, *dif.* 6, pp. 102–3; reprinted, *Works* 6:278.

Yea, he says expressly (p. 42),[8] "That it is not possible for God to act otherwise, than according to this fitness and goodness in things."

**Watts' conclusion: *There is no virtue, nor anything of a moral nature, in the acts and exercises of God. He exercises no moral excellency; exercising no freedom in these things, but only as a kind of mechanical medium of fate.***

So that according to this author, putting these several passages of his *Essay* together, there is *no virtue, nor anything of a moral nature*, in the most sublime and glorious acts and exercises of God's holiness, justice, and faithfulness; and he never does anything which is in itself supremely worthy, and above all other things fit and excellent, but only as a kind of mechanical medium of fate; and in what he does as the judge, and *moral governor* of the world, he exercises no moral excellency; exercising no freedom in these things, because he acts by moral necessity, which is in effect the same with physical or natural necessity; and therefore he only acts by an *Hobbistical* fatality;

> *as a being indeed of vast understanding, as well as power and efficiency [as he said before] but [. . .] without a will to choose, being a kind of almighty minister of fate, acting under its supreme influence.*[9]

For he allows, that in all these things God's will is determined constantly and certainly by a superior fitness, and that it is not possible for him to act otherwise.

And if these things are so, what glory or praise belongs to God for doing holily and justly, or taking the most fit, holy, wise and excellent course, in any one instance? Whereas, according to the Scriptures, and also the common sense of mankind, it doesn't in the least derogate from the honor of any being, that through the moral perfection of his nature, he necessarily acts with supreme wisdom and holiness: but on the contrary, his praise is the greater: herein consists the height of his glory.

**IW: *A wise and good man can choose contrary to the fitness of things, yet he does not but suffers himself to be directed by fitness. Contrarily, God cannot choose nor act contrary to the fitness of things but suffers himself to be directed by fitness.***

The same author (p. 56)[10] supposes, that herein appears the

> *excellent character of a wise and good man, that though he can choose contrary to the fitness of things, yet he does not; but suffers himself to be directed by fitness; and that in this conduct he imitates the blessed God.*

And yet he supposes it is contrariwise with the blessed God; not that he suffers himself to be directed by fitness,

---

8. Watts, *Essay*, sec. 4, *prop.* 11, p. 42; reprinted, *Works* 6:255.
9. Watts, *Essay* (London, 1732), sec. 7, *dif.* 1, pp. 85–86; reprinted, *Works* 6:272.
10. Watts, *Essay*, sec. 5, *adv.* 5, p. 56; reprinted, *Works* 6:260.

when *he can choose contrary to the fitness of things,* but that *he cannot choose contrary to the fitness of things*; as he says (p. 42) . . .. *that it is not possible for God to act otherwise, than according to this fitness, where there is any fitness or goodness in things*:

yea, he supposes (p. 31)[11] that if a man *were perfectly wise and good, he could not do otherwise than be constantly and certainly determined by the fitness of things.*

### JE's Conclusion: It derogates nothing from the glory of God to be necessarily determined by superior fitness in some things.

One thing more I would observe, before I conclude this section; and that is, that if it derogates nothing from the glory of God, to be necessarily determined by superior fitness in some things, then neither does it to be thus determined in all things; from anything in the nature of such necessity, as at all detracting from God's freedom, independence, absolute supremacy, or any dignity or glory of his nature, state, or manner of acting; or as implying any infirmity, restraint, or subjection. And if the thing be such as well consists with God's glory, and has nothing tending at all to detract from it; then we need not be afraid of ascribing it to God in too many things, lest thereby we should detract from God's glory too much.

---

11. Watts, *Essay*, sec. 3, *prop*. 4, p. 31; reprinted, *Works* 6:251.

# Section 8

## Some Further Objections against the Moral Necessity of God's Volitions Considered

**Ar: God's will never perfectly determines one thing above another.**

**JE: *The wise God chooses and acts the most fittest of good things. Eventually, Watts admits that that is not any dishonor to him.***

The author last cited, as has been observed, owns that God, being perfectly wise, will constantly and certainly choose what appears most fit, where there is a superior fitness and goodness in things; and that it is not possible for him to do otherwise. So that it is in effect confessed, that in those things where there is any real preferableness, it is no dishonor, nothing in any respect unworthy of God, for him to act from necessity;

**JE: *But his point objects the common doctrine of such a necessity as Stoics and Hobbes agreed.***

notwithstanding all that can be objected from the agreement of such a necessity, with the fate of the Stoics, and the necessity maintained by Mr. Hobbes.

**JE: *God's will necessarily chooses by preferring to one of many other things, that is never dishonor him.***

From which it will follow, that if it were so, that in all the different things, among which God chooses, there were evermore a superior fitness or preferableness on one side, then it would be no dishonor, or anything, in any respect, unworthy, or unbecoming of God, for his will to be necessarily determined in everything.

**IW: *Divine necessity is dishonor to God and is unsuitable to his nature.***

And if this be allowed, it is a giving up entirely the argument, from the unsuitableness of such a necessity to the liberty, supremacy, independence and glory of the divine

Being; and a resting the whole weight of the affair on the decision of another point wholly diverse; viz.

***IW's Supposition: In God is there no preference like favoritism.***

Whether it be so indeed, that in all the various possible things which are in God's view, and may be considered as capable objects of his choice, there is not evermore a preferableness in one thing above another.

***IW's Supposition: But perfect indifference and equality in his tendency.***

This is denied by this author; who supposes, that in many instances, between two or more possible things, which come within the view of the divine mind, there is a perfect indifference and equality as to fitness, or tendency to attain any good end which God can have in view, or to answer any of his designs. Now therefore I would consider whether this be evident.

The arguments brought to prove this, are of two kinds.

***IW's Argument (1): We all must believe that there is no any difference among objects of choice.***

(1) It is urged, that in many instances we must suppose there is absolutely no difference between various possible objects of choice, which God has in view:

***IW's Argument (2): We all must believe that there is not any little difference among objects of choice.***

(1) that the difference between many things is so inconsiderable, or of such a nature, that it would be unreasonable to suppose it to be of any consequence; or to suppose that any of God's wise designs would not be answered in one way as well as the other.[1]

***JE's Response I. It is normal that there are differences and diversity among objects of choice. If not, all decisions are the same and so they cannot be made. God chooses one thing than the other.***

Therefore,

I. The first thing to be considered is, whether there are any instances wherein there is a perfect likeness, and absolutely no difference, between different objects of choice, that are proposed to the divine understanding?

---

1. [For constructing his natural philosophy, JE imported the main ideas from Isaac Newton, for instance, of atom and its constitution, gravity and its force, time and space, light, color, and planets, and then he used them to depict God as "the first cause," "being in general," and "the Creator," like the Great Geometrician, "the Governor," especially in his "Of Being," "Of Atom," "The Mind," "Natural Philosophy," etc. See *Scientific and Philosophical Writings*, WJE 6.]

And here in the first place, it may be worthy to be considered, whether the contradiction there is in the *terms* of the question proposed, doesn't give reason to suspect that there is an inconsistence in the *thing* supposed. It is inquired, whether *different* objects of choice mayn't be absolutely *without difference*? If they are absolutely *without difference*, then how are they *different* objects of choice? If there be absolutely *no difference* in any respect, then there is *no variety* or *distinction*: for distinction is only by some difference. And if there be no *variety* among proposed *objects* of choice, then there is no opportunity for *variety of choice*, or difference of determination. For that determination of a thing which is not different in any respect, is not a different determination, but the same. That this is no quibble, may appear more fully anon.

### Watts' Argument: Even though there is no difference among things, God often chooses one thing than the other.

The arguments, to prove that the Most High, in some instances, chooses to do one thing rather than another, where the things themselves are perfectly without difference, are two.

### Watts: Even though all things are alike and have no difference, God prefers to and chooses this world than the other.

1. That the various parts of infinite time and space, absolutely considered, are perfectly alike, and don't differ at all one from another: and that therefore, when God determined to create the world in such a part of infinite duration and space, rather than others, he determined and preferred among various objects, between which there was no preferableness, and absolutely no difference.[2]

### JE's Answer: IW had wrong thought that the infinite time before the world was distinguished by successive parts, but it was a whole piece of time before the beginning.

This objection supposes an infinite length of time before the world was created, distinguished by successive parts, properly and truly so; or a succession of limited and measurable[3] periods of time, following one another, in an infinitely long series, which must needs be a groundless imagination. The eternal duration which was before the world, being only the eternity of God's existence; which is nothing else but his immediate, perfect and invariable possession of the whole of his unlimited life, together

---

2. ["This identification of God and space was certainly not original to Edwards. The Cambridge Platonists, who may well have influenced his thinking in this regard, viewed space as a dynamic principle that operated as the divine instrument; at times, they even went farther by equating God himself with space or the void." Paul Copan, "Jonathan Edwards's Philosophical Influences: Lockean or Malebranchean?," *Journal of Evangelical Theological Society* 44, no. 1 (2001): 107–124; see also George Rupp, "The 'Idealism' of Jonathan Edwards," *Harvard Theological Review* 62 (1969): 210. See also Anderson, "Immaterialism in Jonathan Edwards," 184–6.]

3. [Corrected, from "unmeasurable."]

and at once; *vita interminabilis, tota, simul et perfecta possessio.*[4] Which is so generally allowed, that I need not stand to demonstrate it.[5]

## JE: IW's Wrong Supposition of Infinite Space

So this objection supposes an extent of space beyond the limits of the creation, of an infinite length, breadth and depth, truly and properly distinguished into different measurable parts, limited at certain stages, one beyond another, in an infinite series. Which notion of absolute and infinite space is doubtless as unreasonable, as that now mentioned, of absolute and infinite duration. It is as improper, to imagine that the immensity and omnipresence of God is distinguished by a series of miles and leagues, one beyond another; as that the infinite duration of God is distinguished by months and years, one after another. A diversity and order of distinct parts, limited by certain periods, is as conceivable, and does as naturally obtrude itself on our imagination, in one case as the other; and there is equal reason in each case, to suppose that our imagination deceives us. It is equally improper, to talk of months and years of the divine existence, and mile-squares of deity: and we equally deceive ourselves, when we talk of the world's being differently fixed with respect to either of these sorts of measures. I think, we know not what we mean, if we say, the world might have been differently placed from what it is, in the broad expanse of infinity; or, that it might

---

4. [JE's translation: "immediate, perfect and invariable possession of the whole of his unlimited life;" Boethius (ca. 480–524)'s Latin definition of *eternity*. "Aeternitas igitur est interminabilis vitae tota simul et perfecta possessio" (Boethius, De consolatione Philosophiae, V, vi) is well known and often quoted by schoolmen.]

5. [JE, "If all created beings were taken away, all possibility of any mutation or succession of one thing to another would appear to be also removed. Abstract succession in eternity is scarce to be understood. What is it that succeeds? One minute to another perhaps, *velut unda supervenit undam* ["Follows upon" or "succeeds the other."] But when we imagine this, we fancy that the minutes are things separately existing. This is the common notion; and yet it is a manifest prejudice. Time is nothing but the existence of created successive beings, and eternity the necessary existence of the Deity. Therefore, if this necessary Being hath no change or succession in his nature, his existence must of course be unsuccessive.

"We seem to commit a double oversight in this case; *first*, we find succession in the necessary nature and existence of the Deity himself: which is wrong, if the reasoning above be conclusive. And *then* we ascribe this succession to eternity, considered abstractedly from the eternal Being; and suppose it, one knows not what, a thing subsisting by itself, and flowing, one minute after another. This is the work of pure imagination, and contrary to the reality of things. Hence the common metaphorical expressions: 'Time runs apace,' 'Let us lay hold on the present minute,' and the like. The philosophers themselves mislead us by their ILLs; they compare eternity to the motion of a point running on forever, and making a traceless infinite line. Here the point is supposed a thing actually subsisting, representing the present minute; and then they ascribe motion or succession to it: that is, they ascribe motion to a mere non-entity, to illustrate to us a successive eternity made up of finite successive parts . . . [I]f once we allow an all-perfect Mind, which hath an eternal immutable and infinite comprehension of all things, always (and allow it we must) the distinction of past and future vanishes with respect to such a mind. . . . In a word, if we proceed step by step, as above, the eternity or existence of the Deity will appear to be vita *interminabilis, tota, simul et perfecta possession* (*the unending life, the whole soul, and at the same time the perfect possession*); how much so ever this may have been a paradox hitherto." Baxter, *Inquiry*, 3rd ed., 2:409–11.]

have been differently fixed in the long line of eternity: and all arguments and objections which are built on the imaginations we are apt to have of infinite extension or duration, are buildings founded on shadows, or castles in the air.

### IW: *Particles or atoms of a matter perfectly equal and alike make different bodies without the will of God.*

2. The second argument, to prove that the Most High wills one thing rather than another, without any superior fitness or preferableness in the thing preferred, is God's actually placing in different parts of the world, particles or atoms of matter that are perfectly equal and alike. The aforementioned author says (p. 78,[6] etc.),

> If one would descend to the minute specific particles, of which different bodies are composed, we should see abundant reason to believe that there are thousands of such little particles or atoms of matter, which are perfectly equal and alike, and could give no distinct determination to the will of God, where to place them.

He there instances in particles of water, of which there are such immense numbers, which compose the rivers and oceans of this world; and the infinite myriads of the luminous and fiery particles, which compose the body of the sun; so many, that it would be very unreasonable to suppose no two of them should be exactly equal and alike.

### JE: *Even if particles of all things are created alike in their general nature and figure and different in their dimensions and quantity, we must not say they all are exactly equal and alike.*

*Answer* (1). To this I answer: that as we must suppose matter to be infinitely divisible, it is very unlikely that any two of all these particles are exactly equal and alike; so unlikely, that it is a thousand to one, yea, an infinite number to one, but it is otherwise:

### ILL: *Water and fire have similar yet different particles.*

and that although we should allow a great similarity between the different particles of water and fire, as to their general nature and figure; and however small we suppose those particles to be, it is infinitely unlikely, that any two of them should be exactly equal in dimensions and quantity of matter.

### ILL: *The earth and other globes have different nature and particles, respectively.*

If we should suppose a great many globes of the same nature with the globe of the earth, it would be very strange, if there were any two of them that had exactly the same number of particles of dust and water in them.

---

6. [Watts, *Essay*, sec. 6, *ans.* to *obj.* 6, pp. 78–79; reprinted, *Works* 6:269.]

### ILL: Light is composed of infinite many particles.

But infinitely less strange, than that two particles of light should have just the same quantity of matter. For a particle of light (according to the doctrine of the infinite divisibility of matter) is composed of infinitely more assignable parts, than there are particles of dust and water in the globe of the earth. And as it is infinitely unlikely, that any two of these particles should be *equal*; so it is, that they should be *alike* in other respects:

### ILL: The surfaces of globes don't have the same particles.

to instance in the configuration of their surfaces. If there were very many globes, of the nature of the earth, it would be very unlikely that any two should have exactly the same number of particles of dust, water and stone, in their surfaces, and all posited exactly alike, one with respect to another, without any difference, in any part discernible either by the naked eye or microscope; but infinitely less strange, than that two particles of light should be perfectly of the same figure. For there are infinitely more assignable real parts on the surface of a particle of light, than there are particles of dust, water and stone, on the surface of the terrestrial globe.

### JE: That God created same particles or atoms and placed them in different parts of the universe is a mere supposition.

*Answer* (2). But then, supposing that there are two particles or atoms of matter perfectly equal and alike, which God has placed in different parts of the creation; as I will not deny it to be possible for God to make two bodies perfectly alike, and put them in different places; yet it will not follow, that two different or distinct acts or effects of the divine power have exactly the same fitness for the same ends.

### ILL: Two perfectly same bodies are impossible to exist. It is wrong that they can be located in different places or circumstances.

For these two different bodies are not different or distinct, in any other respects than those wherein they *differ*: they are two in no other respects than those wherein there is a difference. If they are perfectly equal and alike *in themselves*, then they can be distinguished, or be distinct, only in those things which are called *circumstances*; as, place, time, rest, motion, or some other present or past circumstances or relations. For it is difference only, that constitutes distinction. If God makes two bodies *in themselves* every way equal and alike, and agreeing perfectly in all other circumstances and relations, but only *their place*; then in this only is there any distinction or duplicity. The figure is the same, the measure is the same, the solidity and resistance are the same, and everything the same, but only the place.

### JE: Watts misunderstands the will of God; God determines his acts wholly without motive or end.

Therefore, what the will of God determines, is this, namely, that there should be the same figure, the same extension, the same resistance, etc., in two different places. And for this determination he has some reason. There is some end, for which such a determination and act has a peculiar fitness, above all other acts. Here is no one thing determined without an end, and no one thing without a fitness for that end, superior to anything else.[7]

***JE ranks Watts' absurd claims: 1st: God has no motive or end; 2nd: He acts the same things in the same time; 3rd: He places the same things in different places.***

If it be the pleasure of God to cause the same resistance, and the same figure, to be in two different places and situations, we can no more justly argue from it, that here must be some determination or act of God's will, that is wholly without motive or end, than[8] we can argue that whenever, in any case, it is a man's will to speak the same words, or make the same sounds at two different times; there must be some determination or act of his will, without any motive or end.

The difference of place, in the former case, proves no more than the difference of time does in the other.

***Ar: Two same bodies are located in the different places.***

***JE: The bodies are created distinct in the beginning and began their existence in different places.***

If anyone should say with regard to the former case, that there must be something determined without an end; viz. that of those two similar bodies, this in particular should be made in this place, and the other in the other, and should inquire why the creator did not make them in a transposition, when both are alike, and each would equally have suited either place? The inquiry supposes something that is not true; namely, that the two bodies differ and are distinct in other respects besides their place. So that with this distinction, *inherent* in them, they might in their first creation have been transposed, and each might have begun its existence in the place of the other.

***ILL: There cannot be two same earths.***

Let us for clearness' sake suppose, that God had at the beginning made two globes, each of an inch diameter, both perfect spheres, and perfectly solid without pores, and perfectly alike in every respect, and placed them near one to another, one towards the right hand, and the other towards the left, without any difference as to time, motion

---

7. [Teleology of Edwards: By the way of Thomas Aquinas, JE proves here the existence of God, by arguing that everything is created by the Creator for His end and God exists, and in it is seen God's being, and also elsewhere mobilizing various arguments Metaphysical, Idealistic, Cosmological, Ethical, and Teleological. See John Bombaro, "The Formulation of Jonathan Edwards's Theocentric Metaphysics," *The Clarion Review* 1 (Oct., 2003): 8–16, 18; George Rupp, "The 'Idealism' of Jonathan Edwards," *The Harvard Theological Review* 62, no. 2 (Apr., 1969): 209.]

8. [Corrected, from "then." Possibly a reference to Exodus 6:3.]

or rest, past or present, or any circumstance, but only their place; and the question should be asked, Why God in their creation placed them so? Why that which is made on the right hand, was not made on the left, and *vice versa*? Let it be well considered, whether there be any sense in such a question; and whether the inquiry doesn't suppose something false and absurd. Let it be considered, what the Creator must have done otherwise than he did, what different act of will or power he must have exerted, in order to the thing proposed. All that could have been done, would have been to have made two spheres, perfectly alike, in the same places where he has made them, without any difference of the things made, either in themselves, or in any circumstance; so that the whole effect would have been without any difference, and therefore just the same. By the supposition, the two spheres are different in no other respect but their place; and therefore in other respects they are the same. Each has the same roundness: it is not a distinct rotundity, in any other respect but its situation. There are also the same dimensions, differing in nothing but their place.

And so of their resistance, and everything else that belongs to them.

### Ar: Two globes are the same in any respects but different numerically.

Here if any chooses to say,

> "that there is a difference in another respect, viz. that they are not *numerically* the same: that it is thus with all the qualities that belong to them: that it is confessed they are in some respects the same; that is, they are both exactly alike; but yet NUMERICALLY they differ. Thus the roundness of one is not the same *numerical, individual* roundness with that of the other."

### JE's Reasonable Objecting Question: Why did he place it there, and did so in a contrary position?

Let this be supposed; then the question about the determination of the divine will in the affair, is, why did God will, that this individual roundness should be at the right hand, and the other individual roundness at the left? Why did not he make them in a contrary position? Let any rational person consider, whether such questions be not words without a meaning;

### JE's Reasonable Objecting Question: God does repeat the same sounds at different times? If you think so, you have to ask why he does so.

as much as if God should see fit for some ends to cause the same sounds to be repeated, or made at two different times; the sounds being perfectly the same in every other respect, but only one was a minute after the other; and it should be asked upon it, why God caused these sounds, numerically different, to succeed one the other in such a manner? Why he did not make that individual sound which was in the first minute, to be in the second? And the individual sound of the last minute to be in the first? Which inquiries would be even ridiculous; as I think every person must see at once, in the case proposed of two sounds, being only the same repeated, absolutely without any difference, but that one circumstance of time.

### JE's Reasonable Objecting Question: Why would God repeat the same thunder?

If the most High sees it will answer some good end, that the same sound should be made by lightning at two distinct times, and therefore wills that it should be so, must it needs therefore be, that herein there is some act of God's will without any motive or end?

### JE's Reasonable Objecting Question: Did God repeat the same word to Moses without any aim?

God saw fit often, at distinct times, and on different occasions, to say the very same words to Moses; namely those, "I am Jehovah."[9] And would it not be unreasonable, to infer as a certain consequence from this, that here must be some act or acts of the divine will, in determining and disposing these words exactly alike at different times, wholly without aim or inducement?

### JE: The most unreasonable word is that God acts without any inducement.

But it would be no more unreasonable than to say, that there must be an act of God's without any inducement, if he sees it best, and for some reason, determines that there shall be the same resistance, the same dimensions, and the same figure, in several distinct places.

### JE's Reasonable Objecting Question: If the two earths were different in number alone, would it not be just to say the same earth could be made at the same place and time?

If in the instance of the two spheres, perfectly alike, it be supposed possible that God might have made them in a contrary position; that which is made at the right hand, being made at the left; then I ask, Whether it is not evidently equally possible, if God had made but one of them, and that in the place of the right-hand globe, that he might have made that numerically different from what it is, and numerically different from what he did make it; though perfectly alike, and in the same place; and at the same time, and in every respect, in the same circumstances and relations?

### JE's Reasonable Objection Question: If so, didn't God make the second earth at the same place and leave it in a state of nonexistence? Moreover, is it impossible for him to make the third one and leave it at the place of the second?

Namely, whether he might not have made it numerically the same with that which he has now made at the left hand; and so have left that which is now created at the right hand, in a state of nonexistence? And if so, whether it would not have been possible to

---

9. [Exodus 6:2, JE prefers the name "Jehovah." Cf. *WJE* 1:390.]

have made one in that place, perfectly like these, and yet numerically differing from both?

### Notion of a Numerical Difference in Bodies

And let it be considered, whether from this notion of a numerical difference in bodies, perfectly equal and alike, which numerical difference is something inherent in the bodies themselves, and diverse from the difference of place or time, or any circumstance whatsoever; it will not follow, that there is an infinite number of numerically different possible bodies, perfectly alike, among which God chooses, by a self-determining power, when he goes about to create bodies.

### JE: When I hold that God in the beginning had created but one perfectly solid sphere, in a certain place, it is normal to ask the following questions:

Therefore, let us put the case thus: supposing that God in the beginning had created but one perfectly solid sphere, in a certain place; and it should be inquired,

> Why God created that individual sphere, in that place, at that time? And
>
> why he did not create another sphere perfectly like it, but numerically different, in the same place, at the same time? Or
>
> why he chose to bring into being there, that very body, rather than any of the infinite number of other bodies, perfectly like it; either of which he could have made there as well, and would have answered his end as well?
>
> Why he caused to exist, at that place and time, that individual roundness, rather than any other of the infinite number of individual rotundities, just like it?
>
> Why that individual resistance, rather than any other of the infinite number of possible resistances just like it?

And it might as reasonably be asked,

> Why, when God first caused it to thunder, he caused that individual sound then to be made, and not another just like it?
>
> Why did he make choice of this very sound, and reject all the infinite number of other possible sounds just like it, but numerically differing from it, and all differing one from another?

I think, everybody must be sensible of the absurdity and nonsense of what is supposed in such inquiries.

### JE: Their objections are weak mainly for the imperfection of metaphysical terms.

And if we calmly attend to the matter, we shall be convinced, that all such kind of objections as I am answering, are founded on nothing but the imperfection of our manner of conceiving of things, and the obscureness of language, and great want of

Section 8—Some Further Objections against the Moral Necessity of God's Volitions Considered

clearness and precision in the signification of terms. If any shall find fault with this reasoning, that it is going a great length into metaphysical niceties and subtleties; I answer, the objection which they are in reply to, is a metaphysical subtlety, and must be treated according to the nature of it.[10]

### IW: There is no difference between things chosen by God and ones not by him.

II. Another thing alleged is, that innumerable things which are determined by the divine will, and chosen and done by God rather than others, differ from those that are not chosen in so inconsiderable a manner, that it would be unreasonable to suppose the difference to be of any consequence, or that there is any superior fitness or goodness, that God can have respect to in the determination.

### JE: It is unreasonable for IW to allege that there is one atom in the whole universe and, for example, the Earth and Jupiter are made without any aim of God.

To which I answer; it is impossible for us to determine with any certainty or evidence, that because the difference is very small, and appears to us of no consideration, therefore there is absolutely no superior goodness, and no valuable end which can be proposed by the Creator and Governor of the world, in ordering such a difference. The aforementioned author[11] mentions many instances. One is, there being one atom in the whole universe more, or less. But I think it would be unreasonable to suppose, that God made one atom in vain, or without any end or motive. He made not one atom but what was a work of his almighty power, as much as the whole globe of the earth, and requires as much of a constant exertion of almighty power to uphold it; and was made and is upheld understandingly, and on design, as much as if no other had been made but that. And it would be as unreasonable to suppose, that he made it without anything really aimed at in so doing, as much as to suppose that he made the planet Jupiter without aim or design.[12]

### JE: According to the physical laws of Isaac Newton: the smallest cause like one atom brings out a minute effect, and yet later the latter will be greater.

It is possible, that the most minute effects of the Creator's power, the smallest assignable differences between the things which God has made, may be attended, in the whole series of events, and the whole compass and extent of their influence, with very great and important consequences. If the laws of motion and gravitation, laid down by Sir Isaac Newton,[13] hold universally, there is not one atom, nor the least assign-

---

10. "For men to have recourse to subtleties, in raising difficulties, and then complain, that they should be taken off by minutely examining these subtleties, is a strange kind of procedure." [Andrew] Baxter, *Inquiry* [*into the Nature of the Human Soul*] 2:331.

11. [Isaac Watts.]

12. ["Of Atom," *WJE* 6:214.]

13. [Rupp notes JE goes beyond farther than Newton a scientist and theologian went. "To preserve both the immediacy of God's presence and the order of natural law, he identifies the spontaneous

able part of an atom, but what has influence, every moment, throughout the whole material universe, to cause every part to be otherwise than it would be, if it were not for that particular corporeal existence. And however the effect is insensible for the present, yet it may in length of time become great and important.

### Three Illustrations: Even a minute difference can make a big effect.

### #(1) Two bodies moving the same way, in straight lines, perfectly parallel one to another, can be diverted just by the attraction of an atom.

To illustrate this, let us suppose two bodies moving the same way, in straight lines, perfectly parallel one to another; but to be diverted from this parallel course, and drawn one from another, as much as might be by the attraction of an atom, at the distance of one of the furthest of the fixed stars from the earth; these bodies being turned out of the lines of their parallel motion, will, by degrees, get further and further distant, one from the other; and though the distance may be imperceptible for a long time, yet at length it may become very great.

### #(2) The revolution of a planet round the sun can go wrong by the influence of the least atom.

So the revolution of a planet round the sun being retarded or accelerated, and the orbit of its revolution made greater or less, and more or less elliptical, and so its periodical time longer or shorter, no more than may be by the influence of the least atom, might in length of time perform a whole revolution sooner or later than otherwise it would have done; which might make a vast alteration with regard to millions of important events.

### #(3) The influence of the least particle in human body and mind can have big effects on them.

So the influence of the least particle may, for ought we know, have such effect on something in the constitution of some human body, as to cause another thought to arise in the mind at a certain time, than otherwise would have been; which in length of time (yea, and that not very great) might occasion a vast alteration through the whole world of mankind. And so innumerable other ways might be mentioned, wherein the least assignable alteration may possibly be attended with great consequences.

### IW: I reject a necessary determination of the divine will by a superior fitness.

Another argument, which the aforementioned author brings against a necessary determination of the divine will by a superior fitness, is, that such doctrine derogates

---

divine activity with the motion not only of resistance but also of gravity, so that every being and every event is directly dependent on the Deity." George Rupp, "The 'Idealism' of Jonathan Edwards," *Harvard Theological Review* 62 (1969): 210. Cf. Isaac Newton, *Philosophiæ Naturalis Principia Mathematica* (Mathematical Principles of Natural Philosophy, 1687), 226; JE, "The Mind," and "Of Being," *WJE* 6.]

from the *freeness* of God's *grace* and *goodness*, in choosing the objects of his favor and bounty, and from the obligation upon men to *thankfulness* for special benefits (p. 89,[14] etc.).

In answer to this objection, I would observe,

### JE: 1. It is meaningless God does his goodness by chance. His will is to be determined by his end and his volition by a prevailing motive.

1. That it derogates no more from the goodness of God, to suppose the exercise of the benevolence of his nature to be determined by wisdom, than to suppose it determined by chance, and that his favors are bestowed altogether at random, his will being determined by nothing but perfect accident, without any end or design whatsoever; which must be the case, as has been demonstrated, if volition be not determined by a prevailing motive.

That which is owing to perfect contingence, wherein neither previous inducement, nor antecedent choice has any hand, is not owing more to goodness or benevolence, than that which is owing to the influence of a wise end.

### JE: 2. Who chose whom? How did he choose them? God does not choose an object by its moral quality, but determines his will by his wisdom and end.

2. It is acknowledged, that if the motive that determines the will of God, in the choice of the objects of his *favors*, be any moral quality in the object, recommending that object to his benevolence above others, his choosing that object is not so great a manifestation of the freeness and sovereignty of his grace, as if it were otherwise. But there is no necessity of supposing this, in order to our supposing that he has some wise end in view, in determining to bestow his favors on one person rather than another. We are to distinguish between the *merit* of the *object* of God's favor, or a moral qualification of the object attracting that favor and recommending to it, and the *natural fitness* of such a determination of the *act* of God's goodness, to answer some wise design of his own, some end in the view of God's omniscience. It is God's own act, that is the proper and immediate object of his volition.

### JE: The one side choosing God does not reduce his freedom and mercy nor diminish the thankfulness of the chosen object.

3. I suppose that none will deny, but that in some instances, God acts from wise design in determining the particular subjects of his favors: none will say, I presume, that when God distinguishes by his bounty particular societies or persons, he never, in any instance, exercises any wisdom in so doing, aiming at some happy consequence. And if it be not denied to be so in some instances, then I would inquire, whether in these instances God's goodness is less manifested, than in those wherein God has no aim or

---

14. [Watts, *Essay*, sec. 5, *adv.* 8, p. 89; reprinted, *Works* 6:262.]

end at all? And whether the subjects have less cause of thankfulness? And if so, who shall be thankful for the bestowment of distinguishing mercy, with that enhancing circumstance of the distinction's being made without an end? How shall it be known when God is influenced by some wise aim, and when not?

### ILL: God's choosing Paul to be an apostle magnifies his freedom and divine grace in his election.

It is very manifest with respect to the Apostle Paul, that God had wise ends in choosing him to be a Christian and an apostle, who had been a persecutor, etc. The Apostle himself mentions one end. 1 Timothy 1:15, 1 Timothy 1:16: "Christ Jesus came into the world to save sinners, of whom I am chief. However, for this cause I obtained mercy, that in me first, Jesus Christ might show forth all long-suffering, for a pattern to them who should hereafter believe on him to life everlasting." But yet the Apostle never looked on it as a diminution of the freedom and riches of divine grace in his election, which he so often and so greatly magnifies. This brings me to observe,

### JE: God determines his will in moral necessity, in which he chooses his elect and receives their superior giving thanks.

4. Our supposing such a moral necessity in the acts of God's will as has been spoken of, is so far from necessarily derogating from the riches of God's grace to such as are the chosen objects of his favor, that in many instances, this moral necessity may arise from goodness, and from the great degree of it. God may choose this object rather than another, as having a superior fitness to answer the ends, designs and inclinations of his goodness; being more sinful, and so more miserable and necessitous than others; the inclinations of infinite mercy and benevolence may be more gratified, and the gracious design of God's sending his Son into the world may be more abundantly answered, in the exercises of mercy towards such an object, rather than another.

### Ar: God also is subject to fatal necessity and he would wisely accommodate his will to this fixed futurity of things because he had foreknown events before he had any decrees about them, i.e., middle knowledge.

One thing more I would observe, before I finish what I have to say on the head of the necessity of the acts of God's will; and that is, that something much more like a servile subjection of the Divine Being to fatal necessity, will follow from Arminian principles, than from the doctrines which they oppose. For they (at least most of them) suppose, with respect to all events that happen in the moral world depending on the volitions of moral agents, which are the most important events of the universe, to which all others are subordinate; I say, they suppose with respect to these, that God has a certain foreknowledge of them, antecedent to any purposes or decrees of his about them. And if so, they have a fixed certain futurity, prior to any designs or volitions of his, and independent on them, and to which his volitions must be subject, as he would wisely accommodate his affairs to this fixed futurity of the state of things in the moral world.

**JE: *The Arminian notion of necessity is close to the heathen doctrine of fate. Men follow the fixed futurity of the state of things instead of a moral necessity of God's will, which accommodates them to the state.***

So that here, instead of a moral necessity of God's will, arising from or consisting in the infinite perfection and blessedness of the Divine Being, we have a fixed unalterable state of things, properly distinct from the perfect nature of the divine mind, and the state of the divine will and design, and entirely independent on these things, and which they have no hand in, because they are prior to them; and which God's will is truly subject to, being obliged to conform or accommodate himself to it, in all his purposes and decrees, and in everything he does in his disposals and government of the world; the moral world being the end of the natural; so that all is in vain, that is not accommodated to that state of the moral world, which consists in, or depends upon the acts and state of the wills of moral agents, which had a fixed futurition from eternity. Such a subjection to necessity as this, would truly argue an inferiority and servitude, that would be unworthy of the supreme Being; and is much more agreeable to the notion which many of the heathen had of fate, as above the gods, than that moral necessity of fitness and wisdom which has been spoken of; and is truly repugnant to the absolute sovereignty of God, and inconsistent with the supremacy of his will; and really subjects the will of the Most High to the will of his creatures, and brings him into dependence upon them.[15]

---

15. [Ramsey, Intro., pt. 5, nos. 19–21, for an analysis and final appraisal of the encounter between Watts and JE.]

# Section 9

## Concerning That Objection against the Doctrine Which Has Been Maintained, That It Makes God the Author of Sin

*Ar: If men commit their sins in the necessity ordered by God, he is the author of sin.*

It is urged by Arminians, that the doctrine of the necessity of men's volitions, or their necessary connection with antecedent events and circumstances, makes the First Cause, and Supreme Orderer of all things, the author of sin; in that he has so constituted the state and course of things, that sinful volitions become necessary, in consequence of his disposal. Dr. Whitby, in his "*Discourse on the Freedom of the Will*,"[1] cites one of the ancients, as on his side, declaring that

> this opinion of the necessity of the will "absolves sinners, as doing nothing of their own accord which was evil, and would cast all the blame of all the wickedness committed in the world, upon God, and upon his providence, if that were admitted by the asserters of this fate; whether he himself did necessitate them to do these things, or ordered matters so that they should be constrained to do them by some other cause."

And the Doctor says in another place,

> "In the nature of the thing, and in the opinion of philosophers, *causa deficiens, in rebus necessariis, ad causam per se efficientem reducenda est.* In things necessary, the deficient cause must be reduced to the efficient. And in this case the reason is evident; because the not doing what is required, or not avoiding what is forbidden, being a defect, must follow from the position of the necessary cause of that deficiency."

Concerning this, I would observe the following things.

---

1. Whitby, *Discourse*, Dis. IV, ch. 4, no. 3, p. 361.

## Section 9—Concerning That Objection against the Doctrine Which Has Been Maintained

### I. *There is difficulty in our doctrine but not disadvantage, and so they could not reasonably object it.*

I. If there be any difficulty in this matter, it is nothing peculiar to this scheme; it is no difficulty or disadvantage wherein it is distinguished from the scheme of Arminians; and therefore not reasonably objected by them.

### DW: *As God did not help men, they could not keep themselves from sinning, and so he is the author of sin.*

Dr. Whitby supposes, that if sin necessarily follows from God's withholding assistance, or if that assistance be not given which is absolutely necessary to the avoiding of evil; then in the nature of the thing, God must be as properly the author of that evil, as if he were the efficient cause of it. From whence, according to what he himself says of the devils and damned spirits, God must be the proper author of their perfect unrestrained wickedness: he must be the efficient cause of the great pride of the devils, and of their perfect malignity against God, Christ, his saints, and all that is good, and of the insatiable cruelty of their disposition. For he allows, that God has so forsaken them, and does so withhold his assistance from them, that they are incapacitated from doing good, and determined only to evil.[2]

Our doctrine, in its consequence, makes God the author of men's sin in this world, no more, and in no other sense, than his doctrine, in its consequence, makes God the author of the hellish pride and malice of the devils. And doubtless the latter is as odious an effect as the former.

### JE: *The fixed foreknowledge of God is the position that both of Calvinists and Arminians insist.*

Again, if it will *follow at all*, that God is the author of sin,[3] from what has been supposed of a sure and infallible connection between antecedents and consequents, it will *follow because of this*, viz. that for God to be the author or orderer of those things which he knows beforehand, will infallibly be attended with such a consequence, is the same thing in effect, as for him to be the author of that consequence. But if this be so, this is a difficulty which equally attends the doctrine of Arminians themselves; at least, of those of them who allow God's certain foreknowledge of all events. For on the supposition of such a foreknowledge, this is the case with respect to every sin that is committed: God knew, that if he ordered and brought to pass such and such events, such sins would infallibly follow.

### JE: *Is God the author of sin in Judas?*

2. Dis. IV, ch. 1, no. 3, pp. 302, 305.

3. [James Dana (1735–1812) insists that Edwards "must either maintain the positive energy and action of the deity in the introduction of sin into the world, or else admit that it arose from a cause in the mind of the sinner in other words, that he was self-determined." James Dana, *An Examination of the Same Continued* (New Haven: Thomas and Samuel Green, 1773), 59.]

As for instance, God certainly foreknew, long before Judas was born, that if he ordered things so, that there should be such a man born, at such a time, and at such a place, and that his life should be preserved, and that he should, in divine providence, be led into acquaintance with Jesus; and that his heart should be so influenced by God's spirit or providence, as to be inclined to be a follower of Christ; and that he should be one of those twelve, which should be chosen constantly to attend him as his family; and that his health should be preserved so that he should go up to Jerusalem, at the last Passover in Christ's life;

and it should be so ordered that Judas should see Christ's kind treatment of the woman which anointed him at Bethany, and have that reproof from Christ, which he had at that time, and see and hear other things, which excited his enmity against his master, and other circumstances should be ordered, as they were ordered; it would be what would most certainly and infallibly follow, that Judas would betray his Lord, and would soon after hang himself, and die impenitent, and be sent to hell, for his horrid wickedness.

Therefore, this supposed difficulty ought not to be brought as an objection against the scheme which has been maintained, as *disagreeing* with the Arminian scheme, seeing it is no difficulty owing to such a *disagreement*; but a difficulty wherein the Arminians share with us. That must be unreasonably made an objection against our differing from them, which we should not escape or avoid at all by agreeing with them.

**II. I oppose to supposing "God the author of sin" to be "the sinner, the agent, or actor of sin, or the doer of a wicked thing," but not "the permitter, or not a hinderer of sin." In this sense, most of the Arminians also agree on this doctrine.**

And therefore I would observe,

II. They who object, that this doctrine makes God the author of sin,[4] ought distinctly to explain what they mean by that phrase, "the author of sin." I know, the phrase, as it is commonly used, signifies something very ill. If by "the author of sin," be meant the sinner, the agent, or actor of sin, or the *doer* of a wicked thing; so it would be a reproach and blasphemy, to suppose God to be the author of sin. In this sense, I utterly deny God to be the author of sin; rejecting such an imputation on the Most High, as what is infinitely to be abhorred; and deny any such thing to be the consequence of what I have laid down.

But if by "the author of sin," is meant the permitter, or not a hinderer of sin; and at the same time, a disposer of the state of events, in such a manner, for wise, holy and most excellent ends and purposes, that sin, if it be permitted or not hindered, will most certainly and infallibly follow:

---

4. [For further study, see John Kearney, "Jonathan Edwards's Account of Adam's First Sin," *Scottish Bulletin of Evangelical Theology* 15: 135–6; Idem, "Jonathan Edwards and the 'Author of Sin' Charge' Account of Adam's First Sin." *The Princeton Theological Review* 15(1998): 10–11.]

I say, if this be all that is meant, by being the author of sin, I don't deny that God is the author of sin (though I dislike and reject the phrase, as that which by use and custom is apt to carry another sense), it is no reproach for the most High to be thus the author of sin.

This is not to be the *actor* of sin, but on the contrary, of *holiness*. What God doth herein, is holy; and a glorious exercise of the infinite excellency of his nature. And I don't deny, that God's being thus the author of sin, follows from what I have laid down; and I assert, that it equally follows from the doctrine which is maintained by most of the Arminian divines. That it is most certainly so, that God is in such a manner the disposer and orderer of sin, is evident, if any credit is to be given to the Scripture; as well as because it is impossible in the nature of things to be otherwise.

**Biblical Instances of God's Permitting Sins: 1) Pharaoh; 2) Joseph's Brothers; 3) Sihon King; 4) Kings of Canaan; 5) Nebuchadnezzar; 6) Shimei; 7) Judas Iscariot; 8) Herod and Phontius.**

*#1) Pharaoh: Hardening his heart*

In such a manner God ordered the obstinacy of Pharaoh, in his refusing to obey God's commands, to let the people go.

> Exodus 4:21, "I will harden his heart, and he shall not let the people go."
>
> Ch. 7:2–5, "Aaron thy brother shall speak unto Pharaoh, that he send the children of Israel out of his land. And I will harden Pharaoh's heart, and multiply my signs and my wonders in the land of Egypt. But Pharaoh shall not hearken unto you; that I may lay mine hand upon Egypt, by great judgments," etc.
>
> Ch. 9:12, "And the Lord hardened the heart of Pharaoh, and he hearkened not unto them, as the Lord had spoken unto Moses."
>
> Ch. 10:1–2, "And the Lord said unto Moses, go in unto Pharaoh; for I have hardened his heart, and the heart of his servants, that I might show these my signs before him, and that thou mayest tell it in the ears of thy son, and thy son's son, what things I have wrought in Egypt, and my signs which I have done amongst them, that ye may know that I am the Lord."
>
> Ch. 14:4, "And I will harden Pharaoh's heart, that he shall follow after them: and I will be honored upon Pharaoh, and upon all his host."
>
> V. 8, "And the Lord hardened the heart of Pharaoh King of Egypt, and he pursued after the children of Israel."

*#2) Joseph's Brothers: Selling Joseph for a servant*

And it is certain that in such a manner, God for wise and good ends, ordered that event, Joseph's being sold into Egypt by his brethren.

> Genesis 45:5, "Now therefore be not grieved, nor angry with yourselves, that ye sold me hither; for God did send me before you to preserve life."
>
> Vv. 7–8, "God did send me before you to preserve a posterity in the earth, and to save your lives by a great deliverance: so that now it was not you, that sent me hither, but God."
>
> Psalms 105:17, "He sent a man before them, even Joseph, who was sold for a servant."

### *#3) Sihon King: Stubborning his spirit*

It is certain, that thus God ordered the sin and folly of Sihon King of the Amorites, in refusing to let the people of Israel pass by him peaceably.

> Deuteronomy 2:30, "But Sihon King of Heshbon would not let us pass by him; for the Lord thy God hardened his spirit, and made his heart obstinate, that he might deliver him into thine hand."

### *#4) Kings of Canaan: Fighting against Israel*

It is certain, that God thus ordered the sin and folly of the kings of Canaan, that they attempted not to make peace with Israel, but with a stupid boldness and obstinacy, set themselves violently to oppose them and their God.

> Joshua 11:20, "For it was of the Lord, to harden their hearts, that they should come against Israel in battle, that he might destroy them utterly, and that they might have no favor; but that he might destroy them, as the Lord commanded Moses."

### *#5) Nebuchadnezzar: Plundering Israel and all other nations*

It is evident, that thus God ordered the treacherous rebellion of Zedekiah, against the King of Babylon.

> Jeremiah 52:3, "For through the anger of the Lord it came to pass in Jerusalem, and Judah, till he had cast them out from his presence, that Zedekiah rebelled against the King of Babylon."
>
> So II Kings 24:20. "And it is exceeding manifest, that God thus ordered the rapine and unrighteous ravages of Nebuchadnezzar, in spoiling and ruining the nations round about."
>
> Jeremiah 25:9, "Behold, I will send and take all the families of the north, saith the Lord, and Nebuchadnezzar my servant, and will bring them against this land, and against all the nations round about; and will utterly destroy them, and make them an astonishment, and a hissing, and perpetual desolations."

Ch. 43:10–11, "I will send and take Nebuchadnezzar the King of Babylon, my servant; and I will set his throne upon these stones that I have hid, and he shall spread his royal pavilion over them. And when he cometh, he shall smite the land of Egypt, and deliver such as are for death to death, and such as are for captivity to captivity, and such as are for the sword to the sword."

Thus God represents himself as *sending* for Nebuchadnezzar, and *taking* of him and his armies, and *bringing* him against the nations which were to be destroyed by him, to that very end, that he might utterly destroy them, and make them desolate; and as appointing the work that he should do, so particularly, that the very persons were designed, that he should kill with the sword; and those that should be killed with famine and pestilence, and those that should be carried into captivity; and that in doing all these things, he should act as his servant: by which, less can't be intended, than that he should serve his purposes and designs.

And in Jeremiah 27:4–6, God declares how he would cause him thus to serve his designs, viz. by bringing this to pass in his sovereign disposals, as the great possessor and governor of the universe, that disposes all things just as pleases him:

"Thus saith the Lord of Hosts, the God of Israel; I have made the earth, the man and the beast that are upon the ground, by my great power, and my stretched out arm, and have given it unto whom it seemed meet unto me: and now I have given all these lands into the hands of Nebuchadnezzar MY SERVANT, and the beasts of the field have I given also to serve him."

And Nebuchadnezzar is spoken of as doing these things, by having his "arms strengthened" by God, and having "God's sword put into his hands, for this end" (Ezekiel 30:24–26).

Yea, God speaks of his terribly ravaging and wasting the nations, and cruelly destroying all sorts, without distinction of sex or age, as the weapon in God's hand, and the instrument of his indignation, which God makes use of to fulfill his own purposes, and execute his own vengeance.

Jeremiah 51:20, etc.,

"Thou art my battle-axe, and weapons of war. For with thee will I break in pieces the nations, and with thee I will destroy kingdoms, and with thee I will break in pieces the horse and his rider, and with thee I will break in pieces the chariot and his rider; with thee also will I break in pieces man and woman; and with thee will I break in pieces old and young; and with thee will I break in pieces the young man and the maid," etc.

It is represented, that the designs of Nebuchadnezzar, and those that destroyed Jerusalem, never could have been accomplished, had not God determined them, as well as they;

> Lamentations 3:37, "Who is he that saith, and it cometh to pass, and the Lord commandeth it not?"

And yet the King of Babylon's thus destroying the nations, and especially the Jews, is spoken of as his great wickedness, for which God finally destroyed him (Isaiah 14:4–6, 12; Habakkuk 2:5–12; and Jeremiah, chs. 50 and J51).

### *#6) Shimei: Cursing David*

It is most manifest, that God, to serve his own designs, providentially ordered Shimei's cursing David.

> II Samuel 16:10–11, "The Lord hath said unto him, curse David. . . . Let him curse, for the Lord hath bidden him."

### *#7) Judas Iscariot: Betraying and selling Christ*

It is certain, that God thus, for excellent, holy, gracious and glorious ends, ordered the fact which they committed, who were concerned in Christ's death; and that therein they did but fulfill God's designs. As, I trust, no Christian will deny it was the design of God, that Christ should be *crucified*, and that for this end, he came into the world. It is very manifest by many scriptures, that the whole affair of Christ's crucifixion, with its circumstances, and the treachery of Judas, that made way for it, was ordered in God's providence, in pursuance of his purpose; notwithstanding the violence that is used with those plain Scriptures, to obscure and pervert the sense of them.

> Acts 2:23: "Him being delivered, by the determinate counsel and foreknowledge of God,[5] ye have taken, and with wicked hands, have crucified and slain."

> Luke 22:21, Luke 22:22,[6] "But behold the hand of him that betrayeth me, is with me on the table: and truly the Son of man goeth, as it was determined."

> Acts 4:27–28, "For of a truth, against thy holy child Jesus, whom thou hast anointed, both Herod, and Pontius Pilate, with the Gentiles, and the people of Israel, were gathered together, for to do whatsoever thy hand and thy counsel determined before to be done."

---

5. "Grotius, as well as Beza, observes, that πρόγνωσις must here signify 'decree'; and Elsner has shown that it has that signification, in approved Greek writers. And it is certain ἔκδοτος signifies one 'given up' into the hands of an enemy." Philip Doddridge, *The Family Expositor, or a Paraphrase and Version of the New Testament*, 6 vols. (London, 1739-48), *in Loc.* Acts 2:23, 3:23n.

6. "As this passage is not liable to the ambiguities, which some have apprehended in *Acts 2:23* and *Acts 4:28* (which yet seem on the whole to be parallel to it, in their most natural construction) I look upon it as an evident proof, that these things are, in the language of Scripture, said to be determined or decreed (or exactly bounded and marked out by God, as the word ὁρίζω most naturally signifies) which he sees in fact will happen, in consequence of his volitions, without any necessitating agency; as well as those events of which he is properly the author." Doddridge, *Family Expositor, in Loc. Luke* 22:22, 2:434n.

Acts 3:17–18, "And now brethren, I wot that through ignorance ye did it, as did also your rulers: but these things, which God before had showed by the mouth of all his prophets, that Christ should suffer, he hath so fulfilled."

### #8) Herod and Pilate: Handing Christ over to be suffered and crucified

So that what these murderers of Christ did, is spoken of as what God brought to pass or ordered, and that by which he fulfilled his own word.

> In Revelation 17:17, "the agreeing of the kings of the earth to give their kingdom to the beast,"

though it was a very wicked thing in them, is spoken of as "a fulfilling God's will," and what "God had put it into their hearts to do."

It is manifest, that God sometimes permits sin to be committed, and at the same time orders things so, that if he permits the fact, it will come to pass, because on some accounts he sees it needful and of importance that it should come to pass.

> Matthew 18:7: "It must needs be, that offences come; but woe to that man by whom the offence cometh."

> With I Corinthians 11:19, "For there must also be heresies among you, that they which are approved, may be made manifest among you."

Thus it is certain and demonstrable, from the holy Scriptures, as well as the nature of things, and the principles of Arminians, that God permits sin; and at the same time, so orders things, in his providence, that it certainly and infallibly will come to pass, in consequence of his permission. I proceed to observe in the next place,

### III. God is the orderer and permitter of sin but not the hinderer, and rather he is neither producer nor agent of it, and so in a strict sense he is not the author.

III. That there is a great difference between God's being concerned thus, by his *permission*, in an event and act, which in the inherent subject and agent of it, is sin (though the event will certainly follow on his permission), and his being concerned in it by *producing* it and exerting the act of sin; or between his being the *orderer* of its certain existence, by *not hindering* it, under certain circumstances, and his being the proper *actor* or *author* of it, by a *positive agency* or *efficiency*. And this, notwithstanding what Dr. Whitby offers about a saying of philosophers, that *causa deficiens, in rebus necessariis, ad causam per se efficientem reducenda est*.

### ILL: As the sun's presence produces light and heat and its departure and withdrawment causes cold and darkness, so any action of God is not cause of the evil of men's wills, but his withdrawment and absence is.

As there is a vast difference between the sun's being the cause of the lightsomeness and warmth of the atmosphere, and brightness of gold and diamonds, by its presence and positive influence; and its being the occasion of darkness and frost, in the night, by its motion whereby it descends below the horizon. The motion of the sun is the occasion of the latter kind of events; but it is not the proper cause, efficient or producer of them; though they are necessarily consequent on that motion, under such circumstances: no more is any action of the Divine Being the cause of the evil of men's wills. If the sun were the proper *cause* of cold and darkness, it would be the *fountain* of these things, as it is the fountain of light and heat: and then something might be argued from the nature of cold and darkness, to a likeness of nature in the sun; and it might be justly inferred, that the sun itself is dark and cold, and that his beams are black and frosty. But from its being the cause no otherwise than by its departure, no such thing can be inferred, but the contrary; it may justly be argued, that the sun is a bright and hot body, if cold and darkness are found to be the consequence of its withdrawment; and the more constantly and necessarily these effects are connected with, and confined to its absence, the more strongly does it argue the sun to be the fountain of light and heat.

**JE: Likewise, if God withdraws his energy, men themselves necessarily commit their sins.**

So, inasmuch as sin is not the fruit of any positive agency or influence of the Most High, but on the contrary, arises from the withholding of his action and energy, and under certain circumstances, necessarily follows on the want of his influence; this is no argument that he is sinful, or his operation evil, or has anything of the nature of evil; but on the contrary, that he, and his agency, are altogether good and holy, and that he is the fountain of all holiness. It would be strange arguing indeed, because men never commit sin, but only when God leaves them *to themselves*, and necessarily sin, when he does so, that therefore their sin is not *from themselves*, but from God; and so, that God must be a sinful being: as strange as it would be to argue, because it is always dark when the sun is gone, and never dark when the sun is present, that therefore all darkness is from the sun, and that his disk and beams must needs be black.

**IV. God orders all important events and all moral acts of men in his good pleasure, according to his wisdom.**

**Ar: They will all be disposed by chance.**

IV. It properly belongs to the supreme and absolute Governor of the universe, to order all important events within his dominion, by his wisdom:

but the events in the moral world are of the most important kind; such as the moral actions of intelligent creatures, and their consequences.

These events will be ordered by something. They will either be disposed by wisdom, or they will be disposed by chance; that is, they will be disposed by blind and undesigning causes, if that were possible, and could be called a disposal. Is it not better, that the good and evil which happens in God's world, should be ordered, regulated, bounded and determined by the good pleasure of an infinitely wise Being, who perfectly comprehends within his understanding and constant view, the universality of things, in all their extent and duration, and sees all the influence of every event, with respect to every individual thing and circumstance, throughout the grand system, and the whole of the eternal series of consequences; than to leave these things to fall out by chance, and to be determined by those causes which have no understanding or aim?

**JE: When there is a better and a worse circumstance in the course of events, God chooses the best one by his wisdom.**

Doubtless, in these important events, there is a better and a worse, as to the time, subject, place, manner and circumstances of their coming to pass, with regard to their influence on the state and course of things. And if there be, it is certainly best that they should be determined to that time, place, etc., which is best. And therefore it is in its own nature fit, that wisdom, and not chance, should order these things. So that it belongs to the Being, who is the possessor of infinite wisdom, and is the creator and owner of the whole system of created existences, and has the care of all; I say, it belongs to him, to take care of this matter; and he would not do what is proper for him, if he should neglect it. And it is so far from being unholy in him, to undertake this affair, that it would rather have been unholy to neglect it; as it would have been a neglecting what fitly appertains to him; and so it would have been a very unfit and unsuitable neglect.

**Ar: Men's moral events happen not by the sovereignty of God but the volitions of men, to which he left them and are perfectly without any cause.**

**JE: Men's will is determined by in circumstances formed in the disposal and wisdom of the Sovereign God.**

Therefore the sovereignty of God doubtless extends to this matter; especially considering, that if it should be supposed to be otherwise, and God should leave men's volitions, and all moral events, to the determination and disposition of blind and unmeaning causes, or they should be left to happen perfectly without a cause; this would be no more consistent with liberty, in any notion of it, and particularly not in the Arminian notion of it, than if these events were subject to the disposal of divine providence, and the will of man were determined by circumstances which are ordered and disposed by divine wisdom; as appears by what has been already observed.

**JE: Men's evil and good morals are necessary acts ordered by God, but their liberty would not be infringed at all. Their evils are done by themselves and so they cannot be attributed to God for they are ordered for his good ends.**

But it is evident, that such a providential disposing and determining men's moral actions, though it infers a moral necessity of those actions, yet it does not in the least infringe the real liberty of mankind; the only liberty that common sense teaches to be necessary to moral agency, which, as has been demonstrated, is not inconsistent with such necessity.

On the whole, it is manifest, that God may be, in the manner which has been described, the orderer and disposer of that event, which in the inherent subject and agent is moral evil; and yet his so doing may be no moral evil. he may will the disposal of such an event, and its coming to pass for good ends, and his will not be an immoral or sinful will, but a perfectly holy will. And he may actually in his providence so dispose and permit things, that the event may be certainly and infallibly connected with such disposal and permission, and his act therein not be an immoral or unholy, but a perfectly holy act. Sin may be an evil thing, and yet that there should be such a disposal and permission, as that it should come to pass, may be a good thing.[7] This is no contradiction, or inconsistence.

**JE: Joseph's brothers did trafficking and Christ's crucifixion that was ordered by God for his good aims, and that cannot blame God to be evil but rather it should be praised his most holy volition.**

Joseph's brethren's selling him into Egypt, consider it only as it was acted by them, and with respect to their views and aims which were evil, was a very bad thing; but it was a good thing, as it was an event of God's ordering, and considered with respect to his views and aims which were good.

> Genesis 50:20, "As for you, ye thought evil against me; but God meant it unto good."

So the crucifixion of Christ, if we consider only those things which belong to the event as it proceeded from his murderers, and are comprehended within the compass of the affair considered as their act, their principles, dispositions, views and aims; so it was one of the most heinous things that ever was done; in many respects the most horrid of all acts: but consider it, as it was willed and ordered of God, in the extent of his designs and views, it was the most admirable and glorious of all events; and God's willing the event was the most holy volition of God, that ever was made known to men; and God's act in ordering it, was a divine act, which above all others, manifests the moral excellency of the Divine Being.

### JE: God's Two Wills

*1) Secret Will: disposing will in disapproving and opposing the evil objects,*

*2) Revealed Will: preceptive will in willing and determining the good ones.*

---

7. [Samuel Hopkins, *Sin, Through Divine Interposition, an Advantage to the Universe; and Yet this No Excuse for Sin, Or Encouragement to it: Illustrated and Proved, in Three Sermons, for Rom. Iii. 5. 6. 7. 8.* (Newport, Rhode Island, 1773). Samuel Hopkins (1721–1803), Edwards's student, wrote the first biography of the latter and as a New Light he represented JE's doctrine of sin as his sermon's title shows.]

## Section 9—Concerning That Objection against the Doctrine Which Has Been Maintained

*Ar: Such wills of God must be inconsistent to the Most High.*

The consideration of these things may help us to a sufficient answer to the cavils of Arminians concerning what has been supposed by many Calvinists, of a distinction between a *secret* and *revealed* will of God, and their diversity one from the other; supposing, that the Calvinists herein ascribe inconsistent wills to the Most High: which is without any foundation. God's *secret* and *revealed* will, or in other words, his *disposing* and *preceptive*[8] will may be diverse, and exercised in dissimilar acts, the one in disapproving and opposing, the other in willing and determining, without any inconsistence. Because, although these dissimilar exercises of the divine will may in some respects relate to the same things, yet in strictness they have different and contrary objects, the one evil and the other good.

*JE: The crucifixion of Christ may be agreeable to the secret will of God, though it is contrary to the revealed one.*

Thus for instance, the crucifixion of Christ was a thing contrary to the revealed or preceptive will of God; because, as it was viewed and done by his malignant murderers, it was a thing infinitely contrary to the holy nature of God, and *so* necessarily contrary to the holy inclination of his heart revealed in his Law. Yet this doesn't at all hinder but that the crucifixion of Christ, considered with all those glorious consequences, which were within the view of the divine omniscience, might be indeed, and therefore might appear to God to be, a glorious event; and consequently be agreeable to his will, though this will may be secret, i.e. not revealed in God's Law. And thus considered, the crucifixion of Christ was not evil, but good.

*JE: The crucifixion by murderers was contrary to the revealed or preceptive will of God that wills good, and also to his secret will that opposes evil, yet it may contradict his will by permitting it for his good end. However, it can't be supposed inconsistent with his will.*

If the secret exercises of God's will were of a kind that is dissimilar and contrary to his revealed will, respecting the same, or like objects; if the objects of both were good, or both evil; then indeed to ascribe contrary kinds of volition or inclination to God, respecting these objects, would be to ascribe an inconsistent will to God: but to ascribe to him different and opposite exercises of heart, respecting different objects, and objects contrary one to another, is so far from supposing God's will to be *inconsistent* with itself, that it can't be supposed *consistent* with itself any other way. For any being to have a will of choice respecting good, and at the same time a will of rejection and refusal respecting evil, is to be very consistent: but the contrary, viz. to have the same will towards these contrary objects, and to choose and love both good and evil at the same time, is to be very inconsistent.

---

8. [This late Middle English word is derived from Latin *praeceptīvus*: preceptive 1. of the nature of or expressing a precept; mandatory; 2. giving instructions; instructive.]

### Part IV—Wherein the Chief Grounds of the Reasonings of Arminians

**JE: Man who commits sin with evil purpose is evil, but God is not evil for he permits it. And so what is evil morally happens, and that can be agreeable with the will of God.**

There is no inconsistence in supposing, that God may hate a thing as it is in itself, and considered simply as evil, and yet that it may be his will it should come to pass, considering all consequences. I believe, there is no person of good understanding, who will venture to say, he is certain that it is impossible it should be best, taking in the whole compass and extent of existence, and all consequences in the endless series of events, that there should be such a thing as moral evil in the world.[9]

**JE: God does choose what is absolutely best as the wisest and holiest disposer.**

---

9. Here are worthy to be observed some passages of a late noted writer, of our nation, that nobody who is acquainted with him will suspect to be very favorable to Calvinism. "It is difficult (says he) to handle the *necessity of evil* in such a manner, as not to stumble such as are not above being alarmed at propositions which have an uncommon sound. But if philosophers will but reflect calmly on the matter, they will find, that consistently with the unlimited power of the supreme Cause, it may be said, that in the best ordered system, *evils* must have place." George Turnbull, *The Principles of Moral Philosophy, an Inquiry into the Wise and Good Government of the Moral World* (London, 1740), 327, 328.

He is there speaking of *moral* evils, as may be seen. Again the same author, in his second Vol. entitled, *Christian Philosophy*, p.35. has these words: "If the author and governor of all things be infinitely *perfect*, then whatever is, is right; of all possible systems he hath chosen the *best*: and consequently there is *no absolute evil* in the universe. . . .. This being the case, all the seeming *imperfections or evils* in it are such only in a partial view; and with respect to the whole system, they are goods.

George Turnbull, 37. "*Whence then comes evil*, is the question that hath in all ages been reckoned the *Gordian* Knot in philosophy. And indeed, if we own the existence of evil in the world in an absolute sense, we diametrically contradict what hath been just now proved of God. For if there be any evil in the system, that is not good with respect to the whole, then is the whole not good, but evil: or at best, very imperfect: And an author must be his *workmanship* is; as is the effect, such is the cause, But the solution of the difficulty is at hand; *That there is no evil in the universe*. What! Are there no pains, no imperfections? Is there no misery, no vice in the world? Or are not these evils? Evils indeed they are; that is, those of one sort are hurtful, and those of the other sort are equally hurtful and abominable: But they are not evil or mischievous with respect to the *whole*."

George Turnbull, 42. "But He is at the same time said to *create* evil, darkness, confusion; and yet to do no evil, but to be the author of Good only. He is called the *Father of Lights, the Author of every perfect and good gift, with whom there is no variableness no shadow of turning, who tempteth no man, but giveth to all man liberally*, and upbraideth not. And yet by the prophet Isaias He is introduced saying of Himself, *I form Light, and create darkness; I make peace, and create evil: I the Lord do all these things*. What is the meaning, the plain language of all this, but that the Lord delighteth in goodness, and (as the Scripture speaks) Evil is *his strange work*? He intends and purifies the universal *good* of His creation: and the *evil* which happens, is not permitted for its own sake, or thro' any pleasure in evil, but because it is requisite to the *greater good* pursued."

[*WJE Online*, It may also be seen that Turnbull justifies the existence of moral evil not only by considering all the consequences which God may have in his view, but by himself viewing moral evil as an unavoidable result and risk of freedom, which great good everyone may witness along with the evil, or else phrase as follows his "complaint against nature": "Nature hath dealt unkindly by us in making our happiness depend in any measure on ourselves, and in making us capable of the pleasures of knowledge, foresight, *self-direction*, and good management" (p. 326; ed. italics).]

## Section 9—Concerning That Objection against the Doctrine Which Has Been Maintained

And if so, it will certainly follow, that an infinitely wise Being, who always chooses what is best, must choose that there should be such a thing. And if so, then such a choice is not an evil, but a wise and holy choice. And if so, then that providence which is agreeable to such a choice, is a wise and holy providence. Men do *will* sin as sin, and so are the authors and actors of it: they love it as sin, and for evil ends and purposes.

### JE: Men do will sin as sin, but God doesn't will sin as sin.

God doesn't will sin as sin, or for the sake of anything evil; though it be his pleasure so to order things, that he permitting, sin will come to pass; for the sake of the great good that by his disposal shall be the consequence. His willing to order things so that evil should come to pass, for the sake of the contrary good, is no argument that he doesn't hate evil, as evil: and if so, then it is no reason why he mayn't reasonably forbid evil as evil, and punish it as such.

### JE: We must distinguish the secret will of God that disposes what is best and the revealed will that orders what he loves and is agreeable to his nature.

The Arminians themselves must be obliged, whether they will or no, to allow a distinction of God's will, amounting to just the same thing that Calvinists intend by their distinction of a secret and revealed will. They must allow a distinction of those things which God thinks best should be, considering all circumstances and consequences, and so are agreeable to his disposing will, and those things which he loves, and are agreeable to his nature, in themselves considered.

### JE: Giving devils up to their own wickedness is agreeable to God's will.

Who is there that will dare to say, that the hellish pride, malice and cruelty of devils, are agreeable to God, and what he likes and approves? And yet, I trust, there is no Christian divine but what will allow, that it is agreeable to God's will so to order and dispose things concerning them, so to leave them to themselves, and give them up to their own wickedness, that this perfect wickedness should be a necessary consequence. Be sure Dr. Whitby's words do plainly suppose and allow it.[10]

### JE: Three Universal Truths: 1. God is the most happy Being; 2. No mischief to Him; 3. All beings including Him are suffering.

These following things may be laid down as maxims of plain truth, and indisputable evidence.

1. That God is a perfectly happy Being, in the most absolute and highest sense possible.

---

10. Whitby, *Discourse*, Dis. IV, ch. 1, nos. 1, 2, 5, pp. 300, 305, 309.

2. That it will follow from hence, that God is free from everything that is contrary to happiness; and so, that in strict propriety of speech, there is no such thing as any pain, grief or trouble in God.

3. When any intelligent being is really crossed and disappointed, and things are contrary to what he truly desires, he is the less pleased, or has less pleasure, his pleasure and happiness is diminished, and he suffers what is disagreeable to him, or is the subject of something that is of a nature contrary to joy and happiness, even pain and grief.[11]

**JE: Misunderstanding occurs when even so Arminians do not distinguish the two wills of God: All sins are contrary to his will and his will conflicts in them. Moreover, he might become the most miserable victim.**

From this last axiom it follows, that if no distinction is to be admitted between God's hatred of sin, and his will with respect to the event and the existence of sin, as the all-wise determiner of all events, under the view of all consequences through the whole compass and series of things; I say, then it certainly follows, that the coming to pass of every individual act of sin is truly, all things considered, contrary to his will, and that his will is really crossed in it; and this in proportion as he hates it. And as God's hatred of sin is infinite, by reason of the infinite contrariety of his holy nature to sin; so his will is infinitely crossed, in every act of sin that happens. Which is as much as to say, he endures that which is infinitely disagreeable to him, by means of every act of sin that he sees committed. And therefore, as appears by the preceding positions, he endures truly and really, infinite grief or pain from every sin. And so he must be infinitely crossed, and suffer infinite pain, every day, in millions of millions of instances: he must continually be the subject of an immense number of real, and truly infinitely great crosses and vexations. Which would be to make him infinitely the most miserable of all beings.

**Ar: Is He immoral and contrary to His nature and will for He orders evils for good ends?**

**JE: As He permits them ultimately for good ends and without any evil disposition, He does not do any evil and so he is not to be blamed.**

If any objector should say; all that these things amount to, is, that God may do evil that good may come; which is justly esteemed immoral and sinful in men; and therefore may be justly esteemed inconsistent with the moral perfections of God. I answer, that for God to dispose and permit evil, in the manner that has been spoken of, is not to

---

11. Certainly it is not less absurd and unreasonable to talk of God's Will and Desires being truly and properly crossed without his suffering any uneasiness, or anything grievous or disagreeable, than it is to talk of something that may be called a *revealed Will*, which may in some respect be different from a secret purpose; which Purpose may be fulfilled, when the other is opposed.

do evil that good may come; for it is not to do evil at all. In order to a thing's being morally evil, there must be one of these things belonging to it: either it must be a thing unfit and unsuitable in its own nature; or it must have a bad tendency; or it must proceed from an evil disposition, and be done for an evil end. But neither of these things can be attributed to God's ordering and permitting such events, as the immoral acts of creatures, for good ends.

### *1. As God unlike men has perfect wisdom, He can control the matter of evils.*

1. It is not unfit in its own nature, that he should do so.

For it is in its own nature fit, that infinite wisdom, and not blind chance, should dispose moral good and evil in the world. And it is fit, that the Being who has infinite wisdom, and is the maker, owner, and supreme governor of the world, should take care of that matter. And therefore there is no unfitness, or unsuitableness in his doing it. It may be unfit, and so immoral, for any other beings to go about to order this affair; because they are not possessed of a wisdom, that in any manner fits them for it; and in other respects they are not fit to be trusted with this affair; nor does it belong to them, they not being the owners and lords of the universe.

### *Illustration of a Wise and Good Man: It would not be contrary to him and his goodness that in the world a moral evil exists, but he is not able to order it.*

We need not be afraid to affirm,
    that if a wise and good man knew with absolute certainty, it would be best, all things considered, that there should be such a thing as moral evil in the world, it would not be contrary to his wisdom and goodness, for him to choose that it should be so. It is no evil desire, to desire good, and to desire that which, all things considered, is best. And it is no unwise choice, to choose that that should be, which it is best should be; and to choose the existence of that thing concerning which this is known, viz. that it is best it should be, and so is known in the whole to be most worthy to be chosen. On the contrary, it would be a plain defect in wisdom and goodness, for him not to choose it. And the reason why he might not order it, if he were able, would not be because he might not desire it, but only the ordering of that matter doesn't belong to him.

    But it is no harm for him who is by right, and in the greatest propriety, the supreme orderer of all things, to order everything in such a manner, as it would be a point of wisdom in him to choose that they should be ordered.

### *JE: The best God chooses His best ordering, for it is impossible for Him to do otherwise.*

If it would be a plain defect of wisdom and goodness in a being, not to choose that that should be, which he certainly knows it would, all things considered, be best should be (as was but now observed), then it must be impossible for a being who has no defect of wisdom and goodness, to do otherwise than choose it should be; and that, for this very reason, because he is perfectly wise and good. And if it be agreeable to perfect wisdom and goodness for him to choose that it should be, and the ordering of all things supremely and perfectly belongs to him, it must be agreeable to infinite wisdom and goodness, to order that it should be. If the choice is good, the ordering and disposing things according to that choice must also be good. It can be no harm in one to whom it belongs "to do his will in the armies of heaven, and amongst the inhabitants of the earth," to execute a good volition.

### JE: God's will and object is good, and so all his acts are righteous.

If his will be good, and the object of his will be, all things considered, good and best, then the choosing or willing it is not willing evil that good may come. And if so, then his ordering according to that will is not doing evil, that good may come.

### 2. To make best by ordering and permitting even evils is from His good tendency.

2. It is not of a bad tendency, for the Supreme Being thus to order and permit that moral evil to be, which it is best should come to pass. For that it is of good tendency, is the very thing supposed in the point now in question. Christ's crucifixion, though a most horrid fact in them that perpetrated it, was of most glorious tendency as permitted and ordered of God.

### 3. If His aim and result was good, the tendency of his order and choice, too, were good.

3. Nor is there any need of supposing, it proceeds from any evil disposition or aim: for by the supposition, what is aimed at is good, and good is the actual issue, in the final result of things.

# Section 10

## Concerning Sin's First Entrance into the World

*If God created Adam and Eve as imperfect and unavoidable to sin, would that mean that by creating us this way he caused us to sin? Isn't God responsible for the sin?*

The things which have already been offered, may serve to obviate or clear many of the objections which might be raised concerning sin's first coming into the world; as though it would follow from the doctrine maintained, that God must be the author of the first sin, through his so disposing things, that it should necessarily follow from his permission, that the sinful act should be committed, etc. I need not therefore stand to repeat what has been said already, about such a necessity's not proving God to be the author of sin, in any ill sense, or in any such sense as to infringe any liberty of man, concerned in his moral agency, or capacity of blame, guilt and punishment.

But if it should nevertheless be said, supposing the case so, that God, when he had made man, might so order his circumstances, that from these circumstances, together with his withholding further assistance and divine influence, his sin would infallibly follow, why might not God as well have first made man with a fixed prevailing principle of sin in his heart?

I answer,

*JE: Sin did arise from Adam's imperfection but not from God as the positive cause and real source of it.*

1. It was meet, if sin did come into existence, and appear in the world, it should arise from the imperfection which properly belongs to a creature, as such, and should appear so to do, that it might appear not to be from God as the efficient or fountain. But this could not have been, if man had been made at first with sin in his heart; nor unless the abiding principle and habit of sin were first introduced by an evil act of the creature. If sin had not arose from the imperfection of the creature, it would not have been so visible, that it did not arise from God, as the positive cause, and real source of

### Part IV—Wherein the Chief Grounds of the Reasonings of Arminians

it. — But it would require room that can't be here allowed, fully to consider all the difficulties which have been started, concerning the first entrance of sin into the world. And therefore,

**Ar: 2. Adam's first sinful volition arose accidentally, without any cause at all, or chose, determined, and produced itself.**

**JE: That is to say, the will was self-determined or determined by free choice, in that sinful volition and the first sinful volition was determined by a foregoing sinful volition.**

2. I would observe, that objections against the doctrine that has been laid down, in opposition to the *Arminian* notion of liberty, from these difficulties, are altogether impertinent; because no additional difficulty is incurred, by adhering to a scheme in this manner differing from theirs, and none would be removed or avoided, by agreeing with, and maintaining theirs.

Nothing that the *Arminians* say, about the contingence, or self-determining power of man's will, can serve to explain with less difficulty, how the first sinful volition of mankind could take place, and man be justly charged with the blame of it. To say, the will was self-determined, or determined by free choice, in that sinful volition; which is to say, that the first sinful volition was determined by a foregoing sinful volition; is no solution of the difficulty. It is an odd way of solving difficulties, to advance greater, in order to it.

**JE: This difficulty would not be solved by such an approach. ILL: "2+2=9"**

To say, two and two makes nine; or, that a child begat his father, solves no difficulty: no more does it, to say, the first sinful act of choice was before the first sinful act of choice, and chose and determined it, and brought it to pass. Nor is it any better solution, to say, the first sinful volition chose, determined and produced itself; which is to say, it was before it was. Nor will it go any further towards helping us over the difficulty, to say, the first sinful volition arose accidentally, without any cause at all;

**JE: This difficulty is harder than the question how the world could be made out of nothing, and it cannot be an answer to it.**

any more than it will solve that difficult question, *how the world could be made out of nothing?* to say, it came into being out of nothing, without any cause; as has been already observed. And if we should allow that that could be, that the first evil volition should arise by perfect accident, without any cause, it would relieve no difficulty, about God's laying the blame of it to man. For how was man to blame for perfect accident, which had no cause, and which therefore, he (to be sure) was not the cause of, any more than if it came by some external cause?

## Section 10—Concerning Sin's First Entrance into the World

***JE: Arminian solutions are no better than ones of mathematical paradoxes and are rather mistakes in making wrong suppositions.***

... Such kind of solutions are no better, than if some person, going about to solve some of the strange mathematical paradoxes, about infinitely great and small quantities; as, that some infinitely great quantities are infinitely greater than some other infinitely great quantities; and also that some infinitely small quantities are infinitely less than others, which yet are infinitely little; in order to a solution, should say, that mankind have been under a mistake, in supposing a greater quantity to exceed a smaller; and that a hundred multiplied by ten, makes but a single unit.

# Section 11

## Of a Supposed Inconsistence of These Principles, with God's Moral Character

The things which have been already observed, may be sufficient to answer most of the objections, and silence the great exclamations of Arminians against the Calvinists, from the supposed inconsistence of Calvinistic principles with the moral perfections of God, as exercised in his government of mankind. The consistence of such a doctrine of necessity as has been maintained, with the fitness and reasonableness of God's commands, promises and threatenings, rewards and punishments, has been particularly considered: the cavils of our opponents, as though our doctrine of necessity made God the author of sin, have been answered;

*JE: Contrary to Arminians' objections to Calvinists, the secret and revealed will of God is not inconsistent but consistent, and as such is with God's perfections.*

and also their objection against these principles, as inconsistent with God's sincerity, in his counsels, invitations and persuasions, has been already obviated, in what has been observed, respecting the consistence of what Calvinists suppose concerning the *secret* and *revealed* will of God: by that it appears, there is no repugnance in supposing it may be the secret will of God, that his ordination and permission of events should be such that it shall be a certain consequence, that a thing never will come to pass; which yet it is man's duty to do, and so God's *preceptive* will, that he should do; and this is the same thing as to say, God may sincerely command and require him to do it. And if he may be sincere in commanding him, he may for the same reason be sincere in counseling, inviting and using persuasions with him to do it. Counsels and invitations are manifestations of God's preceptive will, or of what God loves, and what is in itself, and as man's act, agreeable to his heart; and not of his disposing will, and what he chooses as a part of his own infinite scheme of things. It has been particularly shown (Pt. III, Sec. 4) that such a necessity as has been maintained, is not inconsistent with the propriety and fitness of divine commands; and for the same reason, not

## Section 11—Of a Supposed Inconsistence of These Principles, with God's Moral Character

inconsistent with the sincerity of invitations and counsels, in the corollary at the end of that section.

Yea, it hath been shown (Pt. III, Sec. 7, *Corol.* 1) that this objection of Arminians, concerning the sincerity and use of divine exhortations, invitations and counsels, is demonstrably against themselves. Notwithstanding, I would further observe, that the difficulty of reconciling the sincerity of counsels, invitations and persuasions, with such an antecedent known fixedness of all events, as has been supposed, is not peculiar to this scheme, as distinguished from that of the generality of Arminians, who[1] acknowledge the absolute foreknowledge of God: and therefore, it would be unreasonably brought as an objection against my differing from them.

### JE: Difficulty of Arminian scheme: Why does God make all efforts, perfectly knowing men will not follow his commands?

The main seeming difficulty in the case is this:

### Arminian Difficulty: Why does God make efforts, even after he persuaded men?

that God in counseling, inviting and persuading, makes a show of aiming at, seeking and using endeavors for the thing exhorted and persuaded to;

### Arminian Difficulty: Why does God keep making efforts, even knowing that men would not obey?

whereas, it is impossible for any intelligent being truly to seek, or use endeavors for a thing, which he at the same time knows most perfectly will not come to pass;

### Arminian Difficulty: Why does God keep counseling, even knowing men would not employ his means?

and that it is absurd to suppose, he makes the obtaining of a thing his end, in his calls and counsels, which he at the same time infallibly knows will not be obtained by these means.

### Arminian Difficulty: Why does God let the problem be left, even knowing perfectly?

Now, if God knows this, in the utmost certainty and perfection, the way by which he comes by this knowledge makes no difference. If he knows it by the necessity which he sees in things, or by some other means; it alters not the case.

### JE: Arminians, too, agree that God does so is no evidence of his insincerity; God has a certain foreknowledge of all things.

But it is in effect allowed by Arminians themselves, that God's inviting and persuading men to do things, which he at the same time certainly knows will not be done, is no evidence of insincerity; because they allow, that God has a certain foreknowledge of

---

1. [Corrected, from "which."]

all men's sinful actions and omissions. And as this is thus implicitly allowed by most Arminians, so all that pretend to own the Scriptures to be the Word of God, must be constrained to allow it. . . .

### ILL: *God preknew and predicted the refusals of the King Pharaoh.*

God commanded and counseled Pharaoh to let his people go, and used arguments and persuasions to induce him to it; he laid before him arguments taken from his infinite greatness and almighty power (Exodus 7:16) and forewarned him of the fatal consequences of his refusal, from time to time (ch. 8:1–2, 20–21; ch. 9:1–5, 13–17; and 10:3, 6). He commanded Moses, and the elders of Israel, to go and beseech Pharaoh to let the people go; and at the same time told them, he knew surely that he would not comply to it.

> Exodus 3:18–19: "And thou shalt come, thou and the elders of Israel, unto the king of Egypt, and you shall say unto him; the Lord God of the Hebrews hath met with us; and now let us go, we beseech thee, three days' journey into the wilderness, that we may sacrifice unto the Lord our God": and, "I am sure that the king of Egypt will not let you go."

### ILL: *Jesus preknew and predicted the denial and betrayal of Peter.*

So our blessed Savior, the evening wherein he was betrayed, knew that Peter would shamefully deny him, before the morning; for he declares it to him with asseverations, to show the certainty of it; and tells the disciples, that all of them should be offended because of him that night (Matthew 26:31–35, John 13:38, Luke 22:31–34, John 16:32). And yet it was their duty to avoid these things; they were very sinful things, which God had forbidden, and which it was their duty to watch and pray against; and they were obliged to do so from the *counsels* and *persuasions* Christ used with them, at that very time, so to do (Matthew 26:41), "Watch and pray, that ye enter not into temptation."

### JE: *This difficulty does not belong to Calvinism, and it is related to the doctrine of predestination.*

So that whatever difficulty there can be in this matter, it can be no objection against any principles which have been maintained in opposition to the principles of Arminians; nor does it any more concern me to remove the difficulty, than it does them, or indeed all that call themselves Christians, and acknowledge the divine authority of the Scriptures. Nevertheless, this matter may possibly (God allowing) be more particularly and largely considered, in some future discourse, on the doctrine of predestination.

### Arminianism Claims: *The defenders of that notion of liberty of will, consisting in self-determination, without all necessity, and which is essential to moral agency;*

***that such a determination of the will belongs to moral agents, or in their moral acts; objectors of the doctrine of Calvinists.***

But I would here observe, that however the defenders of that notion of liberty of will, which I have opposed, exclaim against the doctrine of Calvinists, as tending to bring men into doubts, concerning the moral perfections of God; it is their scheme, and not the scheme of Calvinists, that indeed is justly chargeable with this. For it is one of the most fundamental points of their scheme of things, that a freedom of will, consisting in self-determination, without all necessity, is essential to *moral agency*. This is the same thing as to say, that such a determination of the will without all necessity, must be in all intelligent beings, in those things, wherein they are *moral agents*, or in their *moral acts*: and from this it will follow, that

> "God's will is not necessarily determined, in anything he does, as a moral agent, or in any of his *acts* that are of a *moral nature*. So that in all things, wherein he acts *holily, justly* and *truly*, he doesn't act necessarily; or his will is not necessarily determined to act holily and justly; because if it were necessarily determined, he would not be a moral agent in thus acting:"

his will would be attended with necessity; which they say is inconsistent with moral agency:

> "He can act no otherwise; he is at no liberty in the affair; he is determined by unavoidable invincible necessity: therefore, such agency is no moral agency; yea, no agency at all, properly speaking: a necessary agent is no agent: he being passive, and subject to necessity, what he does is no act of his, but an effect of a necessity prior to any act of his."

### *How do you prove God's theodicy: that God certainly will in any one instance do that which is just and holy?*

This is agreeable to their manner of arguing. Now then what is become of all our proof of the moral perfections of God? How can we prove, that God certainly will in any one instance do that which is just and holy; seeing his will is determined in the matter by no necessity? We have no other way of proving that anything *certainly* will be, but only by the necessity of the event. Where we can see no necessity, but that the thing may be, or may not be, there we are unavoidably left at a loss.

### *Chubb's Proof of God's Theodicy:*

*1) God perfectly knows what is best in itself;*

*2) He must see it to be so;*

*3) He cannot have any temptation to reject it;*

*4) He must will it.*

We have no other way properly and truly to demonstrate the moral perfections of God, but the way that Mr. Chubb proves them, in pp. 252, 261–63 of his *Tracts*;[2] viz. that God must necessarily perfectly know what is most worthy and valuable in itself, which in the nature of things is best and fittest to be done. And as this is most eligible in itself, he being omniscient, must see it to be so; and being both omniscient and self-sufficient, cannot have any temptation to reject it; and so must necessarily will that which is best. And thus, by this necessity of the determination of God's will to what is good and best, we demonstrably establish God's moral character.[3]

***Fallacy of Arminian Demonstration: Their argument that without such a freedom of will men can't be proper moral agents nor the subjects of command, promises, rewards, and punishments, etc., and this is confessedly based on the Scriptures begging the question.***

*Corol.* From things which have been observed, it appears, that most of the arguments from Scripture, which Arminians make use of to support their scheme, are no other than *begging the question*[4]. For in these their arguments they determine in the first place, that without such a freedom of will as they hold, men can't be proper moral agents, nor the subjects of command, counsel, persuasion, invitation, promises, threatenings, expostulations, rewards and punishments; and that without such a freedom it is to no purpose for men to take any care, or use any diligence, endeavors or means, in order to their avoiding sin, or becoming holy, escaping punishment or obtaining happiness: and having supposed these things, which are grand things in question in the debate, then they heap up scriptures containing commands, counsels, calls, warnings, persuasions, expostulations, promises and threatenings [as doubtless they may find enough such; the Bible is confessedly full of them, from the beginning to the end]; and then they glory, how full the Scripture is on their side, how many more texts there are that evidently favor their scheme, than such as seem to favor the contrary.

***Weak points of Arminian Demonstration: The things in question are not manifest, propriety of their scheme is not demonstrable, and Scriptures are not used.***

---

2. [JE agrees with his opponent Chubb's ways to prove God's Theodicy. Cf. *FOW,* 349.]

3. [JE like Chubb holds of both *scientia necessaria* or *naturalis,* the so-called necessary or natural *knowledge*; viz., "The knowledge that God, according to his nature, must necessarily have; infinite and perfect knowledge of both the divine being itself and of all possibilities, and *scientia libera or voluntaria, the* free or *voluntary* knowledge; *viz.,* a free or voluntary knowledge of actual things brought freely into existence by the divine will operating within the range of possibility perfectly known to God. Cf. Richard A. Muller, *Dictionary of Latin and Greek Theological Terms Drawn Principally from Protestant Scholastic Theology* (Grand Rapids: Baker, 1985).]

4. ["Begging the question (petitio principii, assming the initial point)" is literally to catch a point by forcefully taking a question or point, a form of logical fallacy in which a statement or claim is assumed to be true without evidence other than the statement or claim itself. e.g., "This phone is junk because it looks valueless."]

But let them first make manifest the things in question, which they suppose and take for granted, and show them to be consistent with themselves, and produce clear evidence of their truth; and they have gained their point, as all will confess, without bringing one scripture. For none denies, that there are commands, counsels, promises, threatenings, etc., in the Bible. But unless they do these things, their multiplying such texts of Scripture is insignificant and vain. It may further be observed, that such scriptures as they bring, are really against them, and not for them.

*Ar: God entrusts the free will of men.*

*JE: But he uses their motives and persuasion and moral means, and acts as the moral Governor with men as the subjects.*

As it has been demonstrated, that it is their scheme, and not ours, that is inconsistent with the use of motives and persuasives, or any moral means whatsoever, to induce men to the practice of virtue, or abstaining from wickedness: their principles, and not ours, are repugnant to moral agency, and inconsistent with moral government, with law or precept, with the nature of virtue or vice, reward or punishment, and with everything whatsoever of a moral nature, either on the part of the moral Governor, or in the state, actions, or conduct of the subject.

# Section 12

## Of a Supposed Tendency of These Principles to Atheism and Licentiousness

***Ar: How is Arminian doctrine close to atheism, even though atheists hold the doctrine of necessity? Isn't Calvinist doctrine close to atheism because it holds the doctrine of necessity?***

If any object against what has been maintained, that it tends to atheism[1]; I know not on what grounds such an objection can be raised, unless it be that some atheists have held a doctrine of necessity which they suppose to be like this. But if it be so, I am persuaded the Arminians would not look upon it just, that their notion of freedom and contingence should be charged with a tendency to all the errors that ever any embraced, who have held such opinions.

The Stoic philosophers, whom the Calvinists are charged with agreeing with, were no atheists, but the greatest theists, and nearest akin to Christians in their opinions concerning the unity and the perfections of the Godhead, of all the heathen philosophers. And Epicurus,[2] that chief father of atheism, maintained no such doctrine of necessity, but was the greatest maintainer of contingence.

***JE: The Best Way to Prove God's Existence: All events are connected with some antecedent divine ground and reason of their existence.***

The doctrine of necessity, which supposes a necessary connection of all events, on some antecedent ground and reason of their existence, is the only medium we have to prove the being of God. And the contrary doctrine of contingence, even as maintained by Arminians (which certainly implies or infers, that events may come into existence,

---

1. ["Practical Atheism" (1731, Psalms 14:1), *WJE* 17:47–57.]

2. [Epicurus (341–271 B.C.), a Greek philosopher, held that the highest good is pleasure, identified with freedom from disturbance or pain, and that the world is a series of fortuitous combinations of atoms.]

## Section 12—Of a Supposed Tendency of These Principles to Atheism and Licentiousness

or begin to be, without dependence on anything foregoing, as their cause, ground or reason) takes away all proof of the being of God; which proof is summarily expressed by the Apostle, in Romans 1:20. And this is a tendency to atheism with a witness.

### JE: Arminian doctrine is prone to atheism.

So that indeed it is the doctrine of Arminians, and not of the Calvinists, that is justly charged with a tendency to atheism; it being built on a foundation that is the utter subversion of every demonstrative argument for the proof of a deity; as has been shown (Pt. II, Sec. 3). And whereas it has often been said, that the Calvinistic doctrine of necessity, saps the foundations of all religion and virtue, and tends to the greatest licentiousness of practice: this objection is built on the pretense that our doctrine renders vain all means and endeavors, in order to be virtuous and religious.

Which pretense has been already particularly considered in the 5th section of this part; where it has been demonstrated, that this doctrine has no such tendency; but that such a tendency is truly to be charged on the contrary doctrine: inasmuch as the notion of contingence, which their doctrine implies, in its certain consequences, overthrows all connection, in every degree, between endeavor and event, means and end.

### JE: Arminian doctrine claims evil inclinations to be necessary but natural, and yet is easy to licentiousness.

And besides, if many other things which have been observed to belong to the Arminian doctrine, or to be plain consequences of it, be considered, there will appear just reason to suppose that it is *that*, which must rather tend to licentiousness. Their doctrine excuses all evil inclinations, which men find to be natural; because in such inclinations, they are not self-determined, as such inclinations are not owing to any choice or determination of their own wills. Which leads men wholly to justify themselves in all their wicked actions, so far as natural inclination has had a hand in determining their wills, to the commission of them.

### Ar: Arminians objected moral necessity and inability to be inconsistent with blame or moral obligation, but they finally admitted that evil acts must have been done by necessary evil inclinations.

Yea, these notions which suppose moral necessity and inability to be inconsistent with blame or moral obligation,[3] will directly lead men to justify the vilest acts and practices, from the strength of their wicked inclinations of all sorts; strong inclinations inducing a moral necessity; yea, to excuse every degree of evil inclination, so far as this

---

3. [Opposing Augustine's viewpoint on total depravity and inability of men, Pelagius denied original sin and emphasized *humans'* unconditional free will and moral *responsibility*. "When I have to discuss the principles of right conduct and the leading of a holy life, I usually begin by showing the strength and characteristics of human nature. . . .. To call a person to something he considers impossible does him no good." Pelagius, "Letter to Demetrias," in *Theological Anthropology, Sources of Early Christian Thought*, ed. and tr. J. Patout Burns (Philadelphia: Fortress, 1981), 40–41.]

has evidently prevailed, and been the thing which has determined their wills: because, so far as antecedent inclination determined the will, so far the will was without liberty of indifference and self-determination.

***Unavoidable Inconsistencies of Arminianism:***

*1) Justifying themselves: "I did not sin without my liberty, and it is not my sin";*

*2) Diminishing the guilt of sin, and the difference between offences;*

*3) Putting off the work of religion and virtue, and turning from sin to God;*

*4) Having men misunderstood to have a sovereign power to determine themselves to just when they please;*

*5) Excusing their sin due to their inability.*

Which at last will come to this, that men will justify themselves in all the wickedness they commit. It has been observed already, that this scheme of things does exceedingly diminish the guilt of sin, and the difference between the greatest and smallest offences:

and if it be pursued in its real consequences, it leaves room for no such thing, as either virtue or vice, blame or praise in the world. And then again, how naturally does this notion of the sovereign self-determining power of the will, in all things, virtuous or vicious, and whatsoever deserves either reward or punishment, tend to encourage men to put off the work of religion and virtue, and turning from sin to God; it being that which they have a sovereign power to determine themselves to, just when they please; or if not, they are wholly excusable in going on in sin, because of their inability to do any other.

***JE: Even if the doctrine of necessity were abused and then it could be prone to licentiousness, it would not be so, but many sinners attempt to justify themselves by making the doctrine improved and by doing many good things.***

If it should be said, that the tendency of this doctrine of necessity, to licentiousness, appears by the improvement many at this day actually make of it, to justify themselves in their dissolute courses; I will not deny that some men do unreasonably abuse this doctrine, as they do many other things which are true and excellent in their own nature: but I deny that this proves, the doctrine itself has any tendency to licentiousness.

I think, the tendency of doctrines, by what now appears in the world, and in our nation in particular, may much more justly be argued from the general effect which has been seen to attend the prevailing of the principles of Arminians, and the contrary principles; as both have had their turn of general prevalence in our nation.

***JE: The misjudgment to Calvinism, which undermines the very foundation of all religion and morality and disannuls all rational motives; and to Arminianism, which induces virtue and goodness, rationalizes religion, and enforces it.***

## Section 12—Of a Supposed Tendency of These Principles to Atheism and Licentiousness

If it be indeed, as is pretended, that Calvinistic doctrines undermine the very foundation of all religion and morality, and enervate and disannul all rational motives, to holy and virtuous practice; and that the contrary doctrines give the inducements to virtue and goodness their proper force, and exhibit religion in a rational light, tending to recommend it to the reason of mankind, and enforce it in a manner that is agreeable to their natural notions of things:

**JE: Paradoxical consequences of Calvinism, which was said to be inconsistent with virtue and religious practice, but it rather promoted almost universally; and of Arminianism, which seems to be well consistent with virtue and religious practice, but rather so does all sorts of wickedness, and holds contempt of all religion.**

I say, if it be thus, it is remarkable, that virtue and religious practice should prevail most, when the former doctrines, so inconsistent with it, prevailed almost universally: and that ever since the latter doctrines, so happily agreeing with it, and of so proper and excellent a tendency to promote it, have been gradually prevailing, vice, profaneness, luxury and wickedness of all sorts, and contempt of all religion, and of every kind of seriousness and strictness of conversation, should proportionally prevail; and that these things should thus accompany one another, and rise and prevail one with another, now for a whole age together.

**JE: A curious speculation of Calvinism, which is inconsistent with religion, and tending to banish all virtue from the earth; tending to banish religion and virtue, and prevailing licentiousness.**

It is remarkable, that this happy remedy [discovered by the free inquiries, and superior sense and wisdom of this age] against the pernicious effects of Calvinism, so inconsistent with religion, and tending so much to banish all virtue from the earth, should on so long a trial, be attended with no good effect; but that the consequence should be the reverse of amendment; that in proportion, as the remedy takes place, and is thoroughly applied, so the disease should prevail; and the very same dismal effect take place, to the highest degree, which Calvinistic doctrines are supposed to have so great a tendency to; even the banishing of religion and virtue, and the prevailing of unbounded licentiousness of manners. If these things are truly so, they are very remarkable, and matter of very curious speculation!

# Section 13

## Concerning That Objection against the Reasoning, by Which the Calvinistic Doctrine is Supported, That It is Metaphysical and Abstruse

*Ar: Calvinist reasonings are scholastic and abstruse metaphysical.*

*JE: They are not, but rather so are Arminian schemes.*

It has often been objected against the defenders of Calvinistic principles, that in their reasonings, they run into nice scholastic distinctions, and abstruse metaphysical subtleties, and set these in opposition to common sense. And it is possible, that after the former manner it may be alleged against the reasoning by which I have endeavored to confute the Arminian scheme of liberty and moral agency, that it is very abstracted and metaphysical. Concerning this, I would observe the following things.

*Ar: Calvinist reasoning is very metaphysical, or the science of metaphysics.*

*JE: Their objection is very impertinent and not worthy of any dispute.*

I. If that be made an objection against the foregoing reasoning, that it is *metaphysical*, or may properly be reduced to the science of metaphysics, it is a very impertinent objection; whether it be so or no, is not worthy of any dispute or controversy. If the reasoning be good, it is as frivolous to inquire what science it is properly reduced to, as what language it is delivered in: and for a man to go about to confute the arguments of his opponent, by telling him, his arguments are "metaphysical," would be as weak as to tell him, his arguments could not be substantial, because they were written in French or Latin. The question is not, whether what is said be metaphysics, physics, logic, or mathematics, Latin, French, English, or Mohawk?[1] But, whether the reasoning be good, and the arguments truly conclusive?

---

1. [One of the Indian tribes, to which JE was a missionary at Stockbridge while writing the *Inquiry*.]

### JE: *Metaphysical reasoning is useful to disprove Roman Catholic doctrine of transubstantiation.*

The foregoing arguments are no more metaphysical, than those which we use against the Papists, to disprove their doctrine of transubstantiation; alleging, it is inconsistent with the notion of corporeal identity that it should be in ten thousand places at the same time. It is by metaphysical arguments only we are able to prove, that the rational soul is not corporeal; that lead or sand can't think; that thoughts are not square or round, or don't weigh a pound.

### JE: *Metaphysical reasoning is useful to prove the existence of God.*

The arguments, by which we prove the being of God, if handled closely and distinctly, so as to show their clear and demonstrative evidence, must be metaphysically treated.

It is by metaphysics only, that we can demonstrate,

> that God is not limited to a place, or is not mutable; that he is not ignorant, or forgetful; that it is impossible for him to lie, or be unjust; and that there is one God only, and not hundreds or thousands.

### JE: *Metaphysical reasoning is useful for demonstrating anything, except mathematical truths.*

And indeed we have no strict demonstration of anything, excepting mathematical truths, but by metaphysics. We can have no proof, that is properly demonstrative, of any one proposition, relating to the being and nature of God, his creation of the world, the dependence of all things on him, the nature of bodies or spirits, the nature of our own souls, or any of the great truths of morality and natural religion, but what is metaphysical.

I am willing, my arguments should be brought to the test of the strictest and justest reason, and that a clear, distinct and determinate meaning of the terms I use, should be insisted on; but let not the whole be rejected, as if all were confuted, by fixing on it the epithet "metaphysical."

### Ar: *Calvinist metaphysical reasoning is abstruse and ambiguous.*

### JE: *The reasoning depends on no abstruse definitions or terms, nor abstruse speculation.*

II. If the reasoning which has been made use of, be in some sense metaphysical, it will not follow, that therefore it must needs be abstruse, unintelligible, and akin to the jargon of the schools. I humbly conceive, the foregoing reasoning, at least as to those things which are most material belonging to it, depends on no abstruse definitions or distinctions, or terms without a meaning, or of very ambiguous and undetermined signification, or any points of such abstraction and subtlety, as tend to involve the attentive understanding in clouds and darkness.

There is no high degree of refinement and abstruse speculation,

in determining,

that a thing is not before it is, and so can't be the cause of itself; or that the first act of free choice, has not another act of free choice going before that, to excite or direct it;

or in determining,

that no choice is made, while the mind remains in a state of absolute indifference; that preference and equilibrium never coexist; and that therefore no choice is made in a state of liberty, consisting in indifference: and that so far as the will is determined by motives, exhibited and operating previous to the act of the will, so far it is not determined by the act of the will itself; that nothing can begin to be, which before was not, without a cause, or some antecedent ground or reason, why it then begins to be; that effects depend on their causes, and are connected with them; that virtue is not the worse, nor sin the better, for the strength of inclination, with which it is practiced, and the difficulty which thence arises of doing otherwise; that when it is already infallibly known, that a thing will be, it is not a thing contingent whether it will ever be or no; or that it can be truly said, notwithstanding, that it is not necessary it should be, but it either may be, or may not be.

And the like might be observed of many other things which belong to the foregoing reasoning.

### Ar: *Calvinist reasoning is metaphysical sophistry, a seeming force of persuasion.*

If any shall still stand to it, that the foregoing reasoning is nothing but metaphysical sophistry; and that it must be so, that the seeming force of the arguments all depends on some fallacy and wile that is hid in the obscurity, which always attends a great degree of metaphysical abstraction and refinement; and shall be ready to say,

### Ar: *Calvinist reasoning tends to confound the mind, to blame or praise acts unconnected to volitions of men, to depend on abstract notions, and to insist irrational doctrines.*

"Here is indeed something that tends to confound the mind, but not to satisfy it: for who can ever be truly satisfied in it, that men are fitly blamed or commended, punished or rewarded, for those volitions which are not from themselves, and of whose existence they are not the causes. Men may refine, as much as they please, and advance their abstract notions, and make out a thousand seeming contradictions, to puzzle our understandings; yet there can be no satisfaction in such doctrine as this: the natural sense of the mind of man will always resist it."[2]

2. A certain noted author [Ramsey concludes the author is George Turnbull], of the present

***JE: My objectors have no humility and calmness of spirit, but a mere prejudice and inadvertent use of words.***

I humbly conceive, that such an objector, if he has capacity and humility and calmness of spirit, sufficient impartially and thoroughly to examine himself, will find that he knows not really what he would be at; and that indeed his difficulty is nothing but a mere prejudice, from an inadvertent customary use of words, in a meaning that is not clearly understood, nor carefully reflected upon. Let the objector reflect again, if he has candor and patience enough, and don't scorn to be at the trouble of close attention in the affair.

***Ar: A man's volition is from himself voluntarily; that is, it origins from his choice. If not so, why should he be blamed or praiseworthy?***

---

age, says, the arguments for *necessity* are nothing but "quibbling, or logomachy, using words without a meaning, or begging the question." I don't know what kind of necessity any authors he may have reference to, are advocates for; or whether they have managed their arguments well, or ill. As to the arguments I have made use of, if they are "quibbles," they may be shown to be so: such knots are capable of being untied, and the trick and cheat may be detected and plainly laid open. If this be fairly done, with respect to the grounds and reasons I have relied upon, I shall have just occasion for the future to be silent, if not to be ashamed of my argumentations. I am willing, ray proofs should be thoroughly examined; and if there be nothing but "begging the question," or mere "logomachy," or dispute of words, let it be made manifest, and shewn how the seeming strength of the argument depends on my "using words without a meaning," or arises from the ambiguity of terms, or my making use of words in an indeterminate and unsteady manner; and that the weight of my reasons rest mainly on such a foundation; and then, I shall either be ready to retract what I have urged, and thank the man that has done the kind part, or shall be justly exposed for my obstinacy.

The same author is abundant in appealing, in this affair, from what he calls "logomachy and sophistry," to "experience." A person can experience only what passes in his own mind. But yet, as we may well suppose, that all men have the same human faculties; so a man may well argue from his own experience to that of others, in things that the nature of those faculties, and the manner of their operation. But then one has as good right to allege his experience, as another. As to my own experience, I find, that in innumerable things I can do as I will; that the motions of my body, in many respects, instantaneously follow the acts of my will concerning those motions; and that my will has some command of my thoughts; and that the acts of my will are my own, i.e. that they are acts of my will, the volitions of my own mind; or in other words, that what I will, I will. Which, I presume, is the sum of what others experience in this affair. But as to finding by experience, that my will is originally determined by itself; or that my will first choosing what volition there shall be, the chosen volition accordingly follows; and that this is the first rise of the determination of my will in any affair; or that any volition arises in my mind contingently; I declare, I know nothing in myself, by experience, of this nature; and nothing that ever I experienced, carries the least appearance or shadow of any such thing, or gives me any more reason to suppose or suspect any such thing, than to suppose that my volitions existed twenty years before they existed. It is true, I find myself possessed of my volitions before I can see the effectual power of any cause to produce them (for the power and efficacy of the cause is not seen but by the effect) and this, for ought I know, may make some imagine, that volition has no cause, or that it produces itself. But I have no more reason from hence to determine any such thing, than I have to determine that I gave myself my own being, or that I came into being accidentally without a cause, because I first found myself possessed of being, before I had knowledge of a cause of my being.

### Part IV—Wherein the Chief Grounds of the Reasonings of Arminians

**JE: *The original and first choice are not from his choice; his following choice cannot be the cause of it. Thus, his evil is not of himself but his choice, and he must be blamed.***

He would have a man's volition be *from himself*. Let it be *from himself*, most primarily and originally of any way conceivable; that is, from his own choice: how will that help the matter, as to his being justly blamed or praised, unless that choice itself be blame or praiseworthy?

And how is the choice itself [an ill choice, for instance] blameworthy, according to these principles, unless that be from himself too, in the same manner; that is, from his own choice? But the original and first determining choice in the affair is not from his choice: his choice is not the cause of it. And if it be from himself some other way, and not from his choice, surely that will not help the matter: if it is not from himself of choice, then it is not from himself voluntarily; and if so, he is surely no more to blame, than if it were not from himself at all. It is a vanity, to pretend it is a sufficient answer to this, to say, that it is nothing but metaphysical refinement and subtlety, and so attended with obscurity and uncertainty.

**JE: *Even the natural sense of our minds admits that what is blameworthy in a man must be from himself, from something wrong in himself, a bad choice, or bad disposition. That is because it is evil.***

If it be the natural sense of our minds, that what is blameworthy in a man must be from himself, then it doubtless is also, that it must be from something bad in himself, a bad choice, or bad disposition. But then our natural sense is, that this bad choice or disposition is evil in itself, and the man blameworthy for it, on its own account, without taking into our notion of its blameworthiness, another bad choice, or disposition going before this, from whence this arises; for that is a ridiculous absurdity, running us into an immediate contradiction, which our natural sense of blameworthiness has nothing to do with, and never comes into the mind, nor is supposed in the judgment we naturally make of the affair.

**JE: *Our simple natural sense does not admit that moral evil is from the cause of our volitions and dispositions, but from our nature, but that a thing is from the choice of our will or heart, but not "from" us, and so it can be blameworthy. To say properly an evil thing is from an evil man is to signify that it is from his bad will or inclination.***

As was demonstrated before, natural sense doesn't place the moral evil of volitions and dispositions in the cause of them, but the nature of them. An evil thing's being FROM a man, or from something antecedent in him, is not essential to the original notion we have of blameworthiness: but it is its being the choice of the heart; as appears by this, that if a thing be "from" us, and not from our choice, it has not the nature of blameworthiness or ill desert, according to our natural sense. When a thing is *from* a man, in that sense, that it is from his will or choice, he is to blame for it, because his will is IN IT: so far as the will is *in it*, blame is *in it*, and no further. Neither do we go any further in our notion of blame, to inquire whether the bad will be "from" a bad will: there is no consideration of the original of that bad will; because according to our natural apprehension, blame *originally consists in it*.

**JE: *That a thing is from a man means that it is from our will or choice because we are in it, i.e., our will is in it.***

Therefore, a thing's being "from" a man, is a secondary consideration, in the notion of blame or ill-desert. Because those things in our *external* actions, are most properly said to be *from* us, which are *from* our choice; and no other *external* actions but those that are from us in this sense, have the nature of blame; and they indeed, not so properly because they are *from* us, as because we are *in them*, i.e. our wills are in them; not so much because they are from some *property* of ours, as because they are our *properties.*

**JE: *It is true that all external actions are from us, as their cause. But philosophers have incautiously used common sense and misapprehended acts of men and run into the dreadful confusion.***

However, all these external actions being truly *from us*, as their cause; and we being so used, in ordinary speech, and in the common affairs of life, to speak of men's actions and conduct that we see, and that affect human society, as deserving ill or well, as worthy of blame or praise; hence it is come to pass, that philosophers have incautiously taken all their measures of good and evil, praise and blame, from the dictates of common sense, about these *overt acts* of men; to the running of everything into the most lamentable and dreadful confusion. And therefore I observe,

**JE: *Arminianism misuses metaphysical terms and notions by depending on the plain dictates of common sense, and eventually it introduces a new strange liberty.***

III. It is so far from being true (whatever may be pretended) that the proof of the doctrine which has been maintained, depends on certain abstruse, unintelligible, metaphysical terms and notions; and that the Arminian scheme, without needing such clouds and darkness, for its defense, is supported by the plain dictates of common sense; that the very reverse is most certainly true, and that to a great degree. It is fact, that they, and not we, have confounded things with metaphysical, unintelligible notions and phrases, and have drawn them from the light of plain truth, into the gross darkness of abstruse metaphysical propositions, and words without a meaning. Their pretended demonstrations depend very much on such unintelligible, metaphysical phrases, as "self-determination" and "sovereignty of the will"; and the metaphysical sense they put on such terms, as "necessary," "contingency," "action," "agency," etc., quite diverse from their meaning as used in common speech; and which, as they use them, are without any consistent meaning, or any manner of distinct consistent ideas;

as far from it as any of the abstruse terms and perplexed phrases of the peripatetic philosophers[3], or the most unintelligible jargon of the schools, or the cant of the wildest fanatics.

Yea, we may be bold to say, these metaphysical terms, on which they build so much, are what they use without knowing what they mean themselves; they are pure metaphysical sounds, without any ideas whatsoever in their minds to answer them; inasmuch as it has been demonstrated, that there cannot be any notion in the mind consistent with these expressions, as they pretend to explain them; because their explanations destroy themselves.

No such notions as imply self-contradiction, and self-abolition, and this a great many ways, can subsist in the mind; as there can be no idea of a whole which is less than any of its parts, or of solid extension without dimensions, or of an effect which is before its cause. Arminians improve these terms, as terms of art, and in their metaphysical meaning, to advance and establish those things which are contrary to common sense, in a high degree.

*Ar: Liberty consists in indifference, contingency, and self-determination.*

*JE: Theirs is contrary to common sense, which places virtue and vice in bias and inclination.*

Thus, instead of the plain vulgar notion of liberty, which all mankind, in every part of the face of the earth, and in all ages, have; consisting in opportunity to do as one pleases; they have introduced a new strange liberty, consisting in indifference, contingence, and self-determination; by which they involve themselves and others in great obscurity, and manifold gross inconsistence. So, instead of placing virtue and vice, as common sense places them very much, in fixed bias and inclination, and greater virtue and vice in stronger and more established inclination; these, through their refinings and abstruse notions, suppose a liberty consisting in indifference, to be essential to all virtue and vice. So they have reasoned themselves, not by metaphysical distinctions, but metaphysical confusion, into many principles about moral agency, blame, praise, reward and punishment, which are, as has been shown, exceeding contrary to the common sense of mankind; and perhaps to their own sense, which governs them in common life.

---

3. [Aristotle founded his school at Athens in BC 335 called Lyceum, which had a cloister called "peripatetics" in which he walked and taught his disciples. So the "peripatetic philosophers" indicates Metaphysicians who adopted Aristotelian philosophy and arguments.]

# The Conclusion

*Edwards's Science of the Will Articulates Calvinist Soteriology, the So-Called "Five Points of Calvinism."*[1]

Whether the things which have been alleged, are liable to any tolerable answer in the ways of calm, intelligible and strict reasoning, I must leave others to judge: but I am sensible they are liable to one sort of answer.

*Weak Points of the Modern Fashionable Divinity*

It is not unlikely, that some who value themselves on the supposed rational and generous principles of the modern fashionable divinity, will have their indignation and disdain raised at the sight of this discourse, and on perceiving what things are pretended to be proved in it. And if they think it worthy of being read, or of so much notice as to say much about it, they may probably renew the usual exclamations, with additional vehemence and contempt, about the "fate of the heathen," "Hobbes' necessity," and "making men mere machines"; accumulating the terrible epithets of "fatal," "unfrustrable," "inevitable," "irresistible," etc. and it may be, with the addition of "horrid" and "blasphemous";

and perhaps much skill may be used to set forth things which have been said, in colors which shall be shocking to the imaginations, and moving to the passions of those who have either too little capacity, or too much confidence of the opinions they have imbibed, and contempt of the contrary, to try the matter by any serious and circumspect examination.[2]

---

1. [See "9. Edwards's Conclusion: 'Five Points of Calvinism,'" in Editor's Introduction.]

2. A writer of the present age, whom I have several times had occasion to mention, speaks once and again of those who hold the doctrine of *necessity*, as scarcely worthy of the name of "philosophers." I don't know, whether he has respect to any particular notion of necessity, that some may have maintained; and if so, what doctrine of necessity it is that he means. Whether I am worthy of the name of a philosopher, or not, would be a question little to the present purpose. If any, and ever so many, should deny it, I should not think it worth the while to enter into a dispute on that question; though at the same time I might expect, some better answer should be given to the arguments brought for the truth of the doctrine I maintain; and I might further reasonably desire, that it might be considered, whether it don't become those who are *truly worthy* of the name of philosophers, to be sensible, that there is a difference between *argument* and *contempt*; yea, and a difference between the contemptibleness of the

Or difficulties may be started and insisted on which don't belong to the controversy; because, let them be more or less real, and hard to be resolved, they are not what are owing to anything distinguishing of this scheme from that of the Arminians, and would not be removed nor diminished by renouncing the former, and adhering to the latter. Or some particular things may be picked out, which they may think will sound harshest in the ears of the generality; and these may be glossed and descanted on, with tart and contemptuous words; and from thence, the whole treated with triumph and insult.

***Summary of the Doctrine of Necessity, the main point of controversy between Calvinists and Arminians: whether the freedom of the will is necessary to a moral agency?***

It is easy to see how the decision of most of the points in controversy, between Calvinists and Arminians, depends on the determination of this grand article concerning *the freedom of the will requisite to moral agency*; and that by clearing and establishing the Calvinistic doctrine in this point, the chief arguments are obviated, by which Arminian doctrines in general are supported, and the contrary doctrines demonstratively confirmed.

***Ar: Is it inconsistent with that God makes men as the objects of his commands, counsels, calls, warnings, etc., while he determines and disposes of all events?***

Hereby it becomes manifest, that God's moral government over mankind, his treating them as moral agents, making them the objects of his commands, counsels, calls, warnings, expostulations, promises, threatenings, rewards and punishments, is not inconsistent with a determining disposal of all events, of every kind, throughout the universe, in his providence; either by positive efficiency, or permission.

***JE: The futurity of all events is infallibly determined by the moral necessity because they are related to morals.***

Indeed, such a *universal, determining providence*, infers some kind of necessity of all events; such a necessity as implies an infallible previous fixedness of the futurity of the event: but no other necessity of moral events, or volitions of intelligent agents, is needful in order to this, than *moral* necessity; which does as much ascertain the futurity of the event, as any other necessity. But, as has been demonstrated, such a necessity is not at all repugnant to moral agency, and the reasonable use of commands, calls, rewards, punishments, etc. Yea, not only are objections of this kind against the doctrine of a

---

*person* that argues, and the inconclusiveness of the *arguments* he offers.

[Ramsey, George Turnbull affirms that the error of that great genius Leibniz "consists in his saying most unphilosophically, that God could not do otherwise than he hath done"; he urges that "we keep to experience, and use words in a determinate, clear sense, as philosophers ought to do"; and he asserts that the inward feeling of freedom "is only called in question by some pretended philosophers" (*Christian Philosophy*, 38–39, 198).]

universal determining providence, removed by what has been said; but the truth of such a doctrine is demonstrated.

*JE: The sovereign Creator God determines all necessity of all beings and their circumstances.*

As it has been demonstrated, that the futurity of all future events is established by previous necessity, either natural or moral; so it is manifest, that the sovereign Creator and Disposer of the world has ordered this necessity, by ordering his own conduct, either in designedly acting, or forbearing to act. For, as the being of the world is from God, so the circumstances in which it had its being at first, both negative and positive, must be ordered by him, in one of these ways; and all the necessary consequences of these circumstances, must be ordered by him.

*JE: Even after God ordered all things, he still operates or interposes them, or forbears to do so.*

And God's active and positive interpositions, after the world was created, and the consequences of these interpositions; also every instance of his forbearing to interpose, and the sure consequences of this forbearance, must all be determined according to his pleasure. And therefore every event which is the consequence of anything whatsoever, or that is connected with any foregoing thing or circumstance, either positive or negative, as the ground or reason of its existence, must be ordered of God; either by a designed efficiency and interposition, or a designed forbearing to operate or interpose. But, as has been proved, all events whatsoever are necessarily connected with something foregoing, either positive or negative, which is the ground of its existence.

*Necessary Connection Chain: God's immediate conduct ⇨ something preceding ⇨ the whole series of events.*

It follows therefore, that the whole series of events is thus connected with something in the state of things, either positive or negative, which is original in the series; i.e. something which is connected with nothing preceding that, but God's own immediate conduct, either his acting or forbearing to act. From whence it follows, that as God designedly orders his own conduct, and its connected consequences, it must necessarily be, that he designedly orders all things.

The things which have been said, obviate some of the chief objections of Arminians against the Calvinistic doctrine of the *total depravity and corruption of man's nature*, whereby his heart is wholly under the power of sin, and he is utterly unable, without the interposition of sovereign grace, savingly to love God, believe in Christ, or do anything that is truly good and acceptable in God's sight. For the main objection against this doctrine is, that it is inconsistent with the freedom of man's will, consisting in indifference and self-determining power; because it supposes man to be under a necessity of sinning, and that God requires things of him, in order to his avoiding eternal damnation, which he is unable to do; and that this doctrine is wholly inconsistent with the sincerity of counsels, invitations, etc.

## The Five Points of Calvinism

### 1. "The total depravity and corruption of man's nature"

Now this doctrine supposes *no other necessity* of sinning, than a moral necessity; which, as has been shown, doesn't at all excuse sin; and supposes *no other inability* to obey any command, or perform any duty, even the most spiritual and exalted, but a moral inability, which, as has been proved, doesn't excuse persons in the nonperformance of any good thing, or make them not to be the proper objects of commands, counsels and invitations. And moreover, it has been shewn, that there is not, and never can be, either in existence, or so much as in idea, any such freedom of will, consisting in indifference and self-determination, for the sake of which, the doctrine of original sin is cast out; and that no such freedom is necessary, in order to the nature of sin, and a just desert of punishment.

### 2. *Efficacious grace is the same as irresistible grace.*

The things which have been observed, do also take off the main objections of Arminians against the doctrine of *efficacious grace*; and at the same time, prove the grace of God in a sinner's conversion (if there be any grace or divine influence in the affair) to be efficacious, yea, and *irresistible* too, if by irresistible is meant, that which is attended with a moral necessity, which it is impossible should ever be violated by any resistance.

The main objection of Arminians against this doctrine is, that it is inconsistent with their self-determining freedom of will; and that it is repugnant to the nature of virtue, that it should be wrought in the heart by the determining efficacy and power of another, instead of its being owing to a self-moving power; that in that case, the good which is wrought, would not be *our* virtue, but rather *God's* virtue; because it is not the person in whom it is wrought, that is the determining author of it, but God that wrought it in him. But the things which are the foundation of these objections, have been considered; and it has been demonstrated, that the liberty of moral agents does not consist in self-determining power; and that there is no need of any such liberty, in order to the nature of virtue; nor does it at all hinder, but that the state or act of the will may be the virtue of the subject, though it be not from self-determination, but the determination of an extrinsic cause; even so as to cause the event to be morally necessary to the subject of it. And as it has been proved, that nothing in the state or acts of the will of man is contingent; but that on the contrary, every event of this kind is necessary, by a moral necessity; and has also been now demonstrated, that the doctrine of a universal determining providence, follows from that doctrine of necessity, which was proved before: and so, that God does decisively, in his providence, order all the volitions of moral agents, either by positive influence or permission:

and it being allowed on all hands, that what God does in the affair of man's virtuous volitions, whether it be more or less, is by some positive influence, and not by mere permission, as in the affair of a sinful volition: if we put these things together, it will follow, that God's assistance or influence, must be determining and decisive, or must be attended with a moral necessity of the event; and so, that God gives virtue, holiness and conversion to sinners, by an influence which determines the effect, in such a manner, that the effect will infallibly follow by a moral necessity; which is what Calvinists mean by efficacious and irresistible grace.

### 3. Absolute, eternal, and personal election is the same as unconditional election.

The things which have been said, do likewise answer the chief objections against the doctrine of God's *universal* and *absolute decree*, and afford infallible proof of that doctrine; and of the doctrine of *absolute, eternal, personal election* in particular. The main objections against these doctrines are, that they infer a necessity of the volitions of moral agents, and of the future moral state and acts of men; and so are not consistent with those eternal rewards and punishments, which are connected with conversion and impenitence; nor can be made to agree with the reasonableness and sincerity of the precepts, calls, counsels, warnings and expostulations of the Word of God; or with the various methods and means of grace, which God uses with sinners, to bring them to repentance; and the whole of that moral government, which God exercises towards mankind: and that they infer an inconsistence between the *secret* and *revealed will* of God; and make God the author of sin.

But all these things have been obviated in the preceding discourse. And the certain truth of these doctrines, concerning God's eternal purposes, will follow from what was just now observed concerning God's universal providence; how it infallibly follows from what has been proved, that God orders all events, and the volitions of moral agents amongst others, by such a decisive disposal, that the events are infallibly connected with his disposal. For if God disposes all events, so that the infallible existence of the events is decided by his providence, then he doubtless thus orders and decides things *knowingly,* and *on design.* God doesn't do what he does, nor order what he orders, accidentally and unawares; either *without,* or *beside* his intention. And if there be a foregoing *design* of doing and ordering as he does, this is the same with a purpose or *decree.* And as it has been shown, that nothing is new to God, in any respect, but all things are perfectly and equally in his view from eternity; hence it will follow, that his designs or purposes are not things formed anew, founded on any new views or appearances, but are all eternal purposes.

And as it has been now shewn, how the doctrine of determining efficacious grace certainly follows from things proved in the foregoing discourse; hence will necessarily follow the doctrine of particular, eternal, absolute election. For if men are made true saints, no otherwise than as God makes them so, and distinguishes them from others, by an efficacious power and influence of his, that decides and fixes the event; and God thus makes some saints, and not others, on design or purpose, and (as has been now observed) no designs of God are new; it follows, that God thus distinguished from others, all that ever become true saints, by his eternal design or decree. I might also shew, how God's certain foreknowledge must suppose an absolute decree, and how such a decree can be proved to a demonstration from it: but that this discourse mayn't be lengthened out too much, that must be omitted for the present.

### 4. Die for All Yet Particular Redemption is equal to limited atonement.

From these things it will inevitably follow, that however Christ in some sense may be said to *die for all*, and to redeem all visible Christians, yea, the whole world by his death; yet there must be something *particular* in the design of his death, with respect to such as he intended should actually be saved thereby. As appears by what has been now shown, God has the actual salvation or redemption of a certain number in his proper absolute design, and of a certain number only; and therefore such a design only can be prosecuted in anything God does, in order to the salvation of men. God pursues a proper design of the salvation of the elect in giving Christ to die, and prosecutes such a design with respect to no other, most strictly speaking; for it is impossible, that God should prosecute any other design than only such as he has: he certainly doesn't, in the highest propriety and strictness of speech, pursue a design that he has not. And indeed such a particularity and limitation of redemption will as infallibly follow from the doctrine of God's foreknowledge, as from that of the decree. For it is as impossible, in strictness of speech, that God should prosecute a design or aim at a thing, which he at the same time most perfectly knows will not be accomplished, as that he should use endeavors for that which is beside his decree.

### 5. The infallible and necessary perseverance of saints is equal to the perseverance of the saints.

By the things which have been proved, are obviated some of the main objections against the doctrine of the infallible and necessary *perseverance* of saints, and some of the main foundations of this doctrine are established. The main prejudices of Arminians against this doctrine seem to be these; they suppose such a necessary, infallible perseverance to be repugnant to the freedom of the will;

that it must be owing to man's own self-determining power, that he *first becomes* virtuous and holy; and so in like manner, it must be left a thing contingent, to be determined by the same freedom of will, whether he will *persevere* in virtue and holiness; and that otherwise his continuing steadfast in faith and obedience would not be his virtue, or at all praiseworthy and rewardable; nor could his perseverance be properly the matter of divine commands, counsels and promises, nor his apostasy be properly threatened, and men warned against it.

Whereas we find all these things in Scripture: there we find steadfastness and perseverance in true Christianity, represented as the virtue of the saints, spoken of as praiseworthy in them, and glorious rewards promised to it; and also find, that God makes it the subject of his commands, counsels and promises; and the contrary, of threatenings and warnings. But the foundation of these objections has been removed, in its being shown that moral necessity and infallible certainty of events is not inconsistent with these things; and that, as to freedom of will lying in the power of the will to determine itself, there neither is any such thing, nor any need of it, in order to virtue, reward, commands, counsels, etc.

And as the doctrines of efficacious grace and absolute election do certainly follow from things which have been proved in the preceding discourse; so some of the main foundations of the doctrine of perseverance are thereby established. If the beginning of true faith and holiness, and a man's becoming a true saint at first, don't depend on the self-determining power of the will, but on the determining efficacious grace of God; it may well be argued, that it is so also with respect to men's being continued saints, or persevering in faith and holiness. The conversion of a sinner being not owing to a man's self-determination, but to God's determination, and eternal election, which is absolute, and depending on the sovereign will of God, and not on the free will of man; as is evident from what has been said: and it being very evident from the Scriptures, that the eternal election which there is of saints to faith and holiness, is also an election of them to eternal salvation; hence their appointment to salvation must also be absolute, and not depending on their contingent, self-determining will. From all which it follows, that it is absolutely fixed in God's decree, that all true saints shall persevere to actual eternal salvation.

### *The first Reformers and their successors were Calvinists.*

But I must leave all these things to the consideration of the fair and impartial reader; and when he has maturely weighed them, I would propose it to his consideration, whether many of the first Reformers, and others that succeeded them, whom God in their day made the chief pillars of his church, and greatest instruments of their deliverance from error and darkness, and of the support of the cause of piety among them, have not been injured, in the contempt with which they have been treated by many late writers, for their teaching and maintaining such doctrines as are commonly called Calvinistic.

### *JE: Some Arminians were contrary to common sense and misrepresented the doctrines of ancient and eminent divines.*

Indeed, some of these new writers, at the same time that they have represented the doctrines of these ancient and eminent divines, as in the highest degree ridiculous, and contrary to common sense, in an ostentation of a very generous charity, have allowed that they were honest well-meaning men: yea, it may be some of them, as though it were in great condescension and compassion to them, have allowed that they did pretty well for the day which they lived in, and considering the great disadvantages they labored under: when at the same time, their manner of speaking has naturally and plainly suggested to the minds of their readers, that they were persons, who through the lowness of their genius, and greatness of the bigotry, with which their minds were shackled, and thoughts confined, living in the gloomy caves of superstition, fondly embraced, and demurely and zealously taught the most absurd, silly and monstrous opinions, worthy of the greatest contempt of gentlemen possessed of that noble and generous freedom of thought, which happily prevails in this age of light and inquiry. When indeed such is the case, that we might, if so disposed, speak as big words as they, and on far better grounds. And really all the Arminians on earth might be challenged without arrogance or vanity, to make these principles of theirs wherein they mainly differ from their fathers, whom they so much despise, consistent with common sense; yea, and perhaps to produce any doctrine ever embraced by the blindest bigot of the church of Rome, or the most ignorant Mussulman, or extravagant enthusiast, that might be reduced to more, and more demonstrable inconsistencies, and repugnancies to common sense, and to themselves; though their inconsistencies indeed may not lie so deep, or be so artfully veiled by a deceitful ambiguity of words, and an indeterminate signification of phrases. I will not deny, that these gentlemen, many of them, are men of great abilities, and have been helped to higher attainments in philosophy, than those ancient divines, and have done great service to the church of God in some respects: but I humbly conceive, that their differing from their fathers with such magisterial assurance, in these points in divinity, must be owing to some other cause than superior wisdom.

### The Unhappy Change lately in many Protestant countries by exploding Calvinist Doctrines

It may also be worthy of consideration, whether the great alteration which has been made in the state of things in our nation, and some other parts of the Protestant world, in this and the past age, by the exploding so generally Calvinistic doctrines, that is so often spoken of as worthy to be greatly rejoiced in by the friends of truth, learning and virtue, as an instance of the great increase of light in the Christian Church; I say, it may be worthy to be considered, whether this be indeed a happy change, owing to any such cause as an increase of true knowledge and understanding in things of religion; or whether there is no reason to fear, that it may be owing to some worse cause.

### JE: Extreme Arminians condemn God as an irrational being who ignores reason and interpret the Bible in an irrational way.

And I desire it may be considered, whether the boldness of some writers may not be worthy to be reflected on, who have not scrupled to say, that if these and those things are true (which yet appear to be the demonstrable dictates of reason, as well as the certain dictates of the mouth of the Most High) then God is unjust and cruel, and guilty of manifest deceit and double-dealing, and the like. Yea, some have gone so far, as confidently to assert, that if any book which pretends to be Scripture, teaches such doctrines, that alone is sufficient warrant for mankind to reject it, as what cannot be the Word of God. Some who have not gone so far, have said, that if the Scripture seems to teach any such doctrines, so contrary to reason, we are obliged to find out some other interpretation of those texts, where such doctrines seem to be exhibited.

**JE: There are moderate Arminians who admit the moral government of God, accept biblical doctrines, and acknowledge the infallibility of our decisions.**

Others express themselves yet more modestly: they express a tenderness and religious fear, lest they should receive and teach anything that should seem to reflect on God's moral character, or be a disparagement to his methods of administration, in his moral government; and therefore express themselves as not daring to embrace some doctrines, though they seem to be delivered in Scripture, according to the more obvious and natural construction of the words. But indeed it would show a truer modesty and humility, if they would more entirely rely on God's wisdom and discerning, who knows infinitely better than we, what is agreeable to his own perfections, and never intended to leave these matters to the decision of the wisdom and discerning of men; but by his own unerring instruction, to determine for us what the truth is; knowing how little our judgment is to be depended on, and how extremely prone, vain and blind men are, to err in such matters.

**JE: The greatest difficulty of Arminians is the fact that Calvinist doctrines, which they oppose, are supported by the Scriptures and also are agreeable to the most natural dictates of reason.**

The truth of the case is, that if the Scripture plainly taught the opposite doctrines, to those that are so much stumbled at, viz. the Arminian doctrine of Free Will, and others depending thereon, it would be the greatest of all difficulties that attend the Scriptures, incomparably greater than its containing any, even the most mysterious of those doctrines of the first Reformers, which our late Free-thinkers[3] have so superciliously exploded. Indeed, it is a glorious argument of the divinity of the holy Scriptures, that they teach such doctrines, which in one age and another, through the blindness of men's minds, and strong prejudices of their hearts, are rejected, as most absurd and unreasonable, by the wise and great men of the world; which yet, when they are most carefully and strictly examined, appear to be exactly agreeable to the most demonstrable, certain, and natural dictates of reason. By such things it

---

3. [There was a "Free-Thinking" sect in 18th century England and its scheme. Anthony Collins was a representative of "Free Thinker[s]." He meant by "Free-thinking" that "The Use of the Understanding, in endeavoring to find out the Meaning of any Proposition whatsoever, in considering the nature of the Evidence for or against it, and in judging of it according to the seeming Force or Weakness of the Evidence." In his view "Freethinking" was a right and the only means of attaining knowledge of truth. In England this essay was then assessed as a plea for deism. Anthony Collins, *A Discourse of Free-thinking, occasion'd by the Rise and Growth of a Sect call'd Free-Thinkers* (London, 1713).]

appears, that the "foolishness of God is wiser than men," and God does as is said in I Corinthians 1:19–20,

> "For it is written, I will destroy the wisdom of the wise; I will bring to nothing the understanding of the prudent. Where is the wise! Where is the Scribe! Where is the disputer of this world! Hath not God made foolish the wisdom of this world?"

And as it used to be in time past, so it is probable it will be in time to come, as it is there written, in vv. 27–29,

> "But God hath chosen the foolish things of the world, to confound the wise: and God hath chosen the weak things of the world, to confound the things that are mighty: and base things of the world, and things which are despised, hath God chosen: yea, and things which are not, to bring to naught things that are; that no flesh should glory in his presence." Amen.

# Appendix 1

(Edwards's) Remarks on the "Essays on the Principles of Morality and Natural Religion (by Henry Home, Lord Kames, 1751)," in a Letter to a Minister of the Church of Scotland [1]

Stockbridge, July 25, 1757

Rev. Sir,

The intimations you have given me of the use which has, by some, been made of what I have written on the Freedom of the Will, etc. to vindicate what is said on the subject of liberty and necessity by the author of the *Essays on the Principles of Morality and Natural Religion*, has occasioned my reading this author's *Essay* on that subject, with particular care and attention. And I think it must be evident to everyone, that has read both his *Essay* and my *Inquiry*, that our schemes are exceeding reverse from each other. The wide difference appears particularly in the following things.

*Kames: The necessity and liberty are contrary to each other. Edwards: Man is free, and so necessity is consistent with liberty.*

This author supposes, that such a necessity takes place with respect to all men's actions, as is inconsistent with liberty,[2] and plainly denies that men have any liberty in

---

1. [*Essays on the Principles of Morality and Natural Religion* was published as a single volume in Boston in 1754(1st), 1762(2nd and reprinted in London), 1768(3rd and as an appendix to the 3rd edition of *FOW*), and 1775(4th). Besides, there were some other objections against Kames' *Essays*, such as Phileleutherus, *A Letter to a friend, upon occasion of a late book, intitled, Essays on the Principles of Morality and Natural Religion* (Edinburgh, 1751); George Anderson's *An estimate of the profit and loss of religion personally and publically stated: illustrated with references to Essays on the Principles of Morality and Natural Religion* (Edinburgh, 1753) "*The complaint made to the presbytery of Edinburgh verified*," (Edinburgh, 1756); Hugh Blair's *Objections Against the Essays on Morality and Natural Religion Examined* (Edinburgh, 1756).]

2. [Anonymous (Henry Home, Lord Kames), *Essays on the Principles of Morality and Natural*

Appendix 1

acting. Thus in p. 168 after he had been speaking of the necessity of our determinations, as connected with motives, he concludes with saying,

> "In short, if motives are not under our power or direction, which is confessedly the fact, we can at bottom have — *no liberty*."

Whereas I have abundantly expressed it as my mind, that man, in his moral actions, has true liberty; and that the moral necessity which universally takes place, is not in the least inconsistent with anything that is properly called liberty, and with the utmost liberty that can be desired, or that can possibly exist or be conceived of.[3]

### JE: I allow a sort of liberty, yet ARs hold a higher sort of freedom than I do.

I find that some are apt to think, that in that kind of moral necessity of men's volitions, which I suppose to be universal, at least some degree of liberty is denied; that though it be true I allow a sort of liberty, yet those who maintain a self-determining power in the will, and a liberty of contingence and indifference, hold an higher sort of freedom than I do: but I think this is certainly a great mistake.

### JE's Notion of Liberty: All men have freedom, by which they do as they please, or which is a power to do so.

Liberty, as I have explained it, in p. 38[4] and other places, is

> "the power, opportunity, or advantage that anyone has to do as he pleases," or
> "conducting, *in any respect*, according to his pleasure";

without considering how his pleasure comes to be as it is. It is demonstrable, and I think has been demonstrated, that no necessity of men's volitions that I maintain, is inconsistent with this liberty: and I think it is impossible for anyone to rise higher in his conceptions of liberty than this:

### Abnormal Notion of Liberty: a higher and greater liberty than one that a man has of conducting in any respect as he pleases, viz. a l freedom of choosing as he pleases.

if any imagine they desire higher, and that they conceive of a higher and greater liberty than this, they are deceived, and delude themselves with confused ambiguous words, instead of ideas. If anyone should here say,

> "Yes, I conceive of a freedom above and beyond the liberty a man has of conducting in any respect as he pleases, viz. a liberty of *choosing* as he pleases":

---

*Religion* (1st ed. Edinburgh, March, 1751), 160, 161, 164, 165, etc. Confuted by objections like above, Kames made the changes in the second and third editions of 1758, and in the fourth one 1779, for that one shall see his own prefaces.]

3. [*FOW*, 163–66, 272–73, 343–49, 358–9, 363, 377–83.]

4. [JE or the first editor (1754)'s "38" is mispaginated "27." See "Pt. I, St. 5, Concerning the Notion of Liberty and of Moral Agent," *FOW*, 163.]

such an one, if he reflected, would either blush or laugh at his own instance. For, is not choosing as he pleases, conducting, *in some respect*, according to his pleasure, and still without determining how he came by that pleasure? If he says,

> "Yes, I came by that pleasure by my own choice":

if he be a man of common sense, by this time he will see his own absurdity: for he must needs see that his notion or conception, even of this liberty, doesn't contain any judgment or conception how he comes by that choice, which first determines his pleasure, or which originally fixed his own will respecting the affair.
Or if any shall say, that

> "a man exercises liberty in this, even in determining his own choice, but not as he pleases, or not in consequence of any choice, preference, or inclination of his own, but by a determination arising contingently out of a state of absolute indifference";

this is not rising higher in his conception of liberty: as such a determination of the will would not be a voluntary determination of it.

### Ar: Extreme Notion of Liberty: Doing as he pleases, or acting from his election.

### JE: The Normal Concept of Freedom: Power of doing something not according to his choice, or from his choosing.

Surely he that places liberty in a power of doing something not according to his own choice, or from his choice, has not a higher notion of it, than he that places it in doing as he pleases, or acting from his own election. If there were a power in the mind to determine itself, but not by its choice or according to its pleasure, what advantage would it give? And what liberty, worth contending for, would be exercised in it?

### JE: Arminian, Pelagian, or Epicurean conceptions of liberty is impossible to be higher than JE holds.

Therefore, no Arminian, Pelagian, or Epicurean, can rise higher in his conceptions of liberty, than the notion of it which I have explained: which notion is, apparently, perfectly consistent with the whole of that necessity of men's actions, which I suppose takes place. And I scruple not to say it is beyond all their wits to invent a higher notion, or form a higher imagination of liberty; let them talk of sovereignty of the will, self-determining power, self-motion, self-direction, arbitrary decision, liberty *ad utrumvis*, power of choosing differently in given cases, etc., etc. as long as they will. It is apparent that these men, in their strenuous affirmation, and dispute about these things, aim at they know not what, fighting for something they have no conception of, substituting a number of confused unmeaning words, instead of things, and instead of thoughts. They may be challenged clearly to explain what they would have: they never can answer the challenge.

### Appendix 1

***Liberty of Kames, the Author of the Essays: Real liberty is a freedom that is opposed to moral necessity, and is an acting without and against motives, any view, purpose, etc.***

The author of the *Essays*, through his whole "Essay on Liberty and Necessity," goes on that supposition, that, in order to the being of real liberty, a man must have a freedom that is opposed to moral necessity: and yet he supposes (p. 175) that

> such a liberty "must signify a power in the mind of acting without and against motives, a power of acting without any view, purpose or design, and even of acting in contradiction to our own desires and aversions, and to all our principles of action"; and is "an absurdity altogether inconsistent with a rational nature."

Now whoever imagined such a liberty as this, a higher sort or degree of freedom, than a liberty of following one's own views and purposes, and acting agreeable to his own inclinations and passions? Who will ever reasonably suppose that liberty, which is an absurdity altogether inconsistent with a rational nature, to be a kind of liberty above that which is consistent with the nature of a rational intelligent designing agent.

***LK: Necessity is a "power of arbitrary choice," and a way of our actions being performed in our power, from ourselves, or dependent on ourselves.***

The author of the *Essays* seems to suppose such a necessity to take place, as is inconsistent with some supposable "power of arbitrary choice";[5] or that there is some liberty conceivable, whereby men's own actions might be more "properly in their power,"[6] and by which events might be more "dependent on ourselves":[7] contrary to what I suppose to be evident, in my *Inquiry*.[8]

What way can be imagined, of our actions being more *in our power, from ourselves*, or *dependent on ourselves*, than their being from our power to fulfill our own choice, to act from our own inclination, pursue our own views, and execute our own designs?

Certainly, to be able to act thus, is as properly having our actions in our power, and dependent on ourselves, as a being liable to be the subjects of acts and events, contingently and fortuitously, "without desire, view, purpose or design, or any principle of action" within ourselves; as we must be, according to this author's own declared sense, if our actions are performed with that liberty that is opposed to moral necessity.

***LK: A Necessary Action: It is unavoidably occasioned by the prevailing motive, in which our actions lie, and it is impossible for us to act otherwise.***

---

5. *Essays*, 169.
6. *Essays*, 191, 185, 197, 206.
7. *Essays*, 183,
8. See above, pp. 426–8.

This author seems everywhere to suppose, that necessity, most properly so called, attends all men's actions; and that the terms "necessary," "unavoidable," "impossible," etc. are equally applicable to the case of moral and natural necessity.

In p. 173, he says, "The idea of *necessary* and *unavoidable* equally agrees, both to moral and physical necessity." And in p. 184, "All things that fall out in the natural and moral world are alike necessary." P. 174: "This inclination and choice is *unavoidably* caused or occasioned by the prevailing motive. In this lies the necessity of our actions, that in such circumstances it was *impossible* we *could* act otherwise."

He often expresses himself in like manner elsewhere, speaking in strong terms of men's actions as "unavoidable," what they "cannot" forbear, having "no power" over their own actions, the order of them being "unalterably" fixed, and "inseparably" linked together, etc.[9]

***JE: LK's necessity is fatalistic, but the actual one in the acts of men's wills can be called connection or certainty between antecedent things and the following ones.***

On the contrary, I have largely declared, that the connection between antecedent things and consequent ones, which takes place with regard to the acts of men's wills, which is called moral necessity, is called by the name of "necessity" improperly; and that all such terms as "must," "cannot," "impossible," "unable," "irresistible," "unavoidable," "invincible," etc. when applied here, are not applied in their proper signification, and are either used nonsensically, and with perfect insignificance, or in a sense quite diverse from their original and proper meaning, and their use in common speech:[10] and that such a necessity as attends the acts of men's wills, is more properly called "certainty," than "necessity"; it being no other than the certain connection between the subject and predicate of the proposition which affirms their existence.[11]

***JE: Arminian misconception of necessity: It impedes our liberty like an immovable mountain of brass.***

Agreeable to what is observed in my *Inquiry*, I think it is evidently owing to a strong prejudice in persons' minds, arising from an insensible habitual perversion and misapplication of such like terms, as "necessary," "impossible," "unable," "unavoidable," "invincible," etc. that they are ready to think, that to suppose a certain connection of men's volitions without any foregoing motives or inclinations, or any preceding moral influence whatsoever, is truly and properly to suppose such a strong irrefragable chain of causes and effects, as stands in the way of, and makes utterly vain, opposite desires and endeavors, like immovable and impenetrable mountains of brass; and impedes our liberty like walls of adamant, gates of brass, and bars of iron: whereas all such representations suggest ideas as far from the truth, as the east is from the west.

9. *Essays*, 180, 188, 193, 194, 195, 197, 198, 199, 205, 206.
10. *Inquiry*, 149–55, 158–62, 308, 350–53, 355–56, 361–64, 428–29.
11. *Inquiry*, 351–3.

### JE: Arminian misconception of necessity: Calvinist necessity is like a fatalism; men cannot act freely.

Nothing that I maintain, supposes that men are at all hindered by any fatal necessity, from doing, and even willing and choosing as they please, with full freedom; yea, with the highest degree of liberty that ever was thought of, or that ever could possibly enter into the heart of any man to conceive. I know it is in vain to endeavor to make some persons believe this, or at least fully and steadily to believe it: for if it be demonstrated to them, still the old prejudice remains, which has been long fixed by the use of the terms "necessary," "must," "cannot," "impossible," etc.: the association with these terms of certain ideas inconsistent with liberty, is not broken; and the judgment is powerfully warped by it; as a thing that has been long bent and grown stiff, if it be straightened, will return to its former curvity again and again.

### JE: LK rather insists fatalistic necessity, for which men are not responsible for their actions.

The author of the *Essays* most manifestly supposes, that if men had the truth concerning the real necessity of all their actions clearly in view, they would not appear to themselves, or one another, as at all praiseworthy or culpable, or under any moral obligation, or accountable for their actions:[12]

which supposes, that men are not to be blamed or praised for any of their actions, and are not under any obligations, nor are truly accountable for anything they do, by reason of this necessity; which is very contrary to what I have endeavored to prove, throughout the third Part of my *Inquiry*.

### LK: True liberty is the liberty of indifference and contingence; men act without any principles or motives.

I humbly conceive it is there shown, that this is so far from the truth, that the moral necessity of men's actions, which truly take place, is requisite to the being of virtue and vice, or anything praiseworthy or culpable: that the liberty of indifference and contingence,[13] which is advanced in opposition to that necessity, is inconsistent with the being of these; as it would suppose that men are not determined in what they do, by any virtuous or vicious principles, nor act from any motives, intentions or aims whatsoever; or have any end, either good or bad, in acting. And is it not remarkable, that this author should suppose, that, in order to men's actions truly having any desert, they must be performed "without any view, purpose, design, or desire," or "any principle of action," or anything "agreeable to a rational nature"? As it will appear that he does, if we compare, pp. 206, 207, with p. 175.

---

12. *Essays*, 207, 209, and other places.
13. *Inquiry*, pp. 151–3.

**LK: *God has deeply implanted in man's nature, a strong and invincible apprehension, or feeling. But they are deceitful; they make men believe they are free, when they are not.***

The author of the *Essays* supposes, that God has deeply implanted in man's nature, a strong and invincible apprehension, or feeling, as he calls it, of a liberty, and contingence of his own actions, opposite to that necessity which truly attends them; and which in truth doesn't agree with real fact,[14] is not agreeable to strict philosophic truth,[15] is contradictory to the truth of things,[16] and which truth contradicts,[17] not tallying with the real plan:[18] and that therefore such feelings are deceitful,[19] are in reality of the delusive kind.[20] He speaks of them as a wise delusion,[21] as nice artificial feelings, merely that conscience may have a commanding power:[22] meaning plainly, that these feelings are a cunning artifice of the Author of nature, to make men believe they are free, when they are not.[23] He supposes that by these feelings the moral world has a disguised appearance.[24] And other things of this kind he says. He supposes that all self-approbation, and all remorse of conscience, all commendation or condemnation of ourselves or others, all sense of desert, and all that is connected with this way of thinking, all the ideas, which at present are suggested by the words "ought," "should," arise from this delusion, and would entirely vanish without it.[25]

**JE: *Common sense of necessity and liberty: the moral necessity in men's actions is consistent with reward and punishment.***

All which is very contrary to what I have abundantly insisted on and endeavored to demonstrate in my *Inquiry*; where I have largely shown, that it is agreeable to the natural sense of mankind, that the moral necessity or certainty that attends men's actions, is consistent with praise and blame, reward and punishment;[26] and that it is agreeable to our natural notions, that moral evil, with its desert of dislike and abhorrence, and all its other ill-deservings, consists in a certain deformity in the nature of

---

14. *Inquiry*, 200.
15. *Inquiry*, 152.
16. *Inquiry*, 183.
17. *Inquiry*, 186.
18. *Inquiry*, 205.
19. *Inquiry*, 203, 204, 211.
20. *Inquiry*, 183.
21. *Inquiry*, 209.
22. *Inquiry*, 211.
23. *Inquiry*, 153.
24. *Inquiry*, 214.
25. *Inquiry*, 160, 194, 199, 205, 206, 207, 209.
26. *Inquiry*, see above, pt. IV, sec. 4, throughout.

the dispositions and acts of the heart, and not in the evil of something else, diverse from these, supposed to be their cause or occasion.[27]

### JE's Objecting Questions 1:

*Do men act without any motive, desire, or principle of action?*

*Do they have a sense or feeling of that?*

*Do they act well like that and is it more praiseworthy?*

I might well ask here, whether anyone is to be found in the world of mankind, who is conscious to a sense or feeling, naturally and deeply rooted in his mind, that, in order to a man's performing any action that is praise or blameworthy, he must exercise a liberty that implies and signifies a power of acting without any motive, view, design, desire, or principle of action? For such a liberty this author supposes that must be which is opposed to moral necessity, as I have already observed once and again. Supposing a man should actually do good, independent of desire, aim, inducement, principle or end, is it a dictate of invincible natural sense, that his act is more meritorious or praiseworthy than if he had performed it for some good end, and had been governed in it by good principles and motives? And so I might ask, on the contrary, with respect to evil actions.[28]

### JE's Questions 2: What do natural men answer to the liberty without necessity? "Contingence/chance." Then they ask, What was their intention, what did influence them, and how far are they justified or condemned?

The author of the *Essays* supposes that the liberty without necessity which we have a natural feeling of, implies *contingence*: and speaking of this contingence, he sometimes calls it by the name of "chance." And it is evident, that his notion of it, or rather what he says about it, implies things happening "loosely," "fortuitously," by "accident," and "without a cause."[29]

Now I conceive the slightest reflection may be sufficient to satisfy anyone, that such a contingence of men's actions, according to our natural sense, is so far from being essential to the morality or merit of those actions, that it would destroy it; and that, on the contrary, the dependence of our actions on such causes, as inward inclinations, incitements and ends, is essential to the being of it. Natural sense teaches men, when they see anything done by others of a good or evil tendency, to inquire what their intention was; what principles and views they were moved by, in order to judge how far they are to be justified or condemned; and not to determine, that, in order to their being approved or blamed at all, the action must be performed altogether fortuitously,

---

27. *Essays*, Sec. 1, throughout, and 426–8.
28. See this matter illustrated in ibid., sec. 4, esp. 360–62.
29. *Essays*, 156, 157, 158, 159, 177, 178, 181, 183, 184, 185.

proceeding from nothing, arising from no cause. Concerning this matter, I have fully expressed my mind in the *Inquiry*.[30]

**LK: The liberty is essential to men's morality or demerit, then indifference is essential to the former. JE: Natural men have no notion of such liberty; that is very contrary to natural sense.**

If the liberty which we have a natural sense of as necessary to desert, consists in the mind's self-determination, without being determined by previous inclination or motive, then indifference is essential to it, yea, absolute indifference; as is observed in my *Inquiry*.[31] But men naturally have no notion of any such liberty as this, as essential to the morality or demerit of their actions; but, on the contrary, such a liberty, if it were possible, would be inconsistent with our natural notions of desert, as is largely shown in the *Inquiry*.[32] If it be agreeable to natural sense, that men must be indifferent in determining their own actions; then, according to the same, the more they are determined by inclination, either good or bad, the less they have of desert: the more good actions are performed from good dispositions, the less praiseworthy; and the more evil deeds are from evil dispositions, the less culpable; and in general, the more men's actions are from their hearts, the less they are to be commended or condemned: which all must know is very contrary to natural sense.

**JE: Moral necessity is to be given by the inclination of the heart, excited by motive.**

Moral necessity is owing to the power and government of the inclination of the heart, either habitual or occasional, excited by motive; but, according to natural and common sense, the more a man does anything with full inclination of heart, the more is it to be charged to his account for his condemnation, if it be an ill action, and the more to be ascribed to him for his praise, if it be good.

**LK: Three Notions of Liberty: 1) Actions are determined by contingence, in indifference; 2) This indifference is liberty; 3) Indifference to good and evil is fault.**

**JE: Such a liberty, as essential, is inconsistent.**

If the mind were determined to evil actions by contingence, from a state of indifference, then either there would be no fault in them, or else the fault would be in being so perfectly indifferent, that the mind was equally liable to a bad or good determination. And if this indifference be liberty, then the very essence of the blame or fault would lie in the liberty itself, or the wickedness would, primarily and summarily, lie in being a free agent.

If there were no fault in being indifferent, then there would be no fault in the determination's being agreeable to such a state of indifference: that is, there could no

---

30. See above, 326–28, 332–33, 360–61, and other places.
31. *Essays*, 203–05.
32. *Essays*, esp. in pt. III, secs. 6 and 7.

fault be reasonably found with this, viz. that opposite determinations actually happen to take place *indifferently*, sometimes good and sometimes bad, as contingence governs and decides.

And if it be a fault to be indifferent to good and evil, then such indifference is no indifference to good and evil, but is a determination to evil, or to a fault; and such an indifferent disposition would be an evil, faulty disposition, tendency or determination of mind. So inconsistent are these notions of liberty, as essential to praise or blame.

**LK: Men's natural delusive sense of liberty makes them put all their labor, care and industry, and also one of necessity does make them inactive and hopeless.**

The author of the *Essays* supposes men's natural delusive sense of a liberty of contingence to be, in truth, the foundation of all the labor, care and industry of mankind;[33]

> and that if men's "practical ideas had been formed on the plan of universal necessity, the *ignava ratio*, the inactive doctrine of the Stoics, would have followed"; and that "there would have been no *room* for forethought about futurity, or any sort of industry and care":[34]

plainly implying, that, in this case, men would see and know that all their industry and care signified nothing, was in vain, and to no purpose, or of no benefit; events being fixed in an irrefragable chain, and not at all *depending* on their care and endeavor; as he explains himself, particularly, in the instance of men's use of means to prolong life:[35]

**JE: LK superficially seems to agree, but he is fundamentally opposite to me.**

not only very contrary to what I largely maintain in my *Inquiry*,[36] but also very inconsistently with his own scheme, in what he supposes of the ends for which God has so deeply implanted this deceitful feeling in man's nature; in which he manifestly supposes men's care and industry not to be in vain and of no benefit, but of great use, yea, of absolute necessity, in order to the obtaining the most important ends and necessary purposes of human life, and to fulfill the ends of action to the "best advantage"; as he largely declares.[37]

**JE: Like LK says, don't men need their effort? The great wisdom and goodness of God prompts them to pour out all their care and industry for their good, and he receives his glory from them.**

Now, how shall these things be reconciled? That, if men had "a clear view of real truth," they would see that there was "no room" for their care and industry, because they

33. *Essays*, 184.
34. *Essays*, 189.
35. *Essays*, 184, 185.
36. *Inquiry*, esp. pt. IV, sec. 5.
37. *Essays*, 188–92, and in many other places.

would see it to be in vain, and of no benefit; and yet that God, by having a clear view of real truth, sees that their being excited to care and industry, will be of excellent use to mankind, and greatly for the benefit of the world, yea, absolutely necessary in order to it: and that therefore the great wisdom and goodness of God to men appears, in artfully contriving to put them on care and industry for their good, which good could not be obtained without them; and yet both these things are maintained at once, and in the same sentences and words by this author.

### LK: Why has God put a deceitful feeling into men?

The very reason he gives, why God has put this deceitful feeling into men, contradicts and destroys itself; that God in his great goodness to men gave them such a deceitful feeling, because it was very useful and necessary for them, and greatly for their benefit, or excites them to care and industry for their own good, which care and industry is useful and necessary to that end: and yet the very thing that this great benefit of care and industry is given as a reason for, is God's deceiving men in this very point, in making them think their care and industry to be of great benefit to them, when indeed it is of none at all; and if they saw the real truth, they would see all their endeavors to be wholly useless, that there was "no room" for them, and that the event doesn't at all depend upon them.[38]

And besides, what this author says, plainly implies (as appears by what has been already observed) that it is necessary men should be deceived, by being made to believe that future events are contingent, and their own future actions free, with such a freedom, as signifies that their actions are not the fruit of their own desires, or designs, but altogether contingent, fortuitous and without a cause.

### LK: Everything is contingent or accidental, and man is free. This kind of freedom encourages effort. It is arbitrary and independent without connection between the action and desire and purpose and liberty.

But how should a notion of liberty, consisting in accident or loose chance, encourage care and industry? I should think it would rather entirely discourage everything of this nature. For surely, if our actions don't depend on our desires and designs, then they don't depend on our endeavors, flowing from our desires and designs. This author himself seems to suppose, that if men had indeed such a liberty of contingence, it would render all endeavors to determine or move men's future volitions, in vain: he says, that, in this case, "to exhort, to instruct, to promise, or to threaten, would be to no purpose."[39] Why? Because (as he himself gives the reason) then our will would be "capricious and arbitrary," and we should "be thrown loose altogether," and our arbitrary power could do us good or ill only "by accident."[40] But if such a loose fortuitous

38. *Essays*, 188, 189, etc.
39. *Essays*, 178, 213, 214.
40. *Essays*, 177–78.

state would render vain others' endeavors upon us, for the same reason would it make useless our endeavors on ourselves: for events that are truly contingent and accidental, and altogether loose from and independent of all foregoing causes, are independent on every foregoing cause within ourselves, as well as in others.

**LK: *In our minds are the notion planted by birth, and it can't be erased.***

**JE: *Such a liberty and its notion do not exist.***

I suppose that it is so far from being true, that our minds are naturally possessed with a notion of such liberty as this, so strongly, that it is impossible to root it out, that indeed men have no such notion of liberty at all, and that it is utterly impossible, by any means whatsoever, to implant or introduce such a notion into the mind. As no such notions as imply self-contradiction and self-abolition can subsist in the mind, as I have shown in my *Inquiry*;[41]

**JE: *Such a notion can be rejected even by Arminians if they are mature thinkers.***

I think a mature sensible consideration of the matter, sufficient to satisfy anyone, that even the greatest and most learned advocates themselves for liberty of indifference and self-determination, have no such notion; and that indeed they mean something wholly inconsistent with, and directly subversive of what they strenuously affirm, and earnestly contend for.

**LK: *Humans will have his self-determining power. His mind has a choice and causes his first choice.***

**JE: *I hold a conventional notion of liberty: Men choose an act, i.e., they choose or determine an act according to the preceding inclination or cause.***

By a man's having a power of determining his own will, they plainly mean a power of determining his will, as he pleases, or as he chooses; which supposes that the mind has a choice, prior to its going about to conform any action or determination to it. And if they mean that they determine even the original or prime choice, by their own pleasure or choice, as the thing that causes and directs it; I scruple not most boldly to affirm, that they speak they know not what, and that of which they have no manner of idea; because no such contradictory notion can come into, or have a moment's subsistence in the mind of any man living, as an original or first choice being caused, or brought into being, by choice. After all they say, they have no higher or other conception of liberty, than that vulgar notion of it, which I contend for, viz. a man's having power or opportunity to do as he chooses: or if they had a notion that every act of choice was determined by choice, yet it would destroy their notion of the contingence of choice; for then no one act of choice would arise contingently, or from a state of indifference, but every individual act, in all the series, would arise from foregoing

---

41. *Inquiry*, see above, 325–26. See also 174, 179, 190–91, 196, 270–73, 345–46, 357–60.

bias or preference, and from a cause predetermining and fixing its existence, which introduces at once such a chain of causes and effects, each preceding link decisively fixing the following, as they would by all means avoid.

***JE: The ground of Armenians' confusion and inconsistency: It does not arise from their mind or natural feeling, but from their false philosophy and prejudice.***

And such kind of delusion and self-contradiction as this don't arise in men's minds by nature: it is not owing to any natural feeling which God has strongly fixed in the mind and nature of man; but to false philosophy, and strong prejudice, from a deceitful abuse of words. It is "artificial"; not in the sense of the author of the *Essays*, supposing it to be a deceitful artifice of God; but artificial as opposed to natural, and as owing to an artificial deceitful management of terms, to darken and confound the mind. Men have no such thing when they first begin to exercise reason; but must have a great deal of time to blind themselves with metaphysical confusion, before they can embrace, and rest in such definitions of liberty as are given, and imagine they understand them.

***Three Points in JE's Freedom of the Will: (1) Moral necessity is consistent with human liberty; (2) It is so with praise and blame, and it answers the ground of human actions; (3) It establishes a moral system of the universe and moral government of God.***

On the whole, I humbly conceive, that whosoever will give himself the trouble of weighing, what I have offered to consideration in my *Inquiry*, must be sensible,

[(1)] that such a moral necessity of men's actions as I maintain, is not at all inconsistent with any liberty that any creature has, or can have, as a free, accountable, moral agent, and subject of moral government; and

[(2)] that this moral necessity is so far from being inconsistent with praise and blame, and the benefit and use of men's own care and labor, that on the contrary it implies the very ground and reason, why men's actions are to be ascribed to them as their own, in that manner as to infer desert, praise and blame, approbation and remorse of conscience, reward and punishment; and

[(3)] that it establishes the moral system of the universe, and God's moral government, in every respect, with the proper use of motives, exhortations, commands, counsels, promises, and threatenings; and the use and benefit of endeavors, care and industry: and that therefore there is no need that the strict philosophic truth should be at all concealed from men; no danger in "contemplation" and "profound discovery" in these things.

***Conclusion: 1) The truth of this matter is at risk; 2) The clear and full knowledge of the real fact establishes the true doctrines; 3) The doctrines teach the divine administration in the City of God and the gospel of Jesus.***

So far from this, that the truth in this matter is of vast importance, and extremely needful to be known; and that the more clearly and perfectly the real fact is known, and the more constantly it is in view, the better; and particularly, that the clear and full knowledge of that which is the true system of the universe, in these respects, would greatly establish the doctrines which teach the true Christian scheme of divine administration in the *City of God*, and the gospel of Jesus Christ, in its most important articles; and that these things never can be well established, and the opposite errors, so subversive of the whole gospel, which at this day so greatly and generally prevail, be well confuted, or the arguments by which they are maintained, answered, till these points are settled: while this is not done, it is, to me, beyond doubt, that the friends of those great gospel truths, will but poorly maintain their controversy with the adversaries of those truths: they will be obliged often to dodge, shuffle, hide, and turn their backs; and the latter will have a strong fort, from whence they never can be driven, and weapons to use, which those whom they oppose will find no shield to screen themselves from; and they will always puzzle, confound, and keep under the friends of sound doctrine; and glory, and vaunt themselves in their advantage over them; and carry their affairs with an high hand, as they have done already for a long time past.

I conclude, sir, with asking your pardon for troubling you with so much said in vindication of myself from the imputation of advancing a scheme of necessity, of a like nature with that of the author of the *Essays on the Principles of Morality and Natural Religion*. Considering that what I have said is not only in vindication of myself, but, as I think, of the most important articles of moral philosophy and religion; I trust in what I know of your candor, that you will excuse,

Your obliged friend and brother,<br>
J. EDWARDS<br>
*Stockbridge,*<br>
*July 25, 1757.*

# Appendix 2

## (Edwards's) Letter to John Erskine, August 3, 1757, "To Mr. Erskine"[1]

To Mr. Erskine [2]
Stockbridge, August 3, 1757

Rev. and Dear Sir,

In June last, I received a letter from you, dated January 22, 1757, with *Mr. Anderson's complaint verified*,[3] and *Objections to the "Essays" examined*.[4] For these things, I now return you my hearty thanks.

The conduct of the vindicator of the *Essays*, from objections made against them, seems to be very odd. Many things are produced from Calvin, and several Calvinistic writers, to defend what is not objected against. His book is almost wholly taken up about that, which is nothing to the purpose; perhaps only to amuse and blind the common people. According to your proposal, I have drawn up something, stating the difference between my hypothesis, and that of the *Essays*; which I have sent to you, to be printed in Scotland, if it be thought best; or to be disposed of as you think proper. I have written it in a letter to you: and if it be published, it may be as "A letter from me to a minister in Scotland."

---

1. [*WJE* 16:718–24.]

2. [For a comment on the significance of the argument of this letter, see above, Intro., pt. 5, no. 2, esp. pp. 71–73; for a more definitive version of this letter based on JE's partial MS draft, see Letter A228, in *WJE* 16:718–24.]

3. [The complaint made to the presbytery of Edinburgh verified. By George Anderson. *The Scots Magazine* (Oct. 1756), 528.]

4. ["Objections Against the Essays on Morality and Natural Religion Examined," Prepared by Hugh Blair (1718–1800) (Edinburgh, 1756), with assistance from George Wishart, Robert Hamilton, and Robert Wallace.]

## Appendix 2

***Lord Kames: God has deeply implanted in man's nature, a strong and invincible apprehension, or feeling. But they are deceitful; they make men believe they are free, when they are not.***

Lord Kames' notion of God's deceiving mankind, by a kind of invincible or natural instinct or feeling, leading them to suppose, that they have a liberty of *contingence* and *self-determination of will*, in order to make them believe themselves and others worthy to be blamed or praised for what they do, is a strange notion indeed; and it is hard for me to conjecture, what his views could be, in publishing such things to the world.

However, by what I have heard, some others seem to be so far of the same mind, that they think, that if it be really true, that there is no self-determining power in the will, as opposed to any such moral necessity, as I speak of, consisting in a certain connection between motives and volitions, it is of mischievous tendency to say anything of it; and that it is best that the truth in this matter should not be known, by any means. I cannot but be of an extremely different mind. On the contrary, I think that the notion of liberty, consisting in a *contingent self-determination of the will*, as necessary to the morality of men's dispositions and actions, is almost inconceivably pernicious; and that the contrary truth is one of the most important truths of moral philosophy, that ever was discussed, and most necessary to be known; and that for want of it, those schemes of morality and religion, which are a kind of infidel schemes, entirely diverse from the virtue and religion of the Bible, and wholly inconsistent with, and subversive of, the main things belonging to the gospel scheme, have so vastly and so long prevailed, and have stood in such strength.

### *JE: Fatal Influences of Doctrinal Errors*

And I think, whoever imagines that he, or anybody else, shall ever see the doctrines of grace effectually maintained against these adversaries, till the truth in this matter be settled, imagines a vain thing. For, allow these adversaries what they maintain in this point, and I think they have strict demonstration against us. And not only have these errors a most pernicious influence, in the public religious controversies, that are maintained in the world; but such sort of notions have a more fatal influence many ways, on the minds of all ranks, in all transactions between God and their souls. The longer I live, and the more I have to do with the souls of men, in the work of the ministry, the more I see of this. Notions of this sort are one of the main hindrances of the success of the preaching of the Word, and other means of grace, in the conversion of sinners. This especially appears, when the minds of sinners are affected with some concern for their souls, and they are stirred up to seek their salvation. Nothing is more necessary for men, in such circumstances, than thorough conviction and humiliation; than that their consciences should be properly convinced of their real guilt and sinfulness in the sight of God, and their deserving of his wrath.

(Edwards's) Letter to John Erskine, August 3, 1757, "To Mr. Erskine"

*JE: The Condition of Souls in the Fatal Influences of Doctrinal Errors*

But who is there, that has had experience of the work of a minister, in dealing with souls in such circumstances, that does not find that the thing, that mainly prevents this, is men's excusing themselves with their own inability, and the moral necessity of those things, wherein their exceeding guilt and sinfulness in the sight of God, most fundamentally and mainly consist: such as, living from day to day, without one spark of true love to the God of infinite glory, and the Fountain of all good; their having greater complacency, in the little vile things of this world, than in him; their living in a rejection of Christ, with all his glorious benefits and dying love; and after all the exhibition of his glory and grace, having their hearts still as cold as a stone towards him; and their living in such ingratitude, for that infinite mercy of his laying down his life for sinners. They, it may be, think of some instances of lewd behavior, lying, dishonesty, intemperance, profaneness, etc. But the grand principles of iniquity, constantly abiding and reigning, from whence all proceeds, are all overlooked.

*LK: The responsibility for sin is not to men but to God.*

*JE: It arises not only from the occasion or determining influence of it, but also from the bad will or evil inclination of heart.*

Conscience does not condemn them for those things, because they "cannot love God of themselves," they "cannot believe of themselves," and the like. They rather lay the blame of these things, and their other reigning wicked dispositions of heart, to God, and secretly charge him with all the blame. These things are very much, for want of being thoroughly instructed, in that great and important truth, that *a bad will, or an evil disposition of heart, itself, is wickedness*. It is wickedness, in its very being, nature and essence, and not merely the occasion of it, or the determining influence, that it was at first owing to. Some, it may be, will say,

> "They own it is their fault that they have so bad a heart, that they have no love to God, no true faith in Christ, no gratitude to him, because they have been careless and slothful in times past, and have not used means to obtain a better heart, as they should have done."

And it may be, they are taught,

> "that they are to blame for their wickedness of heart, because they, as it were, brought it on themselves, in Adam, by the sin which he voluntarily committed, which sin is justly charged to their account";

which perhaps they do not deny. But how far are these things from being a proper conviction of their wickedness, in their enmity to God and Christ.

*JE: The hardness of heart implies moral inability. Religious exercises cannot help men realize it but their fears of hell.*

To be convinced of the sin of something that, long ago, was the occasion of their enmity to God; and to be convinced of the wickedness of the enmity itself; are quite two things. And if sinners, under some awakening, find the exercise of corruption of heart, as it appears in a great many ways; in their meditations, prayers, and other religious duties, and on occasion of their fears of hell, etc., etc.; still, this notion of their inability to help it, excusing them, will keep them from proper conviction of sin herein. Fears of hell tend to convince men of the hardness of their hearts. But then, when they find how hard their hearts are, and how far from a proper sensibility and affection in things of religion; they are kept from properly condemning themselves for it, from the *moral necessity*, or *inability*, which attends it. For the very notion of hardness of heart, implies moral inability. The harder the heart is, the more dead is it in sin, and the more unable to exert good affections and acts. Thus the strength of sin, is made the excuse for sin. And thus I have known many under fears of hell, justifying, or excusing, themselves, at least implicitly, in horrid workings of enmity against God, in blasphemous thoughts, etc.

The Interferences of Conviction and Conversion: Man's self-reliance on his righteousness, his justifying himself by his endeavors, and his excusing by moral inability.

It is of great importance, that they, that are seeking their salvation, should be brought off from all dependence on their own righteousness: but these notions above all things prevent it. They justify themselves, in the sincerity of their endeavors. They say to themselves, that they do what they can; they take great pains; and though there be great imperfection in what they do, and many evil workings of heart arise, yet these they cannot help: here moral necessity, or inability, comes in as an excuse. Things of this kind have visibly been the main hindrance of the true humiliation and conversion of sinners, in the times of awakening, that have been in this land, everywhere, in all parts, as I have had opportunity to observe, in very many places. When the gospel is preached, and its offers, and invitations, and motives, most powerfully urged, and some hearts stand out, here is their stronghold, their sheet-anchor. Were it not for this, they would either comply; or their hearts would condemn them, for their horrid guilt in not complying. And if the law of God be preached in its strictness and spirituality, yet conscience is not properly convinced by it. They justify themselves with their *inability*; and the design and end of the law, as a schoolmaster, to fit them for Christ, is defeated. Thus both the law and the gospel are prevented from having their proper effect.

**Evils of the Doctrine of Self-determining Will #1: It prevents any proper exercises of faith; teaches a kind of absolute independence; depends on our own acts, as self-determined.**

The doctrine of a self-determining will, as the ground of all moral good and evil, tends to prevent any proper exercises of faith in God and Christ, in the affair of our salvation, as it tends to prevent all dependence upon them. For, instead of this, it teaches a kind of absolute independence on all those things, that are of chief importance in this affair; our righteousness depending originally on our own acts, as self-determined. Thus our own holiness is from ourselves, as its determining cause, and its original and highest source.

***Evils of the Doctrine of Self-determining Will #2: It is contrary to the doctrine of 'imputed righteousness,' that is dependent on God.***

And as for imputed righteousness, that should have any merit at all in it, to be sure, there can be no such thing. For self-determination is necessary to praise and merit. But what is imputed from another is not from our self-determination or action. And truly, in this scheme, man is not dependent on God; but God is rather dependent on man in this affair: for he only operates consequentially in acts, in which he depends on what he sees we determine, and do first.

***Evils of the Doctrine of Self-determining Will #3: It gives the glory wholly to man.***

The nature of true faith implies a disposition, to give all the glory of our salvation to God and Christ. But this notion is inconsistent with it, for it in effect gives the glory wholly to man. For that is the very doctrine that is taught, that the merit and praise is his, whose is the original and effectual determination of the praiseworthy deed. So that, on the whole, I think it must be a miracle, if ever men are converted, that have imbibed such notions as these, and are under their influence in their religious concerns.

***Evils of the Doctrine of Self-determining Will #4: It prevents men's ever seeking after conversion; precludes all sense of any great guilt.***

Yea, these notions tend effectually to prevent men's ever seeking after conversion, with any earnestness. It is manifest, that men never will be in earnest in this matter, till their consciences are awakened, and they are made sensible of God's anger, and their danger of suffering the terrible effects of it. But that stupidity, which is opposed to this awakening, is upheld chiefly by these two things: their insensibility of their guilt, in what is past, and present; and their flattering themselves, as to what is future. These notions of liberty of indifference, contingence, and self-determination, as essential to guilt or merit, tend to preclude all sense of any great guilt for past or present wickedness. As has been observed already, all wickedness of heart is excused, as what, in itself considered, brings no guilt. And all that the conscience has to recur to, to find any guilt, is the first wrong determination of the will, in some bad conduct, before that wickedness of heart existed, that was the occasion of introducing or confirming it. Which determination arose contingently from a state of indifference. And how small a matter does this at once bring men's guilt to, when all the main things, wherein their wickedness consists, are passed over. And indeed the more these principles are pursued, the more and more must guilt vanish, till at last it comes to nothing, as may easily be shown.

And with respect to self-flattery and presumption, as to what is future, nothing can possibly be conceived more directly tending to it, than a notion of a liberty, at all times possessed, consisting in a power to determine one's own will to good or evil; which implies a power men have, at all times, to determine them to repent and turn to God. And what can more effectually encourage the sinner, in present delays and neglects, and embolden him to go on in sin, in a presumption of having his own salvation at all times at his command? And this notion of self-determination and self-dependence, tends to prevent, or enervate, all prayer to God for converting grace; for why should men earnestly cry to God for his grace, to determine their hearts to that, which they must be determined to of themselves. And indeed it destroys the very notion of conversion itself. There can properly be no such thing, or anything akin to what the Scripture speaks of conversion, renovation of the heart, regeneration, etc. if growing good, by a number of self-determined acts, are all that is required, or to be expected.

Excuse me, sir, for troubling you with so much on this head. I speak from the fullness of my heart. What I have long seen of the dreadful consequences of these prevalent notions everywhere, and what I am convinced will still be their consequences so long as they continue to prevail, fills me with concern. I therefore wish that the affair were more thoroughly looked into, and searched to the very bottom.

I have reserved a copy of this letter, and also of my other to you, dated July 25, intending to send them to Mr. Burr, to be by him conveyed, by the way of New York or Philadelphia. Looking on these letters as of special importance, I send duplicates, lest one copy should fail. The pacquet, in which I enclose this, I cover to Mr. Gillies, and send to Boston, to the care of Mr. Hyslop, to be conveyed to Mr. Gillies. But yet have desired him, if he has a more direct opportunity, to convey the pacquet to Edinburgh, by the way of London, then to put a wrapper over the whole, inscribed to you; and to write to you, desiring you to break open the pacquet, and take out the letters which belong to you.

You will see, sir, something of our sorrowful state, on this side of the water, by my letter to Mr. M'Culloch.

O, sir, pray for us; and pray in particular, for

> Your affectionate and obliged Friend and brother Jonathan Edwards

# Appendix 3

## The Last Letter from John Erskine to Jonathan Edwards, January 24, 1758.[1]

Reverend and Dear Sir,[2]

About six weeks ago I received your 3 Letters of 12th April, 25 July and 3 August 1757. Some of your religious intelligence in the first of these will be printed by Mr. [John] Gillies[3] which I would not have consented to, not approving such freedom with private Letters, was it not that your mournful tidings of Mr [Aaron] Burr's death allows small hopes of his preparing any regular account of that glorious revival for the Press.[4] Your Letter of 25 July, I immediately transmitted to one Miller[5] a Bookseller in Edinburgh who from his zeal for purity of doctrine and his aversion to Lord Kaims' [sic] hypothesis and his little connection with great Folks I believed would be most ready to undertake, but after Showing the MSS to the Revd Mess. [Robert] Walker of Edinburgh, [John] Bonar and Others, he was of the opinion that the controversy was so far Sopite [put to rest] since January last that your Letter would not meet with due attention, and that except Lord Kames in a new edition he is preparing of his Book

---

1. [This letter is discovered by Jonathan Yeager during researching for his dissertation. See Jonathan Yeager, "An Unpublished Letter from John Erskine to Jonathan Edwards," *JESO* 3, no. 1 (2013).]

2. [This letter was certainly delivered to Edwards's widow because he died on March 22, the same year. See "Letter to the Reverend John Erskine, July 25, 1757" *WJE* 16:705–18. "Letter to the Reverend John Erskine, August 3, 1757" *WJE* 16:718–24.]

3. [Yeager, An Extract of Edwards' Letter to Erskine on April 12, 1757 can be seen in John Gillies, *Historical Collections Relating to Remarkable Periods of the Success of the Gospel* (Edinburgh, 1845), 522–23.]

4. [In his letter on April 12, 1757, Edwards had written to Erskine with news that a revival broke out at the College of New Jersey earlier that year while Burr was president.]

5. [Yeager assumes this might be the Edinburgh bookseller William Miller, who published Erskine's sermon, *Ministers of the Gospel Cautioned against Giving Offence* in 1764. This same bookseller might have changed his mind, for Edwards's "Remarks" was published at Edinburgh in 1758, but without the name of the printer or publisher listed on the imprint.]

*Essays* [6] should claim your Patronage - no more need be said on the subject. I intend however as my own opinion is different to send a letter to Mess: [John] Witherspoon and [Thomas] Walker of Dundonald, hoping thro' their influence, it may be printed at Glasgow.

I am peculiarly indebted to you for your Letter of 3 August. I am fully convinced of the importance of establishing such a necessity as you maintain in your enquiry; that I don't see how Calvinism can be consistently defended on other principles.

The accurate reasoning in your Book [*Freedom of the Will*] has been much applauded even by some good judges in the Arminian Scheme. I've not met with any thorough Calvinists who are displeased with your Scheme. The most violent censurers of it are from Semi Arminians. I have indeed met with one or two zealous Calvinists, who while they approve the rest of your Book disrelish the Argument from Kames to being in a state of trial which they think a harsh expression, but I don't see for what reason.

I wrote six weeks ago both to Edinburgh and Glasgow anent procuring subscribers for your Book on original Sin and from Edinburgh I expect several; but unhappily they have been dilatory in making up the List, so that I wish it may catch the ship by which this is sent.

June last Mr [David] Imrie sent me a copy of some Letters he had wrote to others in which he seems confident that 'ere two years end, Pangs will come on England as of a Woman in travail, whereby God will greatly humble and reform her.[7] And after this will correct and reform France, by thicker and heavier judgments viz. Famine, Pestilence, Earthquakes, civil War and the Sword of a foreign Power different from Britain [sic] which to invade Conquer and Oppress her. But in her distress she will cry to the Lord, and the Lord will send her deliverance and reform her from Popery, and reduce her to the state of an inferior Kingdom dependent on Britain, from which she will not then be separated by a Sea, the now intervening Chanel being filled up by an Earthquake and this he thinks may be looked for 'ere the end of seven years. He thinks that God has promis[e]d to make a proclamation of the approach of Christ's second coming by which he means his coming to introduce a glorious state of the Church prior to the last judgment and to give Signs of [the] 2d proclamation: and that the midnight Cry behold the Bridegroom cometh is already begun to go forth.

He apprehends that Britain and France will soon be made nursing Fathers to the 10 Tribes, who he thinks are the American Indians. This first occurred to him from a Passage which as it stands in our Hebrew Bible is incapable of any sense but by altering

---

6. [*Essays on the Principles of Morality, and Natural Religion*, second edition (London, 1758), in which some of the most exceptionable passages are to be softened.]

7. [Yeager, Edwards had read *A Letter from the Reverend Mr. David Imrie. . . To a Gentleman in the City of Edinburgh* (Edinburgh, 1755; reprinted in Boston and Philadelphia in 1756). See Edwards's letter to William McCulloch on April 10, 1756 in *WJE* 16, letter 215, 684–85. The information that Erskine relates from Imrie does not come out of *A Letter from the Reverend Mr. David Imrie*. Rather, this appears to be new prophetic insight from Imrie that was never published.]

a Letter or two of ours of a similar figure will contain a number of marks agreeing to no People but the 10 Tribes and to no Country, but America he delays mentioning the Passage, 'till the printing of his Book: but hints some collateral Proofs e.g.: Noah's Prophecy about Japheth Gen. 9:27 which he thus paraphrases

> "God shall spread abroad the European, the posterity of Japheth and they shall dwell in the Tents of Shem i.e.: in a land of Pilgrimage possessed by the 10 Tribes the posterity of Shem viz. in America, and in the Land of the African Negroes, the posterity of Canaan shall be slaves to said Europeans, the Posterity of Japheth."

In this way Noah's Prophecy will relate to all the four Quarters of the World. The Wisdom of the Spirit appears in choosing words equally fit for wrapping up the meaning till the proper time and for disclosing when that time comes and also by answering so many different purposes, by such an admirable variety of well chosen words.

The Posterity of Shem in the Prophecy as appears from v. 26 must be a people to whom God had bound himself by a national covenant to be their God; which can only apply to Israel's seed. Canaan was to be a Servant of Servants i.e. a Servant in the lowest and most abject sense to his Brethren. He was so to the seed of Shem in the Land of Canaan. But in no Country has he been under such abject slavery to Japheth's seed as to deserve notice in such a Prophecy except in America where the law [of] slavery of the African Negroe to Japheth's European seed is well known. America is term'd the Tents of Shem, because there his Posterity of the 10 Tribes were long to sojourn, in a state of Pilgrimage and exile from their own Land (2) Balaam's prophecy Numb. 23.9: Lo the people shall dwell alone &c. Balaam's prophecies respect the state of Israel in the latter days and no words can more compendiously describe, the state in which the 10 Tribes of Israel were to live for many ages in America, alone, secreted and concealed from the rest of the world, so as for many hundreds of years not to be reckoned among the nations.

There is an old Jewish tradition 2d Esdras 13 relating to the Elopement of the 10 Tribes from the first places of their exile. Mr. Imrie adds the proof of this will not rest on mere Criticism. God will point out his ancient [sic] People by marvelous works of Providence and Grace foretold in several Scriptures.

Except the late signal victorys [sic] of the King of Prussia public civil affairs continue to wear a mournful aspect and yet amidst all these calls of Providence to Prayer and Fasting, gayety and Frolicks prevail more than ever: and little is minded by the Politer sort but pleasure and diversion. But I must break off.

I send you along with this [John] Mason's *Student and Pastor*. The Plan appears to me greatly better than the execution. I am surprised that except Cotton Mather's *Candidates* [*Student and Preacher*][8] nothing has hitherto been writ for the direction of Students of Divinity. I wish some Minister of suitable parts and literature would do it.

---

8. [Cotton Mather, *Student and Preacher*; or, MANUDUCTIO AD MINISTERIUM; or,

Appendix 3

    I am Reverend and Dear Sir
    Your most affect[ionate] Brother and Servant
    John Erskine

                                                                Culross 24 January 1758

To the Reverend Mr. Jonathan Edwards = (Stockbr.) Sent upon to T[homas]. F[oxcroft]. for perusal - took this copy - And then sent away the Letter and Packet to Reverend Mr. [Gideon] Hawley - to Colonel [Timothy] Dwight of Northampton to be forwarded to Mr. Edwards's Widow -

---

DIRECTIONS FOR A CANDIDATE OF THE MINISTRY; first published in Boston in 1726]

# Appendix 4

## Thomas Reid's Reading Notes on Edwards's *Freedom of the Will*

Introduction

Jonathan Edwards's *Freedom of the Will* was published in Boston in 1754, followed by a second London edition in 1762.[1] The work attracted not only its advocates, such as Andrew Fuller, William Godwin, John Collett Ryland, John Ryland Jr., and Edward Williams, but also its critics: Lord Kames, David Hume, Joseph Priestley, Dugald Stewart, Henry Philip Tappan, and especially the famous Common Sense philosopher Thomas Reid (1710–1796).

Presented here for the first time is the text of Reid's *Reading Notes* on Edwards's *Treatise*.[2] Recently discovered in the collections of the University of Aberdeen, a transcript of Reid's notes is provided after a brief introduction.

Reid most likely read Edwards's *FOW* in 1762 or1763 while in Aberdeen, before he wrote his first major book, and formulated his philosophy by reacting unfavorably to Edwards's key principles. In his notebooks, in which he recorded his thoughts on many books, he summarized, assessed and criticized *Freedom of the Will*.

Reid graduated from Marischal College at Aberdeen in 1726 as a student of George Turnbull, who would be the second antagonist, after John Taylor, in Edwards's *Original Sin*. He was ordained as a minister at New Machar in 1737. Then he taught philosophy in King's College, Aberdeen, from 1752, and moral philosophy in University of Glasgow from 1764, when he published *An Inquiry into the Human Mind on the Principles of Common Sense*.

---

1. [Anonymous, "Review of *Freedom of the Will*," *Monthly Review of Literary Journal* 27 (Dec. 1762): 434–38.]

2. [I am personally indebted to James Harris for directing me to the manuscript (MS 2131/3/II/6), which is housed at Special Collections Centre, The Sir Duncan Rice Library, University of Aberdeen. See James Harris, *Of Liberty and Necessity* (New York: Oxford Univ. Press, 2005), 191.]

Reid might have read the first London edition of *FOW*. In his *Inquiry*, he reacted to his main antagonists such as Descartes, Malebranche, Locke, Berkeley and Hume, and he articulated Common Sense Realism on the basis of an *a priori* epistemology, that is, that knowledge is not deprived from experiences but from inborn sense. So he became best known as the father of philosophical realism, which is exemplified throughout his works.[3] Reid argued that humans were all endowed with common sense from birth, and their feelings and actions are governed by its basic principles. The faculty of common sense gives them immediate knowledge, which is innate, and is confirmed through sensitive perception of the external objects.[4] In this point, he differentiates his position from idealists such as Descartes, Locke, Berkeley, Hume, Arnauld and Leibniz, who, as he put it, "suppose ideas in the brain or in the mind."[5] Specifically, he refuted the idealist assumption that humans directly perceived not the external object but an image or idea of the object.[6] Reid's realism was revealed in statements in his *Reading Notes* on Edwards, such as the following:

> EVERY man is conscious of [have] a power to determine, . . . To this power we give the name of will; and, . . . the term will is often put to signify the act of determining, which more properly is called volition. Volition, therefore, signifies the act of willing and determining; and will is put indifferently to signify either the power of willing or the act.[7]

In his *Essays on the Active Powers of the Human Mind* (1788), Reid agreed with Locke and Edwards in distinguishing the faculties of soul into the understanding and the will. Yet Reid and Edwards disagreed in defining the will: the former as "a power to determine," the latter as "a power or ability to prefer or choose."[8] Furthermore, Reid intensified his definition, adding that humans have "active power," which is the ability to produce a change and self-determining power by which it determines the will. Ironically, he held that a motive must precede acts of the will, a view espoused by most Necessitarians such as Hume, Kames, Tucker, Hobbes, Collins, and Priestley.[9]

Reid also seemed to agree with Edwards in controversial points, because they used same terms and held similar definition of "the freedom of the will," "motive,"

---

3. [Among Reid's major works were *An Inquiry into the Human Mind on the Principles of Common Sense* (1764), *Essays on the Intellectual Powers of Man* (1785), and *Essays on the Active Powers of the Human Mind* (1788).]

4. [Thomas Reid, *An Inquiry into the Human Mind on the Principles of Common Sense* (1764), 2. 10, 43; 4. 1, 49; 6. 21, 177).]

5. [Thomas Reid, *Essays on the Intellectual Powers of Man* (1785), Essays No. 2. The Powers we have by means of our, Ch. XV. 5.]

6. [James Van Cleve, "4 Reid's Theory of Perception." *The Cambridge Companion to Thomas Reid* (2004), 101.]

7. [Thomas Reid, *Essays on the Active Powers of the Human Mind* (1788), Essays No. 2. Of the Will, Ch. I.]

8. [Edwards quotes from Locke's *Essay*, bk. II, ch.21, no. 17.]

9. [Harris, *Of Liberty and Necessity*, 194.]

and "cause." But he conceived them in terms of agent-causal liberty, asserting that the determination of the will must have an agent as its cause,[10] and considering "the determination of the will as an effect," as he clearly stated as follows in his *Active Powers*:

> This effect must have a cause which had power to produce it; and the cause must either be the person himself, whose will it is, or some other being. The first is as easily conceived as the last. If the person was the cause of that determination of his own will, he was free in that action, and it is justly imputed to him, whether it be good or bad.[11]

Reid's position was that individuals have the inborn power to determine their own wills, and so they "own" the liberty of will. For him, moral liberty was a power over the determination of one's own will "to do well or ill";[12] the power was given by God, and yet liberty could be controlled in particular cases by God. Necessity, on the other hand, was the lack of that liberty.[13] Reid states, revealingly, "His hook is in its nose," by which it appears that he did not entirely deny the necessity of the will.

However, it is only in his *Reading Notes* on *FOW* that Reid mentions the name of Edwards, who, as he judged, somewhat puzzlingly, "agrees with Arminians, and departs from the current and general opinion of Calvinists."[14] Furthermore, Reid criticized Locke and Hobbes in particular.. He assented to Edwards's common definitions of the will, its act, and cause, but when he diagnosed Edwards's core doctrine of it, he critically identified Edwards's ideas with the causality principle of Gottfried Wilhelm Leibniz. And even though he applauds Edwards's "Achillean argument" against Arminianism and its causation theory, he sarcastically remarks on Edwards's objection (*FOW*, II.5.190) against the Arminian notion of liberty, which, according to Reid, argues that "willing is an immediate Act of the Mind."[15] If, Reid continued, "any man be so absurd as to affirm this, Mr. Edwards argument is good against him & convicts him of an absurdity." In closing, he reports that Edwards refutes Isaac Newton's theory of absolute and infinite space and time, which, as Edwards put it, "supposes an extent of space beyond the limits of the creation."[16] "Extramundane Time and Space is denied by the author," Reid observes. By that, as Reid interprets it, Edwards implies that God acts always by necessity and so does not need any alteration of it, not to mention another space and time to place it again.

---

10. [Thomas Reid, *Essays on the Active Powers of the Human Mind* (London, 1788), No. IV, Ch. I.]
11. [Thomas Reid, *Essays*, No. IV, Ch. I.]
12. [Thomas Reid, *Essays*, No. IV, Ch. I.]
13. [Thomas Reid, *Essays*, No. IV, Ch. I.]
14. [Thomas Reid, *Reading Notes* on Edwards's *Freedom of the Will*, p. 1.]
15. [Thomas Reid, *Reading Notes* on Edwards's *Freedom of the Will*, p. 1.]
16. [*FOW*, IV. 8. 387. Cf. Jeon Geunho, "The Trinitarian Ontology of Jonathan Edwards: Glory, Beauty, Love, and Happiness in the Dispositional Space of Creation" (Boston University, Th.D. Diss, 2013), 61–70.]

Reid plainly supported an Arminian notion of liberty, by which he conceived, as he stated, that "a previous Act of Volition is not necessary," and he charged Edwards with being a "fatalist & defender of Liberty" and a "Leibnizian."[17] His final view on the will, argued in his works and in his *Reading Notes* on *FOW*, shows that he was not so absurd an Arminian as to hold the self-determining power of the will, as Edwards portrayed in *FOW*; rather, Reid advocated a moderate position, though it nevertheless conflicted with the Necessitarianism of Edwards. In the long run, Reid's Common Sense Realism philosophy was adopted as a theological principle by Princeton Presbyterians such John Witherspoon and Archibald Alexander, and it enormously influenced New England intellectuals in the eighteenth century.[18]

Read. *A careful and strict Enquiry into the Modern Prevailing Notions of that Freedom of Will which is supposed to be essential to Moral Agency, Virtue and Vice, Reward and Punishment, Praise and Blame* by Jonathan Edwards A.M. Pastor of the Church in Stockbridge, Boston N.E. 1754

## THOMAS REID'S READING NOTES ON EDWARDS'S *FREEDOM OF THE WILL*

By Thomas Reid

In the Preface the author treats with good sense & Moderation this question, How far Christians that differ in opinion ought to give to each other the Appellations of Arminian, Calvinist, Socinians, and the like; and makes an apology for his giving the Appellation of Arminians to those whom he opposes in this Book, although he acknowledges that a man who holds the Doctrine which he opposes may not be an Arminian although in that Doctrine he agrees with Arminians, and departs from the current and general opinion of Calvinists.

§ 1 He allows that Will & Desire are not words precisely of the same signification but thinks they can never be contrary.

§ 2 That the Will is always determined by the strongest motive. Although in general he enumerates those things that may contribute to the strength of a Motive, yet he points out no means by which we may determine the comparative strength of contrary Motives, beside that of their prevailing.

§ 3 The word necessary as used in common Speech is relative to some supposed opposition. That is necessary which is or will be notwithstanding all supposable

---

17. [Thomas Reid, *Reading Notes* on Edwards's *Freedom of the Will*, p. 2.]

18. [See James McCosh, *The Scottish Philosophy, Biographical, Expository, Critical, from Hutcheson to Hamilton* (New York: Robert Carter and Brothers, 1875), 183–89; and also James D. Bratt, "Reformed Theology in North America," *The Cambridge Companion to Reformed Theology*, ed. Paul T. Nimmo & David AS Fergusson (Cambridge Univ. Press, 2016), 269–84.]

opposition. That is necessary in respect to us which no opposition of our wills can frustrate. This says the author is the common meaning of necessity. But it is taken in another sense when applied to the divine existence Eternity, &c. Philosophical or Metaphysical Necessity is nothing different from the certainty of the things.

§ 4 The Distinction of Natural and moral necessity.

§ 5 The Notion of Liberty in common Language is doing what we please. The Arminian Notion of Liberty consists in three things:

> 1. That the Will has a sovereignty over itself and its own acts so as not to be determined by anything prior to its own acts.
>
> 2. Indifference, or that the Mind previous to the Act of Volition be in Equilibrio.
>
> 3. Contingence as opposed to all Necessity or any Certain Connection with some previous ground or Reason of the Existence of the thing.

Part 2 §

§1. A self-determining power in the Will is absurd. The argument is to this purpose. If the mind determines the will, it must do it by an Act of Will, for Determination is an act of Will. The last act of the Will therefore must be determined by a preceding act and for the same Reason this must be determined by a third and so on infinitum which is absurd.

§2. The argument defended. The strength of the defense lies on this that there must be a cause or sufficient reason for the Minds determing itself this way rather than another. This, however, is taking for granted the thing in question.

§ (3.) An Act of Will cannot be without a Cause.

§ (4.) This Achillean argument which the Author puts in a variety of lights and defends from objections through the first five sections is the very same which Locke used and Hobbes if I remember right before him and the same answer serves to all to wit. That willing is an immediate Act of the Mind, whereas all external Actions such as speaking walking, and many internal acts such as deliberating, cannot be require an act of will as the mean of producing them. Speaking is not an action of the Man unless he wills to speak nor walking unless he wills to walk. No man deliberates or reasons without willing to deliberate or Reason. And in a word, all these actions, which are imputable to us and of which we are properly the causes, are performed by means of Volition. But although this holds in all other cases it does not hold with regard to Volition itself. I cannot walk without willing to walk nor Reason without willing to Reason. Willing is the Mean by which we act. But it does not follow that willing is the mean by which we will. If any man be so absurd as to affirm this, Mr. Edwards argument is good against him and convicts him of an absurdity. But this absurdity arises solely from his holding that when we will we must will to will, that is, that no act of Volition can be exerted without a previous act of Volition determining us to exert it. It is likewise to be observed that this absurdity is equally chargeable upon fatalists and the defenders of Liberty if they hold the position above mentioned. There is nothing in the Scheme of Liberty that should lead a man to hold that every act of Volition requires a previous act of Volition, any more than in the Scheme of Necessity.

§ (5.) Mr. Locke and Hobbes have shown the absurdity of supposing the will to be voluntary in the same sense as actions depending upon the Will are said to be voluntary. And all that Edwards makes out in these five sections amounts to no more. But after terminating this point the Philosophical question concerning Liberty remained untouched. Mr. Edwards professes not to take any advantage of the inaccuracy of the expression, of the Will's determining itself, yet his argument is founded upon this inaccuracy. When you correct this inaccuracy and say that Volition is an immediate act of the Mind, to which a previous Act of Volition is not necessary, his argument falls to the ground and he betakes himself to another, to wit that this Act of Volition upon this Supposition is an Effect without a Cause and he argues at great length to show this to be impossible. If it should be affirmed that the Mind is the Cause of this Effect; this Argument falls to the ground likewise, and he betakes himself to a third. there must not only be a Cause but a sufficient reason to determine that Cause to act one way rather than another. This is the Leibnizian Principle. The mingling these three arguments together into one gives them an appearance of strength. But they are really unconnected.

§6. To act where we are indifferent is to choose without a choice which is absurd.

§7. For the mind to act while it is undetermined is to give a preference, and no preference, and to choose without a choice which is absurd. Whether Liberty can consist in suspending action till we deliberate? A. This is gross nonsense and ridiculously absurd. For this implies that Liberty consists in suspending the act of Suspension which is absurd, for it leads to an infinite series.

§8. The act of Volition cannot be contingent, because it must have a Cause, and must be necessarily connected with its cause.

§9. Connection of the Will with the Understanding. If the last dictate of the Understanding do not govern the Will and this be proper Notion of Freedom, then the less the connection between the Understanding and the Will the more freedom, and in perfect freedom there will be no connection at all, and so in vain is all Counsel Exhortation and threatening.

§10. Inconsistence of Mr. Chubb's scheme of Liberty.

§11. Proves at great length God's prescience.

§12. Prescience of Events inconsistent with their contingency. The Existence of things past is now necessary, and the Existence of those things which are certainly and infallibly connected with things which are necessary, is necessary; Now the Divine Foreknowledge hath always existed in time past, its existence therefore is necessary; and it is infallibly connected with all future Events, therefore their Existence is necessary.

There can be no Evidence of future Contingencies; for if there could, it must either be that they are self-evident or can be proved. But neither can be all along the author confounds certainty of existence with necessity of existence.

Prescience does not indeed make the foreknown Event necessary but it proves it to be so. It is not the cause but the Evidence of its necessity.

Part 3

§1. God is necessarily good, therefore according to the Reasoning of Arminians deserves no praise for his Goodness.

§2. The same reasoning applied to the Man Christ.

§3. If Moral Inability takes away Guilt, then the inability of Man in his fallen state leaves him still in innocence and he has no need of a Savior.

§4. Acts of the Soul that are free in the Arminian sense cannot be subject of command or Moral Government, because they are necessarily consequent upon the choice or election which precedes them, and this Election upon another Election and so on infinitum. So that it is the Arminian System and not the Calvinist that is utterly inconsistent with all moral Government.

§5. Men cannot desire virtuous Dispositions without having them

§6. The Liberty of Indifference not only not necessary to Virtue but utterly inconsistent with it; and all other Virtuous or Vicious inclinations and Habits inconsistent with this Liberty of Indifference. What is matter of Choice cannot be indifferent; if therefore an action is virtuous, it cannot [be] indifferent because it must be matter of choice. Virtuous or Vicious Habits and Dispositions are not consistent with indifference nor consequently with Liberty, and upon that account there can be neither virtue nor vice where the Mind has any ideas, good or bad before volition.

§7. Liberty of Indifference inconsistent with all influence of Motives, and Inducements

There can be no Virtue in Actions that have no Motive.

Part 4

§1. The Essence of the Virtue and Vice of Dispositions of the Heart and Acts of the Will lies not in their Cause but in their Nature.

§2. The Arminian Notion of Action and Agency false and inconsistent. Action and Passion are according to this author Relative terms. The same thing which is Action in relation to the Effect produced by it is Passion in relation to that which caused it [to] act. Whether it was a Motive or whatever other Cause. Action may be the Effect of some other Cause besides the Agent and the same Agent in the same Action may be both Active and Passive.

§3. The Prejudices which had men to think it unjust that a man should be punished for what he was under an invincible necessity of doing. From our early years we are accustomed to call everything necessary which we cannot avoid though ever so willing. This necessity indeed excludes all blame. Afterwards we apply the word Necessity to moral Necessity. And are thereby led to form the same conclusion with regard to this Necessity as the Natural

§4. It is agreeable to common sense that Necessary actions should deserve praise or blame.

§5. Of the Objection. That the doctrine of Necessity renders all Men's Endeavors Vain and to no Purpose. The Objection supposes that a man reasons thus, why should I be at pains to bring about what is absolutely fixed. But it is to be observed that in this reasoning the man contradicts himself. If it is vain for him to act for any end, why does he propose this and not to take pains that is as much fixed as other events, and it is as vain for him to do or forbear anything in order to attain it.

§6. That the Deity acts always by necessity, and that there is no case wherein he may not have a Motive to act one way more than another. Extramundane Time and Space is denied by the author.[19] The extreme improbability of any two atoms of matter being alike. Supposing they were it is absurd to speak of choice in placing one here and another there. As it would be absurd to ask why God created such a body in such a place and not another individual exactly like it. A single atom added to the Universe or taken from it might in time produce very sensible Effects.

---

19. [See *FOW*, 385–86. JE reputes Newtonian absolute space. Cf. GeunHo Geon, "The Trinitarian Ontology of Jonathan Edwards: Glory, Beauty, Love, and Happiness in the Dispositional Space of Creation," (Boston University, THD Diss, 2013), 61–70.]

Addenda

The Will is that by which the Mind chooses anything. it can never be contrary to desire. Nor can it be distinguished from the Act of understanding judging an Action to be for the present best for us. We always follow the greatest apparent good - Nothing can determine Will but a Motive, and a Motive must be something that is apprehended by the Mind.

# Appendix 5

Proposals[1] for printing *Freedom of the Will*

Boston, April 25, 1753.

A Treatise Intitled,

A careful and strict Enquiry into the modern prevailing Notions of that Freedom of Will, which is supposed to be essential to moral Agency, Vertue and Vice, Reward and Punishment, Praise and Blame.

WHEREIN are examined the main Foundations of the whole Arminian Scheme, as opposed to the Doctrines maintained by those that are called Calvinistic Divines, and the main Grounds of the pretended Demonstrations in which the Defenders of that Scheme have so long gloried & vaunted themselves, insulting those of a contrary persuasion. The particular Arguments and Reasonings of their Authors who have been most celebrated, and esteemed their greatest Masters of Reason, are humbly, yet with careful Exactness enquired into, with their chief Objections and Exclamations against Calvinists; and particularly their boasted Arguments from Common Sense, and their Pretenses that Calvinistic Doctrines are supported by Nothing but abstruse, scholastic and metaphysical Subtleties and Distinctions, and unintelligible Jargon, contrary to the plain Dictates of Reason, and the natural Notions of Mankind. In this Discourse, Endeavours are used particularly to shew the Nature of human Will, and the Manner of its Determination ; the true Foundation and Essence of that moral Agency which renders Men the proper Subjects of moral Government, Commands, Counsels,

---

1. [A broadside, printed by Samuel Kneeland of Boston, for announcing and collecting subscriptions for the publication and distribution of Edwards's *Freedom of the Will*. The imprint, cut up into four parts, was reused for his manuscript notebook, "Defense of the authenticity of the Pentateuch as a work of Moses and the historicity of the Old Testament narratives (Dec. 1756)," and it is discovered by Jonathan Yeager. See Jonathan Yeager, "An Unpublished Letter from John Erskine to Jonathan Edwards," *JESO* 3, no 1 (2013); BRBL, f. 1204, Notebook of "Defense of the authenticity of the Pentateuch as a work of Moses and the historicity of the Old Testament narratives," (written on Dec. 1756, unpublished).]

Invitations, Persuasions, Promises, Threatenings, Praise, Dispraise and Retribution, according to the common Sense of Mankind, and the most demonstrable Evidence; showing the palpable Absurdity of the modern Notions of these Things, their manifold Inconsistence with themselves, and with common Sense. Among many other Things here treated of, the following Particulars are distinctly handled - The Nature of . . . Necessity and Contingence, Ability and Inability; The Nature of Liberty; How these Terms are used by Philosophers, and how in common Speech; The Distinction of natural and moral Ability, Inability and Necessity; The Nature of physical, unintelligible and inconsistent Notions of them. The Nature of GOD's Fore-knowledge; The Evidence of his certain Fore-knowledge of all future Events; Whether infallible Prescience doesn't infer a Necessity of the Volitions of moral Agents, as much as such a Decree as Calvinists suppose; The Nature of the Liberty of the divine Being, and that of the Man Christ Jesus, and their Consequences ; The Consequences of such an Inability of fallen Man as Arminians confess ; What Inability properly renders Persons not the Subjects of Precept, Exhortation, Invitation, &c. and what not, with the Reasons ; The Nature of Sincerity of Will and Endeavour; What Excuses in the Non-performance of a good Thing required, and what not; Concerning the Agreement of the Doctrine of Calvinists with the Stoical Fate and Hobbistical Necessity ; The Grand Objection against the Calvinistic Scheme, that it makes GOD the Author of Sin; The Nature of the divine Sovereignty in disposing Events, and how it reaches the Acts of moral Agents, with the reasons; The cavils of Arminians concerning the Distinction Calvinists suppose between GOD's secret and revealed Will, and concerning the Calvinistic Doctrines being against the moral Perfections of GOD, and their Tendency to Libertinism and Infidelity ; Concerning the Way of Arminians proving their Opinions, and confuting the Calvinists by Scripture, &c. &c.

By JONATHAN EDWARDS, A. M.
Pastor of the Church of Stockbridge.

# Index

Ability, 14, 32, 34, 42, 69, 97, 105, 108
   Moral, 73
   Natural, 74
   to add, 116
   to avoid, 211
   to choose, 113
   to determine our wills, 105
   to make virtuous, 293
   to perform, 213, 215
   to prefer or choose, 392
   to resist, 222
   to will, 220
Absolutism, moral, 63n4
Accident, 61, 65, 66, 109, 110, 374, 377
   perfect, 317, 338
   pure, 219
Act
   of free volition, 144
   of volition, 30
   of willing, 30, 392
   of God's goodness, 317
   of God's sovereignty, 31
   of the will, 41, 43, 48, 53, 64, 69, 79, 81, 96, 100, 221, 234, 246
   act of the creature, 337
   of choosing or choice, 41, 44, 107, 237
   of volition, 41, 48, 79, 83, 85, 121
   of choice, 44, 99, 107, 142, 145, 262
   of obedience, 218
   of self-determination, 115, 120
   of sin, 334
   of the mind, 83
   of the soul, 117, 184, 219
   of the understanding, 101
   of preference, 47, 134, 140
   of suspension, 120, 121, 396
Actions
   God's foreknowledge of, 180
   morality of, 241
   omissions of, 282
   processes of, 21
Affection, 25n175, 41n1, 74n7, 132n5

Agency, moral, 31, 32, 36, 54, 55, 70, 71, 72, 73, 77, 166, 189, 218, 235, 239, 244, 249, 250, 260, 293, 330, 343
Agreeableness, 47, 49, 51, 90, 107, 276
Anglican, Arminian, 16
Apostasy, 25, 155, 156, 166, 167, 362
Arbitrary, 20, 369, 370, 377, - choice, 370
Arbitrium, 15
Arian, 16, 17
Arminian, v-viii, 3–400
Arminian notion
   of act, 263
   of free will, 134
   of freedom, 80, 86, 132, 184, 218, 292
   of indifference, 219
   of internal volition, 257
   of necessity, 319
   of liberty of Will, v, 77, 87, 329, 338, 394, 395, 398
   of self-determination, 288
Arminianism, 3, 17, 22n157, 33n2, 342, 349, 355
   Definition, 3
   Edwards against, 6, 7, 8, 393
   Edwards's understanding of, 9
   inconsistencies of, 348
   jumble of, 5
   landmark of, 19
   New England – 16
   outspoken form of, 2
   primary principle of, 8
   primary tenet of, 122
Arminius, Jacobus, 22, 23, 24, 33, 34, 35, 201n5, 208n7
   *Works of Arminius*, 23n159
Aristotle, 5, 153, 260n1, 356
   *Nicomachean Ethics*, 5n25
Asselt, Willem J. van, 5n31, 16n111
Atheism
   father of, 293, 346
   Principles to, viii, 346
   tendency to, 347

Atom, 309, 398
  attraction of, 316
  combinations of, 346n2
  *Of Atoms*, 116, 306
  One -, 315
  the least -, 316
Augustine (or St. Austin), 1, 4, 11, 14–16, 207n1
  and Pelagius, 25, 347n3
  *De gratia et libero arbitrio*, 4n21, 207n1
  doctrines of, 11n71, 15, 72n4
  Double Predestination, 208n7
  *On the Free Choice of the Will*
  *On Rebuke and Grace*, 5
Autonomous, 2, 10n65, 16, 211n9
Author
  of sin, 23, 31, 32, 320–23, 337, 340, 361, 401
  of the act, 258
Aquinas, Thomas, 11, 18, 137, 311

Balance, 105
  scale of, 117, 142, 210, 211
Baxter, Andrew, 300, 308, 315
Beast, 94
  difference between men and -, 74n6
  Revelation 5:8–12. "The four, 205
  Jeremiah 27:4–6, 325
  Revelation 17:17, 327
Begging the question, 290n2
Being, Divine, 171
  action of, 328
  dispositions and acts of, 57
  knowledge of, 344
  liberty of, 401
  moral excellency of, 330
  perfection and blessedness, 319
  servile subjection of, 318
Being, first, 298
Being in general, 58n4, 92, 306
Bellamy, Joseph, 18, 18n130, 216n1
Beneficence, 192
Beza, Theodore, 326n5
Blame, 3, 9, 30, 73, 74, 77, 189, 208–12, 238–39, 255, 258, 268, 278, 338, 355, 394
Boice, James Montgomery, 53n2
Bombaro, John, 311n7
Bondage of the will, 12n72, 15n107, 21, 68
Breck, Robert, 16, 17n123
Burr, Arron, 386, 387, 387n4

Calvin, John
  11, 12n74, 15, 21n152, 208n7, *Institutes of Christian Religion*, 4n25, 15n104–08, 16n113–14, "Augustine's doctrine of 'free will," 11n71

Calvinism, Five Points of, 22
Calvinist, 23n159, 24, 36, 57n3, 72, 103, 294, 331
  Moderate -, 16
  Perspective, 14
  doctrine of necessity, 21
  doctrine of "total corruption and depravity, 22
  doctrine of will, 21
  metaphysical reasoning, 351
  opinion of -, 102
  scheme of, 219, 343
  Soteriology, 357
  tradition, 21
  the term -, 35
  Whitby against, (anti-) 129, 130
  Against -, 247, 286, 340, 343
Calvinistic Doctrine, 350, 182, 268, 349–50, 359, 364, 400, 401
Calvinistic divines, 35
Calvinistic Necessarianism, 29, 347
Calvinistic principles, 340, 350, 358
Cambridge Platonists, 307n2
Causationist, 80n4
Cause, 11
  of acts, 98, 134, 148, 148, 183, 262, 266
  of another event, 90, 90n2
  of Arminian liberty, 100–01, 119
  of being, 353
  of blameworthiness, 254
  of choice, 11
  of deficiency, 320
  of determination, 98, 393
  of dispositions, 253
  of effects, 97, 145, 394
  of events, 287
  of evil, 327–28
  of exertion of the will, 146
  of existence, 86, 89, 137
  of faultiness, 255
  of God's prescience, 174
  of (im)possibilities, 176
  of knowledge, 176
  of liberty, 122
  of man's salvation, 23
  of moral evil, 255
  of necessity, 176
  of piety, 363
  of pride, 321
  of thankfulness, 318
  of things future, 174, 298, 318
  of vice, 256
  of virtue, 247
  of volition, 99, 354
  positive cause (= God), 337

Certainty
    of Christian Revelation, 298
    of connection and consequence, 286
    of depraved behavior, 31
    of event, 25, 58, 363
    of existence, 60, 267, 397
    of God's promise, 195
    of good, 51
    of inclination and will, 66
    of knowledge, 57, 173, 175, 177
    of moral perfections of God, 136
    of things, 395
Chance, 61, 65, 374
    Arminian definition of -, 185, 219, 328, 377
    Edwards's argument, 317
Chauncy, Charles, 4n18
Cherry, Conrad, 162n5
Chessboard, 108, 109, 112
Choice, act of, 79, 86, 99, 103–118, 129–36,
    141–45, 184, 237, 249, 291, 338, 378
    Free choice = will, 101, 103, 104, 119,
        144–45, 261, 338, 352
    Objects of -, 86, 133, 306–07
Christ
    crucifixion of, 331
    died to satisfy that old law, 214
    followers of, 33
    foretold Peter's sin, 151, 155
    God rewards -, 205
    human soul of, 193
    in the work of redemption, 157
    last Adam, 206
    predictions of, 157
    promised his disciples, 37, 154
    should be crucified, 326
    should suffer, 327
*Christian Philosophy*, (by Turnbull), 126–27
Christian religion, 9, 202, 292
*Christian Revelation*, (by Clark), 298n3, (by
    Whitby, 1705), 18
Chubb, Thomas, 16, 17, 17n122, 134n1,
    137–148, 261, 344
Clark, Samuel, 20n145, 126, 131, 133, 174,
    175n4, 298n3
Clagett, William, 214n19
Coaction = compulsion, 11, 20, 30, 71, 122,
    182, 189, 192, 193, 207, 209–10
Collins, Anthony, 2, 365n3, 392
Command, 216–30
    actions under its -, 80, 132
    difference between command and invitation, 226
    Divine, 362
    God's -, 10, 25, 30, 130, 150, 182, 203, 205,
        212, 229, 340, 342

    influence of -, 74
    objects of his commands, 358, 360
    of my thoughts, 353
    proper and rightful, 223–24
    sovereign, 132
    subject of, 77, 217, 344, 363, 397
Common Sense, 268, 275
    Arguments from -, 400
    Common Sense philosopher Thomas accident, 391
    definition of, 91n4
    dictate of -, 91, 148, 237, 258, 268, 277–80,
        355
    faculty of -, 29, 392
    JE supports -, 56
    of mankind, 256, 278, 282, 290, 303, 356,
        400
    Realism, 91, 392
    principle of, 91n4, 275n1, *Principles of Common Sense* (by Reid, 1764), 29n187, 391
    Thomas Reid's Scottish -, 29
Compatibilist
    JE, 5, 10, 22, 55n1, Jon Calvin, 21n152,
        Girolamo Zanchi, Franciscus Junius,
        Franciscus
    Gomarus, Gisbertus Voetius, Francesco Turrettini, and Bernardinus de Moor, 5n32
Compulsion = force, coaction, 20, 30, 71, 192,
    203–04
Connection
    between action and desire, 377
    between means and end, 285
    between motives and volitions, 382
    between them and the will, 225
    between virtue or vice, and foregoing event,
        287
    Connection Chain, 359
    habitual connection of ideas, 271, 282
    of antecedents and consequents, 284–86
    of all events, 320, 346
    of causes and effects, 284
    of men's volitions, 371
    with anything foregoing, 261, 264
Conscience, 62, 383, 385
    Natural sense, 277
    remorse of -, 373, 379
Contingency, 8, 72n4, 93, 186, 261, 355, 397
    Arminian - excluding wisdom and motive,
        301
    Edwards "combat[ing] -," 2
    liberty of -, 19
    Volitional -, 122
Copan, Paul, *Jonathan Edwards's Philosophical
    influences*, 12n76, 307n2

405

Index

Covenant
  Half-Way -, 8n52
  Holy -, 151
  of the people, 194
  God's -, 197, 198, 200
  National -, 389
  or promise, 202
Creation, 160, q99
  Dispositional Space of, 393n16
  God's -, 171, 312, 332
  of the world, 57, 92, 351
Creator, 92, 312
  and governor and benefactor of the world, 296, 315
  and owner of the whole system of created existences, 329
  sovereign Creator and Disposer of the world, 359
Crisp, Oliver D., 29, 190, 162n5

Dana, James 1, 1n2, 2n3, 2n5, 29
  *De gratia et libero arbitrio* (*On Grace and Free Will*, by Augustine), 207
Decree
  before the foundation of the world, 23,
  Calvinist absolute decrees of God, 3, 173, 174, 181, 199
  Divine -, 31
  eternal design or, 24, 362
  God's decrees, 31, 361–63
  purpose or -, 361
Deism, 3, 175n4
  modern deism, 17n118, 134n1
  *True Deism, the Basis of Christianity*, (by Caleb Fleming), 17n118
*Demonstration of the Being and Attributes of God*, (by Samuel Clarke), 131, 175
Depravity
  habitual depravity of inclination, 239
  of heart, 293
  total -, 22, 72n3, 347n3, 359–60
Descartes, Rene, 4n22, 392
Design, 185
  choice and -, 294, 361
  eternal design or decree, 24, 362
  God's -, 161, 195, 317, 318, 326
  or decree, 24
  original design of the world, 66
Desire
  conquering -, 16
  evil desires, 11
  incline to or, 42
  Sincerity of -, 227–33
  will and -, 43, 44

Determination
  Antecedent -, 113
  as the cause, 97
  cause of the, 98
  choice or -, 120
  free -, 115, 261
  general, 109
  God's -, 1
  God's sovereign determination, 20, 45, 363
  hard determinism, 5
  notion of -, 98
  of God's will, 298, 311, 317, 344, 347
  of the first action, 97
  of mind, 86, 108, 375
  of motion, 86
  of suspension, 121
  of volition, 87
  of the Will, 45, 13, 45–53, 100, 113, 127–39, 369, 385
  of ours, 254, 368
  particular -, 109
  predetermination, 10, 114
  self-determination, 2, 19, 32, 79–81, 114–16, 210, 244–48, 286–88, 343, 382
  soft determinism, 5
  soul's own -, 97
Determinism, 6n37, 44n6
  and fatalism, 2
  Calvinists' theistic -, 2, 8
  casual or theistic, 20, 21
  hard -, 5
  heretical -, 8
  mechanistic -, 21
  necessary -, 30
  Newtonian -, 21
  Thomas Hobbes' philosophical -, 7
  soft -, 5, 6, 55n1
Difficulty
  Arminian -, 341
  degree of -, 209
  Moral -, 209–10
  natural -, 209–10, 269
Dilemma, 84n2
Dispraise, 93, 201, 239
  worthiness of -, 241, 256, 279
*Discourse of Free-thinking*, (by Anthony Collins), 365n3
Doddridge, Philip, 19n133, 326n5–6
Dort, Canons of, 21, 22, 22n153, 25, 201n5
Duns Scotus, 17, 137
Dutch translation of *FOW*, 27
Dwight, Sereno E., *The Life of President Edwards*, 12, 12n77, 26, 176
Dwight, Timothy, 390

Edwards, Jonathan
    against Arminianism, 6
    Augustinian voluntarism, 5
    Calvinist, 7
    Calvinist necessitarianism, 8n49
    classical compatibilist, 6
    determinist or fatalist, 8
    epistemology, 7n46
    Five Points of, 22
    Fundamental Questions, 29
    Idealism of -, 307n2
    John Locke's influences on, 12
    magnum opus, *Freedom of the Will*, 28
    Necessitarianism of -, 394
    Notion of the will, 14
    Philosophical Theologian, 90n2
    position on the relation of the intellect and the will, 5
    Reconciliationist, 6
    reformed, 8
    relationship to John Locke, 78n2
    Theocentric Metaphysics, 311n7
    three main antagonists, 16
    Teleology of -, 311n7
    Trinitarian Ontology of, 398n19
    understanding of Arminianism, 9
    understanding of the will, 4
    writing motivation and process, 8
Effect
    as a volition, 95
    necessary -, 63
    of a foregoing act, 145, 218
    of a predetermining bias, 262
    of antecedent causes, 5
    of choice, 131, 144, 257, 261
    of grace, 23
    of the strongest motive, 264
    of the will, 263
    of their motives, 134
    of volition, 144
Election
    conditional election, 199
    God's Absolute, eternal, personal -, 22, 23
    God's decree of -, 174
    Divine -, 22
    doctrines of -, 25
    eternal election, 363
    general election, 199
    particular, eternal, absolute election, 361
    of nations and societies, 23
    of the soul, 46
    unconditional -, 22, 24, 361
Endeavor
    desires and -, 223, 227
    means and endeavors, 286–89
    opposition or -, 66
    sincere endeavors, 232, 234, 273
    Sincerity of -, 227
    will and -, 68, 273
Epicurean conceptions of liberty, 369
Epicurus, 20
Episcopius, Simon, 201n5
Equilibrium, 219
    equilibrium theory, 44n6
    indifference and -, 135, 236, 262
    neutral balance and -, 105n1
    of mind, 237
    perfect equilibrium, 238, 44, 116–18
Erskine, John
    JE's letter, 16, 381, 387
    JE's Remarks, 367
Epicurean, 20, 369
Epistemology, Priori, 392
Essence
    divine essence, 297
    of the Liberty, 76
    of the Virtue and Vice, 233, 253–54
Eternity, 24, 59, 90, 308n4, of God's existence, 307
Ethics
    *Aesthetics and -*, 204
    in the Late Thirteenth Century, 4
    *Kant's Lectures on -*, 62n1
    *Nicomachean Ethics*, 5n25
    *of Jonathan Edwards*, 204n8
Ethical sense, 190n4
Ethical voluntarism, 4
Eusebius, 103
Event, 89
    As an effect of that cause, 123
    Consequent -, 90
    Contingent -, 170
    Foregoing -, 287
    Foreknown -, 181
    Future -, 401, 170
    Past -, 59
Evidence
    of God's Certain Foreknowledge, 24n165, 149–68, 401
    indisputable evidence, 333
    intuitive -, 92
    moral -, 62
    of future Contingencies, 397
    of its necessity, 397
    of the being of God, 92
    of the existence of anything, 93
    of their truth, 345
    self-evidence, 253

407

Evil
  considered as evil, 13
  evil desires, 11
Exertion
  act or exertion of will, 86
  bodily exertion or effort, 43
  of power, 262–64
  of that determination, 131
  of the act, 86, 138
  of the active faculty, 146–47
  of the members of his body, 42
  of the soul, 218, 264
  of the will, 146
  soul's exertion, 87
Existence
  Cause / ground / reason of its -, 11, 89, 95, 123
  causal influence on its, 99
  future existence, 170–71, 176–78
  God's -, 91, 92
  man's first -, 130
  manner of -, 99
  necessity of his existence, 92, 178, of the events, 180
  of a body, 91
  of all things, 168
  of any event, 177
  of being in general, 58
  of future events, 181
  of sin, 31
  of the "sovereignty of the will, 20
  of volition, 131
  or being of that thing, 58, 91, 178
  particular nature of -, 94
  passive ground of -, 137
  past existence, 168, 176
  present existence, 170–71
  previous ground of -, 138
Experience
  conversion -, 8n52
  fact and -, 111
  knowledge and -, 91n3
  sensory -, 7n46
  spiritual revival and its -, 4n18
Faculty
  active -, 135, 146, 147
  choosing or preferring -, 12
  exercise of -, 78
  faculty and disposition, 35
  faculty or power of will, 11, 41, 82, 114, 217, 290
  faculty psychology, 13
  human -, 7
  in the soul, 41n1
  moral -, 72, 73
  natural -, 224
  of common sense, 29
  of man, 14
  of the mind, 2, 9, 11
  of perception or apprehension, 52
  of understanding
Faith
  and obedience, 362
  beginning of true -, 363
  Christian -, 175n4
  duty, 216n1
  exercises of -, 383
  in Christ, 226, 383
  inability of fallen men to exert -, 226
  justification by, 21, 213n18
  of the promise, 200
  persevering in -, 362–63
Fall, 31
  after the Fall, 16, 74
  from his integrity, 198
  God foresaw -, 166
  liberty before -, 16
  Man's will before the -, 14
  natural ability, 74n7
  of man, 24, 163, 166
  of man and angels, 162
  of sinner, 4
  prior to the Fall, 33n1, 163
Fatalism, 5, 20, stoical, 20
Fate, 103
  almighty minister of, 296, 302
  heathen doctrine of, 319, 357
  mechanical medium of, 296, 303
  Stoical doctrine of -, 20, 21n152, 181, 292–94, 401
Fathers, Church, 102, 207, 212
Fault, 210, 254
  and praise, 255
  essence of the blame or -, 375
  exposedness to sin or -, 210
  notion of -, 276
  or blame, 270
Faust, Clarence Henry, 13n88
Fiering, Norman, 3n13, 63n4
Fittest
  and best, 298, 302, 344
  of good things, 305
Fleming, Caleb, 17n118
Forbearance, 42, 359
Foreknowledge, 149, 168, 361
  determinate counsel and -, 326
  divine -, 169, 397
  evidences of his -, 162

God's certain -, 24, 24n165, 163, 165, 172–81, 318, 341
  of eschatological events, 156
  of men's Future moral Conducts and events, 155, 168, 321
  of the free actions of moral agents, 149, 169
Franklin, Benjamin, 3n17
Freethinkers, 294n3
Free will, 1, 1n1, as free choice, 15n110, "Augustine's doctrine of 'free will,'" 11n71, fourfold state of -, 15, man's, 23, 277, of free will, 3, 134, three positions in, 5, 365, See Freedom of the will
Freedom of the will, as free will, 1
  Arminian doctrine of -, 10, 17, 25, 100, 218
  Daniel Whitby's -, 102, 189
  Edwards's -, 1, 20, 21, 379
  James Dana's -, 1, 2n3, 47n1
  John Locke's -, 13, 119
  Isaac Watts -, 18, 96, 105
  Pelagian notion of, 19
  Thomas Chubb's -, 16, 17, 36, 134
  Thomas Reid's -, 391–92
*Freedom of the Will* by Edwards, 1
  Achillean argument, 393
  Critic, 47n1
  first English edition, 27
  his magnum opus, 8–9
  moral purpose in writing, 2
  Proposals1 for printing, 400
  Publishing History, 25
  Reception and Influence, 28
  Thomas Reid's Reading Notes, 391
  Three Points, 379
  Trajectories in, 10
  Research Trends, 1
  Review (Dec. 1762), 391n1
Futurity, 177
  certain knowledge of, 177
  fixed, 318, 358
  of the event, 284

Gill, John, 295n4, 386–87
God
  acts of -, 189
  as "the first cause," "being in general," and "the Creator," like the Great Geometrician, "the Governor," 306n1
  Attributes of -, 131, 175
  beauty of -, 204n8
  being of -, 91, 346–47
  church of -, 157, 196, 198
  commands of -, 182, 213, 233
  covenant of -, 200
  deceitful artifice of -, 379

  decrees of -, 3, 173–74, 181, 199
  deistic Understanding of -, 160
  dependence of -, 200
  design of -, 326
  Direction and Control of -, 5
  divine constitution of -, 287
  existence of -, 91
  favor of -, 200
  foreknowledge of -, 165, 173, 321
  glory of -, 156, 304
  goodness of -, 192, 317, 377
  grace of -, 214, 360
  holiness of -, 297
  Hopkins, Samuel, 5n29
  inclinations and actions of -, 57
  influence of -, 31
  judgment of -, 153, 209
  kingdom of -, 157
  knowledge of -, 37
  mind of -, 179
  moral government of -, 365
  moral image of -, 74
  moral perfections of -, 10, 136, 343
  natural image of -, 74
  oath of -, 157
  omnipresence of -, 308
  pleasure of -, 311
  promises of -, 196
  revealed or preceptive will of -, 331
  secret will of -, 331–33
  Son of -, 294
  sovereignty of -, 298–300, 39, 329
  Spirit of -, 129, See Holy Spirit
  will of, 203, 239, 296, 309, 317
  wisdom of -, 163
  Word of -, 149, 365
Godhead, 92, 292, 346
Gomarus, Franciscus, 5n32, 15, 16, 201n5
Good, 227
  acts of will, 279
  and evil, 11, 299
  as God's virtue, 23
  chiefest -, 128
  choose the -, 127
  deeds, 73
  degree of -, 51, 127
  disposition of the heart, 236, 243
  end, 247, 306, 331
  future -, 50
  Greater -, 7, 14
  inclination, 242, 269
  intention or aim, 249
  moral good or evil, 258
  greatest apparent -, 13, 47, 48, 52, 126
  man, 335

409

Good *(continued)*
  moral -, 73
  nature, 67
  or bad, 241
  pleasure, 328
  self-chosen -, 106
  works, 24, 163
  will, 30
Grace
  common -, 91n4
  Conversion by -, 14
  Converting, 386
  divine -, 3, 5, 158
  effect of -, 23
  efficacious, 21n152, 22, 130, 182, 183n1, 360
  freedom by -, 15
  in his election, 318
  infused -, 21, 295
  irresistible -, 23, 360
  kingdom of -, 194
  means of -, 4, 361, 382
  moral necessity of -, 23
  new grace from God, 214
  of God, 214, 317
  sovereign -, 359
  subject of -, 23
Grotius, Hugo, 218n2, 326n5
Gerstner, John, 162n5
Guelzo, Allen C., 3, 4n19, 6n35, 55n1

Habit
  Fixed -, 222
  Moral, 64
  of sin, 337
  of virtue, 67
  strength of, 68
Harris, James A., *Of Liberty and Necessity*, 6n43, 275n1
Heart
  and will, 4, 232
  Carnal -, 229
  habitual disposition of -, 239
  Human -, 32,
    inability in the -, 67
  inclination of the -, 236, 288, 331, 398
  of man, 23
  opposition of his -, 281, 331
  vile temper of -, 282
  violent propensity of -, 279
  wickedness of, 385
Helm, Paul, 8n51, 21n152, 78n2, 90n2
Hobbes, Thomas, 2, 20, 21, 294n3, 392, *Leviathan*, 20n148
Hoekem, Anthony, 22n153
Holmes, Stephen R., 162n5

Hume, David, 2, 29, 91n4, 391, 392
Hypothetical proposition, 89n1

Idea
  of beauty or deformity, 51
  of general and universal being, 92
  of liberty, 10
  or sense, 50
  of sensible things, 50
  of the future pleasure, 50
  of the good, 51
  of the object, 392
  of universal infinite entity, 92
Images of God in man, twofold, 74n7
Imagination, 274, 282, 297, 298, 308, 369
Immutability, God's -, 165, 181, 197, 298
Impossible, 23, 54–57
  impossibility = negative necessity, 60
Inability, 62, 208, 216
  in the heart, 67
  Moral -, 66, 67, 209
  Natural -, 69, 209
  of fallen man, 213, 226
  of men, 22
  of unregenerate men, 182
  some stated defect, 68
  to comply with the Gospel, 216n1
  to love wickedness, 67
  to Obey, 216
  to prostitute herself, 67
Inclination
  contrary to his reason and judgment, 16, 66, 219
  evil -, 347
  habitual, 67, 240
  moral, 210
  of created intelligent beings, 57
  of the heart, 241, 257
  of the soul, 64, 229
  of the will, 113
  or motive, 250, 279, 375
  prior -, 114, 243, 348
  to prefer one thing to another, 44
  want of -, 66
Indifference, 44, 72, 395
  absolute -, 20, 09, 352
  and self-determination, 348
  Arminian notion of -, 219
  contingency and -, 19, 368
  Liberty of -, 235, 238
  Liberty of Will Consisting in -, 113
  mind's, 245
  perfect, 108, 111, 306
  state of -, 117, 237
Inducement, 244

moral -, 73, 132
motive, excitement or -, 46, 148, 244–49
preponderating -, 109
prevailing -, 110
Infallible
certainty, 62, 363
connection, 30, 62, 177, 180, 321
existence of the events, 361
foreknowledge, 169
perseverance of saints, 362
Prescience, 168, 401
Promise, 199
Infralapsarian, 23n164, 162n12
Intellectualism, 4, 126n1
Intuitive, Evidence, 92
knowledge in man, 29
Invitation
Counsels and -, = manifestations of God's preceptive will, 340
of a motive to another volition, 138
Irresistible
grace, 22, 360, impossible for the moral necessity of grace, 23

Jesuits, 113, doctrine of -, 293
Jesus
died for all humanity, 24
gospel of, 292, 379, 380
Human Soul of -, 193
preknew and predicted, 342
redemption by, 24, 163
Son of God, 294
temper and behavior of, 203
true religion of, 157
Justification
doctrine of -, 21, 213n18, 295
Justin Martyr, 102

Kames (Henry Home), Lord, 6, 20n145, 29, 368, 387–88
Kane, Robert, 6, *Contemporary Introduction to Free Will*, 6n40, 55n1
Kant, Immanuel, 62n1
Kent, Bonnie, 4n22
Knowledge
Certain -, 29, 57, 169, 173
God's -, 180–81
Immediate -, 392
intuitive knowledge in man, 29
Locke's notion, 7n46
of God, 37, 297
of moral good and evil, 73
of ourselves, 37
of the existence of God, 91–92
true knowledge, 37

Language
benefit of, 34
common -, 60, 395
common use of, 56, 69, 91, 258
defect in -, 34, 266
of thankfulness, 192
obscureness of, 314
Law
end of -, 219, 384
established -, 65
God's -, 157, 331
influence of
moral, 62n1, 73
new -, 213–14
of motion by Isaac Newton, 65, 115n2, 160, 315
of nature, 65, 217, 225
old -, 213–14
subject of -, 193
use of -, 219
Lee, Sang Hyun, 55n1
Leibniz, Gottfried Wilhelm, 20n145
Liberalism, 17, religious, 19n136
Libertarianism, 5
Louis le Blanc de Beaulieu, 174
Locke, John, 1
*An Essay Concerning Human Understanding*, 9
concept of liberty, 9, 11, 42
empiricism, 7
experimentalism, 7
influence on Edwards, 7, 12
method and principles, 7
psychological basis of will, 1
tabula rasa (blank slate), 105n1
Luther, Martin, 11, 66n8, *On the bondage of the will (De Servo Arbitrio)*, 12n72

Machine, Mere, 20, 160, 204, 284, 209
Malebranche, Nicolas, 58n4
Marandiuc, Natalia, 62n1
Mathematical truths, 58
Mathematician, 160
Mastricht, Petrus van, 1, 5, 14, 5, 15, 162, *Theoretico Practica Theologia*, 15n109
Mather, Cotton, 8, 16n117
McClymond, Michael, 162n5, 23n60
McDermott, Gerald, 162n5, 23n60
Means
of every act of sin, 334
of foresight, 61
of grace, 361, 382
of gratifying the vice, 228
of information, 225

Means *(continued)*
    of our knowledge, 93, 365
    of salvation, 234
    of Volition, 395
Mechanism, universal -, 20, 20n148
Messiah, 154
    as a Savior, 197
    kingdom of, 156–57, 198
    of his seed, 197
    salvation of, 158, 197, 200
Metaphysical
    abstraction and refinement, 352
    Arguments, 282, 351
    Confusion, 356
    Distinction, 266, 356
    Method, 6
    Necessity, 302, 395
    niceties and subtleties, 315, 350
    propositions, 355
    sense, 58, 272
    sophistry, 352
    terms, 356
    Notion of Action, 260
    Notion of liberty, 277
    or philosophical necessity, 57, 59
Metaphysics, 260n1, 297, 351
Miller, Perry, 7, 28n183, *Jonathan Edwards*, 9n54
Mind
    Cause of this effect, 396
    choice of, 52
    chooses, 111, 399
    *Descartes's Concept of*, 4n22
    determination of, 132
    evil temper of, 34
    faculty or power or principle of, 9, 41
    liberty of, 121
    of Christ, 33
    of God, 179, 297
    of man, 104, 352, 378
    prefers, 111
    understanding of the, 2
    view of, 53, 105
Minkema, Kenneth P., 62n1
Mixed modes, 272, 272n2
Mohawk, 350
Moral
    God's, 189, man's moral acts, 1, moral nature, 3, moral perfections of God, 10, Moral Philosophy, 4, moral responsibility, 3, moral theology, 3, Moral Thought, 3n13, moral worthiness and demerit, 74
Moral ability, 73, source of, 73
Moral absolutism, 63n4

Moral agency, 70, Arminian notion of -, 244, Moral agents, 76
Moral evidence, 62n3
Moral inability, 66, 216, instances of, 67, to love wickedness, 67, See inability
Moral necessity, 18, 19, 62, 208, 275, 305, of grace, 23
Moral world, 161, 318, 318–19
    affairs of, 166, as the end of the natural, 7, events in, 328, future state of, 161
    state of, 161, 319
Motive
    and excitements to the action of the will, 17
    as a previous tendency in the mind, 46
    causes the volition, 245
    defect of, 66, 225
    determination by, 9
    good or evil -, 279
    ground and reason of its volition and choice, 30, 148
    in moral actions, 244
    influence of, 134, 244
    moral habit or, 64
    moves, excites or invites the mind to volition, 46
    nature and influence of, 46
    opposite motives, 143
    prevailing, 317
    previous tendency of, 46
    strongest -, 13, 20, 46, 63, 140
    two rivals, 140–41
Muller, Richard, 7n48, 8, 344n3

Natural Religion, 175n4, 298n3, 351, 367, 380, 381n4
Nature
    good or evil dispositions implanted by nature itself, 51, 212, 279, 379, laws of, 65, 225, 286, light of, 102, 235, 292, order of, 84–86, 98, 272, 297–98
Necessary
    Action, 267, as some supposed opposition, 394, causes, 302, connection of a series of antecedents and consequents, 286, dependence or connection, 261, divine will, 301, effects of the acts of the will, 218, 245, existence of the Deity, 308, holiness, 257, means of salvation, 234, volitions, 248, perseverance of saints, 362, purposes of human life, 376
Necessity
    absolute, 63, doctrine of, 20, 21, 126, 290, extrinsical, 30, 192, fatal -, 318, general, 60, Hobbes' doctrine of, 181, moral, 18, 62, 274, 318, natural, 63, 269, of being

blameworthy, 212, of breaking some commands, 213, of grace, 23, of connection and consequence, 30, 134, 168, of constraint or coaction, 122, of nature, 144, 170, of supernatural illumination, 295, of the Divine Will, 296, of the effect, 243, of the event, 177, of the truth, 179, of volition, 131, of the will, 186, term, 54–61, metaphysical necessity, 59, Philosophical, 58, 272, Whitby's sense of, 208

Neele, Adriaan C., *Petrus van Mastricht: Reformed Orthodoxy: Method and Piety*, 15n109

Negligence, 289

No-Cause, 93–94

Noll, Marl, 29n190

Nominal

Noncomplying act, 220–21

Nonconformist, 19

Obedience
Christ's -, 202, 204, Command, and Obligation to, 216, imperfections of our -, 30, 213, imperfect sincere, 213, perfect -, 203, reward for his, 206, to the dictates of the understanding, 127, way of -, 195, wonderful instance of his, 205

Object
immediate, 48, of choice, 49, of God's favor, 317, of honor and regard, 191, of precept or command, 217, of predestination, 162n5, of reward or punishment, 145, of the will, 42, 233, 336, of the volition, 44, 317

Obligation
moral -, 347, 372, necessity of -, 62, to Obedience, 216–25

Occam, William of, 78n3

Occasionalism, 90n.2

Order, of nature, 272, 297, 84, of natural law, 315n13, of things, 65, of time, 84, 101

Origen (Origenes Adamantius), 11, 102, 174, 207

Papists, 351

Passion, 143, notion of action and -, 184, 192, 265, metaphysical distinction between, 266

Passive, ground or reason of that action, 17, 137, ground of its existence, 137, subject, 4

Pelagian, 10, 11, 16, 71, 72n3, 113, 369, notion of the freedom of the will, 19, semi-Pelagians, 113

Pelagianism, 3

Pelagius, 25, 72n3, 347

Perception, mind's present -, 52, 110, of the external objects, 392, of the greater good, 7, passivity of -, 7

Perkins, William, 23n159

Persecution, 18n129, Christ often foretold, 155

Perseverance
doctrine of, 363, infallible and necessary, 25, in true Christianity, 362, of the saints, 18n129, 22, 25

*Personal Narrative*, by JE, 24n171

Physical and natural necessity, 18, 302n4, 303, 371

Physical causes, 139

Physical laws of Isaac Newton, 315

Physical operation of the Spirit, 129, 248

Physical or moral influence, 248

Philosopher
British and Continental, 3, Common Sense, 391, European theologians and -, 29, Greek and roman -, 292, 346, heathen -, 292, 346, "peripatetic -, 356n3, philosophers like Samuel Langdon, 4, Stoic -, 292, 346

Philosophy
Aristotelian, 356n3, British, 6, Christian, 126, Moral, 4n21, 264, 382, Natural, 16, 306

*Mathematical Principles of Natural Philosophy*, (by Newton), 116n2, Reid's Common Sense realism 394, Scottish, 394

Piety, 103, cause of, 363, impiety, 152

Plato, 153n1, 211, his ideas, 65n6, his allegory of the cave, 283n2, *Phaedrus*, 5n25

Pleasure
degree of, 49, displeasure, 234, exercise of, 144, future -, 50, idea of, 50, present -, 48, of willing and choosing, 79, or uneasiness, 5

Power
of action, 19, of choosing = the will, 14, self-determining, 105, 116, 348, of thinking =the understanding, 37n4, of volition, 71

Praise, 268, 275
of men,194, and Blame, 275, Praise or Blame, 268, praise or dispraise, 193, worthiness of, 73

Precept, 193, 217–18, 247, proper object of, 217, proper subject of, 219

Predestination, 5
divine, 55n1, doctrine of, 6, 25, 342, Double -, 208n7, object of, 162n5, of St. Augustine, 72n3, ship, 19

Predicate, of the proposition, 59–62, 176–77, 371
Preference
Choice or preference, 107, 114, 118, whether preference and volition be precisely the same things or no, 43–44
Prescience
God's, 174, 181, 396, in the most High, 149, of Cause and effect, 92, of events, 395, of the future actions of moral agents, 158, of the volitions of moral agents, 158
Preservation, 159
Priestly, Joseph, 7n49, 29, 57n3, 391
Principle, =principium = arché, 65n6
Principle
Arminian -, 210, 224, 287, 318, 340–48, Calvinistic -, 350, Locke's method and -, 7, moving -, 146, of Arminianism, 8, of common sense, 91, of human liberty, 186, of mind, 9, *of Morality and Natural Religion* ( by Henry Home), 367, of motion and action, 65, of nature, 74, of sin in his heart, 337, to Atheism and licentiousness, 346
Professing Christian, 33, 33n1
Promise
absolute, 195, first gospel -, 158, of a future redemption, 200, of blessings, 201, of glorious rewards, 202, of glorious success, 203, of God, 157, 195–96, of great things, 201, of salvation, 233
prophecies, 151–62, 389
Alexander's, 160, as humility, meekness, patience, mercy, gratitude, generosity, heavenly-mindedness, 241
Psychology, faculty -, 13
Pynchon, William, 17n121

Qualities of a moral agent, essential, 74, of a clock, 241

Ramsey, Paul, 2n9
Reason, dictate of, 52, sense and common reason of mankind, 102, wounded through sin, 11
Reasoning
Lock's, 9
Chubb's, 134
Arminians's, 251–308
Redemption, by Jesus Christ, 24, Israel's, 161, Particular, 24, the work of, 157, 163, universal, 24
Reformation, of the Jews, 167
Reformers, first, 33n2, 363, Calvinistic, 22, doctrines of, 365

Refusing
as act of the will, 42, act of choosing and refusing, 129, to obey God's commands, 323, to hearken to the word of the lord, 151
Relation
between nature and human choice, 65, between one thing and another, 123, of the intellect and the will, (between the two faculties), 4, 13
Relative terms, 398
*Religious Affections*, 25n175, 41n1, 74n7, 132n5
Remonstrant, 21, 201n5, Contra-remonstrant, 21
Remorse, of conscience, 373, 379
Repent, 151, 164, repentance, 154, of sin, as spiritual duty, 227
Responsibility, for sin, 383, moral, 3, 347n3
Restraint, 67, 71, 105, necessity of constraint or -, 269, or diminution of freedom, 299
Revealed will of God, 331, 340
Revival, Broke at the College of New Jersey, 387, spiritual, 4n18
Reward, 275, object of, 146, of virtue and righteousness, 158, promises of, 202
Righteousness, his loving -, 57, imputed -, 385, Man's self-reliance on his, 384, of saints, 157
Ryken, Philip Graham, 53n2

Sadducees, doctrine of the, 293
Saints
behavior of, 156, Conversion of, 14, Perseverance of, 22, 25, 362, righteousness of, 157, salvation of, 200, true, 362, virtue of, 25
Schaff, Philip, 22n153
Scotus, Duns, 17, 137
Scriptures, as the Word of God, 149, 342, revealed in the, 199, 268
Secret, and revealed will, 340, delusion and prejudice, 282, will of God, 330–33
Self-determining, power, 1, 9, 25, 72, 84, faculty, 2, freedom, 10, in the will, 19, 96, 99
Self-determination, 19, 32, in the will, 210, notion of, 386, sovereign, 288, the will's, 80–81
Self-existent, 90, 95, 298
Self-moving, 116, as self-determining, 81
Semi-Pelagians, 113
Sensation, immediate, 50, Natural, 276, subjects of particular -, 63

Sin, Adam's, 31, 322n4, doctrines of original, 72n3, God the Author of, 320, of Pilate, 209

Sincerity
of Desires and endeavors, 227, of God, 130, 340, of God's counsels and invitations, 226, of virtue, 236, insincerity, 249, virtuous =true, 233

Socinians, 33, 113, 394

Socinus, 33

Socrates, 283n2

Sophistry, 171, 353, metaphysical, 352

Sovereign power of the will, 238, 279, self-determination, 288

Sovereignty of God, 299n3, 300, 319, 329

Spinoza, 72n4

Spirit, Holy, 16, 37, 53, 74, 129, 194, 322

Spring, Samuel, *Moral Disquisitions and Strictures*, 5n28

Stebbing, Henry, 214, 214n19

Stiles, Ezra, 4n18

Stoical, Doctrine of Fate, 21n152, 181, 292, fatalism, 5, 20

Stoddard, Solomon, 8n52

Storm, Sam, 66n8

Subject
of command or counsel, 77, of God's commands or warnings, 25, of grace, 23, of human liberty, 53, 143

Subtleties, metaphysical and philosophical, 275, 315n10, 400

Sufficient reason, 96, 395-96

Supralapsarian, 24n168

Suspend, power to - the act of the will, 14, 120-21

Sweeney, Douglas A., *Nathaniel Taylor, New Haven Theology, and the Legacy of Jonathan Edwards*, 163n5

Tappan, Henry Philip, 29, 78n2, 391

Taylor, John, 257, 257n2, 391

Teleology of Edwards, 311n7

Tendency
general – to action, 97, natural, 35, previous, 46, to libertinism and infidelity, 401, to uphold distance and disaffection, 34

Theodicy, God's, 343, 344n2

Thomas Aquinas, 11, 18, 137, 311n7

Time, and space, 306-07, 393, 398, order of, 84, 86, 107

Tierra del Fuego, 263

Trial, Man in a state of, 18, 193, 206, 388

Trinitarian Ontology, 393n16, 398

T.U.L.I.P., 22, see Calvinism

Turnbull, George, 3, 20n145, 27, 91n4, 126, 127n2, 175n6, 332n9, 352, 358n2, 391

Unable
morally - to avoid those exercises, 223, to conduct as he will, 70, to do a thing, 219, to exert the acts of the will themselves, 69, to go against the motive , 220, to perform the conditions of salvation, 182, to perform perfect obedience, 213

Unavoidable, 269, 274-75, 282, 332, 337, 371

Understanding
and the will as two faculties, 37, 41n1, dictates or views of -, 14, 52, 126-29, last dictate of, 45, Locke's *Essay on the Human* -, 12, 71, principles of, 21

Uneasiness, 7
as determining the will, 47, avoiding or removal of, 47, pleasure or, 51, present ,14, 105, the greatest, 50

Unitarianism, 4, 5n27

Vice
in habits of the mind, 240, 243, men's, 156, notion of, 249, 302, of covetousness, 228, of Dispositions of the Heart, 253, virtue or, 77, 150

Virgin Mary, 198

Virtue
term, 190, abolition of , 269, Arminian liberty necessary to -, 239, Arminian requisite to -, 219, benefit of , 204, Christ's -, 200, degree of , 240, destitute of , 229,-30, endeavors for Obtaining -, 284, dominion of -, as the Kingdom, 156, foundation of, 190, form and essence of -, 233, God's -, 23, habit of -, 67, in God , 192, inherent -, 241, love of, 256-57, men's -, 156, nature of -, 236, 239, 241, of temperance , 228, of the saints, 25, of will, 229, rewards of -, 158, *The Nature of True Virtue*, by Edwards, 3n12, true -, 157, 233, positive -, 231, *Whitby's notions of,* 212

Volition
As the act of willing and determining, 392
Act of, 117, 119, 137
Adam's first sinful volition, 338
Antecedent, 139
Connected with the influence of Motives, 134
determination of, 131
effect of, 144
existence of, 131
first, 139
free, 144
freedom of, 119

415

Index

Volition *(continued)*
  future, 164, 171–81, 222
  God's -, 305–19, 331
  ground of, 136
  men's -, 320–29, 354, 368
  motives in, 148
  necessity of, 131
  of moral agents, 183, 358–61
  previous act of, 396
  suspending of, 120, 121
Voltaire, 17n118
Voluntarism, 4, Edwards's Augustinian, 5, ethical -, 4, intellectualism and, 4, three forms of, 4n22

Watts, Isaac
  as hymn writer, 18, as not properly Pelagian[s] nor Arminian[s], 16, 18, God determines his acts end, 310, held to the Pelagian notion, 19, 96, necessity is dishonor to God, 305, his work, *Essay on Freedom of Will in God and in Creatures*, 19, 175, John Wesley influenced by Watts's, 19n137, Watts' conclusion, 303
West, Samuel, criticized Edwards, 2
Whitby, Daniel, 18, 175, 190
  as first an evangelical Arminian, and then gradually a Unitarian, 18, evidences of persons being in a state of trial, 206, he alleges the agreement of the Stoics with Calvinists and Arminians, 20, 293, his *Discourses on the Five Points*, as major focus in Edwards's FOW, 18, freedom from coaction and necessity, 207, John Gill answers to, 295n4, opposes Calvinism, 102, his Supposition, 127, his questions, 10, liberty, 211, "mere" knowledge, 177, necessity, 208, 241, notion of freedom, 130
Whittelsey, Chauncey, 1
Will
  as power of soul, 105, as property of agents, 70–71
  Act of, 41, 44, 47, 48, 82, 83, 87, 107, 119, 120, 218, 223, 243, 249, 255, 258, 395
  Antecedent act of, 104, 258, Arminian notion of, 78n2, free -, 36, 54, 61, 119, 133, 165, 167, 201, 212, 277, Free act of, 101, 103, 132, Direct object of, 42, 229, 233, Nature of, 41, of man, 72, 130
Wilson, Stephen, 55n1
World, moral, 161, 166, 319, 328, 371, 373, natural, 134n1, 161, of mankind, 157, 160, 316, 374
Word of God, 149, 342, 361, 365
Wright, Conrad, 2, 2n4, 162n5, 294n3

Yeager, Jonathan, 387n1

Zanchi, Girolamo, 15,

www.ingramcontent.com/pod-product-compliance
Lightning Source LLC
Chambersburg PA
CBHW081147290426
44108CB00018B/2465